PHILIP II OF MACEDONIA

PHILIP II
OF MACEDONIA

IAN WORTHINGTON

YALE UNIVERSITY PRESS
NEW HAVEN AND LONDON

For information about this and other Yale University Press publications, please contact:

U.S. Office: sales.press@yale.edu   www.yalebooks.com
Europe Office: sales@yaleup.co.uk   www.yaleup.co.uk

Set in Minion by SX Composing DTP, Rayleigh, Essex
Printed Great Britain by MPG Books Ltd, Bodmin, Cornwall

Library of Congress Cataloging-in-Publication Data

Worthington, Ian.
  Philip II of Macedonia / Ian Worthington.
     p. cm.
  Includes bibliographical references and index.
  ISBN 978-0-300-12079-0 (ci : alk. paper)
  1. Philip II, King of Macedonia, 382–336 B.C. 2. Greece—History—Macedonian Expansion, 359–323 B.C. 3. Macedonia—History—To 168 B.C. 4. Greece—Kings and rulers—Biography. 5. Macedonia—Kings and rulers—Biography. I. Title.
  DF233.8.P59W67 2008
  938'.07092--dc22
  [B]
                                                                    2008008330

A catalogue record for this book is available from the British Library.

10 9 8 7 6 5 4 3 2 1

CONTENTS

ILLUSTRATIONS AND MAPS

Plates

Figures

Maps

Unless otherwise stated all photographs are by Ian Worthington.

PREFACE

The most famous king of ancient Macedonia has still to be Alexander the Great. However, Alexander's spectacular successes, especially on the battlefield, have considerably downplayed the achievements of his father Philip II, who ruled from 359 to 336 BC. For without Philip, and what he did for Macedonia politically, militarily, economically, socially and culturally, Alexander could not have achieved what he did. Historical figures are a product of their predecessors. However, when we study the reign and achievements of Philip we see that he too was a great king, but that because of the paucity of evidence about him he has lived far too long in the shadow of his more famous, and better-documented, son.

Macedonia, in northern Greece, was teetering on the brink of collapse when Philip became king in 359. It had no centralised government, only a weak conscript army, no economy, no unity, and it had been victim to invasions and dynastic interference from neighbouring tribes and Greek states further afield, such as Athens and Thebes. The chaos was further intensified when Philip's immediate predecessor and four thousand troops were killed in battle, two powerful tribes massed to invade, and the Athenians and Thracians chose to support two different pretenders to the throne. Had Macedonia been a ship, the reasonable expectation at this point in time was that it would sink without a trace.

Philip saved Macedonia in its hour of need, and in forging what would be the first nation-state in Europe he created a first-class army that became the best in the Greek world, united his kingdom, stimulated the economy and laid the foundations of what would become the vast Macedonian empire under Alexander. In 336, when he was dramatically assassinated, his empire comprised the north of modern Greece, the south of the former Yugoslavia, much of Albania, most of Bulgaria and all of European Turkey. He had also planned the invasion of Asia, which Alexander inherited.

In this book I show how Philip accomplished all of these things and more by a combination of diplomacy (including several polygamous marriages), deceit, bribery, military force and an uncanny knack for playing his enemies off against each other. In battles and sieges he lost an eye, shattered a collarbone and suffered a near-fatal leg wound that made him limp for the rest of his life, but he remained a traditional warrior king to the end. As a man, he lived hard, loved hard and was utterly loyal to his kingdom and its position in the Greek world. I am also concerned with his influences, motives and aims, and with his effect on Alexander. Was he the imperialist who aimed to rob Greece of its liberty, as his arch-enemy, the Athenian orator Demosthenes, would have us believe? Or did he simply want to weld together a kingdom for too long torn apart by civil strife and foreign incursion, create prosperity for his people and make Macedonia into the superpower of the ancient word? Or was he both of these and more?

While my book is meant to be authoritative, it is also written to be accessible to a non-specialist readership. The bibliographic essay discusses some of the important modern works on Philip and on Greek history of the fourth century.

All dates are BC except where indicated.

ACKNOWLEDGEMENTS

I have a number of debts to record. First, there is Heather McCallum, my editor at Yale University Press. For her support while I worked on this book, especially during some rough times, and for her comments on my text (even the 'cut this' and 'reduce that' ones), I am enormously grateful. The same feeling applies to Robert Shore, the copy-editor, whose myriad suggestions and queries on my text vastly improved it. My thanks also go to Rachael Lonsdale, who did the lion's share and then some of the thankless task of obtaining permissions to reprint the plates.

I would like to thank the scholars and friends who, over the years, have put up with me, supported me, talked shop with me, and from whom I have learned much: Lindsay Adams, Ernst Badian, Liz Baynham, the late Peter Bicknell, Gene Borza, Brian Bosworth, John Buckler, Ed Carawan, Beth Carney, Craig Cooper, Jack Ellis, Ernst Fredricksmeyer, Michael Gagarin, Mark Golden, the late Nicholas Hammond, Waldemar Heckel, Marianne McDonald, Peter Rhodes, Joseph Roisman, Tim Ryder, Nick Sekunda and Carol Thomas. The person who has endured me the most, outside of my family, is Peter Toohey: the past two decades would have been far less tolerable and fun without his support and friendship. It goes without saying that my colleagues and friends in my own department, especially those with whom I share a much-needed beer or three on Fridays, are greatly valued.

I am also indebted to Professors Jonathan Musgrave and John Prag, who kindly sent me photos of the skeletal remains and reconstructed face of Philip II and an article on the remains in the royal tombs at Vergina in advance of publication, and in various emails generously gave me the benefit of their expertise and vast experience with the skeletal remains. My thanks also go to David Boggs for allowing me to use his splendid drawing of the Philippeion (Figure 3) and for sending me a photo of it.

My deepest debt as always is to Tracy, Oliver and Rosemary, my long-suffering wife, son and daughter, for pretending to accept what I do, and for trying to pull me away from the computer for only 75 per cent of the time I need to be on it. As some minor recompense, I dedicate this book to them.

Ian Worthington
University of Missouri-Columbia
October 2007

PHILIP'S LIFE AND REIGN: THE MAIN EVENTS

383 or 382
Birth of Philip, son of Amyntas III and Eurydice.

368–365
Philip a hostage in Thebes.

364?
Philip given control of Amphaxitis (?). Marries Phila of Elimeia (first wife)(?)

359
Death of Perdiccas III in battle against the Illyrians. Philip II becomes king. Concludes deal with Illyrians not to invade; marries Audata (second wife). Bribes Paeonians not to invade and Thracians not to support their pretender. Dupes Athenians not to support their pretender by withdrawing garrison from Amphipolis. Army reforms begin.

358
Defeats Paeonians and Illyrians. Unites Upper and Lower Macedonia. Intervenes in Larisa (Thessaly); marries Philinna (third wife).

357
Birth of Arrhidaeus (?). Alliance with Epirus; marries Olympias (fourth wife). Retains Amphipolis; Athens declares war on Philip. Alliance with Chalcidian League.

356
Birth of Alexander. Annexation of Crenides; refounded as Philippi. Phocis seizes Delphi. Possible intervention in outbreak of Social War against Athens.

355

Outbreak of Third Sacred War. Siege of Methone begun.

354

Philip blinded in right eye at Methone; city capitulates. Agreement with Cersebleptes in Thrace.

353

Intervention in Thessaly. Philip defeated by Onomarchus of Phocis; army flees back to Macedonia. Repercussions of defeat: Cersebleptes allies with Athens; possible incursions from Illyrians, Paeonians, Epirotes; Olynthus seeks alliance with Athens.

352

Battle of the Crocus Field: Philip defeats Onomarchus. Philip elected *archon* of Thessaly and marries Nicesipolis (fifth wife). Expedition of Nausicles from Athens blocks Philip at Thermopylae. Campaign in Thrace; allies with Byzantium, Perinthus and Amadocus against Cersebleptes.

351

Return from Thrace. Issues warning to Olynthians to stay loyal. Demosthenes in Athens delivers first *Philippic* speech.

350

Possible campaigns in Paeonia and Illyria. Invades Epirus and curtails Arybbas' power; removal of brother-in-law Alexander to Pella for safekeeping.

349

Philip invades the Chalcidice. Returns to Thessaly to deal with Pherae again. Demosthenes delivers first two *Olynthiac* speeches; Athens makes alliance with Olynthus.

348

Philip returns to the Chalcidice. Possible intervention in Euboea against Athens. Demosthenes' third and final *Olynthiac* speech. Fall of Olynthus; Philip takes Athenian prisoners to Pella. Ctesiphon indicates Philip wants peace with Athens. Philocrates proposes embassy to Philip but is indicted (and acquitted).

347

Challenge to Macedonian influence in Thrace from activities of Cersebleptes and Athens.

346

End of Third Sacred War; Philip given the two Phocian votes on the Amphictyonic Council. End of war between Philip and Athens over Amphipolis; Peace of Philocrates. Philip releases Athenian prisoners from Olynthus (taken in 348). Philip elected president of the Pythian Games. Demosthenes' speech *On the Peace*. Isocrates' *To Philip* urges Philip to unite the Greeks and invade Asia.

345

Transpopulation movements within Macedonia for security and economic reasons. Campaign against Pleuratus of Illyria.

344

Philip intervenes in Thessaly and re-creates the tetrarchic system of administration. Philip sends Python to Athens to amend the Peace of Philocrates. Demosthenes' second *Philippic* speech: persuades people to reject Philip's proposals.

343

Philocrates impeached in Athens and flees. Aeschines put on trial for treason during peace talks with Philip in 346; he is acquitted. Arybbas deposed in Epirus; brother-in-law Alexander installed as king of Epirus.

342

Aristotle hired to tutor Alexander. Philip invades Thrace. Defeats Getae in the north; marries Meda (sixth wife). Beginning of involvement in disputes between Cardia (his ally) and Athenian cleruchs in the Chersonese.

341

Diopeithes of Athens campaigns in the Thracian Chersonese against Cardia, hence against Philip. Philip protests formally. Demosthenes successfully delivers *On the Chersonese* and third *Philippic* speeches (possibly also fourth *Philippic*) in support of Diopeithes and against Philip. Philip defeats Cersebleptes and Teres and deposes them. Appoints a Governor of Thrace. Campaigns on west coast of Black Sea.

340

Alexander appointed regent of Macedonia. Philip returns to Thrace. Siege of Perinthus and Byzantium. Philip's letter to the Athenians in which he declares war on Athens; this is not immediately clear to the people. Philip captures the Athenian corn fleet. Athens declares war on Philip.

339

Philip campaigns in Scythia. Philip is defeated by the Triballi. Outbreak of the Fourth Sacred War. Philip seizes Elatea; controls Thermopylae. Alliance between Athens and Thebes against Philip; defence force blocks Philip twice near Cephisus.

338

Battle of Chaeronea. End of war between Athens and Philip. Settlements with Greek states that opposed Philip; pro-Macedonian oligarchy installed in Thebes; Second Athenian Naval Confederacy dismantled. End of Fourth Sacred War. Delegates from all Greek states summoned to Corinth to hear about Philip's Common Peace settlement. Work on Philippeion at Olympia begins (?).

337

Second meeting of all Greek states (minus Sparta) at Corinth; League of Corinth formally constituted with Philip as *hegemon*. Plan to invade Asia revealed and endorsed by Greeks. Marriage of Philip to Cleopatra (seventh wife) at Aegae. Alexander and Olympias leave court for a time. Pixodarus affair.

336

Advance force leaves for Asia Minor. Marriage of Cleopatra (Philip's daughter) to Alexander of Epirus at Aegae. Assassination of Philip (July). Burial of Philip at Aegae. Alexander succeeds to the throne as Alexander III ('the Great'). Revolt of the Greeks ended by Alexander. Macedonian hegemony of Greece re-established.

QUOTATIONS AND ABBREVIATIONS

Quotations from the following ancient sources are taken from these translations (translations of other ancient sources are specified in the notes; where no translator is given, the translation is my own).

Aeschines
C. Carey, *Aeschines*. The Oratory of Classical Greece, Vol. 3 (Austin, TX: 2000)

Demosthenes, *On the False Embassy* and *On the Crown*
H. Yunis, *Demosthenes Speeches 18 and 19*. The Oratory of Classical Greece, Vol. 9 (Austin, TX: 2005)

Demosthenes, all other speeches
A.N.W. Saunders, *Greek Political Oratory*. Penguin Classics (Harmondsworth: 1970; repr. 1984)

Diodorus
C.L. Sherman, *Diodorus Siculus 16.1–65*. Loeb Classical Library, Vol. 7 (Cambridge, MA: 1952; repr. 1971)
C. Bradford Welles, *Diodorus Siculus 16.66–95*. Loeb Classical Library, Vol. 8 (Cambridge, MA: 1963; repr. 1970)

Justin
R. Develin and W. Heckel, *Justin: Epitome of the Philippic History of Pompeius Trogus* (Atlanta, GA: 1994)

Plutarch
Ian Scott-Kilvert, *Plutarch, The Age of Alexander*, Penguin Classics (Harmondsworth: 1973)

These frequently cited modern works are abbreviated in the notes as follows:

Borza, *Shadow of Olympus*	E.N. Borza, *In the Shadow of Olympus: The Emergence of Macedon* (Princeton, NJ: 1990)
Buckler, *Aegean Greece*	J. Buckler, *Aegean Greece in the Fourth Century BC* (Leiden: 2003)
Cawkwell, *Philip*	G.L. Cawkwell, *Philip of Macedon* (London: 1978)
Ellis, *Philip II*	J.R. Ellis, *Philip II and Macedonian Imperialism* (London: 1976)
Errington, *History of Macedonia*	R.M. Errington, *A History of Macedonia*, trans. C. Errington (Berkeley and Los Angeles, CA: 1990)
FGrH	F. Jacoby, *Die Fragmente der griechischen Historiker* (*The Fragments of the Greek Historians*) (Berlin/Leiden: 1926–)
Griffith, *Macedonia* 2	N.G.L. Hammond and G.T. Griffith, *A History of Macedonia* 2 (Oxford: 1979)
Hammond, *Macedonia* 2	N.G.L. Hammond and G.T. Griffith, *A History of Macedonia* 2 (Oxford: 1979)
Hammond, *Macedonian State*	N.G.L. Hammond, *The Macedonian State: Origins, Institutions, and History* (Oxford: 1989)
Hammond, *Philip*	N.G.L. Hammond, *Philip of Macedon* (London: 1994)

Map 1: Greece

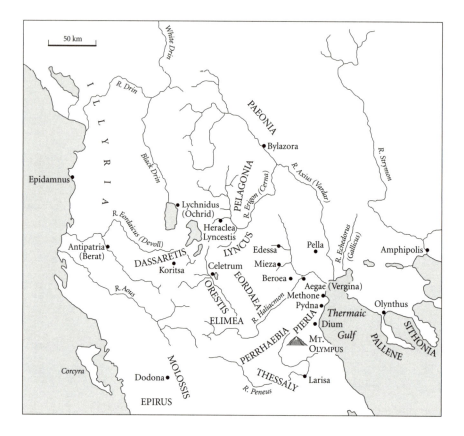

Map 2: Macedonia

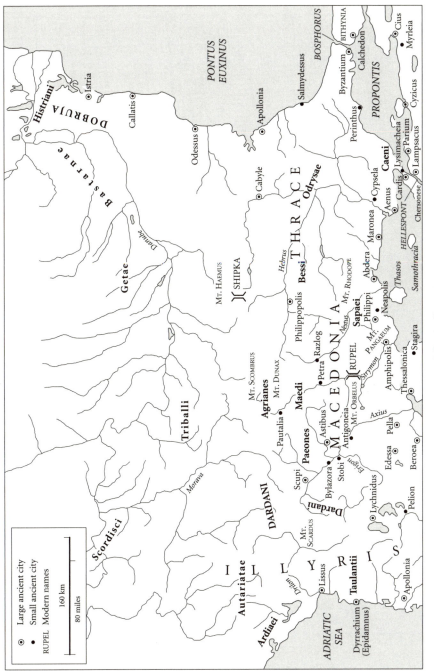

Map 3: The Balkan Area

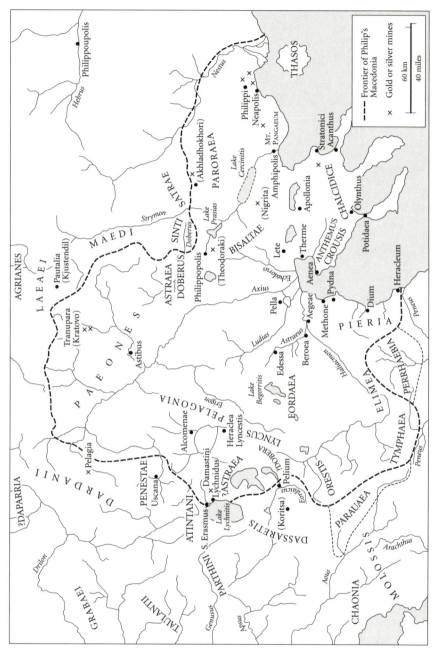

Map 4: Macedonia's Frontiers and Philip's Mines

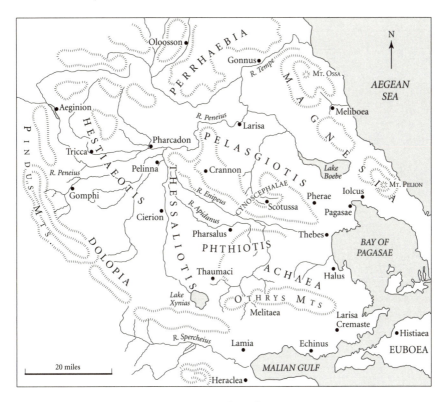

Map 5: Thessaly

1

PREAMBLE:
'THE GREATEST OF THE KINGS IN EUROPE'?

In the summer of 338 BC arguably the most decisive battle in ancient Greek history took place at Chaeronea in Boeotia, as a result of which thousands of Greeks were killed or captured. It was fought between a coalition of Greek states and Philip II of Macedonia, and its outcome would decide the fate of Greece. If the Greeks won, they would retain their autonomy and might even check what was by now Philip's naked imperialism. If the king won, Greek liberty would be lost, and he would add the Greek mainland to his rapidly growing empire. Victory went to Philip, and the course of Greek history, north and south of Mount Olympus (the geographical frontier between Macedonia and Greece in antiquity), was for ever altered.[1] As one ancient source soberly puts it, 'for the whole of Greece this day marked the end of its glorious supremacy and of its ancient independence.'[2]

Philip was now master of Greece. However, the man who had transformed Macedonia from a disunited, weak backwater into an imperial power in a mere two decades of rule would not live much longer. Two years later, in 336, as he was about to invade Asia, he was brutally cut down at the height of his power by an assassin's sword. The throne passed to his son Alexander, who inherited his father's plan to invade Asia and brought it to spectacular fruition. In a reign that lasted for only thirteen years (336–323), he extended Macedonia's empire from Greece in the west to include Asia Minor, the Levant, Egypt, Central Asia and what the Greeks called India (modern Pakistan and Kashmir) in the east. He was not yet thirty-three years old when he died, was worshipped as a god by some of his subjects, and had already planned an invasion of Arabia. Given that he created an empire that was for a long time unparalleled in extent, it is easy to see why history calls him Alexander the Great.

We can therefore understand why Philip is not a household name as Alexander already was in antiquity and continues to be today, and why he still lives in the shadow of his more famous son. But, would there have been an

Alexander the Great without Philip II before him? It goes without saying that all historical figures are a product of their predecessors. Yet in evaluating the relationship of the lesser-known Philip to Alexander, and thus the significance of Philip's reign in Greek history, the question becomes crucial. Alexander's successes, especially in battle, were brilliant, and his reign is one of the most exciting in any period of history. He is arguably the most famous of the ancient world's kings and generals, and the best-known person from antiquity after Jesus Christ. However, without what Philip had already done for Macedonia, for its army, for its nationalistic pride, for its economy, for its cultural life, and for its expansion into an imperial power, Alexander's reign and the world he left behind would have been quite different. He would not be the sort of king to excite popular imagination even today, have movies made about him, songs written about him, and even hotel rooms named after him.[3]

We do not know more about Philip because the ancient source material on him is not plentiful. The histories of Philip or of that period written by contemporary historians exist today only as fragments, quoted by later writers who used them for their own accounts. Of special importance is the *Philippica* (*History of Philip*) in fifty-eight books by Theopompus of Chios, of which we have a large number of fragments. Our other contemporary literary sources are speeches made by Athenian orators, principally Demosthenes and Aeschines. However, the veracity of the information they contain, given that they were written by orators and not historians, is questionable. The first continuous narrative of Philip's reign is that of Diodorus Siculus (of Sicily), who was working in Rome from 30 to 8 BC. He wrote a *Universal History* in forty books covering from mythical times to Caesar's Gallic Wars, and his account of Philip's reign is the focus of Book 16. Then we have Justin's Latin epitome (written at some point between the second and fourth century AD) of the *Historiae Philippicae* by Pompeius Trogus (a first-century BC writer), which deals with Philip in Books 7–9. Also of note is Plutarch (writing in the second century AD), whose biographies of Demosthenes, Alexander and Phocion are of relevance to Philip's reign. Since Diodorus and Justin are our two major narrative sources for Philip, I cite them more often than other sources in my notes. For more details on the ancient sources, see Appendix 1.

Despite the limitations of the sources, much ancient testimony on Philip indicates anything but a king who deserves not to share centre stage with his son in Macedonian history. 'Philip . . . made himself the greatest of the kings in Europe in his time, and because of the extent of his kingdom had made himself a throned companion of the twelve gods', and relying more on his diplomacy than fighting, he 'won for himself the greatest empire in the Greek world', concludes Diodorus at the end of his narrative of his reign.[4] Aeschines reported that Demosthenes called him 'the cleverest man under the sun',[5] and

Theopompus famously said that Europe had never produced a man like him.[6] Perhaps the greatest praise for his accomplishments, especially on the military and economic sides, comes from a speech supposedly given by his son Alexander before his mutinous troops at Opis (in Mesopotamia) in 324, in which he says:[7]

> Philip took you over when you were helpless vagabonds, mostly clothed in skins, feeding a few animals on the mountains and engaged in their defence in unsuccessful fighting with Illyrians, Triballians and the neighbouring Thracians. He gave you cloaks to wear instead of skins, he brought you down from the mountains to the plains; he made you a match in battle for the barbarians on your borders, so that you no longer trusted for your safety to the strength of your position so much as to your natural courage. He made you city dwellers and established the order that comes from good laws and customs. It was due to him that you became masters and not slaves and subjects of those very barbarians who used previously to plunder your possessions and carry off your persons. He annexed the greater part of Thrace to Macedonia and, by capturing the best placed positions by the sea, he opened up the country to trade; he enabled you to work the mines in safety; he made you the rulers of the Thessalians, who in the old days made you dead with terror; he humbled the Phocian people and gave you access into Greece that was broad and easy instead of being narrow and hard. The Athenians and the Thebans were always lying in wait to attack Macedonia; Philip reduced them so low, at a time when we were actually sharing in his exertions, that instead of our paying tribute to the Athenians and taking orders from the Thebans it was we in our turn who gave them security. He entered the Peloponnese and there too he settled affairs, and his recognition as leader with full powers over the whole of the rest of Greece in the expedition against the Persians did not perhaps confer more glory on himself than on the commonwealth of the Macedonians.[8]

Of course, Philip had his critics. Demosthenes, whose bias against Philip is evident in his political speeches, thought the king's aim was to bring Greek freedom to an end. According to him, Philip only succeeded because all of Greece was corrupted, and he owed most of his triumphs to his use of bribery and the 'crop of traitors' (so many of them that Demosthenes said the day would be over before he could name them all) throughout Greece.[9] Although Theopompus offered a seemingly favourable assessment of Philip (cited above), he goes on to criticise the king for such things as his ruthlessness, drinking, sexual appetite for women, men and boys, incontinence, frittering of money, and disregard for friends and allies.[10]

Moreover, in the Opis speech quoted above Alexander followed what he said about his father with a long harangue about how his own deeds and services to his people were much greater.[11] The content of the entire speech is suspect, and it is more than likely a rhetorical composition.[12] However, Alexander did face a mutiny, and he did deliver a speech to his men in which we might reasonably expect him to refer to his father's achievements. The opening references to Philip's turning all Macedonians from nomads to agriculturalists, and replacing animal-skin clothing with the equivalent of Armani suits, are probably embellishments on his part.[13] Yet the remainder of the extract rings true when we consider Philip's accomplishments set against the dire plight that the Macedonians found themselves in when he became king. In the space of a mere twenty-three years, Philip created the first nation-state in Europe; he is the first 'modern' regent of the ancient world, having much in common with Napoleon. By the end of his reign, his lands would comprise the north of modern Greece, the south of the former Yugoslavia, much of Albania, most of Bulgaria and all of European Turkey. He added Greece to his empire and sent an advance force against the Persian empire, able to do so owing to his creation of one of the most formidable armies the ancient world would see. He united his kingdom, centralised the capital at Pella, and developed the economy for the first time in Macedonia's history – and all of this is just the tip of the iceberg.

How Philip achieved all that he did is a remarkable story. It involved a combination of diplomacy, military skill and force, speed, ruthlessness, and an unscrupulous ability to deceive both opponents and allies as befitted his plans. He fought hard battles and waged tough sieges in Greece, the Balkans and as far east as Byzantium, but ultimately he preferred his own brand of diplomacy over fighting.[14] Also part of that diplomacy – and hence of the story – are his seven polygamous marriages, which played so important a role in his policies that one ancient writer says that he 'made war by marriage'.[15] In his battles and sieges he lost an eye, shattered a collarbone, suffered a near-fatal wound that maimed a leg and made him limp for the rest of his life, but he never missed a beat. His face as it appears in a modern reconstruction is testimony to the hard life he led and the knocks he received in the pursuit of his own glory and that of his kingdom (Plate 1).

It is easy enough to describe what Philip did and what he left behind, but what were his goals as king? What were his influences? What made him tick? How did he see himself? Did he have a dark side to his character, as his critics would have us believe? What was the nature of his relationship with Alexander? Was he an imperialist who aimed to rob Greece of its liberty, as Demosthenes said; an opportunist who cynically exploited circumstances and random events for his own ends?[16] Was he a king who wanted to achieve unity in a kingdom continuously torn apart by civil distress and foreign incursion, to transform the economy and create prosperity for his people, to make Macedonia into the greatest power of the ancient word? Did he intend to transform the monarchy into an absolutist one, and in terms of how he saw himself did he seek divine honours towards the end of his life? If so, to what extent did he influence Alexander in this regard, whose pretensions to personal divinity dictated his actions and policy when he was king?[17]

My aim in my life of Philip is to show that he was a great historical figure, to bring him out of the shadow of his more famous son and to demonstrate the importance of his reign in Greek history – and by extension for Alexander the Great. To do so, I present as full a picture as possible of the events before, during and after his life. I hesitate to use the word 'biography' for my book because it is impossible to write one of Philip given the paucity of the ancient evidence. I have refrained from giving excessively copious references to ancient sources (although my narrative is driven by their evidence) and modern scholars' works in the notes; otherwise they would be endless and packed. Generally, I give references to modern works (mostly in English) when I deal with controversial issues or matters that cannot be treated more fully became of limitations of space. These works cite additional bibliography in their notes and the like, especially of foreign works.

All dates are BC except where indicated.

PHILIP'S MACEDONIA

The Land and the People

At the height of his power, Philip ruled a united kingdom that stretched from mainland Greece to Byzantium. In the course of his reign he dramatically increased its size and more than doubled its population. The scale of these achievements is further magnified when we consider what Macedonia was like before he became king.

Originally, the kingdom was comprised only of the valleys of the rivers Haliacmon (to the west) and Axius (the Vardar, extending up to Skopje) and their various tributaries, which flowed – and flow – into the Gulf of Therme or the Thermaic Gulf (Map 2).[1] For much of the Archaic and Classical periods, the kingdom was made up of two areas, Upper and Lower Macedonia.[2] Upper Macedonia (west of Lower Macedonia), in which the Macedonian king had little influence, was an area of remote cantons inhabited mostly by different tribes, stretching up to the Illyrians. It comprised the areas of Tymphaea, Elimea, Orestis, Eordaea, Lyncus, Pelagonia and Derriopus. Life here was tough and probably for the most part a matter of survival. The people were largely nomadic pastoralists, moving their flocks of sheep, goats and cattle to different pastures depending on the season. Winters were cold, summers hot and rainfall in winter was especially heavy.

Lower Macedonia (east of Upper Macedonia) stretched to the Thermaic Gulf, and much of it was coastal plain. It consisted of the original centre of Olympus and Pieria (which means 'rich land' because of its fertile soil and timber), together with the coastal plain of Emathia and Bottiaea, and the areas called Amphaxitis, Crestonia, Mygdonia, Bisaltia, Crousis and Anthemus. Lower Macedonia's fertile soil and rich, well-watered plains enabled the people to grow cereal crops, vegetables, and grapes and other fruit, as well as to graze sheep, goats, cattle and horses with little difficulty. Its warmer climate also tempted those in Upper Macedonia to move their flocks into parts of it during the harsh winters.

Nowadays, what used to be Lower Macedonia and the southern area of Upper Macedonia are in Greece, while the remainder of Upper Macedonia is in the independent Republic of Macedonia (previously part of Serbia, then Yugoslavia).

Given the various areas, the Macedonian state has been aptly described as 'an inner core and an outer rind'.[3] It was thanks to Philip that the two areas were properly united; he achieved unprecedented centralisation of government at his capital, Pella. The Macedonian capital was originally at Aegae, 'the place of goats' (now Vergina), in the northern foothills of Pieria, by the lower Haliacmon valley, about 30 miles (48 km) inland from the Thermaic Gulf (Plates 2a–b). Perdiccas I, the first king of the Argead dynasty, founded the city after an oracular pronouncement that he would be led to the site by goats (hence its name, for *aix* is Greek for goat).[4] The palace there was built strategically on a hillside, on the west side of the city, so as to command a view over the Haliacmon plain and river beyond in case of enemy attack (Plate 2b).[5] However, in 399 King Archelaus relocated the capital to a new site at Pella (Plates 3a–d), a few miles north-east of Aegae.

There are no reliable population figures for ancient Macedonia, but because of their comparative sizes more people will have lived in Upper than Lower Macedonia (despite the fact that the latter had more fertile land). By the time Philip died in 336, the overall population will have increased dramatically. Based on such factors as the bearing capacity of the land and the number of those serving in the army (35,000 in 334, on the eve of Alexander the Great's invasion of Asia), a total population figure of about 500,000 is possible.[6] However, it should be borne in mind that the death rate might have been quite high because malaria was prevalent in Macedonia (and remained so until quite recently).[7]

Philip stimulated the economy as never before, hence contributing greatly to the people's prosperity. Lower Macedonia had good agricultural land, but Macedonia generally was rich in natural resources. These included silver and gold (in Bisaltia, Crestonia and Mygdonia), copper (in Emathia, Crestonia and Amphaxitis), iron (in Pieria and Amphaxitis), lead (in Amphaxitis) and especially timber throughout.[8] Macedonian timber was the best in Greece (oak, pine, fir and cedar, which are found in about a fifth of its lands today, will have grown in antiquity), and was eagerly coveted for shipbuilding. These abundant supplies played no small role in political contacts between the Macedonians and the Greeks to the south.[9] The kings owned all of the state's natural resources (mines, timber and large tracts of farmland), but they were not wealthy because these natural resources were poorly exploited. Moreover, Macedonia's rugged, mountainous terrain and harsh climate made travel and communications difficult, though at the same time the topography provided something of a natural protection barrier against invaders.[10]

That the Macedonian economy was weak, even nonexistent, is ably illustrated by the coinage of Philip's immediate predecessors and of the various tribes.[11] Alexander II (369–368) coined only in bronze, as did Perdiccas III (368–359) after an initial run of silver didrachms. By contrast, the Dardanians (an Illyrian tribe living between the town of Risan and the river Drin in modern Kosovo) minted in silver, the Thracian kings in silver and bronze, and the Chalcidian League and the former Athenian colony of Amphipolis (to the east) in gold and silver. The coinage of this league and of Amphipolis was the major silver currency in the region. All of that would change with Philip II, as we shall see. He exploited the land's natural resources to a greater extent than any previous king, as a result of which the economy boomed and his coinage (especially in silver and gold) became the foremost in Europe.

Ethnicity Issues and Social Snobbery

In antiquity Mount Olympus, the largest mountain in Greece at about 9,461 feet (2,884 m) (Plate 4), formed the frontier between the Macedonians to its north and the Greeks to its south (Map 2). It provided more than a merely geographical line of division, for Greeks called the Macedonians 'barbarians',[12] and were still doing so as late as the last quarter of the fourth century.[13] This does not mean that the Macedonians were uncivilised in our modern definition of the word. Far from it, as is proved by their exquisite artworks, in metals such as gold, silver and bronze, in paintings on the walls of tombs, and in mosaics.[14] To Greeks a 'barbarian' was someone who did not speak Greek: hence, such a person was not Greek.

The nature of the source materials and modern political arguments complicate the issue of whether the Macedonians were Greek or something else (such as a Slavic people who later adopted Greek culture). Here is not the place to elaborate on this in detail: the evidence is set out and the matter more fully discussed in Appendix 2. However, let me say that I believe there is enough evidence and reasoned theory to indicate that the Macedonians were Greek and so Greek-speaking: they simply spoke a local dialect, just as there were different dialects in different parts of Greece. It was this Macedonian dialect that Greeks could not understand. Let me repeat from Chapter 1 that when I refer to 'Greeks' in this book I mean the people who lived south of Mount Olympus, and when I refer to 'Macedonians' I mean those living to its north. I do so only for the sake of convenience.

The snobbery of Greeks towards the Macedonians is shown in other areas. Macedonia was ruled by a monarchy, the people originally preferred barter to coinage (that would change thanks to Philip), and they worked the lands themselves or were pastoralists rather than using slave labour. While the people of Lower Macedonia lived in towns, those of Upper Macedonia inhabited areas that belonged to their tribes (*ethnoi*). The Greeks, on the other hand, used slaves extensively, had a developed economy and lived in an autonomous *polis* ('city-state') system. Here, for various reasons (economic, defensive, political, geographical even), a city in a particular area dominated the other towns and settlements in that area, having its own government, laws, coinage, weights and measures, and social customs.

The Greeks could not understand why free people performed work that slaves could do, and they thought that those living under a monarchy were not intelligent enough to govern themselves. All of these attitudes must have influenced Philip as he struggled to establish himself in Greece, and perhaps to an extent Alexander too.[15] It would have brought Philip much joy to be elected to various Greek constitutional offices as his reign progressed, including presidency of the august Pythian games, in the Olympic cycle, in 346, knowing how much the Greeks would be grinding their teeth over these appointments.

Social Customs

. . . men of restraint and integrity in other fields, who cannot endure a life of drunkenness and debauchery and indecent dancing, are rejected and passed over by a man like Philip. The rest of his entourage are bandits and flatterers, capable of taking part in drunken revelry which I hesitate to describe. This is clearly true, because the outcasts of our society, who were thought lower than mere street-entertainers, creatures like the slave, Callias, who do comic performances and write low songs at the expense of others to get a laugh, these are the people he likes and keeps around him.

So says Demosthenes (who visited Pella on diplomatic missions), complaining that Philip's court was a den of lewd behaviour and drunkenness that drew the lowest human types to visit it.[16] He was not wrong, for Philip was famous for his alcohol consumption,[17] and seems not to have closed his doors to people whom the Athenians, and indeed all Greeks perhaps, might have considered of low repute. In other words, good drinking companions and storytellers. The Macedonians had some significant social and cultural differences from at least the Athenians, which explains why the Greeks looked down their noses at them. One such difference, picking up on Demosthenes' scornful remark, pertained to the consumption of wine and the symposium or drinking party.

The Greeks mixed their wine with water (either warm or cold), pouring each into a large mixing bowl called a *krater*, whereas the Macedonians drank their wine unmixed or neat (*akratos*), hence in the same fashion as the 'barbarian' Scythians and Thracians. It is not known how strong ancient wine was, but the weather and low yields suggest that its alcoholic content was probably 15–16 per cent as opposed to our contemporary average of 12.5 per cent.[18] Mixed wine was thus potent, and unmixed wine even stronger. It also posed potential health hazards: the story goes that Cleomenes I, a sixth-century king of Sparta, went mad and died after drinking unmixed Scythian wine.[19]

The Athenian symposium was a private gathering of men from the upper stratum of society (those from lower social strata of society would drink in taverns).[20] It began in the late afternoon at someone's house and lasted until the wee small hours. The person in charge of the symposium (the *symposiarch*) determined how much water was to be mixed with the wine (so the mixture was not always fifty–fifty), how much was to be eaten and drunk, and what the topics of conversation would be. The attendees were adult men; the only females present would be courtesans providing entertainment (dancing, flute-playing) and sex, and they did not come cheap. The intellectual level of the gathering was high: politics would almost always be debated, and literary works from poetry to Platonic dialogues were read out and discussed. As the wine flowed, the intellectual goals of the evening fell by the wayside and talk was replaced by sex with the dancing girls – if the drunken attendees could still manage it.

Macedonian symposia differed in important respects. Because the Macedonians drank their wine *akratos*, they presumably became drunk sooner than Greeks who mixed their wine.[21] Like their Athenian counterparts, Macedonian men reclined to eat and drink, although a man had to win the right to recline by spearing his first boar without using a net. Respectable women (i.e., wives) were likewise not allowed to attend symposia, but only courtesans and whores (and boys as cupbearers). Another person who was present was the king, which must have brought an interesting dynamic to the gathering. These symposia would also serve as occasions for courtiers to try to outdo each other in their praise and flattery of the king – we see this often enough when Alexander was king, and Philip's would hardly have been different. It is possible that the presence of the king and his senior staff and advisers would turn the symposium into something of a quasi-constitutional affair when the talk turned to business. If so, discussion of state matters would not have been too prolonged, for men 'were drunk while they were still being served their first courses, and could not enjoy their food'.[22]

Philip (and Alexander) were not alcoholics in the sense of always craving a drink and suffering withdrawal symptoms when they were not drinking.[23] They probably drank more than other people because they were kings: the other men looked to them not merely for leadership but to be best at everything. If Philip's symposia were anything like those of Alexander it is no wonder that the Macedonians had the reputation that they did – and why Demosthenes, who was teetotal, said what he did. For example, we are told that Alexander drank so ferociously that after symposia 'he would sleep without waking for two days and two nights'.[24] As for Philip, at his wedding feast in 337 (celebrating his seventh marriage) an angry argument led to him drawing his sword against Alexander and preparing to rush him. He was foiled because he fell over a table in a drunken stupor (see p. 176).

Another cultural difference was polygamy. The family unit was very strong in Greek society, and at least in Athens polygamy was illegal. In Sparta wife-sharing was permitted if a couple had no children (or not enough), but that was a different matter and did not involve marriage. Polygamy was a normal practice for Macedonian kings, and Philip took seven wives without ever divorcing any. How well the royal wives got on with each other is unknown, for they lived together in the royal palace and shared the duties of being queen.[25] But polygamy obviously had political repercussions when it came to the succession. Multiple wives meant multiple heirs (and thus rival factions) contending for the throne, and when Philip II was killed in 336 his heir Alexander faced potential pretender threats.[26]

These social differences are marked, and perhaps they arose because of the different peoples living on Macedonia's borders.[27] Rather than trying to fit in with the Greeks, so to speak, the Macedonians seem to have embraced their own image with gusto. In doing so, they may have wanted to be seen as different,[28] akin to some modern musicians who live large in order to maintain the rock and roll 'image'. Thus, when Mnesitheus, a doctor working in Athens in the fourth century, advocated that heavy drinking was good for you, the Macedonians chose not to imbibe for health reasons.

Political Institutions[29]

The primary reasons for Macedonia's weakness before the reign of Philip were the hostile peoples and powers who encircled and invaded (especially from Upper) Macedonia and the lack of a centralised government.[30] As noted above, the king was not king of *all* Macedonia owing to the division between the Upper and Lower regions and the virtual independence of the chieftains of Upper Macedonia. This situation prevented Macedonian unity, effective central rule and hence any opportunity for growth. Philip was determined to change all that once and for all when he became king.

In the Macedonian constitution the king wielded immense power, and it was his name alone, usually without the formal title of king (*basileus*), that represented it on official documents.[31] He was responsible for conducting domestic and foreign policy and for making wars. He was the commander of the army, responsible for everything from promotions to discipline (including ordering executions), and as a warrior he was expected to lead his troops in battle. Financially, the king was very wealthy thanks to the large tracts of land that he owned, but he could also raise extraordinary taxes. He was also chief priest, charged with such duties as performing state sacrifices, leading processions and organising festivals. In the judicial sphere he acted as final judge in cases of appeal, and he was also the absolute authority in his own family, which included arranging marriages for its members.

The king was constitutionally only one-half of the Macedonian government (the other being the Assembly of male Macedonian citizens), but in practice his power was absolute, and the state was merely a reflection of him.[32] His person was protected at all times by an armed royal bodyguard of seven men (selected by the king himself), and when a new king came to power the people swore an oath of allegiance to him, and he responded by promising to rule according to the law.[33] The people may also have viewed their kings as semi-divine, as a result of a lineage that could be traced back to Zeus, and they were likely deified on death. We know this happened with Amyntas III, for example,[34] and Philip was most likely deified on death.[35]

For advice the king could turn to his closest friends and advisers, who were called 'Companions' (*hetairoi*).[36] They did not form a constitutional body *per se*, and he certainly did not need to follow their advice. Nor was he bound to follow the decisions of the other half of the government, the Assembly.[37] This was composed of male Macedonian citizens who were serving soldiers, noble and non-noble alike, and was convened by the king. It seems to have met to discuss policy and to hear the king on matters of importance, as well as to judge treason cases (when it met under arms). It also acclaimed a new king by having its members clash their spears on their shields. Where there was a clear successor (usually the eldest son), the Assembly's acclamation was presumably a formality. However, where the succession was disputed or in times of emergency it could elect someone who was not next in line, or at least appoint a regent over a minor. Thus, in 359 the Assembly bypassed the young Amyntas because of the dangers facing Macedonia, and acclaimed his uncle – Philip – king instead (see pp. 20–1).

Macedonia before Philip

Before Philip became king Macedonia was in a dismal state. Internal divisions, the incursions of external enemies and the involvement of foreign powers in its domestic affairs caused political, economic and social disorder.[38] A more thorough discussion of Macedonia before Philip is given in Appendix 3, but to understand Philip's accomplishments properly it is necessary to say a little on the subject here.

The Macedonian army was ill-equipped and consisted of poorly trained conscript farmers, who were unable to resist invaders. The major threat to Macedonian security came from the various tribes that lived in Illyria, with that posed by the Paeonians (in the Axius valley to the north) running them a close second. The Illyrians had dominated Upper Macedonia for centuries and had invaded the Lower areas frequently. Earlier kings such as Alexander I 'the Philhellene' (485–454) and Perdiccas II (454–413) had attempted to bring stability by countering Illyrian influence, but they were largely unsuccessful and incursions from the Illyrians still posed a threat in Philip's day. To Macedonia's east was the Chalcidice (Map 4), on whose ports the Macedonians were dependent for their imports and exports. The cities there were eventually bound together in a Chalcidian League dominated by the city of Olynthus, and relations with Macedonia were often strained.

Further south, Athens and Thebes had a history of interfering in Macedonian politics and supporting pretenders to the throne. In 437 the Athenians established a colony at Amphipolis in western Thrace. This was strategically situated on the lower Strymon river, the natural border between Macedonia and Thrace, close to rich mines and within the timber-producing areas that were vital for the Athenians' powerful fleet.[39] Amphipolis then broke from Athens in 424, and the Athenians were determined to retake it, a determination that led to the outbreak of war between them and Philip II in 357 (see Chapter 5). Further, there was a significant Athenian presence on Macedonia's seaboard, which posed a threat to Macedonian security, something that Philip set out to neutralise in the earlier years of his reign.

Another weakness was the dynastic upheavals that plagued much of Macedonian history from the fifth century. Archelaus, who was king from 413 to 399, had a very successful reign, during which he introduced economic and military reforms, and tried to centralise the monarchy and elevate the cultural standing of his court. It was Archelaus who moved the capital from Aegae to Pella in 399. Aegae continued to be the venue for royal weddings and burials, but Pella soon grew to be the largest city in Macedonia (primarily because of Philip II), and it was known as the 'greatest of the cities of Macedonia' (Plates 3a–d).[40] However, after Archelaus' death there followed around a dozen kings in some thirty years, and their reigns often saw the involvement of states such as Athens, Thebes and the Chalcidice in Macedonian affairs. In fact, during the reign of Alexander II (369–368/7), the Thebans demanded the surrender of fifty sons of noble Macedonians as hostages, including the king's youngest brother, Philip (later Philip II). For Philip, the three years he spent as a hostage in Thebes were of great influence when he became king (see Chapter 3).

Then, in 367, Perdiccas III came to power. The relative calm of his reign was abruptly shattered in the summer of 360 or 359 when the Dardanians of Illyria invaded Macedonia, killing the king and four thousand Macedonian soldiers in battle. The Illyrians went on to seize several Macedonian cities and prepared to move against Pella itself.[41] The scale of this disaster was magnified because the heir to the throne, Perdiccas III's son Amyntas, was still only a minor. In addition to the Illyrian invasion, the Paeonians to the north massed to invade, and the Thracians and the Athenians supported two different pretenders to the throne. Macedonia, as has been aptly described, was in a 'melancholy condition'.[42] Only a miracle, it seemed, would save it; and, as we shall see, one came in the shape of Philip.

PHILIP'S YOUTH AND ACCESSION

Philip's Early Years

Little is known of Philip's birth and upbringing. His father was King Amyntas III and his mother, Eurydice, was most likely a princess in the royal house of Lyncestis in Upper Macedonia.[1] She was also the granddaughter of King Arrhabaeus,[2] who had successfully appealed for Illyrian aid against Perdiccas II in 424. When the Illyrians invaded Macedonia in 392, Philip's father, by then in his sixties, had married Eurydice perhaps in an effort to secure allies against them. Amyntas' ancestor Temenus, the traditional founder of Argos in the Peloponnese, was descended from the hero Heracles, son of Zeus. Philip's family had ruled Macedonia since about 650, when Perdiccas was said to have moved from Argos to Macedonia to found the Temenid dynasty. By extension, Philip's relationship to Heracles gave him links to the two kings of Sparta and to the Aleuadae, a leading family of Larisa in Thessaly (Map 5), which was at the head of a Thessalian League. Thus, his family pedigree was faultless.

Philip was born in either 383 or 382.[3] He was the youngest of three sons, and he also had a sister, Eurynoe.[4] His two older brothers were kings before him, Alexander II (369–368) and Perdiccas III (368–359). Both met with untimely ends, for the usurper Ptolemy of Alorus murdered Alexander and Perdiccas died in battle against the Illyrians, as we saw. Philip also had three half-brothers (Archelaus, Arrhidaeus and Menelaus), the product of his father's marriage to a woman named Gygaea, who was perhaps an Argead.[5] It is unknown how well the males got along, but the half-brothers may have been challengers for the throne when Perdiccas was killed and even later in 349/8 two of them were living (in asylum?) in Olynthus.

We have a fairly full description in the sources of what Alexander the Great, Philip's son, looked like,[6] but next to nothing about Philip's physical appearance. There were statues of him (and Alexander) in Athens, Olympia, Pella and Ephesus, but these have not survived.[7] A gold medallion from Tarsus is believed to have Philip's head on it (Plate 5), and a herm portrait now in Copenhagen could depict him. He is probably the bearded horseman wearing the distinctive Macedonian felt cap (*kausia*) depicted on a silver tetradrachm coin that bears his name (Plate 6).[8] However, the facial features on the coin are too small to be made out properly, assuming that he was naturalistically portrayed in the first place. There is a small ivory head (found in Tomb II at Aegae) that seems to be part of a family group, and it has been convincingly argued in my opinion that it is a portrait of Philip (Plate 7).[9] The ivory head shows a bearded man with a closed right eye to indicate blindness, which is in keeping with the wound Philip received during the siege of Methone in 355/4 (see p. 49). Since the skull that was found in that tomb shows evidence of trauma around the right eye, as is seen in the modern reconstruction of the face in Plate 1, it is plausible that the body in the tomb is that of Philip too. Hence the ivory head shows us what Philip looked like. For further discussion of the skull and injuries to it that aid the identification, see Appendix 6.

Philip was not a tall man, as is shown by the skeletal remains found in what is thought to be his tomb at Vergina (Plate 8, and see Appendix 6). Estimates of his height based on these remains range from 65 to 67 ins (167 to 171 cm). Given the larger-than-life role Philip played in history, it is perhaps startling to realise that he was a short and slender man; certainly having none of the build or height of Val Kilmer, who played him so well in Oliver Stone's movie *Alexander* (2004).

Philip would have been educated at home, as was the Macedonian custom, and trained like any other Macedonian noble boy. We know a little more about Alexander's earlier upbringing, and presumably Philip's was not greatly different.[10] Thus, there would have been the customary emphasis on physical training, such as learning to fight, to ride a horse, to run and to hunt. The hunt was an important social occasion, and Macedonian youths hunted the various animals, no matter how fierce, that inhabited Macedonia. Philip would also have been taught to read the major works of Greek literature, especially Homer, although he does not seem to have modelled himself as much on heroes like Achilles as Alexander was to do. His education at home was interrupted, and indeed his whole life changed dramatically, when he was sent as a hostage to Thebes when he was about thirteen years old. His physical and intellectual education continued in Thebes, under, it seems, teachers who advocated a Pythagorean lifestyle of vegetarian eating, celibacy and pacifism. Philip's later career and lifestyle show his teachers did not inspire him.

Philip grew up attending (and then participating in) the symposia that were part of Macedonian court life. He would have heard all sorts of stories including, no doubt, those that served as warnings about how dangerous the Illyrians were or that explained the attitude of the Greeks to the Macedonians.

He would also have believed in the traditional Greek gods and worshipped them as was customary, but he may also have taken part in the cult of the Great Gods (Cabiri) in Samothrace, a fertility cult that was connected with the gods of the underworld. There is a story that Philip met Olympias (his fourth wife, the mother of Alexander) during a religious festival at the sanctuary in Samothrace, several years before he married her (in 357). He is said to have fallen in love with her then, but the tale is unlikely.[11] Olympias did practise a mystery religion, probably something to do with a Dionysian cult, which involved snake-handling,[12] and which could be connected with the cult of the Cabiri. When she was married to Philip and living at court, we are told that her snakes instilled fear in the men around her.

A Hostage in Thebes

From the age of about thirteen to fifteen, Philip had been a hostage in Thebes, the principal city of Boeotia (Map 1), after the Thebans defeated his brother Alexander II.[13] Hence he was there from about 368 to 365 (following Justin).[14] At that time, despite its relatively small size, Thebes was the dominant power in Greece thanks to its brilliant generals Pelopidas and Epaminondas.[15] The latter's victory over a Spartan army at the Battle of Leuctra in 371 arguably makes Epaminondas the supreme master of warfare before Philip.[16] When Pelopidas died in battle against Alexander of Pherae in Thessaly in 364, Epaminondas took sole charge of Theban affairs. He was killed in battle at Mantinea in 362, against a combined army from Athens, Sparta, Elis and Achaea, and Theban ascendancy in Greece came to an end.

Philip's enforced stay in Thebes influenced him more than anything else; as Justin says, it was this experience 'that most served to develop Philip's exceptional genius'.[17] He stayed at the house of the general and statesman Pammenes, and there is a tradition that he and Pammenes were lovers.[18] It was said that he learned much about military strategy from Pammenes' friend Epaminondas, the hero of Leuctra, especially when it came to the use of shock tactics and the combined deployment of infantry and cavalry in battle.[19] Philip would have watched the training of the famous Sacred Band, an elite corps of three hundred Theban soldiers (supposedly the number came from its being composed of 150 pairs of lovers, who would fight all the more ferociously to protect their partners in battle), and he grew to admire these soldiers.[20]

Thebes itself was inland, but Epaminondas planned to build a hundred triremes, cannily grasping that mastery of Greece lay in military and naval prowess: that meant he would be prepared to face the naval might of Athens. Hence Philip was also made aware of the importance of naval power. This might explain his later attitude to the Athenians, one of courtship and diplomacy for the most part, given that Philip would never have a navy to rival the Athenian. Aside from military influences, Philip was given a first-hand glimpse into what life was like in a Greek *polis* (one that wielded such influence in Greece, to boot), witnessing how it functioned and, in terms of its often xenophobic relations with other Greek states, how it malfunctioned. This experience would pay dividends as he became more actively involved in Greece and played one state off against another with ease.

Thus, Philip learned what military might and unity could do for a state regardless of the power of its opponents. He would have known that the Greeks would continue meddling in Macedonian affairs and that no peace could ever be made and kept by means of normal diplomatic ties. Despite their cultural similarities, military means were the only way to prevent Greeks and others interfering in Macedonia. While the kingdom at that time was hardly in a position to resist any external power, the seeds of what it could achieve in the future may well have been sown in Philip's mind during his time in Thebes.

It may be queried how much a young teenager could learn when he was being kept against his will in a foreign city. Could so young a boy learn anything about complex military strategy and the like, as the sources say he did?[21] However, it must be remembered that Macedonian princes learned by example. From an early age they were trained to fight, to learn about warfare, to admire courage and to aspire to excellence, and they were schooled in Homer and the great battles portrayed in the *Iliad*. When Alexander was only seven, the story goes, he impressed Persian ambassadors in Pella with his detailed questions about the size of the Persian army and communications routes. By the time he turned fourteen and Aristotle arrived to tutor him, he was a tough Macedonian youth and a typical product of his society. He was only sixteen in 340 when Philip appointed him regent of Macedonia, at which time he ended a revolt of the Maedians, a Paeonian tribe on the upper Strymon. Two years later, at the age of eighteen, he commanded the left flank of the Macedonian army at Chaeronea, and more than proved his mettle in battle.

It is hard to believe that Philip, raised in the same tradition, would not have been influenced by his personal contacts with Epaminondas. Indeed, some of his later military tactics regarding his infantry echo those of the Theban general.[22] He would have learned of the need to have secure borders at all times. He saw that while a general could also be a statesman and play an influential role in politics, expansion ultimately needed to be anchored not in diplomacy but in military power. Later he saw Thebes' ascendancy in Greece (371–362) ended suddenly and decisively by its defeat at the Battle of Mantinea. That must have made Philip realise that conquest alone was not enough to establish and maintain superiority. While a well-trained and battle-hardened army was essential, a state needed to be unified and able to keep opponents – actual and potential – from uniting with others against it. When he became king, he put the lessons he had learned at Thebes into practice, and he did not intend either his army or his kingdom to meet with the same fate as the Thebans at Mantinea.

Philip returned from Thebes during the reign of his brother Perdiccas III (368–359). The exact date is not known. He may have been released soon after Perdiccas' accession, perhaps as part of a goodwill gesture by the Thebans since the new king had maintained a pro-Theban, anti-Athenian policy. Certainly Macedonian interests at this time were more dependent on the goodwill of Thebes than of Athens. It is possible that on his return Philip persuaded Perdiccas to allow Thebes access to Macedonian timber for its fleet. This would explain an inscription that records the bestowal of Theban honours on a certain Athenaeus of Macedonia, presumably for his role in delivering much-needed timber.[23] The construction of a Boeotian navy would have given Athens, which boasted the most powerful fleet and was no friend of Thebes, serious cause for concern.

Philip's Governorship

When Philip returned to Pella he did not lead a sedentary life. Perdiccas gave his brother part of the kingdom, probably not to rule in his own right but to administer on behalf of the king.[24] Precisely where this territory was is anyone's guess, but it may have been the strategically important Amphaxitis, which occupied the area from the gates of the Axius to the Thermaic Gulf. Possibly during his years of tenure Philip married his first wife, Phila, the daughter of Derdas II of Elimeia, probably as part of a diplomatic alliance.[25] Philip would marry a total of seven times, and there is some confusion in the sources on the order of his first three wives (Olympias was his fourth).[26] However, it is generally accepted that he married Phila first, either shortly before or after his accession.[27] The latter seems unlikely, I believe, given the chaos that elevated Philip to the kingship and the attention he devoted to ending it which included an almost immediate marriage to an Illyrian princess. A marriage to Phila arranged by Perdiccas (as was his right as king) at a date during Philip's governorship, when it was certainly fitting for the king's brother to marry, is more plausible.

Philip was in charge of his territory during a three- or four-year period of enormous stress. Macedonia's enemies were numerous, and most of his time was taken up with ensuring that the Thracians (between the Aegean and the Danube) and the Paeonians did not penetrate the borders. He was also in control of a force of infantry and cavalry, and it may have been now that he began to experiment with some of the military tactics and the like that he had learned during his stay in Thebes. The timeline from his return to Macedonia to his accession in 359, given the continued problems that he faced in the area he administered, precludes his putative visit to Samothrace and falling in love with Olympias at this stage.

The Circumstances and Date of Philip's Accession

In 360/59 Perdiccas III was killed in battle against invading Illyrians under Bardylis, and his death opened the door to several threats to the kingdom's security.[28] The triumphant Illyrians prepared to push deeper into Macedonia, while the Paeonians under Agis moved down from the upper Axius valley and made ready to invade Lower Macedonia. Indeed, they may have already penetrated its borders.

Moreover, two pretenders to the throne posed serious problems. The Athenians, who had supported a pretender in 429, now threw their weight behind a certain Argaeus. He may be the same man who was installed as king in the 380s with the support of the Illyrians and the Chalcidian League. The Athenians' motive was not so much to take control of Macedonia as to regain possession of their former colony of Amphipolis in Thrace (lost in 427). Perdiccas had offered Amphipolis military aid, although whether this took the form of an actual garrison or merely Macedonian soldiers boosting local numbers is unknown. When news of Perdiccas' death became known, the Athenians sent Argaeus north with three thousand of their own troops as well as some mercenary soldiers under the command of Mantias. They landed at Methone, on the Thermaic Gulf, less than 20 miles (32 km) from Pella and Aegae.

The second pretender threat came from a certain Pausanias, who was most probably supported by Berisades, a king of Thrace. Pausanias may have been the man who had defied Perdiccas III in 368, again with Chalcidian support, and had been expelled by Iphicrates of Athens. Whether the Chalcidian League played any role in supporting this pretender is unknown, but the possibility cannot be excluded. At any rate, Pausanias now marched on the capital Pella from the north-east.

According to Justin, the heir to the throne, Amyntas, was only an infant (*parvulus*).[29] His exact age at the time is unknown,[30] not that this matters too much for he was a minor. Hence Philip, Amyntas' uncle, by now in his twenty-fourth year, may well have expected to be appointed regent until his nephew came of age. That was not to be. Given the threats that faced Macedonia, the Assembly unexpectedly set aside Amyntas without prejudice and, instead of making his uncle regent, acclaimed him king, and the people swore their oath of allegiance to him.[31] Only Justin gives a different account, saying specifically that Amyntas became king on Perdiccas' death: 'so it was that for a long period Philip was guardian for the minor rather than king himself but, facing the threat of more serious wars, and at a time when any assistance to be expected from the infant was too far in the future, he was constrained by the people to take the throne.'[32]

Support for a regency period, however, may also be seen in an extract from the third-century BC Peripatetic biographer Satyrus, who says that Philip was king for twenty-two years. Hence, he was regent for two years and became king in 357.[33] In his account Justin talks about Philip being regent 'for a long period' (*diu*): is two years a long time? In fact, Philip's regency for even a year or two is surely impossible, given the threats facing Macedonia in 359. We hear in our sources of Philip alone overcoming them.[34] Moreover, Diodorus says nothing of any regency in his treatment of Philip's accession.[35] Justin's accuracy is also called into question by his statement that Perdiccas did not die in battle but was assassinated. He is (again) the only ancient source to give this information, and it appears to be quite untrue. Finally, Satyrus displays errors elsewhere in his biography and is guilty of rhetorical embellishment, both of which affect his general credibility.[36]

The decision to bypass the legal heir shows the extreme seriousness of the situation facing Macedonia, for the Argead dynasty believed that the kingship should pass only from father to (eldest) son. If the heir was a minor, a regent was appointed until the child came of age.[37] But it is hard to accept such a scenario in the aftermath of Perdiccas' death, and indeed Philip is supposed to have been challenged by his three half-brothers (the sons of Gygaea).[38] Their opposition (if any) was inconsequential. There is no question that Philip was more experienced in military and administrative affairs than either Amyntas or his half-brothers, and this point would have swayed the Assembly the most. It is also possible that Philip had one of his half-brothers put to death at this time (359) as a warning to the others, for in 348 we find him campaigning against Olynthus, which was offering shelter to two of them. If so, the one killed now was most likely Archelaus.[39] No moves were made against Amyntas, who lived a privileged life throughout the reign and seems not to have minded his uncle enjoying all the power.[40]

These were the circumstances in which Philip became king. The most likely year for his accession is 359, although a date of mid- to late 360 is possible as an inscription from Oleveni (a small village about 3 miles [5 km] south of Monastir [Bitola]) points to 360/59.[41] Also, Diodorus has Philip reigning for twenty-four years,[42] and Justin says he ruled for twenty-five years.[43] However, the figure in Justin is normally read as an ordinal, hence Philip's reign ended in its twenty-fifth year. Furthermore, it is by no means clear that the Oleveni inscription refers to Philip II: it could equally relate to Philip V (221–179). There is also the argument that Philip II's army reforms were so sweeping that they could not possibly have been accomplished in the first year of his reign. However, this assumes that he had to think them all up and start from scratch when he became king. If he had already been experimenting with new tactics in Amphaxitis, based on his experiences in Thebes, during his governorship under Perdiccas, much of the groundwork would already have been laid. Indeed, the forces under his command back then would already be trained in the new tactics and perhaps even weaponry. They might thus have formed the nucleus of the new army even at the time of his accession. This lends weight to Diodorus' statement that Philip enacted reforms as soon as he became king.[44] Thus, Bardylis probably invaded Macedonia in early spring 359 (hence the year 360/59), and Philip became king shortly afterwards.

Philip's inheritance was the worst that any new king could face, and lesser men would have failed miserably in their attempts to save Macedonia. Philip, however, had his experiences in Thebes and in his Macedonian territory, plagued as it had been by external threats, to draw on, and failure was not in his vocabulary. Macedonia, the dormant giant of the Balkan peninsula, was about to be awakened.[45]

THE NEW ARMY AND THE
UNIFICATION OF MACEDONIA

Elimination of the Threats to Macedonia

Speed and money were central to Philip's thinking at this crucial time, factors that he would consistently focus on as king. The Greeks might understand the use of money to get something but, as they would soon find out to their detriment, they would never get to grips with the speed with which Philip could move as a result of power being concentrated in his hands.

According to Diodorus, although the Macedonian people were 'in the greatest perplexity', Philip 'was not panic-stricken by the magnitude of the expected perils, but, bringing together the Macedonians in a series of assemblies and exhorting them with eloquent speeches to be men, he built up their morale'.[1] At the same time he knew that he needed to act quickly. He mustered the remnants of the Macedonian army and recalled the garrison that Perdiccas III had earlier sent to Amphipolis. The situation perhaps forced him to hire mercenaries,[2] although from where he got the money at this critical time is unknown. Even so, the poor state of the army made it an easy prey for any invader. As Justin tells us, 'Philip could not take on these wars all at once, and he decided they should be dealt with separately'.[3] He abandoned any plan to resist the invaders on the field. Instead he switched to diplomacy, at the heart of which was the sort of deception that would become his trademark.

The most urgent threat came from the Illyrians, although fortunately for the Macedonians Bardylis did not press home his advantage following his defeat of Perdiccas. Instead he returned home, thus effectively ending the Illyrian menace. The only explanation for this surprising decision is that the two kings concluded some sort of treaty, or at the very least a truce, which may have included in its terms Philip's marriage to an Illyrian princess, Audata (who may have been Bardylis' granddaughter).[4] This was Philip's second marriage. Since the Macedonians were in no position to refuse anything at this time, Bardylis presumably dictated the terms. The Illyrians probably remained in control of Upper Macedonia, or at least of Lyncus and Pelagonia, and Philip may also have had to agree to continue paying them tribute.

With the benefit of hindsight we can say that Bardylis was guilty of a serious miscalculation, for his next encounter with Philip, a year or so later (see below), would end very differently. At this time, however, he may well have thought that, given the stranglehold he had imposed on Macedonia, and by dint of having the Macedonian king as his son-in-law, there was no need to wage further warfare. His blunder, however, gave Philip the one thing he needed most: time to regroup and turn the tables.

Philip next applied himself to the question of the Paeonians: by simply 'corrupting some with gifts and persuading others by generous promises he made an agreement with them to maintain peace for the present'.[5] In other words, he bribed them not to invade. When it came to the pretender Pausanias, the king was lucky. The previous Thracian king, Cotys (of the Odrysians), had very likely been assassinated shortly before Philip came to the throne, and his son and successor, Cersebleptes, faced threats from two rivals, Berisades and Amadocus. Confusion reigned before the three of them split the Odrysian kingdom: Berisades took western Thrace (probably from the Strymon river to Maroneia), Amadocus central Thrace (Maroneia to the river Hebrus), and Cersebleptes eastern Thrace (Hebrus to the Chersonese). Philip was able to bribe Berisades (who most probably supported Pausanias) to put the pretender to death.[6] For the moment Thrace gave him no trouble but he would have to deal with it again in due course.

Argaeus and the Athenians posed a far more serious problem.[7] It is here that we first see the cunning that is part and parcel of Philip's dealings with the Athenians.[8] He beguiled them into believing that when he had earlier recalled the Macedonian soldiers (who had been sent there by Perdiccas) from Amphipolis he was giving up any claim on it.[9] It is hardly surprising that the Athenians, eager to reclaim their former colony, interpreted his move in this way. Although Diodorus says that Philip declared Amphipolis autonomous,[10] it had actually enjoyed this status for some time; strictly speaking, it was hardly a question for Philip to determine. He operated in a deliberately ambiguous way, however, and would hardly have pointed out that the Athenians were misinterpreting his actions. His tactics paid off: believing he was going to return Amphipolis to them, the Athenians withdrew their support for Argaeus, and Mantias, the Athenian commander, stayed at Methone with his troops.

A desperate Argaeus, supported by his own mercenaries and some Macedonian exiles eager to return home, set off for Aegae. It was pointless marching on the king in Pella itself, given that the Athenian force was no longer with him. Moreover, since Aegae was the old capital, Argaeus may have expected to find nobles there who were against Philip's accession and hence would support him. At Aegae the pretender appealed to the people to accept him as their king, but they refused. The loss of Athenian support may have been a factor, but we should not discount Philip's presence at nearby Pella. If there had been any dissatisfaction with the election of Philip, it was clearly not enough to give Argaeus the edge he needed. In despair he turned back to Methone, but en route Philip and a small force surprised him. After many of his mercenaries had been killed Argaeus either surrendered or was himself killed.[11] With that danger over, Philip sent a letter to Athens seeking an alliance. The Athenians were swayed, and the two sides eventually agreed to a peace treaty. Most significant among its terms was that Philip gave up any claim to Amphipolis, which is perhaps an indication of the seriousness of Argaeus' threat.[12]

The miracle needed to save Macedonia had happened. Within a year of coming to power, Philip had ended the four external threats that had led to his extraordinary accession. He did so by adopting a diplomatic strategy that included deceit, bribery and political marriage, and by the lightning speed of his actions. This combination would all too often baffle his opponents as the years passed.[13]

There was still a potential danger from the Chalcidians, who had a long history of interfering in Macedonian affairs. Perhaps realising that they might be next on Philip's list, and anxious to protect their economic interests in the mines of their region, an embassy from the chief city of Olynthus went to Athens to seek an alliance against Philip. The Athenians at the time were debating what to do about Philip's own request for an alliance with them. Since relations between the Athenians and Chalcidians were already strained, principally because of Athenian moves to recover Amphipolis, and with the carrot of regaining Amphipolis dangling in front of them, the Athenians rejected the Olynthian overtures and voted instead for the treaty with Philip.[14] All that the Chalcidians could do over the next few years was to monitor Philip's movements, no doubt with alarm when he moved into the Crenides area and diverted the income from its mines into his own coffers (see Chapter 5).

Philip must have realised that the deals he struck with his various enemies in 359 had bought him little except time. Bribes would only work in the short term, and besides he did not have the financial resources to keep buying people off or to maintain mercenaries. If the kingdom were to prosper it was essential for him to secure its borders against future invaders, to unite Macedonia and to stimulate the economy. For that he needed an army, and thus it was that the army became central to his policy of unification, border security and economic progress.[15]

Philip's Military Reforms

It was now time to put into practice what Philip had learned while a hostage in Thebes. The peasant levies that made up the Macedonian army were untrained and poorly equipped, and could not therefore effectively repel invasions. Moreover, Philip needed to replenish manpower reserves quickly, for four thousand men had died with Perdiccas in battle against the Illyrians. In this, Philip was spectacularly successful. When he invaded Illyria in 358 (see below), the army numbered 10,000 infantry and 600 cavalry;[16] by 352, 20,000 infantry and 3,000 cavalry;[17] and in 334, on the eve of Alexander the Great's departure to Asia, the Macedonian contingent in the 24,000-strong Greek army was 12,000 infantry and 1,800 cavalry. In addition, Alexander left Antipater, the regent of Greece in his absence, with 12,000 infantry and about 1,500 cavalry.[18] As Diodorus puts it, when Philip died he left an army 'so numerous and powerful that his son Alexander had no need to apply for allies in his attempt to overthrow the Persian supremacy'.[19] There is exaggeration here, for both Philip and Alexander needed allies, and the latter frequently demanded reinforcements from Antipater; but there is no question that Philip dramatically added to the army. The increase would have come principally from the union of Upper and Lower Macedonia and the integration of new areas (and hence peoples) as Macedonia expanded its territories throughout his reign.

It is impossible to say what parts of the army Philip inherited from previous kings, and what he created himself, as the sources say so little on the subject. It is also impossible to provide a timeline for the reforms. Everything did not happen overnight, and military innovations were still being made as Macedonia increased in size and power over the next decades.[20] The Macedonian king was on friendly terms with Thessaly, from where he obtained most of the horses for his cavalry, but the numbers would have increased dramatically when he became *archon* (ruler) of Thessaly in 352 (see p. 65). When Alexander invaded Asia in 334, the Thessalian cavalry was almost as numerous as his own Companion Cavalry. Similarly, Thracian cavalry and javelin men (peltasts) would not become a regular part of the army until Philip conquered Thrace in the late 340s. It is plausible that some of his military reforms grew out of what he had done while he was governor of probably Amphaxitis. At that time, Perdiccas may even have encouraged him in his innovations, not wanting to waste what Philip had learned in Thebes. He may well have seen the advantage of having his governor try out new tactics and even weaponry before adopting them for the Macedonian army as a whole. This would help to explain Diodorus' comment that when Philip became king he could turn to military reforms immediately.[21]

Philip began by switching the main attacking arm of the army from the infantry to the cavalry, which was the reverse of conventional Greek practice. His strategy from now on was to have the cavalry attack the flanks of the enemy, while his infantry bore down on the centre. He (or possibly Alexander II before him) may also have given the name *pezhetairoi*, or foot companions, to the infantry to show they were a complement to the cavalry companions.[22] The massed infantry unit was called the phalanx. It was organised in regiments (*taxeis*), which like the cavalry were based on the territory from which each came.[23]

Instead of the usual short sword that Greek infantrymen carried to stab at the enemy, each Macedonian infantryman would now carry a deadly new weapon, the sarissa. This was a long pike (estimates vary between 14 and 18 feet [4.25 and 5.50 m], though the latter is the length in the Hellenistic period) made of cornel wood with a pointed iron head, and it required both hands to hold and use it.[24] When marching in what was called 'close order' (*pyknosis*), the men carried their sarissas in an upright position. However, when they were about to engage an enemy in battle the first five ranks of the phalanx lowered their sarissas to a horizontal position, pointing forward (Figure 1). As they charged, the others behind them followed suit. They may also have manoeuvred the sarissas forward and back in a jabbing motion when they actually came into contact with the enemy line.

The extreme length of the sarissas (perhaps three times as long as the regular Greek spear) meant that the opposing line had little chance of overcoming the Macedonian line. Even if Greek hoplite soldiers managed to kill some Macedonian soldiers in the first line, they were likely to be impaled by the sarissas of the lines behind them. Thus, the two distinct and new features of this pike were its length and the shape of its head, which was designed not merely to damage an opponent's armour or wound him like a conventional spearhead, but to penetrate the armour and keep going into the enemy's body. On the promenade at Thessaloniki is a magnificent statue of Alexander the Great sitting on a rearing Bucephalas, which is flanked by actual-size sarissas (Plate 9). Only by seeing them can one realise just how long and deadly the sarissa was.

Each Macedonian infantryman carried a small shield (*pelta*), about 24 inches (60 cm) in diameter, which had to be slung over his shoulder as both hands were needed to hold the sarissa. Apparently he did not wear a breastplate, but only a bronze helmet, greaves and a cloth tunic, for the phalanx line, with its massed sarissas, afforded him sufficient protection from the enemy. With its massive array of deadly weapons protruding in front of the soldiers, the Macedonian phalanx must have been a terrifying sight to see.

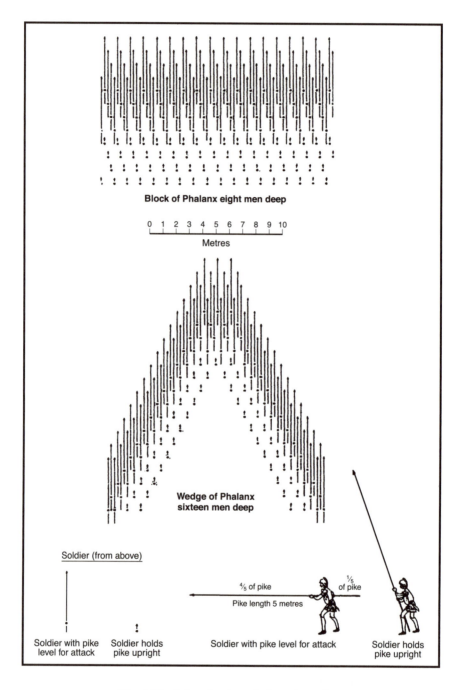

Block of Phalanx eight men deep

0 1 2 3 4 5 6 7 8 9 10
Metres

**Wedge of Phalanx
sixteen men deep**

Soldier (from above)

⁴⁄₅ of pike

¹⁄₅
of pike

Pike length 5 metres

Soldier with pike
level for attack

Soldier holds
pike upright

Soldier with pike level for attack

Soldier holds
pike upright

Fig. 1 The Macedonian phalanx in action

The repeated drilling that the soldiers underwent to ensure that they could march and run with long, heavy sarissas at the ready must have been arduous. The men also trained and exercised before battles, marching thirty stades with full equipment.[25] Moreover, Philip varied the depth of his phalanx formations to meet particular situations. Thus, they could range from eight (the usual number for Greek hoplites) to thirty-two ranks (sixteen was the most common), and the training must have been even more rigorous so that the men could operate with ease and speed at different depths. This flexibility was something that would help to destroy enemies in Greece, and later in Asia under Alexander.

Another unit of the infantry was the hypaspists, the special *corps* of shield-bearing infantry. They were sometimes called *somatophylakes* or 'bodyguards', and this name perhaps indicates their original function as the king's personal bodyguard. It is possible that Philip was not responsible for introducing them, in which case Alexander II may have done so.[26] They were certainly in existence when Alexander became king in 336, for hypaspists fought in his earlier campaigns in 336 and 335, and by 334 they numbered three thousand and were divided into three units. The hypaspists were more lightly armed and trained to move at higher speeds than the regular phalanx, and they may have been handpicked as the elite of the infantry. That would also explain why they were paid a drachma a day, which was more than regular infantrymen.[27]

Philip divided the cavalry into squadrons (*ilai*) based on the areas from which the men were drawn. That would have encouraged each of the *ilai* to fight even more ferociously so that their own areas would come to be identified with their valour. Instead of the usual frontal cavalry charge, Philip trained the cavalry to charge in a wedge formation, which was the Thracian and Scythian practice. The cavalrymen wore iron helmets and a bronze or leather cuirass, and they carried the customary spear (*xyston*) and a short sword. However, one unit of the cavalry (in Alexander's army at least) was called the *prodromoi* or *sarissophoroi*, which indicates that it (unlike the other units) carried the sarissa.[28] It is hard to see how a cavalryman could wield the long sarissa, which needed both hands, while controlling his horse (especially as saddles and stirrups had not yet been invented); perhaps these troops had a longer spear than the regular *xyston*, and so their name was akin to a nickname. The Macedonian cavalry soon became a formidable and much-feared force throughout the Greek world. One contingent was called the Royal Companions, and it fought next to the king in battle; as the elite of the cavalry units, entry into it was presumably subject to intense competition and was dependent on the decision of the king. Philip also seems to have created a corps of mounted scouts (*prodromoi*), a vanguard force that could be deployed quickly.

Philip also incorporated specialist troops into his army from subjugated peoples who became his allies. The inclusion of Thracian troops was noted above, and Paeonian troops seem to have supported the *prodromoi*. There were also the Agrianians, who lived at the head of the Strymon river (west and south-west of Sofia) and who were specialist javelin-throwers, and the *asthetairoi*, infantry units perhaps from Upper Macedonia,[29] although it may have been Alexander who formed them in 334 or 333.[30]

The use of foreign troops (by which I mean those from Upper Macedonia as well as from areas beyond Macedonia's borders) was also motivated by political considerations, for they would transfer their loyalty from their own kings to Philip at Pella. Even so, Philip always had to keep an eye on the foreign element in his army. It is significant that when he was defeated in 353 his army deserted him, and we are told that when he was assassinated some members of his army 'renewed their hopes of liberty, believing they were held in unjust servitude; others, tired of service far from home, were happy to have been spared (going to Persia)', and the attitude of the people towards 'the Illyrians, the Thracians, the Dardanians and the other barbarian tribes' was that they were 'of dubious loyalty and unstable character'.[31] The implications of all this are that as time went on and more foreigners were integrated into the army, the king was not in complete control, a situation that even forced him to change his policy towards the Greeks (see pp. 61–2).

Nevertheless, the Macedonian soldiers came to be not only highly trained fighters but also learned to carry their own arms, equipment and food. This self-sufficiency was crucial at all times, but especially in Philip's later campaigns. It meant that his army could march quickly and easily, especially through narrow mountain passes and over rugged terrain. Moreover, the oxen or mules that normally pulled the wagons could stay in Macedonia and work the land, thereby contributing to economic prosperity.

Gone, then, was the old conscript army of poorly trained peasants supplemented by mercenaries, itself the product of an inadequate military system. In its place came a new army of full-time soldiers, who received regular pay for the first time. The hypaspists were paid the most, at one drachma a day, but there were also 'double-pay men' and 'ten-stater men' as well as others who received less. Philip also introduced a system of rewards. These included cash bonuses and promotion to the enviable ranks of Companion Cavalry and Hypaspists, who might also receive grants of land, as was the case later under Alexander.[32] Land grants may have been given to the rank and file as well, as with the division of the land of Methone in 354.[33]

In addition, a new body was created (or, if it already existed, it was revamped) for the sons of nobles, the Royal Pages (*basilikoi paides*), who became a fixed part of court life.[34] These boys (as many as two hundred of them) entered service at fourteen and left it at eighteen. In addition to receiving an education, they acted as the personal attendants of the king, preparing his horse, accompanying him on hunts and into battle, and keeping watch over him as he slept. Serving as a royal page was a highly coveted position, but there is no question that the emphasis was on military training and the programme may have been a form of officer training for when the pages turned eighteen. The other side of the coin – and this aspect would not have been lost on Philip – was that because these boys lived and were educated at court, they became hostages of sorts to ensure the loyalty of their families to the king. In time, they – and their families – became an integral part of Macedonian society.[35]

Aside from new tactics, Philip was keen to introduce new technological advances, especially in the area of siege engines. There is no question that the innovations introduced by Philip facilitated Alexander's successes in his great sieges, especially at Tyre and Gaza, and progress in areas first explored by Philip continued well into the Hellenistic period after Alexander's death.[36] In about 350, when Philip felt secure enough on the throne, he created a mechanical engineering corps.[37] Given the amateur and conscript nature of the army he inherited, it is unlikely that such a corps existed before he came to power. Philip's new department may have arisen from his interventions in Thessaly, where he came into contact with Polyeides (or Polyidus), a Thessalian experimenting with new designs for siege machinery who later moved to Pella to work.

Exactly what sorts of advances were made in Philip's reign and at what speed are unknown, largely because we lack sufficient source material. Diodorus tells us that Philip used 'machines' and battering rams at the siege of Amphipolis in 357, but what these machines were is anyone's guess (perhaps a form of protective shell to enable men to reach the walls safely). Philip was still using mechanically drawn catapults (Figure 2) to fire bolt-heads (an innovation of Dionysius I of Syracuse in the 390s) at the siege of Olynthus in 348: we know this as a goodly number of these bolt-heads have been found with his name on their stems.[38] The same practice was still in use at the siege of Perinthus in 340, deployed along with battering rams and siege towers (120 feet [37 m] high) as well as the usual field artillery.[39] Then a change took place that revolutionised siege warfare.

The ancient military writer Athenaeus Mechanicus refers to a newly developed type of siegecraft invented by Polyeides, which was used at the siege of Byzantium (also in 340).[40] Here we know that Philip used the torsion catapult for the first time (Figure 2). It was far more powerful than the other catapults of the time, and it could be placed on top of a high siege tower, where its missiles could smash enemy walls. Polyeides wrote a treatise, *On Machines*, that included a reference to *katapeltai Makedonikoi,* perhaps designating those of special design. He and his research and development team also attracted a number of students, and two of them, Diades and Charias, were later to prove a critical part of Alexander's engineering corps.

Significantly the role of the new army was no longer merely defensive, as it had been in the past, but offensive too. For the first few years of his reign Philip probably had to depend heavily on mercenaries. However, that need diminished as time went on and Macedonian manpower was replenished. Led by Philip, general *par excellence,* the Macedonian army would enjoy spectacular successes on the battlefield and in sieges.[41] Of course, in Philip's first few years as king expansion was the last thing on his mind. His goal in these turbulent years was survival (for himself and his kingdom) by dealing with those enemies who had been bought off, either with bribes or diplomacy, but who still posed a threat.

Confident that he had the army's support once his kingship was safely established, Philip now turned to border security. Successful diplomacy was one thing, but he needed a substantive victory in the field in order to test his new army and prove his military leadership. He also wanted to eliminate the threats to his borders that came from Paeonia and Illyria, hence a single campaign against both would kill two birds with one stone.[42]

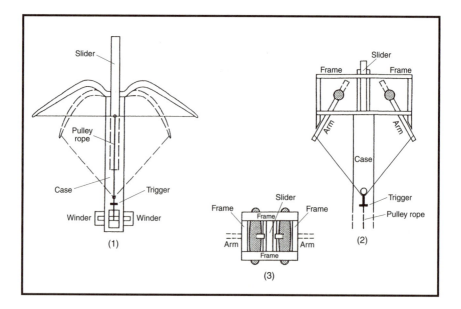

Fig. 2 The mechanical bow and the torsion catapult

Securing the Western Frontier: The Campaign against Paeonia and Illyria

Fighting did not take place during the winter, given the harsh conditions, but in spring 358 Philip marched north against the Paeonians. He probably chose to attack them first because of the confusion caused by the recent death of their king (Agis), and because he suspected they would put up less of a fight than the Illyrians. That is exactly what happened, for Philip's new army defeated the Paeonians easily. The precise details are unknown. However, Paeonia became subject to Macedonia, and some of its people were incorporated into the army, one reason for doing this being to give them a sense of belonging to a larger whole and hence promote loyalty to the king. The area became something of a buffer zone between Macedonia and the tribes of the Danube beyond. Equally importantly, Paeonia lay on the trade route up the Axius valley to Dardania in the north and beyond. This point was surely not lost on Philip even at this early stage of his reign. He was not yet able to exploit Macedonia's own natural resources, but that did not stop him defeating those who threatened his borders and working his way into their spheres of trade.

Philip's army now numbered ten thousand infantry and six hundred cavalry. Spurred on by the defeat of the Paeonians, the king exhorted his troops, perhaps at an official meeting of the Assembly, to march into Illyria. The aged Bardylis does not seem to have had a chance to plan a counter-offensive, and he offered terms. These included keeping the towns that the Illyrians held in Macedonia in return for a guarantee that they would not invade again. Philip refused. He wanted all Illyrian influence expelled from Macedonia. Bardylis had no choice but to fight Philip in pitched battle, and taking ten thousand infantry and about five hundred cavalry he marched to meet the Macedonian king. A year or two earlier the Illyrians had defeated and killed Perdiccas III, plunging Macedonia into chaos, but history would not be repeated.

The two sides met near Lake Lychnitis (Ochrid), possibly close to Heraclea Lyncestis (Monastir).[43] Bardylis must have realised almost immediately that the Macedonian cavalry was far superior to his own: he gambled on his infantry saving the day. He might well have been in his late eighties or even ninety by then, but age had not dimmed his tactical abilities. Expecting Philip to assemble a straight battle line facing him, Bardylis cleverly drew up the Illyrian infantry not in a defensive line but in a hollow rectangular formation. Whichever side Philip attacked with his cavalry it would face Illyrian soldiers. Expecting Philip's infantry to charge head on, Bardylis arranged his toughest and best-trained men on that side of the rectangle.

The best-laid plans, however . . . Rather than face the Illyrian line directly, Philip, on the right flank, marched his phalanx forward, ten men deep, at an angle, so that it protruded further than his left. To Philip's right was his cavalry. When he was satisfied that his line was secure, Philip charged the Illyrians' left side. The infantry for once played the more important tactical role as it had to smash through he enemy line, allowing the cavalry to follow and outflank the enemy. The infantry fought its way through the enemy, and so into the hollow of the enemy rectangle. The cavalry followed the infantry's assault, and now the other three sides of the enemy rectangle were attacked from the rear by enemy infantry and the deadly cavalry. In disarray many tried to flee, including Bardylis, but by the end of the day the Macedonians had killed seven thousand Illyrian soldiers.

Now it was Philip's turn to impose terms. The Illyrians were to pull out of all Upper Macedonian cities: that meant that all of the native tribes as far north as Lake Lychnitis, including those of Orestis, an area controlled by the Molossian kings of Epirus, were now subject to the power of the Macedonian monarchy.[44] New towns were built and Philip also encouraged his people to move there by offering incentives of tax remissions and grants of land. From Lake Lychnitis, a strategic stopping point,[45] Philip would have a route into Epirus to the south and Orestis to the east, thereby allowing him to ward off incursions into Macedonia from the north and west.

The western frontier was now secure as never before: an outstanding achievement given the enmity between the peoples of that region and the court.[46] Philip's victory also generated economic gains for Macedonia, which was now able to take advantage of the Dardanian trading sphere. We saw a similar result with the defeat of the Paeonians. The area also had in it the Damastium mines, with their silver deposits; as late as 337 Philip had to campaign against a renegade chieftain, Pleurias, to protect Dardania and these deposits (Map 4). As we shall see, mining, especially of gold and silver for coinage, became the mainstay of the Macedonian economy.[47]

If there was any opposition from nobles in Upper Macedonia who preferred not to be brought under the power of Pella, it appears to have been inconsequential, at least at this time. Some may have fled, such as a certain Derdas from Elimiotis, who was found fighting on behalf of Olynthus against Philip in 348. Others probably saw the writing on the wall and pledged their loyalty to Philip in return for recognition of their local powers and perhaps other rewards. The latter took the form of important positions in the army. For example, Parmenion, one of the Paeonian chieftains, was made a general soon after coming over to Philip's side. He remained Philip's most trusted general throughout his reign and also served Alexander well, only to be executed on the latter's orders in 330. Then there were three sons of Aeropus of Lyncestis:

Arrhabaeus, Heromenes and Alexander. They were clearly influential because in 336, when Philip was assassinated, we are told that they posed a threat to the succession (see Chapter 14).

Though Philip was still married to the Illyrian princess Audata, the monarchies of the tribal states of Elimeotae, Orestae, Lyncestae and Pelagones were now abolished, and the people became Macedonians, subject to the centralised monarchy in Pella. They also served in the Macedonian army, and Philip immediately began training many of the non-nobles as infantrymen and nobles as cavalrymen. Nonetheless, Upper Macedonia was never completely free of problems, forcing Philip's intervention on a number of occasions.[48]

The significance of Philip's victory over the Illyrians was threefold: first, Macedonia virtually doubled in size; second, manpower for the army was increased within a matter of twelve months, reducing its reliance on mercenaries; and third, and most important, Upper and Lower Macedonia were united as never before, and the king was now king of all Macedonia. Philip did not exactly endear himself to his new western subjects, for he supposedly made Audata change her name to Eurydice in an attempt to mask her Illyrian background, which would have made her unpopular at court. She and Philip had a daughter, Cynnana, who later married Amyntas (Philip's nephew, the real heir in 359) and lived with him at Pella.[49]

Securing the Southern Border: Thessaly

Philip now set his sights on his southern border, which brought him into closer diplomatic contact with Thessaly (Map 5).[50] This powerful state was composed originally of the four tribal areas (tetrads) of Thessaliotis, Pelasgiotis, Hestiaiotis and Phthiotis, each under the control of a tetrarch and ultimately subservient to a single elected king (*tagos*). Its size grew to include the neighbouring areas (*perioikoi*) of Achaea (not the Achaea in the Peloponnese), Magnesia and Perrhaibia (all of which were under the king's control). However, during the fifth century aristocratic factions in the various cities upset the balance of power and so came to dominate Thessalian political life. This situation remained the norm for much of the fourth century.

Two Thessalian cities in particular exerted the most power. One was Pherae (Velestinon), which by virtue of its harbour, Pagasae (Volos), controlled the coastal states. The other was Larisa, which controlled the states of the inland plain and had crafted a Thessalian League under its hegemony. They were bitter enemies. The aristocratic family of Larisa, the Aleuadae, had received support against Pherae from Alexander II before Thebes had intervened. Since there was a connection with the Macedonian monarchy, Larisa now sought an alliance with Philip again in an effort to gain an advantage over Pherae.

Larisa's wish was granted, and in autumn 358 Philip found himself in Thessaly. Two obvious reasons for getting involved there would be to incorporate the expert Thessalian cavalrymen into his new army, for their cavalry force was very large (anything from three to six thousand), and to consolidate his southern border. The passes from Thessaly northwards made Macedonia vulnerable to invasion, and Philip is not likely to have forgotten the imperialistic ambitions of Jason of Pherae, a wealthy tyrant who in the 370s wanted to assert his power over the whole of Thessaly and then further afield (see below). However, a further reason, which may indeed have eclipsed the other two, was that thanks to the traditional contacts with Larisa, Thessaly was about his only ally. At this critical time he needed any friend he could get, and relations between Thessaly and Philip came to play no small role in shaping his policy towards Greece.[51]

Jason, whom Xenophon calls the greatest man of his age,[52] was probably the son of Lycophron who established a tyranny in Pherae. He succeeded his father in about 380 and ruled until 370. In 375 or 374 he proclaimed himself *tagos*, an office that was held for life and may originally have been the title of the first Thessalian monarchs before their power was eclipsed by that of the now dominant cities (see above).[53] As *tagos*, Jason had control of all of Thessaly's considerable military resources, augmented by a mercenary infantry force of six thousand. He was ambitious to increase his own power in Thessaly as well as over Epirus and Macedonia, and is said to have planned an invasion of Persia.[54] His motive was the panhellenic one of liberating the Greeks cities of Asia Minor, then living under Persian rule, and of exacting revenge on the Persians for what they had inflicted on the Greeks in the Persian Wars (480–478). For this venture he would use timber for ships from Macedonia; to this end he had had dealings with Amyntas.[55]

The Thessalian League was no friend of Jason, and it received help against him from Alexander II and Thebes. This led to much disunity in Thessalian affairs, and in 370 Jason was assassinated. His successors, his sons Polyphron and Polydorus, were also elected to the office of *tagos*, but they were never able to unite Thessaly. Polydorus soon died, perhaps at the hands of his brother, and Polyphron was killed a few months later by Polydorus' son Alexander.

Although the power of the tyranny continued to decline (the last tyrants, Lycophron and Peitholaus, were expelled by Philip in 352), Pherae could not forget its previous surge of influence under Jason. Its clashes with Larisa, orchestrated by Alexander of Pherae (elected *tagos* in 369), were a sign that it wanted to regain its influence over Thessaly. Factionalism in Thessaly had the potential to disrupt the security of northern Greece, and hence pose a danger to Macedonia. This was a situation Philip could not allow to continue. Hence, an alliance with the Thessalian League in 358 was a wise move. It would give him a powerful ally and would also present him with an open invitation to take part in Thessalian, and hence central Greek, affairs, because whenever Pherae caused problems Larisa out of necessity would have to turn to the king for help.[56] The alliance was cemented by Philip's marriage (his third) to a Larisan woman called Philinna. She must have been a member of the leading family of the Aleuadae, and not, as Justin says, a common whore.[57] She would bear him a son, Arrhidaeus (who also became known as Philip), the following year.

Epirus and Philip's Marriage to Olympias

After Philip's intervention in Thessaly and his earlier defeat of Bardylis there followed a treaty at some point in 358–357 with Arybbas, the Molossian king of Epirus (Map 2). At this time three large tribes dominated Epirus, the Thesprotians, the Molossians and the Chaonians, of which the Molossians (who spoke a west Greek dialect) were the most powerful and prosperous. They were also the most easterly of the three tribes, hence the closest to Macedonia, and they controlled the summer pastureland of Tymphaea, Parauaea and Orestis. Epirus, like Upper Macedonia, was a land of transhumant pastoralism thanks to its climate, with plenty of winter pastures on the coast and summer ones on the mountainous areas of the North Pindus range.[58]

Since Epirus had also suffered at the hands of Bardylis' Dardanians, the treaty with Macedonia made perfect sense for that kingdom as well as for Philip. Moreover, Epirus had been an ally of Athens since the 370s, and Philip's treaty with the Athenians may also have been a factor, though a less important one than border security. The treaty with Epirus included Philip's betrothal (in 357) to the princess Olympias, his most famous wife (Plate 10). She was the daughter of the recently deceased Molossian king Neoptolemus, hence the niece of Arybbas.[59] As Philip's fourth wife, she gave birth to a son, Alexander (the future Alexander the Great), in 356 and at some later point a daughter, Cleopatra.

By 357, then, Philip's northern, western and southern borders were secure (for the present), his position as king was unchallenged, and his army had more than proved itself as the new force in the Greek world. There were still two major powers that Philip needed to deal with: Athens and the Chalcidian League. Perhaps knowing something of the Athenians' financial straits and of dissatisfactions within their empire at this time, he decided to engage Athens first and placate the geographically closer Chalcidians. It was time to resort to diplomatic deceit once more.

THE WAR OVER AMPHIPOLIS

Athens and Demosthenes

Athens would become Philip's bitterest enemy, and Demosthenes (one of its politicians) his most vocal opponent. In order to understand Philip's dealings with both, we need to survey Athens' power in this period, and look at Demosthenes' background and how he believed Philip could be resisted.

By 359, when Philip became king, Athens was again a military power of some reckoning after a considerable slump following its defeat at the hands of Sparta in the Peloponnesian War (431–404).[1] The Spartans' influence in the Greek world was paramount after their victory, so much so that the period 404 to 371 is called the Spartan hegemony.[2] They soon proved unpopular as leaders, however, and in 378 the Athenians formed an anti-Spartan league, which was called the Second Athenian Naval Confederacy. This became a fourth-century empire, and at its height had over seventy allies.[3] Seven years after the confederacy was founded, Thebes abruptly ended the Spartan hegemony at the Battle of Leuctra. The Thebans then rose to prominence in Greek affairs, thanks to the activities of their generals Epaminondas and Pelopidas, and it was during this time of Theban dominance (371–362) that Philip was a hostage in Thebes. A further clash between Thebes and Athens was inevitable, and it was not long in coming. In 362 the two sides met at the Battle of Mantinea, which ended Thebes' ascendancy, and Athens once again became the predominant power in Greece.

The Athenians' form of government was a direct democracy, meaning that the people had the final say in all matters of domestic and foreign policy.[4] The principal decision-making body under the constitution was the Assembly; several thousand citizens (males only, for women did not have the vote) turned up to the meetings, which were held roughly four times per month and each one lasted a day.[5] Any citizen could speak at the meetings; speakers stood on a *bema* (rostrum) facing the crowd and addressed the issues at hand, and at the end of the debate the people voted by a show of hands. Thus was state policy (including war) decided.

The Assembly met on a huge rocky outcrop called the Pnyx (Plates 11a–c; in the top right-hand corner of Plate 11a can be seen the rostrum from which speakers addressed the people), which was in sight of the Acropolis. Attendees sat by tribes in a semicircular auditorium area of the Pnyx, facing the *bema* and with the Acropolis to their left. The proximity to the latter allowed speakers and audience an unrestricted view of the Athenian citadel with its monumental entranceway and temples on top, of which the Parthenon is still the most famous. The idea was that the people would see the visible signs of Athens' greatness as they met to discuss policy affecting their city. The feelings that this spectacle must have generated can still be felt today when one visits the Pnyx and takes in the spectacular view of the Acropolis when approaching the *bema* (Plate 11b) as well as that over the Agora (the marketplace) from on top of the *bema* (Plate 11c).

Another powerful body was the Boule (often called simply the Council), which set the Assembly's agenda and could advise the Assembly about matters on it.[6] It was composed of five hundred men (after 508) over the age of thirty; they were elected from all areas of Attica, and lived and worked in Athens for one year. This body became vastly influential in Athenian public life, not least because it met almost every day: as a result it took on supervisory powers, oversaw a number of boards that were charged with carrying out various aspects of city life, and made decisions that could not wait until the next Assembly meeting.

There were elected political offices, but in our period influential statesmen did not necessarily hold them. A number of men took advantage of rhetorical training and used their oratorical powers in the Assembly to persuade the people to adopt their policy. Hence, political power came to rest not on political office but on popular support in the Assembly.[7] The men who influenced policy there were referred to as *rhētores* (orators) or demagogues (leaders of the people), and hence real power came to lie in the hands of a few influential speakers.[8]

Against this background Demosthenes became not only Philip's most hardline political opponent but also Greece's foremost orator.[9] The portrait that we have of him today (Plate 12) was sculpted after his death, and shows him at the height of his maturity in reflective mood.[10] Demosthenes was born in about 385. He came from a wealthy family, but when he was seven his father died and the guardians to whom the estate (and Demosthenes himself) were entrusted squandered the money. Faced with financial ruin, he was forced to sue the guardians in court in about 364, when he was roughly twenty.[11] He won his suit convincingly, and that success earned him enough of a reputation to pursue a career as a speechwriter (*logographos*), writing court speeches for prosecutors and defendants for a fee. At some point he decided to move into the political arena. His first speeches in the Assembly were made in the 350s and were unsuccessful, but his fortunes would change when he turned his attention to Philip's involvement in Greece.

Philip, Athens and Amphipolis: Diplomacy, Deceit and the Outbreak of War

As we have seen, by the end of 358 Philip had secured all of his immediate borders, but there were still hostile powers beyond them. The Athenians were nominally Philip's allies, but their eagerness to increase their influence in the north and regain Amphipolis made their loyalty suspect.[12] The Chalcidian League boasted a formidable army of ten thousand infantry and one thousand cavalry, and it had a defensive alliance with Grabus, the king of the Grabaei of Illyria. Fortunately for Philip, the Chalcidians and Athenians were not on friendly terms. In 361 the Athenians had established a cleruchy (a settlement that took over the land and displaced the existing population) at Potidaea, on the neck of the Pallene peninsula (Kassandra), only a little over a mile from Olynthus. This they could use as a naval base. They had also captured Torone on the tip of the middle prong of the Chalcidice. Plus there was Amphipolis, also uncomfortably close to Olynthus, which the Athenians wanted.

Nevertheless, Philip's actions at this time could have drawn Athens and Olynthus together in an 'any enemy of my enemy is my friend' way. The king was in need of money to pay his new army. He had previously secured the rich mines in the Damastium region, north and east of Lychnitis, after his defeat of the Illyrians in 358. The income gained there was also of benefit to the Macedonian economy, and with this in mind Philip now set his sights on the mines of Crenides, which were of economic importance to the Chalcidians. It was also probably now (if not before) that Philip felt safe enough on the throne to decide that the Athenians could not have Amphipolis, despite his earlier agreement with them.[13] Its position, controlling as it did the eastward route into hostile Thrace and being the lowest crossing point of the Strymon (Map 3), made it too important for Macedonia's border security to be in Athenian hands. Also, it lay on several important trade and communication routes, not least of which were to the rich mines at Crenides and the waterway to the Strymon basin and Danube beyond. Philip's decision to keep Amphipolis may well mark the point at which he began to plan the large-scale expansion of the Macedonian economy.[14]

The people of Amphipolis were not impressed by Philip's change of mood. Two men, Hierax and Stratocles, went to Athens and asked the people to 'sail and take over the city'.[15] Their status is unknown; Demosthenes does not call them envoys, although Theopompus does. Thus, they may not have gone to Athens with the official backing of the government in Amphipolis, but merely represented an anti-Macedonian faction that preferred an alliance with Athens to one with Philip. In any case, they arrived too late, for at the start of the next campaigning season (spring 357) Philip led an army to Amphipolis and besieged it. His announced reason – that it was now openly hostile to him – fooled no one.

For the Athenians to send help to Amphipolis they would need a base in the region. The Chalcidic peninsula boasted numerous ports, but the Athenians' earlier rejection of Olynthian overtures for help against Philip meant they would find no friendly harbour there. They may have based a small fleet on the island of Thasos, but if so it did not do much. To make matters worse, they were faced with dissension on the part of some allies in their confederacy and thus with the threat of a serious revolt. Their mind was finally made up when they received a letter from Philip in which, according to some sources, he recognised the city's right to Amphipolis and promised to hand it over to them when he captured it.[16] Hearing of this, the people seem to have thought that they had misjudged Philip. That he was duping them apparently did not occur to them.

Probably in response to the king's letter, if we can believe Demosthenes, the Athenians sent two ambassadors, Antiphon and Charidemus, to him.[17] They were supposed to have concluded a secret agreement, according to Demosthenes in a speech made some years later to the Assembly, by which Philip would hand over Amphipolis in return for the Athenians giving him their ally Pydna (on the coast of Pieria).[18] The secrecy was necessary so as not to alarm the Pydnaeans! This arrangement should not be considered part of the original treaty of 359 because neither side honoured the contract, and besides it is hard to imagine either one patiently waiting two years from 359 until now to receive either place. The supposed 'secret agreement' is an instance of oratorical falsehood on the part of Demosthenes,[19] for only the Assembly could make a treaty and nothing of this nature in the democracy could remain secret.[20] Indeed, when Philip secured Amphipolis he immediately turned to attack Pydna, so it would hardly have figured in negotiations between the two powers.

The siege of Amphipolis did not last long. The Macedonians attacked in a series of frontal assaults using scaling ladders, battering rams and siege 'machines' (it is not known what the last were exactly). Once they had scaled the walls or smashed through their breached sections the defenders were soon overcome, and the city had capitulated by the late summer of 357. The conquering soldiers looted the city, keeping much of the booty for themselves with Philip's permission. Taking walled cities by storm in this period was no easy feat: among other things, the torsion catapult was still at a developmental stage, and would not be used until Philip besieged Byzantium in 340 (Figure 2).[21] Although Demosthenes attributed the fall of Amphipolis to traitors within, we should dismiss his comment and give Philip credit for his accomplishment.[22]

Diodorus tells us that Philip 'exiled those who were disaffected towards him, but treated the rest considerately'.[23] The punishment, however, came from the Amphipolitans themselves, as a decree exiling Stratocles, Philon and their children for ever testifies (if it is to be dated to 357/6).[24] The opening of the decree uses the formula 'resolved by the people', meaning the Assembly, the main political organ. This indicates that Philip allowed the democratic Assembly in Amphipolis to continue functioning. Why the Assembly singled out these two men is not known, for it is hard to believe that they were Philip's only opponents. Stratocles, for instance, had gone to Athens with Hierax to seek aid against Philip, yet there is no mention of Hierax in this decree.

In Athens the news that some (at least) pro-Athenian leaders had been exiled must have caused unease, but the people believed that Philip would honour his word. The truth was quite different. Philip held on to Amphipolis and suddenly besieged Athens' ally Pydna, which fell to him very quickly (again there was talk of treachery from within).[25] The Athenians were now left with nothing but the humiliating realisation that Philip had completely deceived them. It would not be the last time. In an effort to save face, they declared war on him in the latter part of 357. The so-called 'war for Amphipolis' would prove futile.[26]

Philip and the Chalcidice: The Snubbing of Athens

Philip probably expected the Athenians to declare war, and Diodorus tells us that both they and Philip now sought an alliance with Olynthus, given the forces that the latter could muster.[27] Since Athens had made an alliance with Grabus of Illyria as well as with the Thracian and Paeonian kings at about this time (or perhaps in summer 356),[28] an agreement with the Chalcidian League was not impossible. In an effort to prevent this, the king promised to seize Potidaea from Athenian control and give it to the Olynthians, along with Anthemus, a Macedonian possession in the west of the Chalcidice.

Philip's track record of promises made and broken ought to have set alarm bells ringing in Olynthus. It did not. The promise of Anthemus and Potidaea proved too much, and the Olynthians entered into negotiations with Philip. Interestingly, both parties consulted the Oracle of Apollo at Delphi, the most important oracular site on the mainland, about a treaty. This was not a common practice, and it may have been undertaken at Philip's insistence, for if Apollo was in favour of the treaty the god's sanction was something the Olynthians could not ignore. The treaty was made in the winter of 357–356, and it was no small blow to Athenian diplomacy.[29] If either party broke its oath to keep it, then 'many evils should fall on those who committed perjury'. Copies of the treaty were set up at Delphi, at the Temple of Zeus at Olympia, at Dium and in the Temple of Artemis at Olynthus. In keeping with his promise to the Olynthians, Philip began preparations for a siege of Potidaea.

Athens' apparent apathy in its war against Philip is at first sight surprising. We would have expected the city to launch a substantial force against the king when he kept Amphipolis and again when he secured an alliance with the Chalcidian League and moved on Potidaea. The Athenians did send help to their beleaguered garrison in Potidaea, but it failed to arrive in time. They had been involved recently (in 357) in the island of Euboea (off Attica's east coast), where they successfully ended Theban influence and re-established their own.[30] Euboea did not rejoin the Athenian confederacy, but the Athenian victory was important given the strategic importance of the island. However, the real reason for Athens' apathy was the revolt of its allies that it faced in 356–355. This is commonly called the Social War, and in it we may plausibly see Philip at work.

Diverting Athens' Attention: The Social War

There had been dissension on the part of the allies in the Second Athenian Naval Confederacy for some time, apparently as a result of the Athenians' return to the exploitative imperialistic practices of their fifth-century empire and their lack of respect for their allies' autonomy. For example, in 365 the Athenian general Timotheus won back the strategically important island of Samos from the Persians. The Athenians established a cleruchy there in the same year, and two more waves of cleruchs were sent there in 361/0 and 352/1, despite the fact that when creating their confederacy the Athenians had sworn not to resort to this practice. Furthermore, the confederacy was supposed to have an allied council (*synedrion*) free of Athenian interference, but in time this too was disregarded.

In 356 matters came to a head when Chios, Rhodes, Cos and Byzantium accused the Athenians of plotting against them and revolted.[31] They were also encouraged to do so by Mausolus, the satrap of Caria, who had come into contact with them during the Satraps' Revolt and who now sent naval support.[32] Other allies likely followed suit, and the rebels assembled a fleet at Chios. The Athenians were not prepared to let these important places secede from the confederacy, and they sent their generals Chares and Chabrias against them. There must also have been a degree of anxiety over Mausolus' support, which had reinforced the rebel fleet. The Athenian fleet attacked the city of Chios (on the island's eastern side), but Chabrias was killed in fighting at sea, and Chares, who was leading a land assault, only extricated himself with some difficulty. The rebels went on to win over several places, such as Lemnos and Samos.

The Athenians put their dealings with Philip on the backburner for the moment and sent a fleet of another sixty triremes under the generals Iphicrates, Menestheus and Timotheus to Chares' assistance in 355. The two fleets came together at Embata (perhaps off Erythrae), but bad weather with high winds and swells ought to have prevented a battle at this time. Instead, disregarding the advice of his fellow generals, Chares sailed to face the rebels alone. He was defeated, losing many ships in the process owing to the weather, and that defeat effectively ended the war. Athens the *hegemon* was forced to come to terms with its allies in the same year. Chios, Cos, Rhodes and Byzantium became independent (and allies of Mausolus), and were quickly followed by a majority of the other allies. The Second Athenian Naval Confederacy was reduced to a shadow of its former self, for the remaining allies were few, weak and scattered widely across the northern Aegean and the Thracian coast.

Later, probably that winter, Chares prosecuted the other three commanders for taking bribes from the enemy not to engage in battle. Iphicrates and Menestheus were acquitted, but Timotheus was fined the enormous sum of 100 talents. He was unable to pay, and so fled into exile. This trial shows the lack of proper military leadership in the city at this time, not to mention the blindness of the people in supporting Chares, who had acted rashly and greatly to the city's military and financial detriment, over the other three.

Why the Social War broke out when it did is unknown. It is true that the Athenians were not living up to the oaths they had sworn in the confederacy's charter. However, their actions were not as oppressive as they had been under their fifth-century empire, and no widespread revolts had taken place then, despite there being ample opportunity on at least two occasions when the Athenians were on their knees from large-scale manpower losses (following the great plague and the disastrous Sicilian expedition). Another explanation for the Social War lies with Philip (although no ancient source attests to this), for the timing of the revolt with respect to his own activities was too good to be a mere coincidence. It would have been easy to play on the grievances that the allies harboured towards the Athenians, and he may even have offered them Macedonian friendship or protection. His motives would have been to divert Athens' attention away from his exploits in the north, especially his intended siege of Potidaea, and to weaken the city's naval power.[33] He had learned the importance of a navy from Epaminondas, hence he knew that Macedonia would always remain weak and vulnerable if its enemy boasted the strongest navy in the Greek world. This was true, for even after its humiliation in the Social War, Athens was not a spent force.

Economic Advancement and Clashes in the East: The Philippi Mines and Thrace

With the Chalcidian League now his ally, and with Athens preoccupied with the Social War, Philip could turn to Potidaea unhindered. Before he could do so in earnest, however, two events occurred that would expand his power and economic resources further. In early 356 Cetriporis, who had recently succeeded his father Berisades as king of western Thrace, besieged Crenides in the rich gold and silver mines of the Mount Pangaeum region of western Thrace (Map 4). Whether Crenides, which was a colony founded by Thasos in 360, was a town or merely a collection of different mining settlements is unclear. The plural name might indicate the latter, but then many cities had plural names in Greek (including Athens). The area was about 40 miles (64 km) east of Amphipolis, at the head of the Angites valley, and about 8 miles (13 km) north of Neapolis (Kavala). Neapolis was an Athenian ally, and because of its harbour it served as a valuable naval base in that region. As a result Cetriporis' action was viewed with concern.

The people of Crenides appealed to Philip for help, an appeal he could hardly resist given the natural resources of the area. At the same time, he must have realised that if he did take over Crenides he would be redrawing Macedonia's eastern border and involving himself even more inextricably in Thracian affairs – and in eventual showdowns against all of the Thracian kings. Nonetheless, he immediately marched in and defeated a Thracian force. He may also have helped to fortify the area, but he could do no more at the time because he faced sudden and dangerous opposition from a combination of Grabus of Illyria, Lyppeius of Paeonia, and Cetriporis. The Athenians also offered their assistance against Philip (presumably the result of an alliance they had made with Berisades, Amadocus and Cersebleptes in 357),[34] but their aid was ineffectual for they were now being hard pressed in the Social War. There is some confusion in the chronology at this point, but certainly before his enemies could effectively group and invade Macedonia, Philip launched an attack on them. The details are unknown, but by the end of summer 356 the threat was over. Philip defeated Cetriporis' force himself and his general Parmenion brought Grabus to grief.[35] Who defeated Lyppeius is not known, but Diodorus tells us that he was forced to become an ally of the king.[36]

If Plutarch is correct in telling us that Parmenion defeated Grabus, Philip may have headed directly to Potidaea after defeating Cetriporis, leaving his general to mop up elsewhere. As at Amphipolis, the king's siege machinery proved overwhelming, and Potidaea had capitulated by midsummer. Living up to his promise for once, Philip handed over the city to the Chalcidians, although he sold the native Potidaeans as slaves. That left the Athenian cleruchs who had been living there since the 360s. Athens of course was at war with him now, so it was to be expected that Philip would take the Athenians at Potidaea prisoner. Surprisingly, however, he let them go, not even demanding a ransom. Why he did so is unknown: 'he was particularly solicitous towards the people of Athens on account of their importance and repute of their city', says Diodorus,[37] but there must be more to it than this. Philip may well have wanted to cause confusion in the city about his overall intentions towards the Athenians in the war. But his action may also have alerted the Chalcidians to their ally's leniency towards their mutual enemy, and hence persuaded them that they needed to view him with suspicion.

Probably at this point Philip returned to Crenides, taking with him a goodly number of Macedonian settlers. He is unlikely to have taken settlers with him the first time he went to its aid, as the outcome of his intervention would then have been unknown. Philip could afford to involve himself more actively in the area now that he had Olynthus' goodwill and any immediate threat from western Thrace was ended. He renamed (hence refounded) Crenides Philippi after himself, and it became in effect Macedonia's first colony.[38] While Philip was obviously interested in the income from its mines, he also was concerned about increasing the profitability of its agriculture. To this end he ordered the marshy plain of Crenides to be drained and cultivated.[39] Reclaiming swampland and the like was something he attended to elsewhere in his kingdom, always with an eye to strengthening the economy. Philippi was heavily fortified with walls and towers, showing that the Macedonian settlers were expected to defend it should occasion arise. It continued to mint its own coins in bronze and silver, as it had done previously when it was a colony of Thasos, but as one of the Macedonian royal mints at some point after 346 it also increased output of its silver coinage and produced a new gold coinage, the 'Philips'.[40] The new coins that appear throughout Philip's reign offer the best evidence we have for the strong state of the economy.[41]

Mining would remain the major source of revenue for Macedonia, and it transformed its economy almost overnight. For this, Philip deserves praise. From their being 'poor and insignificant' the income from the mines of Philippi alone was more than 1,000 talents per annum.[42] In the first few years of his reign revenue had been as crucial a consideration for Philip as the unification of the kingdom, securing its borders and building up its army. He would have been satisfied with the advances made in all four areas by 356 – a mere three years after coming to power.

The Birth of Alexander the Great

The fall of Potidaea apparently coincided with three other items of news that Philip received on that day. 'The first was that his general Parmenion had overcome the Illyrians in a great battle, the second that his race-horse had won a victory in the Olympic games, and the third that Alexander had been born.'[43] Alexander was Philip's second son (his mother was Olympias of Epirus), the first being Arrhidaeus, who was born about a year earlier from Philip's marriage to Philinna.

From the outset Alexander was the one destined for greatness, for on the day he was born a later source records that:

> the Temple of Artemis at Ephesus burned down. In connection with it, Hegesias of Magnesia uttered something so chilling it was enough to put out that great fire. He said, namely, that the Temple of Artemis' destruction was hardly a surprise because the goddess was busy delivering Alexander into the world. But all the Magi who were at that time at Ephesus saw the temple's destruction as a sign of yet more disaster. They ran around slapping their faces and yelling that destruction and great disaster for Asia had been born on that day.[44]

The prophecy came true. Within half a dozen years of coming to the throne in 336, Alexander had defeated the Great King and was ruling the Persian empire as Lord of Asia.

That the three items of news mentioned above were simultaneously delivered to Philip when Potidaea fell is unlikely. Alexander was born on 20 July 356, probably about the time that Potidaea capitulated; but the Olympic Games were only held in August, possibly even September. It is hard to imagine that news of his son's birth would take months to reach Philip. More likely is that the three items were later grouped together for literary effect, not least to highlight Alexander's birth and to show his superhuman status even at that early time.

The Siege of Methone: Philip Loses an Eye

To commemorate his Olympic victory, Philip had a silver tetradrachm coin minted at Pella. On its obverse was the head of Zeus and on the reverse a victorious jockey and horse, with the inscription *Philippou*, meaning 'of

Philip' (Plate 13). Such coins were not merely produced for propaganda purposes but were also part of Philip's policy to promote the Macedonian economy: the silver tetradrachms were minted in a new weight ($\frac{1}{2}$ oz or 14.5 g) to make them compete with, and eventually eclipse, the then-dominant coinage of the region.

In Philip's campaigns to date, several coastal towns had been won over to Macedonian control. He now planned to eliminate the remaining non-Macedonian presence on his seaboard. Towards the end of 355 he besieged Methone, an independent city on the Thermaic Gulf. Its capture would give him control of the entire coastline, and hence the coastal route to Thessaly. More than that, Methone was located close to a strategic communications route to Dium (Macedonia's main religious sanctuary in the foothills of Mount Piera: Plate 14) and through Tempe to Thessaly. Its location, and the danger it posed to the king in Pella, were amply illustrated when the Athenians landed the pretender Argaeus there in 359.

Why Philip waited so long to move against Methone is unknown, especially when he had seized nearby Pydna in 357. Obviously, he had needed to secure his borders once he became king and this had taken time, during which period he was vulnerable to any attack launched from Methone. Since the Athenians were really the only power that might use it for this reason, and his diplomatic promises and then the Social War were diverting their attention, he may have decided that he could leave Methone alone after he ended the threat from Argaeus. The situation seems to have changed by 355, for there is an enigmatic statement in Diodorus that 'the people of Methone were permitting their city to become a base of operations for his enemies'.[45] Diodorus does not specify who these enemies were, but the Athenians are the obvious choice; later, when the king besieged the town, they sent a force to its aid.

The Athenians' reaction was enough to show Philip that, despite its reversals in the Social War, Athens could not be underestimated. Indeed, some months earlier two ambassadors had gone to the city from its ally Neapolis, now feeling threatened by the king's recent moves in the Chalcidice and Philippi, seeking Athenian support. At the time the Athenians could do nothing more than offer verbal reassurances. However, the implications of Philip's move against Methone at this time, together with Diodorus' comment, suggest that they were looking to use the place once more against Philip. The latter saw this threat as too dangerous to ignore.

Philip gave the people of Methone the chance to surrender; when they refused he besieged them.[46] The siege seems to have proved more difficult than his previous two sieges, perhaps because of Methone's huge walls, and it took several months to succeed. The Macedonians used battering rams to try to breach the walls while men, protected by archers and slingers, attempted to climb them with scaling ladders. As Philip was inspecting the Macedonians' siegecraft, an arrow (*toxeuma*) fired from a catapult (or bow?) by one of the defenders, whose name is given in some sources as Aster,[47] struck him in an eye, usually thought to be the right one.[48] The wound was a terrible one, but thanks to his doctor, Critobulus, he lived, although he lost the sight in that eye.

One of the small ivory heads found in what is believed to be Philip's tomb at Vergina has a facial disfigurement around the right eye, which also appears sightless (Plate 7). In the modern reconstruction of the skull from the tomb, trauma is evident around the right eye (Plate 1), which played no small role in the reconstruction of Philip's face. The head is believed to be that of Philip, and since we know that he was shot in an eye at Methone the trauma to the right eye on the head has given rise to the belief that he was shot in that one. The facial characteristics are also similar to those in the portraits of Philip we have on coins (Plates 5 and 6).

Of all Philip's injuries, the eye wound gets the most attention in the sources; some later authors embellished the incident and added fictionalised details to spice up the biographical tradition about Philip. One variant has it that he lost his eye because of divine retribution: he offended Zeus when he spied on the god, disguised as a snake, having sex with his wife Olympias, who became pregnant with Alexander![49] This story was one of a number circulating about Alexander's divine parentage.

Eye injuries cause considerable bleeding, and Philip's injury probably appeared more terrible because of the blood flow. It is likely to have halted the Macedonian attack while the men waited to find out the fate of their king. Hence, this is likely to be the period when an Athenian relief force was able to breach the Macedonian line. An Athenian decree of about December 355 honours a certain Lachares of Apollonia for entering Methone.[50] It is hard to imagine him being able to accomplish this when the besieging Macedonians were not so diverted.

The siege continued throughout the winter of 355 and came to an end in probably the early summer of 354.[51] The Athenians in the Assembly voted to send another force to Methone, but it only set sail in the spring and so arrived too late.[52] Despite Philip's injury, when the people 'sued for peace he granted it, and showed not merely restraint but leniency in dealing with the defeated enemy'.[53] Those who were still alive were allowed to leave the city, but they could take with them only one item of clothing. Methone's walls and buildings were completely razed to the ground so that even today 'its site is still difficult to find',[54] and the king gave the land to the Macedonians.[55] Why Philip treated the people with such (comparative) magnanimity is unknown, but, as has been suggested, on a personal level he was no doubt keen to leave a place where he had been so badly hurt.[56]

Athens and Eubulus

Macedonia's coastline was now free of independent Greek cities. The acquisition of the Mount Pangaeum mines vastly stimulated the economy, and the Chalcidice was bound to Macedonia in a treaty of alliance. Philip could finally return to Athenian matters. If he had indeed engineered the Social War in order to weaken his foe, his strategy had paid off with dividends. At its end Athens was financially exhausted thanks to the defection of its allies (and the loss of their tribute) and the departure of a number of metics (resident aliens), who contributed significantly to the economy. Indeed, Demosthenes says that the state revenues were down to merely 137 talents per annum 'not long ago' as opposed to 1,000 at the start of the Peloponnesian War in 431, nearly a century earlier.[57] Revenues had by this time increased to 400 talents,[58] but Macedonia by now was getting 1,000 talents annually from the mines at Philippi alone.

An even more marked example of Athens' financial plight was that in 348 the courts had to be suspended because there was insufficient money to pay the jurors their three obols a day.[59] Several contemporary works show that the Athenians were aware of their dismal financial situation and attempted to fix it. In 354 Demosthenes' first political speech in the Assembly, *On the Symmories*, dealt with foreign policy and financial matters. A treatise by Xenophon called *Poroi* (*Ways and Means*) was aimed at improving state revenues and promoting trade. Both were unsuccessful in having many of their proposals adopted, but Athens' financial situation was much improved by Diophantus and especially Eubulus.[60] The latter had been an *archōn* in 370/69, but he shot to prominence when he negotiated the peace that ended the Social War in 355. Under Eubulus, Athenian finances were returned to a secure footing and the ground was laid for the Athenians to expand their empire once more. He oversaw the construction and expansion of the Piraeus dockyards, and stimulated trade. More importantly, he organised the Athenian budget in such a way that part of the surpluses from the various accounts were paid into a Military Fund to help pay for war efforts (these being the largest drain on the city's finances). Most likely he (not Pericles in the previous century) also created a new fund, at some point in the 350s. This was called the Theoric Fund, overseen by a treasurer who was in office for a four-year term, into which was paid a fixed annual amount as well as the remainder of the annual budget surpluses. The Theoric Fund was meant to distribute money to the poor so that they could attend the dramatic performances at the festivals. However, the lion's share was reserved for the city and its port, the Piraeus, for the purpose of economic stimulation, which is why it was often referred to as 'the glue of democracy'.[61] It could not be used for any other purpose (such as military action) unless Eubulus' legislation was first repealed. Since the fund was inviolable, the orators in the Assembly had to be very careful not to propose anything that might either have a detrimental impact on it or cause its holdings to be allocated elsewhere. If they did, they would find themselves indictable.

The Theoric Fund grew into a huge financial resource, and its treasurers came to wield great political power. Hence, Eubulus played a vastly influential role in not only Athenian finances but also political life generally in the 350s and early 340s. His times were remembered as something akin to 'the good old days' in the oratory that followed Macedonia's subjugation of Greece at Chaeronea. In his prosecution speech of Demosthenes of 323, Dinarchus offers a series of comparisons with Eubulus:[62]

> What triremes are there which have been built by this man [Demosthenes] for the city, as in the time of Eubulus? What dockyards have been constructed under his administration? When has this man either by decree or law increased the cavalry? When such opportunities presented themselves after the Battle of Chaeronea, what force did he levy, either by land or by sea? What ornament to the goddess has this man carried up to the Acropolis? What building did Demosthenes construct in your Exchange, or in the city, or anywhere else in the country? No one could show one anywhere!

At the core of the works of Demosthenes and Xenophon referred to above was the idea that in foreign policy Athens needed to keep away from aggressive alliances and to maintain peace, from which would come economic prosperity. Thanks to Eubulus, the Athenians did indeed pursue a cautious foreign policy and avoided costly or imprudent ventures abroad. Thus, in 353, when the city of Megalopolis in Arcadia approached Athens for help in its struggle against Sparta, the appeal was rejected. When exiled Rhodian democrats sought Athenian assistance to return home in 352, a return that might well have brought Rhodes back into the Athenian empire, Eubulus persuaded the people to say no. Demosthenes had delivered speeches in both of these cases urging Athenian help, but both were unsuccessful.[63]

It is interesting to note that neither Demosthenes nor Xenophon mentions Philip at this time although Athens was at war with him. Eubulus was of course aware of the danger from Philip (perhaps more so than Demosthenes in this period), and was prepared to act if necessary. That was why the Athenians had tried to defend Methone; furthermore, as we shall see, they secured possession of the Thracian Chersonese in 353, and in 352 they forced Philip to withdraw from Greece and return to Macedonia.

Philip probably had every intention of dealing with the Athenians once he had brought the Macedonian coastline into his sphere of influence. However, events were now taking place in central Greece that made him abandon that plan. In 356 the state of Phocis seized Delphi, home of Apollo's oracle, and a Sacred War was declared against it in the following year. In establishing border security for Macedonia and providing economic progress, Philip's moves to date had been the first steps on the path to empire, although he may not have suspected as much at the time. His involvement in the Sacred War, in which he significantly dubbed himself Apollo's Saviour, would dramatically boost Macedonia's power south of Mount Olympus. The era of the Macedonian empire was fast approaching. For now, Philip allowed the first war with Athens to run its uneventful course.

APOLLO'S SAVIOUR:
PHILIP AND THE SACRED WAR

Delphi was the home of the oracle of Apollo, and hence one of the most sacred sites on the Greek mainland.[1] The Greeks considered such oracular sites too important for a single state to control, and so an association of states called an Amphictyonic League (which had a council as its executive arm) protected them. The name comes from the word amphictyony ('those that dwell around or near'), and the league has been described, not inaccurately, as a very old club and rather old-fashioned.[2] If the oracle was violated in some way, then the Amphictyonic Council could declare a Sacred War (on behalf of the god) against the offending state, and call to arms the other league members.

Because of the importance of Delphi in Greek religion (and then central Greek politics), its Amphictyonic League (of some twenty-four states by the classical period) was probably the most famous. It was originally formed to protect the shrine of Demeter at Anthela near Thermopylae, but later extended its influence south to include Delphi, probably during the First Sacred War of 595–586. This war was fought against Cirrha (on the plain beneath Mount Parnassus and Delphi), and at its conclusion the town was razed and the council assumed administrative control of the Delphic oracle.[3]

The Amphictyonic Council convened for a meeting called a Pylaea twice a year, first at Anthela, and then at Delphi. The council was composed originally of members of twelve nearby tribes, which included the Ionians and Dorians, and stretched from the Perrhaebians and Thessalians in the north to the Athenians in the south. Each tribe had two votes, but the distribution of votes within the tribes is not clear. The Athenians, for example, had one of the Ionian tribe's two votes (the other was in the hands of Euboea). The tribes north of the strategically important Pass of Thermopylae (providing access from Thessaly to the south) controlled about half of the votes, but they were dominated by the powerful Thessalian League. Thessaly seems always to have been president of the council. However, Theban intervention in Thessaly in

364 ensured that Thebes, at the head of the Boeotian League, probably had more clout than anyone else in the council (controlling perhaps as many as sixteen of the twenty-four votes). Like Athens, Thebes enjoyed *promanteia*, priority rights in consulting the oracle.

Prelude to the Third Sacred War

The Third Sacred War of 355–346 was fought over the occupation of Delphi by Phocis, a small, central Greek state of about twenty-two cities that bordered on Boeotia (Map 1).[4] What made it different from the two previous wars was that it involved a foreign power, Macedonia.[5]

The incidents leading up to the Third Sacred War occurred in 356. At the spring Pylaea, the Thebans brought up the matter of council fines imposed on certain Phocians and other states, including Sparta, which were still unpaid. The Phocian crime appears to have been cultivating sacred land, the plain of Cirrha, on which the oracle's sacrificial animals were kept.[6] Phocis was an ally of Thebes, but, in an example of the divisiveness of the *polis* system, recent internal division in Phocis resulted in the expulsion of the anti-Theban element in the state, which caused concern in Thebes. So also did Phocian contacts with the anti-Theban Athenians.

While the crime was religious in nature, the motives of the Thebans in drawing attention to it were not, for they had the Spartans in their sights.[7] The latter had illegally seized the Cadmea (the Theban Acropolis) in 382 during the period of the Spartan hegemony, installed a garrison and exiled some three hundred of the leading citizens. These exiles took refuge in Athens and, in 379/8, with Athenian help, they expelled the Spartan garrison.[8] After the end of the Spartan hegemony of Greece in 371, the Thebans invaded the Peloponnese, liberated the helots in Messenia (slaves of Sparta, on whom the Spartans were dependent for their economic survival), and refounded their capital at Messene as well as Megalopolis. Their actions increased the influence of Thebes in the Peloponnese. Although the Spartans had been fined for their seizure of the Theban Cadmea, the fine was evidently still unpaid almost three decades later. The matter of the Phocians' lack of payment was thus a timely excuse that the Thebans used to point the finger at Sparta as well. Since all of these fines were outstanding, the Amphictyonic Council ordered them to be doubled.

To everyone's surprise, Philomelus of Phocis persuaded his fellow citizens not to pay the increased fine. Further, he put forward the bold plan of seizing Delphi in order to protest against Thebes' attack on his state. He did so based on some lines of the *Iliad*, which indicate that the Phocians had a claim to Delphi that went back to the time of the Trojan War:[9] 'And the Phocians were ruled by Schedius and Epistrophus, sons of big-hearted Iphitus, son of Naubolus; these were they who lived in Cyparissus and in rocky Pytho, and sacred Crisa.' The Phocians elected Philomelus general and he went to Sparta to seek help. He promised to reverse the council's decision to fine the Spartans, and in response the Spartan king Archidamus secretly gave him 15 talents to hire mercenaries.[10] In the summer of 356 Philomelus seized Delphi.[11] When a Locrian force (the Locrians in the council were then in charge of Delphi) came to expel him he defeated it, and he ordered the captives to be thrown from the nearby Phaedriades cliffs, the traditional punishment for sacrilege. He also apparently forced the Pythia (the priestess of Apollo) to consult the god about his actions, and received the response that he could do as he pleased, which he interpreted to mean that Apollo was on his side. An eagle was spotted which seemed to confirm this.[12] Of course, the Pythia's response had nothing to do with Apollo, but rather with the fact that Philomelus – and a substantial force of five thousand mercenaries – was in control of Delphi.

It should be noted that a mercenary in the classical Greek world was not a soldier of fortune in the modern sense. Mercenaries formed a distinct group that was an accepted part of Greek society; they had their own identity as a group regardless of where they came from, and they played a political and economic role in relations between states. States and generals who provided or led mercenary armies for rulers and the like made political and trading contacts with them. The Greeks had no word for 'mercenary' as such, but instead used terms like *epikouros*, 'fighter-alongside', *misthophoros*, 'wage-earner' and *xenos misthophoros*, 'foreign wage-earner'. Strictly speaking, our word, given its connotations, ought not to be applied to classical 'mercenaries' (although I will continue to do so for convenience).[13]

The sacrilegious nature of Philomelus' act is obvious, and it would have caused the Greeks great consternation given their strong religious sentiments. Perhaps that is why Philomelus had to pay his mercenaries half again more than the going rate.[14] At the same time the constant internecine fighting between the Greek *poleis* and Thebes' underhand attempt to punish Phocis and Sparta would have gained the Phocians some sympathy. Indeed, some states, including Athens and Sparta, would support Phocis, though not so much out of sympathy with the Phocian cause as to keep Thebes at bay. Sparta may have thought that with Thebes' attention diverted it could re-establish its influence in Messenia and dominate the Peloponnese again. In the winter of 355 Philomelus sent out embassies to the Greek states explaining his actions and promising to protect the treasuries at Delphi. These housed money and precious objects (such as votive offerings) provided by various states, and the Greeks were probably as anxious for their safety as for that of the oracle. The embassies failed to convince their hosts, however. At its autumn meeting of 355 the Amphictyonic Council, at the behest of Thebes, which had sent out embassies to Thessaly and other members, voted by a majority to declare a Sacred War against Phocis.[15]

The Early Stages of the War: Philomelus and Onomarchus

Philomelus was not going to give in easily, nor was he sitting idly on his hands. Given the size of the forces mounting against him, he was 'compelled', says Diodorus, to seize some temple treasuries so as to be able to afford to hire more mercenaries, and he soon had ten thousand 'of the worst knaves, and those who despised the gods, because of their own greed', with him at Delphi.[16] With these men, he invaded Locris, where he defeated a force of Locrians and Thebans. This victory was followed by another over some six thousand Thessalians and their allies at Argolas in eastern Locris. This defeat split Thessaly in two, with Pherae turning to seek an alliance with Athens and the Thessalian League headed by Larisa beseeching Philip for help.

Thus Philomelus had not lived up to his earlier promise of protecting the temple treasuries.[17] However, with an impudence worthy of Philip, when challenged he said that he had indeed promised to protect the treasuries, but that that did not necessarily include what was in them! Using the treasuries to finance military operations was something that many Greek states, including Athens, had done in the past.[18] Many Greeks, though, outraged by the Phocians' embezzlement, were terrified that Apollo would inflict terrible retribution on one and all. Some contributed greatly to the Boeotian war effort, presumably in an effort to keep in the god's good books.[19] To make matters worse, it appears that the Phocian leaders did not plunder just to hire mercenaries but also gave votive offerings and the like to their favourite courtesans and dancing girls.

The Phocians would not enjoy military success much longer. In 354 an Amphictyonic force led by the Theban general Pammenes[20] defeated them at the Battle of Neon (by the Cephissus valley) and the survivors were forced up the slopes of Mount Parnassus. These included Philomelus, who realised that all was lost and committed suicide by jumping off the mountainside – 'his impious blood paid the price for his sacrilege'.[21] Down but not out, the Phocians appointed Onomarchus as their new commander-in-chief and his brother Phayllus as a general.[22] They were able to rally the Phocians, helped immensely by the Amphictyonic force's failure to mop up operations by marching on Delphi after Neon and liberating the site.

In the following year (353), Onomarchus plundered further from the sacred treasuries to hire more mercenaries and even struck his own coinage, which he used mostly for bribes.[23] He bought off the Thessalians (who seemed intent on marching against him), reinvaded Locris (where he captured Thronion and sold its people into slavery), reduced Doris and invaded Boeotia. His plan was to isolate Thebes from Thessaly, essentially by controlling the routes that led to Thermopylae, and hence to reduce the fighting power of the Amphictyonic army. He seized the town of Orchomenus; his success may in part have been due to the fact that the Thebans had recently sent Pammenes (the victor of Neon) with five thousand soldiers to the aid of the rebellious Persian satrap Artabazus in Asia Minor. Chaeronea was next, but a Theban force was able to thwart his attempt to take this important town. This outcome may in part have resulted from the return of Philip to Thessaly and the defeat of Phayllus (see below), which caused Onomarchus to leave Boeotia immediately.

When the Third Sacred War was declared, Philip was busy with the siege of Methone, which stretched on over the winter of 355 and lasted until the early summer of 354. He followed this successful siege by taking the towns of Pagae, Abdera, Maroneia and Neapolis.[24] The last three in particular further strained his relations with the Athenians, for his control of the key coastal towns in Thrace might have an impact on the corn route from the Black Sea. The Athenians were dependent on imported corn from the Black Sea region. Each spring an armada of merchant vessels, escorted by warships, would fill up with corn from the Danube and Maritza basins, and sail via Byzantium through the Hellespont, across the Aegean, and on to Athens. Any disruption of this convoy would cause serious hardship in Athens, and the city was thus careful to maintain a presence and allies in the Hellespont and Thracian Chersonese regions.

Thessaly and Philip's Entry into the Sacred War

In the summer of 353 the Aleuadae of Larisa switched Philip's attention to the Sacred War when they appealed for his assistance against Pherae. The Thessalians had not been especially active in the war: they had been defeated by Philomelus and then apparently bribed by Onomarchus not to intervene further.[25] However, their inactivity was more likely due to the exploits of Lycophron of Pherae, who seized the opportunity of Philip's campaigning in Thrace to move against Larisa again. He was most likely in alliance with Onomarchus by now, the latter anticipating that if Lycophron won over Thessaly he would move to dismiss the Theban charges against Phocis in the Amphictyonic Council.

This internal turmoil kept Thessaly out of the Sacred War, but at the same time it brought the Macedonian king into it. Larisa's appeal for help was a call that Philip could not ignore, for it was essential to keep Pherae's power at bay so that Macedonia's southern border would not be compromised.[26] There was also a political advantage to be gained by allying with an enemy of Phocis (in turn an ally now of Pherae), and hence becoming involved himself in the Sacred War. This would prove to be a convenient stepping stone to more formal involvement in central Greek politics. Putting on hold the war with Athens once more, Philip marched into Thessaly prepared to do battle.

We do not know exactly when Philip arrived, or precisely what he did, but evidently Lycophron was sufficiently hard pressed to appeal for help to Phocis. Presumably Philip's forces had linked with Thessalian ones (at Larisa?) and both had besieged Pherae. Onomarchus immediately ordered his brother Phayllus to take troops to Pherae, but Philip defeated this force almost as soon as it arrived. Intent on reversing this outcome, as well as on offsetting the danger posed by a combination of Thessaly and Philip moving against Phocis itself, Onomarchus led his entire force north from Boeotia to Thessaly. He arrived there in the late summer or early autumn of 353 with an army of some twenty thousand infantry and five hundred cavalry. Given that the fighting ability of the Macedonian army was well established, this was a bold move.

To everyone's surprise, certainly Philip's, the Phocian army defeated the Macedonians in not one battle but apparently two. The military writer Polyaenus tells us how the Phocians won the first by outfoxing the king.[27] Some Phocian infantry took up a position on level ground at the entrance to a narrow valley surrounded by a crescent-shaped hill. When Philip charged, they retreated into the valley, where unknown to the Macedonian king further infantry units and stone-throwing catapults were hidden on the slopes of the hill. (The use of siege machinery may indicate that Onomarchus intended to campaign against Thessalian cities afterwards.)[28] The retreat was a ruse. Once the Macedonians were inside they were attacked from above, while the supposedly retreating infantry turned and attacked them face on. The Macedonians escaped with no small difficulty, leaving behind a large number of dead and injured. Onomarchus' stratagem was worthy of the future Alexander the Great, and for once Philip fell into an enemy trap.

A surprising consequence of this defeat was that Philip 'was reduced to the uttermost perils and his soldiers were so despondent that they had deserted him, but by arousing the courage of the majority, he got them with great difficulty to obey his orders'.[29] Rather than remain in Thessaly, he prudently returned home, no doubt using the approach of winter as a face-saving excuse. He was supposed to have said that he was leaving 'like a ram, which next time would butt harder'.[30] The details of the Macedonians' other defeat are unknown, but it may have been only a skirmish involving retreating Macedonian soldiers. The repercussions of all this were far-ranging, and I believe they changed the relations Philip had envisaged with the Greeks up to that point.

We should not downplay the achievement of Onomarchus in defeating Philip. For almost six years the Macedonian army had been an invincible force that had marched inexorably onwards, defeating all in its path regardless of terrain or quality of foe. Now its winning streak was broken, and apparently broken twice. Philip learned never to underestimate an enemy again, regardless of whether it was composed of citizens or, as with the Phocian force, mercenaries. In terms of the bigger picture of the Sacred War the Phocians' success was minor, but at the time they would have celebrated their victory as a great one, and rightly so.

Onomarchus did not follow up by waging a campaign in Thessaly, however, and so he let slip the very real opportunity his victory gave him for elevating Pherae's influence there, and hence for distracting the Thessalians from the Sacred War. Instead he resumed his interrupted campaign in Boeotia with renewed vigour. He was victorious in fighting there, and also seized the town of Coronea.[31] However, the Phocians would not bask in their glory for long. Within a year, the ram would indeed return to butt harder, and with a markedly different agenda.

Repercussions of Philip's Defeat and Athenian Moves in the Chersonese

Onomarchus' victory over Philip had dramatic repercussions for the latter's relations with Cersebleptes, King of Eastern Thrace, the Chalcidian League and the Athenians. There may also have been incursions into Macedonia by the Paeonians and Illyrians, and potential problems from Epirus, to judge by Philip's involvement in these areas a couple of years later. It looked as though the whole fabric of Philip's power was starting to disintegrate, pointing to an inevitable decline in Macedonian power.

When Philip first left for Thessaly, an Athenian general, Chares, sailed to the Thracian Chersonese (Gallipoli peninsula). In a campaign against Cersebleptes in the spring or summer of 353, he captured the town of Sestos. With the endorsement of the Assembly, he killed all of its male citizens and sold all the women and children as slaves. Sestos was an important port on the corn route from the Black Sea to Athens; numerous cleruchies had been established in the Chersonese in the fifth century, and the Athenians did the same again now.

The Athenians had some justification for acting as they did, for their claim to the area had been recognised in a decree of the Greek states of 365. However, it was currently under the control of Cersebleptes, the neighbouring Thracian king. Although he had been an ally of Athens since 357, he was a fickle one. He was intent on reducing Athens' influence in the region and on resurrecting the kingdom that Cotys had ruled before Thrace was divided into three realms in 359. He had also entered into diplomatic contact with Philip. The other kings of Thrace, Berisades and the aged Amadocus, of necessity had stayed loyal to Athens to counter the threat from Cersebleptes.

Chares' treatment of Sestos was meant to be a warning to Cersebleptes to adhere to the spirit of his 357 treaty with Athens. The warning might have been ignored had it not been for Philip's defeat at the hands of Onomarchus, for when news of this became known Cersebleptes turned his back on Philip. He agreed to support Athens in its attempts to regain Amphipolis and recognised Athenian rights over the Chersonese apart from the town of Cardia on the isthmus. Athens now in effect controlled the cities along the Thracian coast and hence that part of the vital corn route. In order to maintain their presence there, the Athenians sent cleruchs to Sestos and other cities in the Chersonese beginning in the summer of 352,[32] and an Athenian general at the head of a substantial force also set up a base in the region.

The renewal of the alliance with Cersebleptes was a substantial gain for Athens, and it was the first real blow to Philip's clever diplomatic policy since he had become king. Worse was to follow, however, as far as his relations with the Chalcidian League were concerned. Perhaps taking his cue from Cersebleptes' change of heart and gambling that Philip would not recover from his defeat, Olynthus sought an alliance with Athens. This was in direct violation of the league's treaty with Philip of 357. It is unknown whether the move was supported by the people as a whole or was engineered by an anti-Macedonian faction in the city, but Philip was in no position to block negotiations this time. Not that it mattered, for no treaty was made between Athens and the league, perhaps because of Eubulus' caution. Philip would not forget Olynthus' attempted defection, however, and its days as his ally were numbered.

Whatever problems the king had had with his men in 353 were resolved by the following year when he marched south again. It was vital for Philip to restore the morale of his army and to re-establish its confidence in him as king and commander by defeating the Phocians. There was also a personal element in wanting to avenge the defeat at Onomarchus' hands and reverse the ensuing problems he had faced from his allies and others. Where he fought Onomarchus – Thessaly, Boeotia or elsewhere – was thus immaterial. In fact, it would be in Thessaly again. As soon as he heard of Philip's advance at the head of over twenty thousand infantry and three thousand cavalry, Lycophron of Pherae sent word to Onomarchus. Philip's army was considerable, and so Phocis enlisted the aid of Athens, probably by means of bribes.[33]

The Athenians were keen to support Phocis against their enemy Philip, and any bribes helpfully ensured (more importantly for the likes of Eubulus) that they would not have to spend money on the campaign from their own coffers. The Assembly voted to send Chares and a fleet into the Gulf of Pagasae to prevent Pagasae (near Volos), Thessaly's principal harbour, from falling to Philip. Pagasae was also the only harbour that the Athenian fleet could put into in order to link up with Onomarchus' force. Thus, we finally hear of actual Athenian involvement in the Sacred War; clearly the situation was serious enough for the cautious Eubulus finally to engage troops.

When Philip marched into Thessaly in 352, he ordered his men to wear crowns of laurel as they went into battle – 'as though the god were going before'.[34] This highly symbolic wearing of laurel wreaths was to show that Philip was fighting not merely for revenge and on behalf of his Thessalian allies, but now for a religious reason, on behalf of Apollo.[35] In that respect, the god was marching before the Macedonian army. Pious though Philip undoubtedly was, the key reason for his return is to be found elsewhere: to expand Macedonia's sphere of influence.

Philip as Apollo's Saviour: A New Macedonian Policy towards Greece

The manner of Philip's return, I would argue, marked a significant change in his plans for a Macedonian presence in Greece. His policy until now had been to protect Macedonia's borders from enemy incursion, to unite the kingdom, to stimulate the economy and to neutralise, by diplomacy or other means, foreign powers that had previously interfered in Macedonian politics. Principal among these were the Athenians, the Thebans and the Chalcidian League. In this policy he had succeeded, as we have seen, but in 353 he met with an unexpected military defeat. The army was hardly annihilated, but his men had fled; as Diodorus was quoted above as saying, they had turned against him and forced his return home. In this act, we can reassess Philip's relations with his army and his designs on Greece.[36]

Onomarchus defeated the Macedonians, but he did not destroy them. The Macedonian army ought to have retreated with its tail between its legs, but not defied its king and fled back to Macedonia. There must have been something going on behind the scenes here, one plausible explanation lying in the actions of the foreign troops in the army, especially those from Illyria and Paeonia. One of the repercussions of the defeat was a possible invasion of Macedonia from the Paeonians and Illyrians. Philip had defeated these peoples soon after coming to power, but the areas were never really conquered: Upper Macedonia was still causing problems in the last years of his reign.[37] When Philip was assassinated in 336, Justin tells us that the army's reaction 'varied with the different nationalities of which it was composed. Some renewed their hopes of liberty believing they were held in unjust servitude; others, tired of service far from home, were happy to have been spared the expedition [to Persia]', while the late king's friends were worried about 'the Illyrians, the Thracians, the Dardanians and the other barbarian tribes of dubious loyalty and unstable character – a simultaneous uprising by all these peoples would be impossible to check'.[38]

The message is obvious: soldiers from Upper Macedonia and elsewhere did not want to be part of the army either because they believed service had been forced on them or because they were tired of campaigning. Moreover, as mentioned above, the loyalty of the peoples named in the passage who had been forced into service (the Thracians must be excluded from consideration in 353 as Philip did not conquer them until the late 340s) was always suspect. In light of these considerations, I suggest that troops from Upper Macedonia and Paeonia seized upon Philip's unexpected defeat to return to their homes, and that when they did so the rest of the army, now denuded of manpower, followed suit. There is no firm evidence to support this theory, but it does explain why the army fled rather than merely retreated.

If this is the case, then Philip probably now realised not so much that the army's confidence could be shaken by defeat but that troops from areas other than Lower Macedonia could, and would, take advantage of any such defeat. It was with no small difficulty that he had managed to rouse his men after Onomarchus' victory: what if he had failed? The widespread repercussions of the defeat showed how easily Macedonia could be plunged back into the sort of chaos that had engulfed it before he became king – especially if the Illyrians and others broke free from him. Philip knew of the swift termination of Thebes' ascendancy in Greece following its defeat at Mantinea in 362, and he had no wish for the same to happen to Macedonia. Thus was shown the precarious nature of his kingship and by extension of Pella as the centre of government in his united Macedonia. In creating his new army, Philip had also created the problem of keeping it united and loyal to him.

To solve that problem he needed to keep the army on campaign and winning. Border security therefore could no longer be his sole aim – border expansion in Greece, and eventually in Persia, would be adopted as a new goal.[39] In the dust of his defeat at Onomarchus' hands was born the need to establish an empire in order to shore up his moves to unite Macedonia. That meant taking on the Greeks,[40] and the wearing of laurel wreaths was the first overt sign of this new determination.

The Battle of the Crocus Field: Phayllus Succeeds Onomarchus

Rather than wait for Onomarchus to arrive and face him in battle, the king turned his attention to Pagasae. The Athenians had mobilised Chares to protect the port town, but he had not yet arrived, and it quickly fell to Philip. Denied a safe haven to land, all that Chares could do was to sail down the western coast of the gulf: hence Athenian aid was rendered ineffectual. Onomarchus, at the head of a large force of Phocians and mercenaries, had by now arrived in Thessaly, and the two sides faced each other in the Krokion Plain or Crocus Field. Philip had perhaps three thousand cavalry and twenty thousand infantry, wearing their laurel crowns as Apollo's warriors, to Onomarchus' five hundred cavalry and twenty thousand infantry.

It was the late spring or summer of 352 when the two sides met. We have little information about the course of the battle, but the Macedonian cavalry, supported by Thessalian cavalry, carried the day.[41] The cavalry's superior numbers and tactics quickly annihilated its Phocian counterpart, and it then attacked the infantry phalanx on its wings and to its rear while the Macedonian phalanx bore down on its front. A large number of Phocian troops, so the story goes, abandoned their line out of guilt when they saw the crowned Macedonians fighting on behalf of the god.[42] The Phocian line was forced towards and then into the gulf, and the Phocian soldiers tried to swim out to Chares' ships, which were holding to offshore. Many were drowned in the attempt or were killed as they shed their armour before trying to swim to the fleet.

Over six thousand Phocians and mercenaries were killed in the battle. These included Onomarchus, who Diodorus says was trying to swim to the Athenian fleet when he died.[43] Three thousand were captured and then drowned as punishment for the sacrilegious crime of seizing Delphi. Onomarchus' body was brought to Philip, and the king ordered it to be crucified and, like those he ordered to be drowned, denied burial. This denial of burial was in accordance with the sacrilegious nature of their crimes. Philip thus made it clear whose side Macedonia was on in the Sacred War – and how he was out to avenge Apollo and to save his sacred site.

The Phocians lost almost half of their army at the Crocus Field, but despite this their tenacity and resilience were not dashed: when news of Onomarchus' death reached them, they promptly elected his brother Phayllus as commander. Like his predecessors, Phayllus immediately used sacred money from Delphi to hire more mercenaries, this time paying double the normal rate.[44]

Although the Sacred War was far from over, over the next few years it consisted mostly of indecisive skirmishes between Phocian and Boeotian forces, the details of which do not concern us in this book.[45] The Athenians, more concerned about Philip's activities in Thessaly, withdrew much of their support for the Phocians, who in turn started to rely more heavily on Sparta, Corinth and other anti-Theban states such as Epidaurus and Phlius. However, they too were expected to support their allies, which could be costly. For example, later that same year when the Spartans tried to recover Messenia and attacked Megalopolis (in Arcadia), the Phocians sent three thousand reinforcements to assist them. These troops did little good, and were a financial burden on Phocis. Worse still, despite significant Phocian gains in Locris, the victorious Boeotian army that had supported Megalopolis went on to reverse Phocian successes in Boeotia and to devastate Phocian lands.[46]

Philip's victory over Onomarchus restored the confidence of the Macedonian army. Apart from a serious reversal against the Thracian Triballi tribe late in 339, it did not lose again, testimony to its training and Philip's leadership as general.[47] The victory also meant that Lycophron of Pherae lost his Phocian support, with the result that he surrendered himself and Pherae to Philip. The king accepted his terms, and allowed him and his fellow tyrant, Peitholaus, to leave unharmed along with their two thousand mercenaries. This was a mistake: Lycophron and his men marched immediately to join Phayllus, and some of them would later support Sparta. The latter's campaign came to an inconsequential end in 350, and this may explain why, with no ostensible need to support Sparta, in 349 Peitholaus returned to Pherae to stir up trouble at a critical time during Philip's invasion of the Chalcidice (see Chapter 7).

Thessaly and Philip's Election as *Archon*

If the Greeks expected the Macedonians to march against Phocis (presumably the Thebans did), they were mistaken. For Philip, the most pressing problem was the stability of Thessaly, which by extension affected the security of Macedonia's borders. Hence he remained in Thessaly for at least the early part of summer 352, his aim being to promote the Thessalian League and to isolate Pherae. He took severe measures against cities that attacked others, in some cases banishing suspect leaders (as at Tricca and Pharacadon), and in others giving lands to loyal members of the league (as at Pelinna, Crannon and Gomphi). As far as Pherae was concerned, Philip had made an agreement with its people to offset any resentment they might harbour over his sudden increase in power and for their loss of Pagasae. The settlement may have also included his marrying a Pheraean woman named Nicesipolis, and naming their daughter Thessalonice.[48] Nicesipolis was said to have died twenty days after giving birth. The chronology for this marriage is open to doubt (it could have been later), but good arguments have been put forward for it taking place in 352.[49] This was Philip's fifth marriage. The daughter's name (which meant 'Thessalian Victory') obviously refers to a military triumph, and the most logical one would be Philip's defeat of Onomarchus (which was also to

Thessaly's advantage in the Sacred War).[50] That Nicesipolis was a niece of Jason, the earlier tyrant of Pherae (who had attempted to secure a similar control of Thessaly), would not have been lost on the people. Unfortunately, Philip's plan failed, for the people of Pherae did not rally around him as he hoped.

While the Thessalian League formally decided the fate of the cities that had defected, it was obvious that Philip was pulling the strings. The message was clear: defection from the Thessalian League, and hence from Philip, would not be tolerated. It was probably now, having convincingly defeated the Phocians and proved himself a supporter of the league, that Philip was elected to the constitutional lifelong office of *archon*.[51] His son Alexander succeeded him to this office on his succession as king in 336.[52] Exactly what being *archon* entailed is unknown.[53] It evidently allowed the holder to exert influence in the league's affairs and to have some command over the Thessalian army (which boasted significant numbers of first-class infantry and especially cavalry), powers that were akin to those of the earlier monarch, or *tagos*, of Thessaly. As *archon*, Philip received formal control of Pagasae, which he had seized earlier in the year, and the income from the Thessalian harbour and various other taxes.[54] Such moneys were welcome and greatly benefited the Macedonian economy. Philip also had some say in the voting of Thessaly, or at least of its *perioikoi*, in the Amphictyonic Council.

It is important to note that Philip's election was extraordinary, for he was not a Thessalian; at no time did he refer to himself as *tagos*, a gesture that might have caused resentment among the Thessalians.[55] On the other hand, he may have been made a citizen of Larisa, perhaps after his marriage to Philinna so that their children would be legitimate.[56] Philip did not bribe his way to the appointment,[57] nor was it 'a gesture of alarm' because of the alliance between Pherae and Phocis.[58] The league bestowed it on him because of his power in the Greek world and as a reward for his support (especially for trying to end the civil war between Larisa and Pherae).[59] Indeed, like other kings before him, Philip was always careful to maintain amicable relations with Thessaly, and the state would play no small role in his central Greek policy. Thessaly would still prove troublesome, however, and little more than three years later he was forced to intervene there again (see pp. 76–7),[60] an indication perhaps that his policies were directed more towards short-term remedies than longer-term projects.[61]

Coupled to the king's increase in influence in Thessaly was his rising power in the Amphictyonic League. Philip had recently acquired territory in at least two neighbouring territories, Perrhaibia and Magnesia, each of which had two votes on the league council. Perrhaibia controlled both of the communications routes into southern Macedonia, so its strategic importance is obvious. The people were subject to Larisa, but the tribute they had previously paid to the tyrant there was now paid into Philip's coffers. Most of Magnesia was mountainous, with ranges running between the Pass of Tempe in the far north and the Aegean coast. In both areas Philip established garrisons in various towns, while Macedonian settlers were moved to Gonnoi (the gateway to the vitally important Pass of Tempe) in order to ensure Macedonian control.

Philip's Attempt to Breach Thermopylae

With Thessaly now his (at least for the moment), Philip could finally turn his attention further south, to Phocis and Athens. He prepared to march the nearly 90 miles (144 km) to Thermopylae (the 'Gates of Greece'), a strategic pass that controlled the route south from Thessaly. It had the sea to its north and was surrounded by mountains to its south. Moreover, the pass was very narrow, a defensive virtue reinforced by a wall through which the only passage was provided by a gate. Thus, whoever controlled Thermopylae controlled access to southern Greece, as was famously illustrated in 480 when a Greek force successfully held off a numerically superior one of invading Persians. For two days the Persians were thwarted in their attempt to penetrate Thermopylae. When a path leading behind the Greek force was betrayed to the Persians on the third day, the soldiers fled, with the exception of three hundred Spartans. Thus was fought the famous Battle of Thermopylae: the Spartans were annihilated, but their bravery still impresses us today.[62] Nowadays, the pass is quite different, transformed into a wide flat plain as a result of the silting up of the gulf. The spectacular hot sulphur springs from which it derives its name are still there, however.

Once through Thermopylae, Philip would have an easy route not only to the Phocian stronghold at Delphi but even, through Boeotia, to Attica. If this *was* his plan, it was about to come unstuck. In anticipation of his push southwards, Phayllus, as noted above, had been busy at Delphi robbing from the sacred treasuries to recruit more mercenaries. He would also receive two thousand troops from Achaea, one thousand from Sparta, five thousand infantry and four hundred cavalry from Athens,[63] and about two thousand from those fleeing with Lycophron from Pherae. This support was provided not out of any sympathy for the Phocian cause, but as a means of survival. If Philip penetrated Thermopylae, he would not be alone in advancing against the Athenians, but would be joined by Thessaly and perhaps also its longstanding enemy, Thebes, both of which were intent on Athens' reduction. The Spartans and Achaeans feared a possible invasion of the Peloponnese, in which a hostile Thebes already exerted no small influence. The xenophobic nature of the Greeks' behaviour towards each other, one of the unfortunate idio-syncrasies of the *polis* system, manifested itself yet again.

Eubulus for once opened the state coffers. Despite the high cost (200 talents), he ordered the general Nausicles, as noted above, to take five thousand infantry and four hundred cavalry, transported by fifty triremes, to Thermopylae to block Philip's advance, and so support Phocis.[64] Eubulus' measure shows that the Athenians viewed the threat from Philip as serious, but they were also afraid of Thebes joining the king. Thus, when Philip's army, supported only by a small force of Thessalians, arrived at the north-west entrance to the Pass of Thermopylae in August 352, it found itself faced by a large coalition army. The narrowness of the pass made it impossible for Philip to deploy his cavalry, and an infantry charge against the enemy could have serious consequences if it failed. He had learned this hard lesson from his defeat at the hands of Onomarchus in 353.

One military solution would be to attack the opposing force in the rear, from the southern entrance to the pass. Caught between the Macedonian army at one end and a hostile force at the other, the Phocians and their supporters would have been rendered suddenly vulnerable. In reality, the only state that might have aided Philip in this way was Thebes, as the other Greeks clearly expected it to do. But it was not to be. The Phocian campaigns in Boeotia made the Thebans think twice about marching out to support the Macedonian king. More than that, the Thebans were suspicious of Philip, given that he had not immediately marched into Phocis after defeating Onomarchus but had increased his power in Thessaly instead. Thebes therefore decided to stay neutral.

Philip was left with only two options: to march to Phocis by another route, perhaps via Doris (so risking attack by the Phocians), or to return home to Pella. Since the former would have been arduous and dangerous, the king chose the latter. A factor in his thinking may have been to keep Thebes at a distance and not to antagonise Athens. His decision not to penetrate the pass shows he was not all that determined to enter central Greece at this time.[65] Thus, the central Greeks won a respite from Philip's advance south and the Phocians lived to fight another day in the Sacred War. Also, the Athenians had shown that, when roused, they were an enemy not to be underestimated. Philip's presence at Thermopylae had panicked the Athenians, but Nausicles' expedition had shown that with the right support (and speed) Philip could be checked.[66]

Eubulus had acted decisively to bar Philip from Greece, but his days of political influence in Athens were numbered. Demosthenes had been addressing the Assembly since 355, although he had never referred to any threat from Philip. His speeches to date had been unsuccessful, largely because of Eubulus' political influence. On Nausicles' return, Eubulus had stood down his force, naively believing that with Philip out of Greece there was no further need for it. But Demosthenes realised that fiscal conservatism was one thing and Philip's military strength was quite another, so he began to develop an anti-Macedonian policy anchored in maintaining a citizen army to resist the king.

Philip's Campaigns in Thrace and the Chalcidice

Philip did not remain at Pella for very long, and by November 352 he was back in Thrace. While he had been in Greece Macedonian interests in Thrace had suffered a reversal, essentially stemming from their earlier defeat by Onomarchus. As we have seen, Chares had successfully re-established Athenian influence in the Chersonese, Cersebleptes had abandoned Philip and was busy fighting to rebuild a single kingdom, and Olynthus had sued for peace with Athens. It was therefore essential for Philip to reassert his authority in Thrace, and an opportunity presented itself in late 352 when a coalition of Byzantium, Perinthus and Amadocus (the king of central Thrace) asked for his support in its fight against Cersebleptes. Byzantium and Perinthus were in Cersebleptes' territory, and the coalition at that time was besieging Cersebleptes at Heraion Teichos, one of his east Thracian fortresses on the coast of the Sea of Marmara close to Perinthus (Marmaraeregli). It was there that Philip now marched with his army.

Calculating that Philip's position was weak because he was fighting far from home and in an area in which his influence had rapidly declined, the Athenians immediately decided to take advantage of the situation. They voted in an Assembly to send an expedition of forty triremes, manned by citizens aged between the ages of twenty and forty-five, and funded by an *eisphora* (extraordinary tax) of 40 talents.[67] It seems unlikely that they were initially aware of the involvement of Byzantium, Perinthus and central Thrace, for when they did find out they had a change of heart. Cersebleptes had been a fickle friend of Athens, and Byzantium boasted too powerful a fleet for the Athenians' liking. Cooler heads in the Assembly pointed out the dangers of committing such a large force in the circumstances, and so the Athenians abandoned the venture.

It seemed as though they had made a rash decision when news reached them that Philip was either dead or ill.[68] Once more rushing to capitalise on the king's (apparent) misfortune, they mobilised a force that set out in about September 351. It was significantly smaller than the one proposed earlier and was composed of only ten ships crewed by mercenaries under the command of Charidemus, Cersebleptes' former general, who took with him only five talents. The intention, presumably, was that more money would be forth-coming from Cersebleptes.

Philip was not dead, and his illness proved short-lived so that he soon resumed the siege of Heraion Teichos. When the city fell to him in about November, he returned it to Perinthus (perhaps its original owner). This was a blow to the Athenians, who now viewed the king's activities in Thrace as a threat to their corn route from the Black Sea (Map 3). When Philip was satisfied that Cersebleptes had been duly cowed, perhaps because he seized his son and transported him to Pella as a hostage,[69] he turned to deal with the defiant Olynthians. The fate of Amadocus is unknown but it is possible that Philip replaced him with his son Teres.

Exactly what Philip did in the Chalcidice and how long he was there are unknown. He obviously did not besiege any cities: if he had, our sources would be more explicit in what they tell us. In the context of a general state-ment about Philip's campaigns against the Illyrians, Paeonians, Arybbas of Epirus (see below) 'and anywhere else one may say', Demosthenes states that he 'made an attempt on' Olynthus.[70] This may mean nothing more than that he resorted to diplomatic means to regain the Olynthians' loyalty. Support is lent to this interpretation by a fragment from a contemporary source that talks of his delivering a stern warning to the leaders.[71] Since his position now, in early 351, was far stronger than in 353 when Olynthus had turned against him, he may well have thought that a verbal warning was enough to counter any anti-Macedonian factionalism, and not long afterwards the anti-Macedonian leader, Apollonides, was expelled from the city and went to Athens (where he was given citizenship).[72] Further, two pro-Macedonians, Lasthenes and Euthycrates, were elected to the important military command of the hipparch (commander of the cavalry).

The Olynthians' gesture proved hollow: when Philip invaded the Chalcidice in 349 he did so because they were harbouring two of his half-brothers, potential claimants to the throne. As Philip left the area in 351–350 he was not yet ready to launch a full-scale invasion of the Chalcidice. For now, border problems to his west and north-west were again demanding his attention.

Renewed Involvement in Paeonia, Illyria and Epirus

Paeonia, Illyria and possibly also Epirus may have taken advantage of Philip's defeat by Onomarchus to set their sights once more on Macedonia. The continuing problems that he faced with these areas indicate the difficulty of integrating them into a unified Macedonia.[73] When he returned to Pella he now concentrated his attention on these areas.

The details of any campaign against the Paeonians and Illyrians are unknown. However, something must have taken place, for a little over four years later, in 346, Isocrates tells us that Philip had enforced his rule over these (and other) people.[74] Isocrates is possibly referring to the campaign in Philip's second year as king, though this evidently did not end the discontent there. A later campaign must have taken place in 351–350, for Philip was busy elsewhere after this time.

King Arybbas of the Molossians in Epirus (Map 2) also posed a problem. Philip had been married to his niece Olympias since 357, but Arybbas was no stalwart supporter of the king.[75] That he may have conspired against Philip in 353 when Onomarchus defeated him is perhaps shown by Philip's declaration of war on him in 350. The details of this short war are unknown, but at its end Macedonia emerged triumphant. Philip allowed Arybbas to remain on the throne, but he took steps to limit his power and to extend his own in Epirus. One such step was removing Alexander, Arybbas' nephew (and Olympias' younger brother, so Philip's brother-in-law), from his uncle's court to live in Pella.[76] Alexander at the time was about twelve years old and he was next in line to the Epirote throne. Arybbas was now made in effect regent of his nephew until he came of age and succeeded to the throne. Philip also abolished the Molossian bronze coinage and substituted his own, which was a further means of stimulating Macedonia's economy.[77] These coins remained in circulation until 342 when Alexander (of Epirus) became king.

There is a story that Philip had a homosexual relationship with the young Alexander (of Epirus). Justin tells us that Philip:[78]

> made every effort to seduce him, holding out the promise of his stepfather's throne, and pretending to be in love with him, until he drove the boy into a homosexual liaison with him. His motive was to gain greater submissiveness from the boy, whether through a guilty conscience or the prospect of the throne . . . he made him a catamite first, and then a king.

We simply do not know if this is true. Philip was not averse to sex with both women and men (his assassin would turn out to be a former male lover). However, this account of his interest in children could well be the product of a hostile literary tradition that began with Theopompus, who criticised the king's morals in general, and that continued through to Trogus and Justin beyond.

Demosthenes' First *Philippic*

The Athenians had successfully thwarted Philip, and Demosthenes' political importance in the city was on the rise. Into the period 351–350 must be fitted the latter's first major speech against Philip, the first *Philippic* (the title is a modern one), which marked a turning point in Demosthenes' development both as an orator and as a politician.[79] Although he had mentioned Philip a little earlier in his speech *Against Aristocrates*, he had only done so *en passant*.[80] In contrast to his speeches for the lawcourts, his earlier political orations (for example, on behalf of Rhodes and Megalopolis of 354) had been failures. The time was thus ripe for him to change tack if he wanted to pursue a political career, and change he did. From 351 he would focus his attention fully on the Macedonian king, characterising him as a despot and a threat to Greek freedom. To Demosthenes, Philip was a tyrant to be resisted at all costs, and the only way to defeat him was by a citizen (not mercenary) army. As his career progressed, Demosthenes stressed that he was the only person who had seen the danger posed by Philip from the outset and that if his advice had been followed the Greeks would not have suffered the loss of their freedom.

Of course, much of this was mere rhetoric designed to elevate Demosthenes' influence in political history. The fiery oratory of his speeches, especially in the four *Philippics*, has justly earned him a reputation as the greatest Greek writer of speeches, but whether he was a true patriot or cynically exploited the danger from Philip as a means to political power is arguable.[81] So too is whether his anti-Macedonian policy was really in the best interests of Athens (and Greece). Might he have grasped instead that the *polis* system was outdated and that the Athenian form of democracy could not run a war when its enemy was a king who controlled each and every decision? Or should he have pursued a policy (as his rival Aeschines was later to advocate) of allying with Philip on equal terms when the king gave the Athenians the chance? These questions cannot be finally answered, but one thing is certain: after 351 Demosthenes became a political force with which to be reckoned, and Athenian foreign policy would take a dramatic turn from that advocated by Eubulus.

The context of the first *Philippic* was the question of how the war for Amphipolis should be conducted and how Philip could be opposed most effectively. It contains a powerful rallying cry to rouse the Athenians from their defeatism and apathy, to persuade them that they were wrong to think that Philip was invincible, to censure them for allowing the king to grow so powerful, and to put forward specific proposals to combat him in the north. Demosthenes says that, if the Athenians in the Assembly would follow his advice, Philip could be defeated. Since these are the sorts of things that Demosthenes repeats often, it is appropriate here to include a lengthy quotation that illustrates his rhetorical style, his vision of Philip and other points he returns to again and again in his speeches:[82]

If the belief is held that Philip is an enemy hard to face in view of the extent of his present strength and the loss to Athens of strategic points, it is a correct belief. But it must be remembered that at one time we had Pydna, Potidaea, Methone, and the whole surrounding district on friendly terms, and that a number of communities now on his side were then autonomous and unfettered, and would have preferred our friendship to his. If Philip had then adopted this belief in the invincibility of Athens in view of her control of points commanding Macedonian territory, while he himself lacked support, he could not have achieved any of his present successes nor acquired the strength he has. As it was, he observed with insight that these strategic points were the prizes of war, that they were open to the contestants, and it is a natural law that ownership passes from the absentee to the first-comer, from the negligent to the energetic and enterprising. This is the spirit which has won him the control of what he holds, in some cases by the methods of military conquest, in others by those of friendship and alliance. Indeed, alliance and universal attention are the rewards to be won by obvious preparedness and the will to take action. If, then, this country is prepared to adopt a similar outlook and to break with the past, if every man is ready to take the post which his duty and his abilities demand in service to the state, and set pretensions aside, if financial contribution is forthcoming from the well-to-do, and personal service from the appropriate group, in a word, if we are prepared to be ourselves, to abandon the hope to evade our duty and get it done by our neighbours, we shall recover what is our own with God's will, we shall regain what inertia has lost to us, and we shall inflict retribution upon Philip. You must not imagine that he is a superhuman being whose success is unalterably fixed. He has enemies to hate, fear and envy him, even in places very friendly to him. His associates, one must suppose, have the same human feelings as anyone else. But now all this is beneath the surface. It has nowhere to turn because of the slowness, the inactivity of Athens. It is this that I urge you to lay aside.

Philip has the ability to make a decision and act on it at once, in contrast to Athenian slowness in making up its mind about issues when it is already too late. Demosthenes marvellously illustrates this by comparing the Athenians to a 'barbarian' boxer, who 'if he is hit, he hugs the place, and if you hit him somewhere else, there go his hands again. He has not learnt, and is not prepared, to defend himself or look to his front.'[83]

The speech is not just rhetoric. Demosthenes was right to stress the need for citizen as opposed to mercenary soldiers, for citizens fighting for their own state tend to make better fighters. Also sensible was his call to equip and maintain two forces, the first to be a standby one of soldiers and five hundred cavalry (half of the total number), to be transported by an armada of fifty triremes and the requisite number of supply ships, and the second a strike force to 'wage war constantly' in the north and be launched immediately. It would consist of two thousand infantry and two hundred cavalry, a quarter of whom would be citizens and the rest mercenaries, transported on ten fast triremes. Its job would be to harass Philip's fleet, raid his coastline and seize his merchant ships, and it would be based at Lemnos, Thasos and Sciathos so that it could attack Philip even in winter were he to make any moves then.

Demosthenes' financial measures to provide for the maintenance of these forces are less sound. Keeping a force on standby for the best part of the year would cost a fortune, and the smaller one, with its estimated cost of 92 talents (a figure that did not include pay for the men), was hardly cheap. It was partly for economic reasons, then, that the speech was unsuccessful. Another reason was logistical. An Athenian fleet in the north would need to be stationed in one of the ports of the Chalcidian League, but there was no guarantee that the league would permit this or, given its fickleness in the past, that it would not turn on the Athenians if Philip offered it a deal. Yet another reason for the speech's failure was the continuing influence of Eubulus, whose fiscal conservatism made this type of troop deployment utterly impossible. In Demosthenes' defeat in the Assembly we can hear the voice of Eubulus at work.

Demosthenes' idea of taking the war to Philip had merit compared to the arguments of Eubulus, who unrealistically thought that Philip could be opposed effectively in central Greece. But in truth Apollo's Saviour was already unstoppable. The king had superior numbers in his own army, and he could also draw on the forces of Thessaly and other allies. Distracted by the Third Sacred War, because it was on their own doorstep, the Greeks had allowed Philip's power to grow. When the war ended, the reality was that no force could stop him, and it was only a matter of time before Greece fell under his control.

THE FALL OF OLYNTHUS

Events in the Third Sacred War had reached a stalemate. The Amphictyonic Council had been suspended – it had struggled to meet with only a few member states in attendance anyway – and would not reconvene until the end of the war in 346. Philip at this stage does not seem to have planned to involve himself in the war again until he had dealt with the Athenians, whose renewed influence in the north he viewed with some concern. Instead of attacking Athens, however, he invaded the Chalcidice (Map 4). Despite the treaty of 357 and the warning he delivered on his way back from Thrace in 351, the Olynthians had been up to their old tricks again.

It seems that Olynthus had offered asylum to two of Philip's three half-brothers from his father Amyntas' marriage to Gygaea. These were most likely Menelaus and Arrhidaeus since Philip may have killed Archelaus when he assumed the throne in 359.[1] Apparently, Machatas, the exiled brother of Philip's first wife, Phila, was also present in Olynthus.[2] If the Olynthians thought that Philip would allow them to give shelter to Menelaus and Arrhidaeus they were mistaken, for he demanded their surrender. His action indicates that ten years after he came to the throne he was still taking steps to eliminate potential rivals and hence to ensure the security of his kingship.[3] According to Justin, when the Olynthians refused his demand he launched a full-scale invasion of the Chalcidice.[4] It was now midsummer 349.

Olynthus was a logical place for the king's rivals to seek refuge. It was powerful, heading a league of some thirty-two cities, it had abundant wealth from its natural resources and trade, and it had a long history of interference in the Macedonian throne. That the Olynthians admitted the two half-brothers is a sign that by 350, or 349 at the latest, they were preparing to interfere in the kingdom's domestic politics again. Hence Philip decided that the time had come to put an end to Chalcidian independence once and for all. The treaty of 357 had clearly been disregarded, so Philip had right on his side as he prepared, in keeping with the consequence of one party breaking the treaty's oath, to wreak 'many evils' on the people.

Philip's First Invasion of the Chalcidice: Demosthenes' *Olynthiacs*

In the autumn of 349 Philip crossed by Lake Bolbe into Chalcidian territory. His strategy was to pick off the other cities of the league one at a time, both west and east of Olynthus, and thus leave Olynthus isolated. He besieged the north-eastern city of Stageira (the birthplace of Aristotle), although there is a corruption in the texts of our sources which means that the identification is not entirely secure.[5] When it fell, he razed it to the ground (later, Aristotle would persuade Alexander to restore it). Its fate was meant to serve as a warning to other cities that contemplated resistance as Philip marched westwards to Olynthus, and it seemed to do the trick. Other towns such as Stratonicia, Acanthus, Apollonia and Arethusa surrendered without a fight and so saved themselves from destruction.

Meanwhile the Olynthians had not been idle. In September or October 349 they sent an embassy to Athens appealing for an alliance.[6] Despite being offered the opportunity of gaining the help of the Chalcidian League against Philip, the Athenians gave the envoys a lukewarm reception. Perhaps this was because of the continuing influence of Eubulus, who was as cautious as ever about getting involved in foreign ventures. Nevertheless, this did not stop Demosthenes from addressing the Assembly. He did so not just in one speech but in three, the *Olynthiacs*, the first two of which were delivered while the Olynthian envoys were still in the city. In these speeches Demosthenes appealed to the Athenians to go to the aid of not merely Olynthus but the Chalcidians as a whole. The rhetoric of all three speeches is masterful, but it illustrates once again the unreliability of oratory as historical evidence, for Demosthenes deliberately presents a distorted picture of Philip's weaknesses, movements and aims in order to strengthen his case.[7]

In the first *Olynthiac* Demosthenes argued that as part of its war effort against Philip it was essential for Athens to act quickly in order to preserve a free and friendly Chalcidian League. He repeated his call from the first *Philippic* for two forces, one to save the cities of the league and another to attack Philip in the north. Aid to Olynthus would also tie in with his plea to keep a strike force operating in the north. To combat Eubulus' caution, he resorted to scare-tactic rhetoric, warning the Athenians that they would have to fight Philip eventually, so better now in the Chalcidice than later in Attica, when Thebes would doubtless support him. More radically, Demosthenes urged the people to consider using the Theoric Fund to finance their support. This was a daring move given that the fund was in principle inviolable and those who suggested using it for anything but its formal purpose risked indictment in the courts. At some earlier point, a certain Apollodorus had proposed diverting its surpluses into the Military Fund, for which he was fined the large sum of one talent.[8] Hence Demosthenes did not mention the fund by name but instead hinted that the city had a fund that could be used. There was certainly plenty of money in it, and he returned to his suggestion in the third *Olynthiac*.[9]

The first *Olynthiac* failed; the second followed perhaps only a few days later.[10] In it, Demosthenes argued that Philip was in a weak position because he was unpopular at home and with his army, and that his power would collapse at any moment! This was more than wishful thinking on his part: it was deliberate deception of the people, a good example of an orator pursuing his agenda at the cost of the truth. Demosthenes also urged the Athenians to exploit the king's enemies. If he had in mind an alliance with the Spartans and the Thebans, that again was wishful thinking, given the current relations between these states. Alternatively, he may have had in mind the king's two stepbrothers, then in Olynthus. One interesting aspect of this speech is his call for the various politicians to end their enmity. Perhaps he had Eubulus, with whom he clashed continually on matters of foreign and financial policy, in mind.

This speech was successful, and the Athenians voted to make an alliance with Olynthus. They sent a large force of two thousand peltasts (named after the *pelta* or wicker shield they carried) or javelin-throwers and thirty ships under the command of Chares.[11] The peltasts were mercenaries (originally from Thrace), so this expeditionary force was not composed of citizens as Demosthenes had wanted. It is unknown what Chares did when he got to the Chalcidice: probably not much since Philip was no longer there, having been forced to return once more to Thessaly to settle matters with a rebellious Pherae.

Philip Returns to Thessaly

It seems that almost as soon as Philip left for the Chalcidice the Thessalians (i.e., the people of Pherae) demanded the restoration of Pagasae (his retention of it was a bone of contention), stopped the Macedonians from fortifying Magnesia, and were withholding the harbour and market dues payable to Philip as their *archon*. It seems that by now Peitholaus, one of the tyrants expelled with Lycophron, had returned to Pherae and was actively advancing its interests in Thessaly.[12] Presumably Lycophron, the other previous tyrant, had died by this time.

Philip could probably have left Thessaly to its own devices while he campaigned in the Chalcidice, had it not been for the potential for an alliance between Pherae and Athens. More than that, in the Sacred War the Phocians currently had the upper hand over the Boeotians, which worried the

Thessalians. They now invited Philip to rejoin the war and put an end once and for all to the Phocian menace. Philip was only too happy to be invited into central Greece again, but he could not turn to the Sacred War yet because of his ongoing campaign in the Chalcidice. Thus, for the moment he marched to Pherae to deal with Peitholaus.[13] The details of the campaign are unknown, but Philip defeated him easily enough (probably because he received no support from other cities in Thessaly or from Athens) and then returned to the task of reducing Olynthus.

Philip's Second Invasion of the Chalcidice: Demosthenes' Third *Olynthiac*

By March 348 Philip was back in the Chalcidice. The Athenians answered a second Olynthian call for help by sending another force. Commanded by Charidemus, the general based in the Chersonese, it was composed of eighteen triremes, four thousand mercenary peltasts and 150 cavalry.[14] What Chares and the earlier Athenian force were doing is unknown, but he must have returned to Athens, for some months later he led another force to Olynthus. Charidemus' troops and a Chalcidian army of one thousand cavalry and ten thousand infantry were able to attack some cities in the Pallene promontory that had recently fallen to Philip, but they could do nothing to stop his advance against Olynthus.

Ultimately, the Athenians' attempt to dislodge Philip from the Chalcidice was a failure. He continued his policy of reducing Chalcidic towns one by one, taking Apollonia easily enough, Torone and not long after, in either late spring or early summer 348, Mecyberna, the port of Olynthus. Diodorus says that Mecyberna and Torone were betrayed to him.[15] With the loss of their port, the Olynthians were cut off from receiving reinforcements and thus very vulnerable, so Philip now moved in for the kill. He issued an ultimatum that either they abandon Olynthus or he abandon Macedonia. Since he had no intention of giving up Macedonia, the meaning was obvious.[16] If he hoped that his earlier treatment of Stageira would cow the people into submission, he was mistaken. The besieged Olynthians sent off a third appeal for help to Athens, this time asking for citizen soldiers. Demosthenes rose once more in the Assembly and delivered his third and final *Olynthiac* oration.

The speech attacks the political leaders and the people for their apathy, which Demosthenes contrasts with the great deeds of their ancestors, a common topos in Greek oratory. More importantly, Demosthenes thought the situation serious enough to suggest that the Athenians consider amending Eubulus' law whereby annual budget surpluses were paid into the Theoric Fund. He had already hinted at using Theoric monies for military purposes in the first *Olynthiac*, but in the third he advanced the appeal less shyly, though still with care.

In the event nothing was done to touch the Theoric Fund, but another Athenian force was sent to help Olynthus. Under the command of Chares, it consisted of seventeen triremes, two thousand citizen infantry and three hundred cavalry (30 per cent of Athens' total cavalry force).[17] Why the Athenians decided to commit so many troops when Philip was at the gates of Olynthus is unknown. Demosthenes' rhetoric about Philip's weak position was perhaps a factor. Another may have been the belief that a grateful Olynthus would help the Athenians regain Amphipolis. However, mainly because of the northerly Etesian Winds (the Meltemi), which blow between May and September and severely hamper sailing, the Athenian force only arrived after Olynthus had already fallen.[18] This was in August or September 348, before the Macedonian Olympic festival in September.[19]

The Fall of Olynthus

According to Demosthenes, who is echoed by Diodorus, the two pro-Macedonian hipparchs earlier elected by the people, Euthycrates and Lasthenes, were bribed to betray the city to Philip.[20] Diodorus adds that Philip had made several assaults on Olynthus and lost a number of men before he finally bribed these men to betray the city to him. Sling bullets and bolt-heads from non-torsion catapults inscribed with Philip's name (*Philippou*) on their stems have been found during excavations, showing the Olynthians put up a fight.[21] This corroborates Diodorus' statement about the fighting, but good arguments have been advanced to discredit Demosthenes' allegation (and hence Diodorus here) of Philip's success being due to bribes.[22] Demosthenes' disparaging comment was in much the same vein as the one he made after the fall of Amphipolis in 357, and was intended to belittle Philip's achievement.

When the Macedonians took Olynthus they went on a bloody rampage, killing indiscriminately. The Olynthians who survived the carnage were enslaved and forced to work in the Macedonian mines and fields, or fled into exile, and Olynthus was razed to the ground.[23] The Chalcidian League, another of the outside powers that had a history of interference in Macedonian domestic politics, came to an end, as did Athens' chances of recovering Amphipolis, although the Athenians did not necessarily see this at the time.

Philip acquired the region's rich timber and mineral resources (especially the gold and silver mines at Stratonici), thus adding further to Macedonian prosperity (Map 4). The Chalcidian coinage that had for long dominated the region was replaced by Macedonian coinage, especially the silver tetradrachms and later the gold staters. These circulated all over the ancient world. Some of Philip's senior staff and Companion Cavalry received portions of land and money as a reward. Whether this was part of a reorganisation of the Chalcidice is unknown, but it is unlikely, not least because there was no resettlement 'programme' of Macedonians such as we find taking place in the kingdom in about 345 (see pp. 109–10).[24] Lastly, Philip would have ordered the execution of his two half-brothers.[25]

In a speech delivered in 341, Demosthenes stated that Philip razed the thirty-two cities of the Chalcidian League: 'I do not mention Olynthus, Methone, Apollonia, and thirty-two cities of the Thracian district [= the Chalcidice], all of which he destroyed so brutally that it is hard for a visitor to tell if they were ever inhabited.'[26] His claim is made as part of a rhetorical effort to rouse the Athenians again against Philip. However, Diodorus and Justin have nothing to say about any such wholesale destruction,[27] and since they detail Philip's treatment of Olynthus and its people, they would surely also have referred to any other violent acts. They only record one other city as being razed, and that was Stageira (accepting this as the city's name) at the start of the campaign. In any case, since Philip wanted to use the Chalcidice as a source of revenue, it made no economic sense to devastate the entire region.[28]

Those Athenians present at Olynthus were taken to Pella as prisoners. In the past Philip had released Athenian prisoners, but not this time: they would play a role in the negotiations leading to the conclusion of the first war between Athens and himself in 346 (see Chapter 8). The Athenians passed a decree condemning Philip's action in reducing Olynthus, and granted asylum to Olynthian refugees who were allowed to join the ranks of resident aliens (metics) living and working in Athens. In a generous gesture the Athenians exempted them from the forms of taxation paid by other metics.

Why did Philip destroy Olynthus? He may have wanted to offer an example to the other Greeks of what happened to those who resisted him. The fact that the city had broken the terms of the treaty of 357 gave him an excuse to move against it as he did, but Olynthus' days were probably numbered once it gave refuge to possible claimants to the Macedonian throne and that caused him to raze it. Philip needed to issue a clear message that any such interference in Macedonian politics would be punished in the harshest manner. Here, an analogy may be drawn with Alexander the Great's decision to raze Thebes to the ground over a decade later, in 335. He divided its territory among neighbouring states, enslaved those Thebans who were not killed when the city capitulated and seized a substantial amount of money.[29] The fate of both Olynthus and Thebes was often cited and became something of a literary topos. For example:

Olynthus and Thebes . . . were plundered by Alexander and Philip and razed to the ground, and the horror of the destruction caused great alarm to many of the Greeks for their all and gave many orators an opportunity to explain in due manner the details of the calamity by their oratory. They have spoken on this subject, some in allegorical fashion, and with redundance in their several dictions, as they seem (to have done). But some have spoken with greater depth, though without avoiding literal and ordinary language in treating a horrible subject.[30]

It is interesting to note the common belief that Alexander destroyed Thebes because it had revolted against him and he wanted to send out a warning to any cities that were thinking of defying him. For example, Diodorus says that his action 'presented possible rebels among the Greeks with a terrible warning', and Plutarch states that 'Alexander's principal object in permitting the sack of Thebes was to frighten the rest of the Greeks into submission by making a terrible example'.[31] Yet inscriptional evidence suggests that the Thebans were supporting a pretender to the throne, none other than Amyntas, the legal heir in 359.[32] While Alexander did punish Thebes as a warning, in actually razing it he was taking a leaf out of his father's book by making it clear what would happen to those who had a history of interfering in Macedonian politics. His action lends weight to Philip's having moved against Olynthus for the same reason.

Athenian Help, or Lack Thereof, for Olynthus

The Athenians, as we have seen, sent three fairly large expeditions to aid Olynthus, the first of which (commanded by Chares) seems to have done little or nothing. The Chalcidice was the last Greek enclave on Macedonian soil, and it seemed logical that once Philip had conquered it he would turn his attention to Athens. Therefore, should the Athenians have done more to save it? Why did they not take up Demosthenes' proposals? A number of reasons can be cited.[33]

To begin with, once an ally did not mean always an ally. In Athens, Eubulus and his supporters doubted the reliability of the Olynthians and so did not want to send a large force so great a distance to assist them. Moreover, the true military situation in the Chalcidice did not become evident until it was too late. There was a very slow initial build-up in the eastern Chalcidian region, then a brief campaign in Thessaly (at Pherae), and finally a very fast attack on Olynthus. Philip timed this last to coincide with the northerly Etesian Winds (the Meltemi). These winds blow from the north in the central Aegean and from the north-east in the eastern Aegean, beginning in mid-June, and are so strong that any ship is hampered by them. For over forty days they prevented an Athenian fleet sailing to the Chalcidice. With no fleet of his own to speak of, Philip used the winds to prevent the Athenian fleet bringing help.

Furthermore, the Athenians could not match the king's speed or, more importantly, second-guess what his next move would be. If they had sent a large number of troops north and split them up to support the various cities of the league, as Demosthenes urged, Philip could conceivably have picked off the forces one by one. Alternatively, he might simply have left the Athenians alone until they ran out of money and had to return home. Even worse, he could have varied his strategy by marching back to Thermopylae and advancing on Athens, now denuded of troops. He had been blocked from passing through Thermopylae in 352, a failure he did not want to repeat.[34] Therefore, the Assembly decided to wait, but by then the situation had deteriorated too much and it was too late for active help.

A final factor in the Athenians' decision was their involvement in the island of Euboea, which they had won over to their side in 357. In early 348 Callias, the tyrant of the town of Chalcis, sought to unite the cities of Euboea into some sort of league under him. Plutarchus, the tyrant of Eretria, opposed him and appealed for help to Athens.[35] If Callias had been successful, his new league would almost certainly have remained aloof from Athens' naval confederacy. This was a situation that the Athenians could not ignore, for Euboea's location made it of vital strategic importance for security purposes. Lying as it did so close to Attica's eastern coastline, it afforded Philip easy access to Attica if Thermopylae were blocked to him again. People in Athens must have thought that Philip would be quick to capitalise on Callias' success, so the situation there appeared more desperate than the fate of the Chalcidian cities.

On the proposal of Eubulus, the Athenians sent a force under the command of the general Phocion to Euboea.[36] Demosthenes also served on this campaign, although he would soon return to Athens because of his role in the festival of the Great Dionysia (in honour of the god Dionysus).[37] Phocion did not receive the expected help from Plutarchus when he arrived, and he found himself besieged by enemy forces at Tamynae.[38] He extricated himself with no small difficulty, and expelled Plutarchus from Eretria. Shortly after, Phocion was recalled and sent to Lesbos. He was succeeded by Molossus, but Plutarchus quickly reappeared on the scene and defeated him (probably in July). Molossus and the Athenians on Euboea were taken prisoner, and only released when the Athenian state paid a ransom of 50 talents. The island as a whole, apart from the town of Carystus at its southern end, then became independent of Athens.[39]

The Euboean issue was clearly a critical one for Athens, and we have to wonder whether the timing of Callias' activities, coming as they did when

Athenian attention was turning to the Chalcidice and Philip, was coincidental. It is not stretching the imagination too far to see Philip's hand at work in Euboea, and Aeschines tells us that Callias 'summoned additional forces from Philip'.[40] The king's objective was to divert Athens' attention from his own exploits in the north, as he had earlier done with the Social War.[41]

Philip Proposes Peace to Athens

After the fall of Olynthus, Philip went to Dium and there celebrated the autumn festival in honour of Zeus of Olympus. Lavish sacrifices, raucous symposia and spectacular artistic competitions took place. It may have been at this point that Philip issued another silver tetradrachm, this time with the king's portrait on it showing him with an upraised hand as if addressing a crowd in victory. The coin was struck to commemorate his victory over Olynthus.[42] With the Chalcidice now part of Macedonia, the only real cloud on Macedonia's horizon was the war with Athens. The first move to dissipate that cloud came from Philip, and surprisingly it was a diplomatic one.

In the summer of 348 Macedonian pirates captured an Athenian citizen from the township of Rhamnus. His name was Phrynon, and his seizure was illegal as it took place during the Olympic truce (the period when those travelling to and from the Olympic Games were protected from attack or capture). Phrynon provided his own ransom and was released. When he returned to Athens he demanded that an embassy be sent to Philip to protest against his capture and to ask for his ransom. The demand was reasonable given the legalities of the case, and the Athenians voted to send Ctesiphon to Philip.

Philip had taken Olynthus by the time Ctesiphon returned from his mission. Surprisingly, Ctesiphon brought back with him a message saying that the king regretted the war with Athens; he had been forced into it, he said, and now he wanted it to end and for peace to be made between Athens and Macedonia. He assured the people that he was their friend and had no hostile intentions towards them. The Athenians had been duped by Philip's apparent sincerity before, but that was forgotten now. They were so relieved that they bestowed an unofficial vote of praise on Ctesiphon, and Philocrates of Hagnus proposed in the Assembly that Philip should send an envoy to Athens to outline his peace terms and that the Assembly should discuss them.[43]

Although Philocrates' proposal was passed unanimously, it was afterwards declared unlawful. Why is unknown: perhaps it breached a clause in Athens' agreement with Olynthus, by which no signatory could enter into negotiations with the other's enemy without the agreement of the other party.[44] If this is the case, it shows that at this time news of Olynthus' demise had not yet reached the Athenians. In accordance with Athenian law, Philocrates was prosecuted for bringing an unconstitutional motion to the Assembly. His ally Demosthenes defended him, and he won such a convincing victory that Philocrates' accuser, Lycinus, was fined 1,000 drachmas and lost the right to bring similar suits in the future.[45]

In defending Philocrates, Demosthenes was not suddenly changing his attitude to Philip and advocating peace with the king. Rather he was seizing the chance to distance himself further from Eubulus' group and so step into the political limelight as his own man. Eubulus' reaction to the situation was to warn the Assembly of the danger posed by Philip to Greek autonomy. He even produced an Arcadian named Ischander, who dramatically (and wrongly) warned that Philip was gathering support everywhere, even in the Peloponnese.[46] Consequently, Eubulus' proposal to send an embassy to all Greek states calling for them to unite in a war against Philip was passed. Demosthenes would have been content with this Athenian response, but he did not go on the embassy because his recent support of Philocrates (who was proposing peace with Philip) would affect its chances of success. Aeschines, a former teacher and actor, and now an orator, who had an odious past according to Demosthenes,[47] supported the motion and went on the mission.[48] He would soon become Demosthenes' most ardent opponent and the most fervent supporter of peace with Philip on equal terms, but for now peace with Macedonia seemed as far away as ever.

APOLLO RESCUED, AND THE PEACE OF PHILOCRATES

The Athenian embassy to the Greek states calling for war against Philip met with complete failure. This was hardly a surprise given the Athenians' track record of leadership, made worse now by its unpopular role in the Third Sacred War and approval of Philip's (apparent) stance towards the Phocians.[1] Eubulus' decree achieved nothing except to damage Athens' relations with Philip. The king had opened the door to peace, but the Athenians were obstructing the threshold. Philip's gesture of goodwill may well have been a covert ruse, as was his wont, but the Athenians' overt action showed Philip exactly what – and whom – he was up against.

Philip's Courtship of Athens: The Isolation of Thebes

With the Chalcidian League disbanded, Philip was in a position to call his allies in Thessaly and Boeotia to arms and so march to end the Sacred War. The possibility of Athens being next on his list of targets was also there. In reality, the Athenians could summon only Sparta and Phocis to their aid,[2] and the former was in dire straits financially and militarily as a result of its war against Megalopolis. Athens could not have put up much of a fight, so why would Philip seek a peace treaty with it at this time?

The answer lies in the king's wish to curb Theban influence in central Greece, to which end he used Athens and Phocis.[3] The danger of an alliance between Athens and Thebes was always present (the fact that Athens was Phocis' ally and Thebes its enemy meant little in inter-state politics), and the combination would present Philip with a serious military threat to any settlement he wanted to see take place in central Greece. The Athenians had not exactly welcomed his peace overtures with open arms, as Eubulus' reaction and the embassies to the Greek states showed. Also, it was inevitable that once Phocis was defeated in the Sacred War Thebes would regain power in central Greece, presenting a scenario for conflict with other powers. Justin tells us that the Thebans were distrusted, and blames them for their weak hegemony and for provoking the Third Sacred War,[4] and especially (with the Spartans) for reducing Greece from being 'world leader in military strength and reputation . . . the conqueror of kings and nations . . . the mistress of many cities' to 'waiting patiently at the court of a foreigner to beg for peace or war'.[5]

Why did Philip thus turn against Thebes and not Athens? The answer, I suggest, is personal: his bad memories of his years there as a hostage. While he may have learned much from the likes of Pelopidas or from watching the Sacred Band train, the fact was that his stay in Thebes was an enforced one, lasting about three years, and during his formative years as a teenager. Relations between Macedonia and Thebes had always been uneasy, but once Philip became king and found himself involved in central Greece, the opportunity to reduce Thebes in revenge for what he had suffered proved irresistible. Thus, the basis of his strategy became the isolation of Thebes by advancing Athenian interests and in the process working to save – as far as possible – Phocis.[6]

Hence he opened negotiations with the Athenians, and perhaps even in these early stages he secretly let them know of his plan to protect Phocis and to defy Thebes. Of course, Philip could not openly threaten Thebes, for that would send it scurrying into the Athenian camp, so he had to beguile the Thebans into thinking he was sympathetic to their cause. In order to achieve this, he began to work behind the scenes with the Thessalian League (an ally of Thebes) and with Athens to bring about a settlement in Greece that would leave Thebes weak. That would involve his ending the Third Sacred War and the war over Amphipolis with Athens. As Demosthenes saw, the final months of the Sacred War and the negotiations for peace between Philip and the Athenians might relate to two separate wars, but the politics involved meshed them together so closely that the divide was not always obvious.[7]

Events in the Sacred War: Phalaecus Succeeds Phayllus

By now, the Sacred War had deteriorated into a series of skirmishes between an exhausted Phocis and a lacklustre Thebes. Athens and Sparta showed little interest in the conflict because of their own problems.[8] In late 352 Phayllus had died 'of a wasting disease, after a long illness, suffering great pain as befitted his impious life',[9] and Phalaecus (Onomarchus' son) succeeded him as commander-in-chief, assisted by another general, Mnaseas. Phalaecus had not taken recent Phocian reversals at the hands of the Thebans lying down, and had gone on the offensive. Although Mnaseas had died during a Boeotian night attack, by 349 or 348 he had inflicted a series of defeats on Boeotian forces and seized Coronea, Corsiae and Orchomenus.[10] His victories had turned the war in favour of the Phocians and had provided the cue, at Thessalian urging, for Philip to re-enter the war. At the time the king was involved in his campaign in the Chalcidice; however, Pherae was again causing problems thanks to the return of its tyrant Peitholaus. The situation was evidently serious enough for Philip to break off his campaign and march against Peitholaus, after which he returned to the Chalcidice.

Then in the spring or early summer of 347, apparently as a result of 'internal fighting' in Phocis,[11] Phalaecus was removed from his command – the official reason being for plundering the temple treasuries. Since the previous Phocian generals had done the same thing without suffering any consequences, something was obviously going on behind the scenes. Phalaecus and the other Phocian commanders (with the exception of Philomelus) along with the state treasurer Philon were found guilty of corruption and embezzlement on a huge scale. The Athenians and Spartans, whose troops had been paid by the Phocian commanders out of temple funds, also came under scrutiny.[12] A disgraced Phalaecus was replaced by three generals, Deinocrates, Callias and Sophanes, who immediately campaigned in Boeotia. Faced with these renewed attacks, the Thebans, with no one else to turn to, appealed to Philip for help.

Diodorus tells us that Philip was 'pleased to see their discomfiture and disposed to humble the Boeotians' pride after Leuctra', which suggests that all he had in mind was keeping the Thebans down.[13] He could not show that delight openly and perhaps risk losing Thebes to Athens, nor could he fail to send help to Thebes and so risk being seen as siding with the sacrilegious Phocians: in the end he sent a token contingent of troops under Parmenion.

Philip's move set alarm bells ringing in Athens. The people thought, logically enough, that the Thebans would appeal for more military support, perhaps against Athens next time. They also thought that once Philip marched through Thermopylae they would be at his mercy and forced to accept any terms he might impose. This was hardly a wild notion since we have seen Philip unscrupulously playing one ally off against another and reducing allies to submission when his plans called for it. At this stage no Greek state knew exactly what Philip had in mind, though, which gave their imaginations a breeding ground.

Athenian Resistance to Philip

Demosthenes, a member of the Boule for that year, urged the Athenians to send an expedition to protect their interests in Thrace and the Hellespont (Dardanelles), for Philip would want to bring the city's influence there to an end. Several influential statesmen including Eubulus heeded Demosthenes' advice, and troops under the command of Chares were sent to the Chersonese.

Once there, they joined forces with the wily turncoat Cersebleptes and established several garrisons, probably manned by Cersebleptes' own men, along the coastline of the Propontis and northern Aegean. For his part Philip ordered Antipater to set up a base close to one of the garrisons at Hieraion Ochos (on the Propontis), though at this stage it was really only to keep an eye on Athenian movements in the region.

Back in Greece, the Thebans, helped by the small Macedonian force, had inflicted a defeat on the Phocians as they were fortifying Abae, where there was a shrine to Apollo. The wrath of the god apparently descended on five hundred of them who rushed for refuge to the temple: a chance fire broke out and burned them alive. As Diodorus says, somewhat tongue in cheek, of their fate: 'the gods do not extend to temple-robbers the protection generally accorded to suppliants.'[14] At the end of his narrative of the Sacred War, Diodorus also recounts the divine retribution that fell on the Phocian generals who plundered the temple treasuries, as well as on their wives, who took jewellery and also met with nasty ends.[15]

The Phocians now appealed to Sparta and Athens for help, in return offering to cede the fortified towns of Alponus, Thronium and Nicaea, which controlled Thermopylae. Not surprisingly, the Athenians and the Spartans jumped at the chance to control this crucially strategic pass. The Spartans sent a thousand men under their king, Archidamus, and the Athenians deployed a force of fifty ships, manned by all fit males up to the age of forty under the command of Proxenus. This combined force, supported by the Phocians, could now bar Philip from entering central Greece (as Nausicles had in 352) and go on to defeat the Boeotians.

Further, the Athenians decided to commit a force to Thessaly. Their nominal reason for doing this was to assist the port town of Halus, which was situated south of the Crocus Field and on the main route south from Larisa, Pherae and Pagasae. Halus at the time was embroiled in a dispute with Pharsalus (about 30 miles [48 km] to its north-west), which was one of the more important cities in the Thessalian League and on the main route to Lamia. No formal alliance was made with Halus, but any Athenian gains in that region would, as in Thrace, put further pressure on Philip. Moreover, the potential disruption to Thessalian unity would also have repercussions for the king.

The opportunities to control Thermopylae and to threaten Philip's interests in Thessaly were the reasons why, at the end of 347 or the beginning of 346, the Athenians sent another embassy to the Greek states. The first such mission, proposed by Eubulus over a year earlier, had been a general call to arms, and it had failed miserably. This second one was different in the sense that the Athenians were calling upon states to send representatives to Athens to discuss whether there should be peace with Philip or an Athenian-led war against him. Like its predecessor, however, it failed, although the outcome would not be known for several months.

If Philip still wanted to settle central Greece to his liking, he would need to move quickly. He thus ordered Parmenion to besiege Halus. This gave him the opportunity to have one of his top generals and a Macedonian force close to Thermopylae. For the moment he steered clear of the pass as he had no wish to risk a coalition of Greek states against him (which might happen if the second embassy to the Greeks was successful). It was imperative to win over Athens and to keep Thebes at bay, and therefore in January or February 346 Philip released Iatrocles, one of the Athenians taken captive when Olynthus fell in 348, with the message that he wanted peace.

The Athenian Prisoners from Olynthus: Philip's Weak Link

The fate of the Athenians captured at Olynthus was a burning issue in Athens, and needs further comment here. Philocrates and Demosthenes had spoken in the Assembly on several occasions about the prisoners. They probably told the people that if they could secure their return Philip would be denied a valuable bargaining chip in any discussions about peace. Eventually, the Assembly was swayed, and Aristodemus, an actor and friend of Philip, was sent to Pella to enquire what he intended to do with them. This was in early 346, before Philip had released Iatrocles, and hence before the Athenians knew of his desire for peace. To some extent, then, the messages that Iatrocles and Aristodemus brought from Philip overlap.

Philip had a dilemma. If he released the prisoners he would indeed lose a valuable bargaining counter. On the other hand, if he held onto them, he would play into the hands of the likes of Demosthenes who were portraying him as untrustworthy and as acting against Athenian interests. Exactly what Philip said to Aristodemus is unknown, but when he returned to Athens he was to present his report to the Boule. He did not, however, putting forward the weak excuse that he was kept busy by private business. Demosthenes may have been behind this delaying tactic so as to give the second embassy to the Greek states more time.

Finally, Aristodemus was ordered to report to the Boule.[16] He now told its members that Philip wanted not only peace but also an alliance with Athens, and the Boule communicated this report to the Assembly. Instead of euphoria the response was one of anguish and anxiety, however, for the same Assembly heard the sudden and shocking news that none other than Phalaecus had dismissed the Athenian and Spartan troops sent to Phocis to secure Thermopylae. It seems that at some point during the second embassy to the Greek states Deinocrates, Callias and Sophanes had been deposed and out of the blue Phalaecus had been reinstated as the Phocian commander.[17]

The Turn to Peace

In this surprising turn of events we see Philip at his cunning best. Macedonia's involvement in the Sacred War spelled Phocis' end, and Philip may well have begun secret negotiations with the deposed Phalaecus and probably also with the Phocian government in an effort to send the Athenian and Spartan troops packing and to open Thermopylae to him.[18] The only way to achieve the latter was by arranging for the Phocians to surrender to him and not to the Amphictyonic Council, probably in return for a promise to moderate their punishment when the war ended. Phalaecus' reinstatement was necessary to fulfil Philip's plan.

Philip's was a dangerous strategy, for he would have had no wish to be seen as a friend of temple-robbers, not least because this could alienate his Thessalian allies on whom so much depended. Then again, it was important to detach Athens from Phocis (and vice versa) so as to bring the war with Athens to a close. It was another of his big gambles, but again it worked for him. Although the second embassy to the Greek states did not return to Athens for another two months or more, news of Phalaecus' action rendered its mission pointless. Everyone in Athens, including Demosthenes, now realised that Philip was about to end the Sacred War, and thus it was essential to make peace with him quickly before he made any more conquests. The Athenians were especially concerned about their interests in Thrace and their alliance with Cersebleptes, but both would be dead issues if Philip got through Thermopylae before the two sides had made peace.

Philocrates, who had wanted to send an embassy to Philip in 348 after the fall of Olynthus, now proposed that an embassy of ten men be sent to the king to discuss 'peace and the common interests of Athens and Philip'.[19] The Assembly enthusiastically supported the idea. This would be the first of four embassies to Philip. In an attempt to show goodwill towards Philip, Demosthenes proposed that Aristodemus receive a crown for what he had achieved on his mission (we hear of nothing being bestowed on Iatrocles).[20]

Cautionary Note on the Sources[21]

The chronology of the various twists and turns of the next few months which led to the end of the Third Sacred War and to the Peace of Philocrates (which concluded the war between Athens and Philip over Amphipolis) is confusing. The principal sources for the peace negotiations and the end of the Sacred War are the two speeches called *On the False Embassy*, delivered by Demosthenes and Aeschines at the trial of the latter in 343 (see pp. 115–16). Additional (and repeated) information is also given in their prosecution and defence speeches in the Crown trial of Demosthenes in 330 (see pp. 191–2).[22] I have been deliberately selective in the references I give to these four important contemporary speeches: had I not been, virtually every sentence of this chapter and the rest of the book would be referenced. The speeches of Demosthenes and Aeschines should be read in full to amplify events not only in 346 but also in the following years.

The information about the peace in these speeches is often deliberately misleading because of the two orators' personal enmity and especially because by 343 both were trying to distance themselves from the roles they had played in securing it.[23] Demosthenes gives the impression that Philip was out to destroy Athens and Phocis and to advance Theban interests in central Greece, but this is part of his campaign of character denigration against Philip and is untrue. Diodorus provides a good, comprehensive account of the end of the Sacred War but says nothing about the negotiations that led to the Peace of Philocrates. Justin adds some information on events in Macedonia before the Athenians swore to the peace in 346. Thus, trying to piece together the details with any degree of accuracy is extremely difficult.

The First Embassy to Philip

The ten envoys, who included Philocrates, Nausicles, Demosthenes (proposed by Philocrates)[24] and Aeschines, on the first embassy to Philip travelled north to Pella, arriving there a week or so later in mid-March 346. Their route took them from Athens to northern Euboea, thence to Larisa, where an official envoy of the king met them to escort them to Pella. Each envoy was to deliver a prepared speech on the subject of the proposed peace and alliance, to which Philip would respond at the end of business. When they came before the king the eldest spoke first, as was the custom, and then the remainder in order of descending age. Demosthenes spoke last, so he was the youngest ambassador; Aeschines gave the penultimate speech.

When it was Demosthenes' turn to address the king Aeschines says he lost his nerve and froze. He began speaking:[25]

in a voice dead with fright, and after a brief narration of earlier events suddenly fell silent and was at a loss for words, and finally abandoned his speech. Seeing the state he was in, Philip encouraged him to take heart and not to suppose that he had suffered a complete catastrophe. . . . But Demosthenes . . . was now unable to recover; he tried once more to speak, and the same thing happened. In the ensuing silence the herald asked us to withdraw.

Aeschines' story may be substantially true, given that the other ambassadors were witnesses to what happened and could have contradicted him, but he probably embellished the extent of Demosthenes' fumble to embarrass his opponent.[26] Demosthenes' oratorical prowess in the Assembly, especially after 346, showed he lived down the incident, but the origins of the enmity these two orators had for each other go back to this embassy.

The Athenians' speeches to Philip must have dealt with Athenian influence in Thrace, the city's access to the Black Sea area (vital for its annual corn fleet), the Sacred War, and Athens' ongoing aid to Halus in Thessaly. Aeschines says he argued that Athens should have Amphipolis, making the case that Philip's predecessors had recognised the city to be Athenian.[27] But Amphipolis was a lost cause, and it is hard to understand why the Athenians did not see that. Philip must have listened to Aeschines' speech with quiet amusement. Phocis and Halus could not play any formal role in negotiations to end Athens' war over Amphipolis, of course, as they were not part of it, so the attempts to include them by Demosthenes and others (and the same goes for Cersebleptes) were foolish. Thrace was perhaps the most crucial issue for both sides.

Philip had several terms: each party should recognise the areas held by the other at that time (an important qualification); as well as a peace there should also be an alliance between him and Athens with no time limit; the peace and alliance were to be defensive and binding on each party's allies; and, finally, given the rampant problem of piracy in the Aegean, no ally was to offer support to pirates, and there may have been plans for a joint expedition to rid the seas of them. Peace and alliance meant that Philip wanted to organise a treaty in which he and the Athenians were equals: this must have surprised the ambassadors. The treaty would thus be a bilateral one between Philip and his allies and the Athenians and their allies in the Second Naval Confederacy. Whether Philip was sincere in making this offer is hard to say. He may have cynically exploited the possibility of an alliance to allow himself to end both the conflict with Athens and the Sacred War to his liking.

If the Athenians hoped to maintain their influence in Thrace and hold onto the independent coastal forts, then the implications of the wording of the first condition were ominous. Philip of course could not allow the Athenians influence there for his own security, just as he could not allow them to continue their support of Halus or Phocis (see below). By 346 he had decided to campaign against the disloyal Cersebleptes, but for the moment he told the ambassadors that he recognised Athens' claim to the Chersonese, and hence its route to the Black Sea. He even went so far as to say that he would keep his army out of the Chersonese while peace negotiations were in progress.

Athens' support for Halus was not a matter for discussion: Philip said bluntly that it had to stop. That left the Sacred War. Resorting to his old trick of diplomatic hoodwinking, Philip seems to have indicated that he would consider protecting the Phocians, but that could not happen until he knew he had Athens' total support. In other words, Phocis had to be excluded from any peace negotiations, hence any eventual treaty between Philip and Athens.

The continued retention of the Athenian prisoners taken at Olynthus must also have been discussed. Philip had to tread carefully here, but he seems to have indicated his willingness to release them without ransom once Athens had accepted his terms. Thus, their fate was deftly put into the Athenians' hands. To sweeten the deal further, he promised to reaffirm Athenian influence in Euboea, to restore the border town of Oropus (then controlled by Thebes), and to cut a channel across the neck of the Chersonese, thus making it easier for the Athenians to protect and defend it against any incursion from the mainland.

All of these concessions came as music to the embassy's ears, as Philip intended. The envoys prepared to return to Athens on 20 Anthesterion (about 18 March), and they would probably have arrived back in the city by 27 Anthesterion at the latest (about 25 March).

Philip Campaigns in Thrace

As soon as the first embassy left Pella, so did Philip, bound for Thrace, but not before he had ordered Antipater, Parmenion and Eurylochus to lead a Macedonian embassy to Athens. Its mission was to repeat the king's sentiments about peace, to confirm his terms and to receive the appropriate oaths to the peace from the Athenians.

Within a month, by 23 Elaphebolion (about 20 April), Philip had reached Cersebleptes' stronghold at the Heraion Orus fort and defeated him.[28] He allowed Cersebleptes to remain king, though Philip made him a vassal and he also took his sons as hostages to ensure his good behaviour.[29] Philip spent about another two months reducing the independent coastal Thracian forts, a task completed by 23 Thargelion (about 18 June), at which time he returned to Pella. The eastern frontier of Macedonia now extended to the Nestus river, and Philip could occupy himself once more with Athens and with the Sacred War.

The Athenians Debate Peace with Philip: Demosthenes' Stance

The first embassy to Philip made its report to the Boule and the Assembly on 8 Elaphebolion (about 6 April). The Macedonian embassy arrived soon afterwards. Given the gravity of the situation, Demosthenes successfully proposed that the peace and alliance with Macedonia should not be debated and voted on at one Assembly meeting but (unusually) at two meetings on consecutive days. On the first day the Athenians should discuss Philip's terms, and on the second day, with Philip's envoys present, they should vote. The allied *synedrion* (of the Athenian Naval Confederacy) put forward a proposal that the Athenians should wait until the second embassy to the Greek states (about possible war with Philip) returned. The suggestion was ignored. Since the Dionysia Festival was about to start (9–13 Elaphebolion), and hence all non-religious business was suspended, it was decided to hold this critical debate on 18 and 19 Elaphebolion (about 15 and 16 April).

In the meantime, as a goodwill gesture Demosthenes proposed *proedria* (a front seat in the theatre, hence VIP treatment) at the festival theatrical performances for Philip's envoys. He went overboard, if we can believe Aeschines, in hiring 'mule teams for them when they were leaving and accompanied them on horseback, not shrinking into the shadow like some people but making a public display of his favour for their cause'.[30]

On the first day of the Assembly meeting (18 Elaphebolion) Philocrates proposed that the Athenians should accept peace as well as alliance with Philip according to the king's terms – in other words, abandoning their support of both Phocis and Halus (not to mention Cersebleptes) and finally recognising that Amphipolis was a lost cause.[31] The people certainly wanted peace, but an alliance on Philip's wide-ranging terms was a different matter. Athenian interests in Thrace had been left in limbo; while Cersebleptes was not a member of the Athenian Naval Confederacy (so the Athenians were not abandoning a formal ally), his goodwill was essential for any continuing Athenian presence there. Exactly what was said in the debate is unknown, but Theopompus apparently quotes part of Philocrates' speech, which put things bluntly:

> Bear in mind then that this is not the time to engage in contentious rivalry, that the affairs of the state are not in a good situation, that many grave dangers surround us. For we know that the Boeotians and the Megarians are at enmity with us, the Peloponnesians are courting some of the Thebans and others the Spartans, the Chians and the Rhodians, and their allies are hostile to our state, and they are negotiating with Philip for his friendship.[32]

Philocrates' proposal was not the only one before the Assembly that day: the allied *synedrion* had called for a Common Peace (*koine eirene*) with Philip. As its name suggests, this would involve a general agreement of all Greek states, each one making an alliance with all the others. If one member state acted in an inappropriate manner towards another (if it attacked it, for example), the others would come to the latter's defence. The xenophobia of the Greek cities towards each other, and the bitter infighting that plagued their history, made a Common Peace something of a deterrent, for the other allies would relish the chance to move legitimately against an offending state. The *synedrion* further proposed that any Greek state could become part of the Common Peace during the next three months, which meant of course that Phocis, Halus and any other state (including any of Philip's allies) were free to join the peace.[33] Since the Athenian people were wavering over their support for Phocis and Halus (and we should not factor out the desire to get Amphipolis back), both Demosthenes and Aeschines supported the *synedrion*'s motion. Demosthenes successfully persuaded the Assembly that the idea of a Common Peace be put to Philip's envoys at the Assembly the following day, thus ignoring Philocrates' proposal.[34]

The Assembly's support of the *synedrion*'s proposal indicates that when the first embassy to Philip reported to the Boule and Assembly it did not detail the king's actual terms for a bilateral peace – otherwise Demosthenes would not have been able to exploit the people's anxiety as easily as he did. As one of the ten ambassadors to Philip, he would have known that the idea of a Common Peace would be unacceptable to the king, for the places he had specifically excluded could become members of it. Thus, Demosthenes switched direction and broke with his ally Philocrates, thereby beginning a breach that ended in 343 when Philocrates was impeached for the policy that he was now advocating.

On the second day Antipater was summoned before the Assembly and asked whether Philip would agree to a Common Peace. Naturally, he answered in the negative. If the Athenians were set on a Common Peace, that meant they would have to continue the war against Philip. At this point, Aeschines (according to Demosthenes)[35] seems to have changed tack from the previous day, for he, Eubulus and another politician, Cephisophon, began to speak in favour of Philip's terms (hence for Philocrates' motion); only Aristophon, one of Eubulus' more vocal opponents, spoke against them. Demosthenes, who was president of the Assembly meeting for that second day, did not take part in the discussion. Theopompus has a fragment from Aristophon's speech, which contains a good deal of rhetorical bluster:

Bear in mind that the most cowardly thing of all that we could do would be to accept the peace while conceding Amphipolis, we who live in the greatest of the Greek states, have most allies, possess 300 triremes and receive almost 400 talents in revenue; which being so, who would not condemn us for making concessions contrary to our just rights because we are scared of the power of Macedonians?[36]

In the end, the Athenians opted for Aristophon's 'cowardly' course, helped by Eubulus' blunt warning (its tone reminiscent of that of Philocrates on the previous day): the people must either accept the king's terms for peace and alliance, with the exclusions it entailed, or go to war – immediately, paying taxes and bearing the cost alone.[37] War meant raising manpower (and the inevitable losses), and potentially diverting money from the Theoric Fund to the Military Fund. The Assembly agreed to adopt Philocrates' motion, but put forward some of its own terms as well, viz., each side should keep the possessions it already held, and only Philip and his allies and Athens and its allies were party to the treaty. The definition of the term 'ally' was left deliberately vague and comprised those that gave their oaths on the day. That meant the door was being kept open for Halus and Phocis to join with Athens and so swear to a peace as their allies. In practice the Assembly was rejecting Philip's exclusion clause – and hoping he would not realise it! At some point a request came from Cersebleptes, under attack from Philip, to join the Athenian Naval Confederacy (and thus be counted as an Athenian ally), but the Assembly rejected it.

The Athenians and their allies now swore their oaths to the peace and alliance to the Macedonian envoys. Although the latter left the city, they did not return immediately to Pella but went to Thebes first instead. It was vital for Philip's plan that the Thebans be lured into a false sense of security while he negotiated with Athens and Phocis. Thebes had taken aggressive steps against other cities in Boeotia in order to keep them loyal to the Boeotian League, and it would have no wish to see its power diminished. Presumably the Macedonian envoys reported that Philip did not intend to take any action against the city, thereby confirming their hegemony in Boeotia. For the moment this piece of diplomacy did the trick.

The Second Embassy to Philip

It was now time for the Athenians to receive Philip's oath to the peace. However, for some reason there was a delay. Over a week went by before Demosthenes carried a resolution in the Boule that those Athenians who had served on the first embassy to Philip should go on a second embassy to obtain his oath. This second embassy left on 3 Mounychion (about 29 April). Since the king was now in Thrace, it took its time travelling to Pella, and twenty-three days went by before it arrived there (in later May). It waited there for a further twenty-seven days before Philip returned on 23 Thargelion (about 17 June). Demosthenes was not a happy man, and he made his dissatisfaction with this waiting around plain.[38] However, there was no saying where Philip was in Thrace, and if the embassy had gone to find him there yet more time might have elapsed before the oath was taken.

The Athenian embassy was not alone in Pella. Other envoys 'from virtually the whole of Greece', as Aeschines said,[39] were also there. These envoys may not quite have come from all over the Greek world, but certainly from at least Sparta, Thebes and Thessaly, and possibly from Phocis.[40] These states would have wanted to know – as might have been expected – what the king planned to do as far as the Third Sacred War and Greece in general went. The Thebans may well have started to see the writing on the wall regarding Philip's intentions towards them, and the presence of the Thessalian and Spartan embassies would only have exacerbated their fears. There was no love lost between the Thebans and Spartans, and the latter had made it clear that they wanted to reduce Theban influence in the Peloponnese, where they viewed Thebes' friendly relations with Argos, Messenia and Arcadia with great suspicion.[41] The Spartan war with Megalopolis had escalated into one involving the whole Peloponnese, with the likelihood of intervention by Philip, and that too boded ill for the Thebans.

The issue of the Peloponnese must have been a burning one in Pella, for everything depended on what Philip did. If, with the support of the Thebans, their Peloponnesian allies (Messenia, Megalopolis, Argos and Arcadia), the Thessalians and now the Athenians, he defeated the Phocians, he would confirm Thebes' power in central Greece and the Peloponnese. However, if he settled the Sacred War as he wanted to by joining with Sparta, Athens, Thessaly and Phocis, Thebes' power came to an end. Again, we see the very real influence Philip exerted in central Greek and now Peloponnesian affairs, an influence all the more remarkable given his fragile position when he became king only thirteen years earlier.

Tensions were running high at the Macedonian court. Philip heard the speeches of the Thebans and Thessalians first. They demanded that he end the Sacred War and punish the Phocians. The envoys from Phocis not surprisingly urged him not to attack their state. Then it was the Athenians' turn, with Aeschines dominating proceedings. He tells us that he urged Philip to accept the Amphictyonic Council's duty to move against any member that acted in a harmful way to another and to punish those who had despoiled Apollo's shrine at Delphi.[42] Now this is very interesting. If Aeschines really did take this line (and did not later in his speech elevate his role), he was referring not only to the Phocians but also the Thebans. Even more importantly, as far as the former was concerned, his reference to those who had despoiled Apollo's shrine shows that he was laying the blame not on the entire Phocian state but only on those Phocians and their mercenaries who had actually occupied Delphi. That was why Athens (and Sparta) supported the Phocians' appeal not to attack their state. In this way, Aeschines was removing Athens from having to take part in any wholesale punishment of Phocis.[43]

Thus, a clever scenario for bringing the Third Sacred War to an end without action against the state of Phocis begins to emerge, and one that also allowed moves against the Thebans. This plan seems to have been in Philip's mind too, and he may well have made his intentions clear to the Athenian ambassadors in private, for he 'granted private audiences to embassies from both sides, promising the one not to open hostilities and binding the ambassadors with an oath not to divulge his response to anyone, and assuring the other that he would join them and bring them assistance'.[44] If this is the case, Aeschines may have embellished his role in the proceedings. On the other hand, the king may have duped Aeschines into thinking he would move against Thebes and support Phocis, for after this time Aeschines became an ardent supporter of Philip's peace proposals. That meant of course that he accepted that Halus, Phocis and Cersebleptes would never become allies of Athens, as Philip intended.[45]

The welcome Philip extended to the Athenian embassy was particularly warm. There is no doubt that he entertained all foreign ambassadors lavishly throughout his reign; more than wanting to be known as an excellent host, he may also simply have wanted to be liked. Demosthenes refused his hospitality, though, and later accused the king of bribery.[46] He may well have viewed the presence of the other embassies with alarm, but Philip's courtship of the Athenians indicated that he thought more highly of them than the others – certainly Demosthenes' fellow envoys thought so. Plans were falling nicely into place for Philip, but then he unwittingly played into the orator's hands.

The Athenian Prisoners: Demosthenes Exploits Philip's Weak Link

Demosthenes was a very different person now from the man supposedly overcome by nerves on the first embassy. Almost as soon as Philip officially greeted the second embassy Demosthenes launched into the question of the Athenian prisoners from Olynthus. The story goes that he had taken a silver talent with him to Pella, which he dramatically flourished before the king as a token payment for the prisoners' release. Philip had wanted to discuss only his strategy to end the Sacred War and was making good progress, but Demosthenes' bold gesture changed all that. The king had managed to deflect attention from this controversial issue before, when he had returned Iatrocles to Athens. However, now that the Athenians had sworn to accept peace there was no reason, as Demosthenes would have argued and as Philip (and everyone else for that matter) must have seen, to keep the Athenian prisoners at Pella any longer.

Philip was again in a quandary. If he released the prisoners now, before he had sworn to the peace, he would lose a substantial bargaining counter in any continuing negotiations. On the other hand, if he refused to hand the prisoners over his plan to end the Sacred War and to nullify Theban power would come unstuck as he needed Athenian support for it. He would be seen as untrustworthy and everything else that his opponent Demosthenes said he was. In the end, the king refused to surrender them immediately, but promised to return them by the time of the festival of the Panathenaea (in honour of Athens' patron deity, Athena), which was about two months away. This decision gave Demosthenes just the ammunition he needed.

Philip now had to move fast and in an entirely new direction dictated by his refusal to release the prisoners immediately. Perhaps he began to see Demosthenes in a different light and to realise the folly of having under-estimated him. Philip (but not his allies) gave his oath to the peace with Athens in Pella.[47] He then announced that he needed to march immediately to Halus to end the ongoing siege there. In reality he had decided to bring about his desired central Greek settlement by force if necessary before Demosthenes had the chance to rouse the Athenians against him. The embassies from the various Greek states left with him. At Pherae, only two or three days' march from Thermopylae, the king's allies swore their oaths to the Athenian ambassadors, and the Peace of Philocrates came into being.[48]

The Peace of Philocrates

Thus ended the war between Athens and Philip over Amphipolis. Cersebleptes, Phocis and Halus were excluded from the peace, and the Athenians also had to swallow the bitter pill of abandoning all hope of retrieving Amphipolis and recognising the independence of Cardia.[49] The Peace of Philocrates also marked Demosthenes' ascendancy in Athenian political life: in light of his role in negotiating it, some would even call it the Peace of Demosthenes.[50] The city's policy towards Macedonia would soon enter a new phase, one in which it was guided by Demosthenes.

There is no question that the Athenians could have suffered more under the terms of the peace. Throughout his reign Philip always showed a different attitude to them than to the other Greeks, and the fact that he wanted an alliance as well as peace with Athens in 346 speaks volumes.[51] The reason lies in his wish to limit Thebes' influence in central Greece. If Philip had imposed harsh terms on the Athenians – such as the dismantling of their fleet (which he needed anyway for his plan to combat piracy and eventually to invade Asia), or the abolition of their democracy (even the surrender of anti-Macedonian politicians like Demosthenes) – there would have been no Greek state strong enough to counterbalance the might of Thebes.[52]

The Death Throes of the Third Sacred War

So much for Philip and Athens, but what of the Third Sacred War, in which Athens played a role through its support of Phocis? At least some in the city feared that the Athenians could still face reprisals from other Amphictyonic states and even Philip.[53] Such fears could only have escalated when Philip left Pherae and marched easily through the Pass of Thermopylae, thanks to his previous agreement with Phalaecus. The latter handed over this crucially important pass to Philip, who set up camp probably at Thermopylae itself. He had used the siege of Halus as an excuse to leave Pella with an army and so avoid arousing suspicion about his true intentions. Indeed, Parmenion may have been acting under orders to prolong the siege: Halus was, after all, a relatively small place.[54] If Philip had marched out with an army without his expedition to Halus as a cover, the Greeks might have realised what he was up to and so had the time to mobilise troops to defend Thermopylae against him one more time.

The second embassy to Philip had returned to Athens on 13 Skirophorion (about 9 July), by which time the king was already at Thermopylae. That item of news was probably not yet known in Athens. When the ambassadors reported to the Boule, Demosthenes went into top gear to discredit them, especially Aeschines, whom he believed Philip had won over with bribes.[55] He criticised the amount of time that the embassy had wasted in travelling to Pella, that it had gone by land instead of by sea (against the orders of the Boule), that it had not gone to get Philip's oath in Thrace, and that it had failed to obtain the oaths of all of the king's allies. He emphasised his own attempts to persuade the king to release the Athenian captives while the other ambassadors had allowed themselves to be lavishly entertained. Finally, he urged that at no cost should the Athenians abandon Phocis.

In one respect his tirade was successful, for the Boule did not pass the customary vote of thanks to the envoys. However, Demosthenes' plea to support Phocis was not: the Boule did not even bring it up at the Assembly meeting held on 16 Skirophorion (about 11 July). Although Demosthenes again vehemently urged that Phocis (and Thermopylae) should not be abandoned, Aeschines and Philocrates read out a letter from Philip (sent with the second embassy), in which he stressed his friendship with the Athenians and his desire for peace and alliance with them. The letter seems to have done the trick, and the Athenians even extended the peace to include his descendants. Moreover, they voted that 'Phocians' – not *the* Phocians, an important distinction – should surrender Delphi to the Amphictyonic Council, and that they would march against anyone who prevented this.[56] The Assembly also voted to send a third embassy to Philip, composed of the same men as the previous two, with news of the resolution. A messenger with unofficial news of its decision went to Philip immediately.

The Third Embassy to Philip and the End of the Sacred War

As was noted above, it was probably not known in Athens at this time that Philip was actually at Thermopylae. This would explain Demosthenes' call not to abandon it, thinking that Philip could still be stopped there. Demosthenes also refused to serve on the third embassy to Philip, still convinced that he could stir up public opinion against the king. That he had a very good chance of succeeding is shown by Aeschines' decision not to go on the embassy either, but to stay in the city to keep an eye on his rival. The third embassy set out on 17 Skirophorion (about 12 July), but it never reached the king.

When Philip (at Thermopylae) received the unofficial news of the Assembly's decision, he sent a letter to the Athenians asking for their infantry to join him against the Phocians. The Spartans had already sent a land army to Thermopylae, and his request for Athenian help served both military and diplomatic purposes. His covert plan for Thebes now became overt, and it was probably at this point that the Thebans ordered their land army to be deployed. According to Demosthenes, Philip was put under pressure when he 'found himself caught between the Thessalian cavalry and the infantry of Thebes, and was therefore led to make concessions'.[57] One explanation may be that the king was actually confronted by a Theban army, especially as Demosthenes goes on to say that he was 'suspicious of Thebes'. If so, events were escalating rapidly.

Philip's request for troops was debated at an Assembly held on 20 Skirophorion, thus three days after the third embassy had left the city. If we can believe Demosthenes, it appears that long after Philocrates' proposal had been passed people were still debating the pros and (especially) the cons of Philip's plans in central Greece – 'for with things still up in the air and the future unclear, all kinds of views were being expressed by people gathering in the Agora'.[58] Demosthenes was no friend of the Thebans, but he saw that if Philip succeeded in eroding Theban power only Athens would stand in the way of his conquering the whole of Greece. That Philip may not have had this intention (certainly in 346) either did not occur to him or was disregarded by him. Demosthenes and another anti-Macedonian politician, Hegesippus, now spoke against the king's request, taking advantage of his refusal to surrender the Athenian prisoners immediately. More than anything else, Philip's decision to hold onto the prisoners wrecked his plans now. When Demosthenes warned that if Athens agreed to send troops he might hold them as hostages as well, the people were persuaded. Anything that Aeschines said was clearly ineffectual.

In the meantime the third embassy reached Chalcis in Euboea, and there it stayed. It did so, plausibly, because news reached it that Philip was at Thermopylae and (perhaps) that the Athenians had just defied his request for troops. How he would react to this, given his current whereabouts, was unknown, and the envoys had no wish to place themselves at his mercy. Once Philip was through Thermopylae the earlier agreement with Phalaecus would be common knowledge. Phalaecus and his army of around eight thousand mercenaries were allowed to depart unharmed (first to the Peloponnese and eventually to fight as mercenaries in Crete, where Phalaecus was killed),[59] and Phocis surrendered not to the Amphictyonic Council but to Philip.[60] This was on 23 Scirophorion (about 18 July). When news of this became known, the third embassy returned to Athens.

The self-styled Apollo's Saviour thus ended the Third Sacred War and freed Delphi. The latter's two votes on the Amphictyonic Council, which Phocis had suspended, were restored. Needless to say, the news caused panic in Athens, given its recent defiance. Demosthenes expected Philip to attack the city, perhaps in conjunction with Thebes. An emergency decree was passed to evacuate the people from the countryside to the city, to repair the forts on the borders and attend to the Piraeus' defences, and to hold the approaching rural festival of Heracles in the city.

The Fourth Embassy to Philip and the Fate of Phocis

No attack came. Soon after, when the Amphictyonic Council met to debate the Phocian issue, probably at Thermopylae itself, the Athenians voted to send a fourth (and final) embassy to Philip. It consisted of those chosen for the third embassy, except that this time Aeschines would serve on it; Demosthenes again stayed behind.

Athens and Sparta did not send formal delegates to the Amphictyonic Council that met to decide the fate of the Phocians; instead, the Athenian fourth embassy attended the meeting.[61] Several member states, such as Oetaea, wanted to impose the legal penalty for sacrilege, which was the execution of all males by throwing them from the top of the nearby Phaedriades cliffs. Philip, although not a member of the council, stood by his promise to Phalaecus and used his influence with his allies on the council to moderate the punishment. Pragmatically, of course, Philip was less concerned with the Phocians' fate in itself than with the loss of so useful an anti-Theban ally if Phocis were wiped off the face of Greece.

The Phocian punishment was severe, but it could have been far worse.[62] Those who had occupied Delphi, or who had assisted in its occupation, and who had fled, were to be under a curse and could be arrested wherever they were found. Their property was confiscated. As far as Phocis itself was concerned, it was excluded from consulting the Delphic oracle and had its membership of the Amphictyonic Council revoked. The Phocians en masse were to be disarmed and their weapons thrown down ravines (they were considered polluted because of the blasphemous crime with which they were associated). The horses that the Phocians owned when the war ended were sold, and the people were forbidden to buy new horses (and arms) until they had repaid the money that they had stolen from Apollo's sanctuary. This was to be paid in annual instalments of 60 talents. All Phocian towns (apart from Abae, the most easterly, which had consistently opposed the occupation of Delphi) were to be razed. The people were to be relocated to villages consisting of no more than fifty houses, each about a stade (approximately 200 yards or 180 m) apart from each other. The Amphictyonic Council was to oversee all aspects of the punishment, but Philip based troops in the Phocian towns to ensure that no state (Thebes in particular) victimised the people unduly. At the same time, these troops afforded Philip the means of having soldiers on hand in central Greece just in case Thebes (or Thessaly) required his attention again; their presence also intimidated the Athenians.[63]

Exactly how much money had to be repaid is unknown. The estimated cost of hiring mercenaries, depending on how we read the evidence, was either 1,622 or 3,244 talents.[64] However, the generals sometimes had to pay double the going rate, and there were also the costs of the treasures that had been given as gifts to their wives and favourite whores – for example, Philomelus had given a gold crown, dedicated by the city of Lampsacus, to Pharsalia, a Thessalian dancing girl,[65] and the wives had been given gold necklaces and other jewellery. Divine retribution fell on them, and they suffered terrible fates – for example, one wife was burned to death in her house after her son went mad and set fire to it.[66]

Had it not been for the moderating influence of Philip, the opponents of Phocis would have seized the opportunity to destroy all and sundry. This was shown in the cases of Orchomenus, Coronea, Corsiae and Halus. The first three cities were in Boeotia and were still controlled by Phocis. The council ordered their defensive walls to be razed, but their ultimate fate was put in the hands of the Boeotian League. The latter showed no mercy, for it sold the people of all three cities into slavery. As for Halus, when the Athenians abandoned their aid to it, Philip gave it back to Pharsalus, who enslaved and deported the entire population. Also, although those Phocians who fled were under a curse and could be arrested, they were not to be killed. Some made their way to Athens and were given asylum there. Further, the indemnity of 60 talents per annum was not enforced until 343, and inscriptions show that in 341 it was reduced to 30 talents and, at some point after 337, to only 10 talents per annum.[67] Nor were the measures against Phocian supporters unduly harsh. The Athenians were deprived of their right of *promanteia* (priority rights in consulting the Delphic oracle), but they were not expelled from the Amphictyonic Council, and nor were the Spartans.

Philip's Influence in Central Greece

As a reward for the liberation of Apollo's shrine, the Thessalian delegation proposed that Phocis' two votes on the council be given to Philip. As *archon* of Thessaly, he automatically controlled at least half of the votes held by the Thessalian *perioikoi* in the council anyway, but these were part of the 'package' of rights and powers he held as *archon*. Now he personally received two votes, thereby becoming a formal member of the league in his own right. He was also made one of the *naopoioi* (a board charged with rebuilding the temple) and was given the Athenians' right of *promanteia* (no small snub to Athens). Finally, he was elected President of the Pythian Games (part of the Olympic cycle), which had not been celebrated for twelve years because of the Third Sacred War.[68] Along with the Boeotians and Thessalians, he was to organise them as a thank-offering to Zeus for the liberation of Apollo's shrine.

The 'barbarian' Macedonian king was now a member of the august Greek Amphictyonic Council and was to preside over the wholly Greek institution that was an Olympic festival. In 352 his election as *archon* of Thessaly had marked the start of his move into central Greek political life. The two honours of 346 significantly increased his relations with *all* the Greeks. It is no surprise that in order to proclaim his freeing of Delphi and his presidency of the games Philip probably had a special gold stater coin minted at this time. This bore the head of Apollo with a laurel wreath on the obverse and a two-horse chariot with a charioteer, above the inscription *Philippou* ('of Philip'), on the reverse (Plate 15). The coin probably appeared in 345. Like his commemorative silver tetradrachms earlier, the gold stater had a financial role as well as a propaganda one, for it was meant to replace the Persian daric (the main gold coin in northern Greece), and hence be a further boost to the Macedonian economy.

Although the Peace of Philocrates was a bilateral agreement secured on Philip's terms, thanks to Demosthenes the situation in central Greece was not what the king wanted. Thebes' resentment of Philip was on the rise because it knew it could no longer use the Amphictyonic Council as a political weapon against its enemies and it had not received the benefits from him that it had expected. Moreover, it owed its continuing influence to the Athenians, of all people, for they had refused Philip the military help he needed at Thermopylae when apparently threatened by a Theban force. If Philip were to make a move against either Thebes or Athens, the side affected would as a matter of survival turn to the other. The king might not have lost sleep at this time over an alliance between Thebes and Athens, but all the same it was something he did not want, and he strove to prevent it.

It is interesting that Philip did not take a leaf out of his own book of political marriage by marrying an Athenian woman as a means of maintaining amity with the city. Whether we can read anything into this is hard to say, but one explanation is that a marriage to a woman from Athens would not have endeared itself to Philip's own people. Despite the power he now wielded, and the potential for discord between the larger Greek powers, Philip was clearly taking care to maintain appearances back in his own kingdom. In any case, he seems only to have married (except for the seventh time perhaps) for military reasons, for the protection of Macedonia and/or when at war. His most recent marriage had taken place in 352 (to the Thessalian Nicesipolis) and his next would not be until 342, to the Thracian Meda (during his Thracian campaign). During the intervening decade, his power was consistently on the rise in Greek affairs, and his own kingdom was secure. Thus, in 346 no threat faced him that called for a marriage.

The tense situation in Greece did not mean that every city was seething with discontent and waiting for the chance to rise against Philip. For one thing, a number of smaller states welcomed his intervention (as shown by their presence at Pella in 346), tired as they were of the activities of the bigger Greek powers and of the 'secrets of more powerful states' (like Athens and Thebes).[69] Indeed, even in Athens there was some support for Philip among the intellectuals of the day, as is shown by the letter that Speusippus (who succeeded Plato as head of the Academy) sent to Pella requesting his patronage (see pp. 121–2). Moreover, in the Peloponnese Philip had a number of allies, not least Messene and Arcadia, who were afraid of a possible resurgence of power on the part of Sparta.[70] These factors show the extent to which Philip was now inextricably part of central and southern Greek politics – and we should note that he had achieved this more by diplomacy than by warfare with the major powers. Nevertheless, in 346 the (inevitable) questions were: how long would the peace in Greece last, and who would be the first to break it?

THE HOSTILE AFTERMATH

The peace between the Athenians and Philip got off to a very rocky start, as it appears that the general feeling among the Athenian people was not to take part in the Pythian Games. Although Philip had released the Athenian prisoners from Olynthus in time for the festival of the Panathenaea (about mid-August) as he had promised the second embassy, the Athenians were far from reassured about his intentions towards them. The king was not prepared to take this rebuff lightly, and he was probably behind an Amphictyonic embassy that went to Athens to suggest the people change their minds.

Demosthenes' *On the Peace*: Greek Attitudes to the Peace

The Assembly met to decide what to do. Demosthenes ascended the rostrum on the Pnyx to face the thousands of his fellow citizens gathered there (cf. Plates 11a–c), and delivered his speech *On the Peace*.[1] Neatly transferring the blame onto others, he argued that the Peace of Philocrates was a bad one from the Athenians' point of view, but that it had to be maintained – and the Athenians had to attend the games – otherwise the city might face a Sacred War:[2]

> The first prerequisite, in my view, is that any alliance or contribution which anyone wishes to secure for Athens shall be secured without breaking the peace. Not that it is anything remarkable, or in any way worthy of Athens. But whatever can be said of it, better for our position that it had never been made, than made and then broken by this country. We have lost many assets whose retention would have made war safer and easier then than it is now. Our second need is to avoid giving the assembly of the so-called Amphictyonic Council the need, or a common pretext, for war against us. Personally, in the event of a fresh war between us and Philip over Amphipolis or on any other private ground not shared by Thessaly, Argos, or Thebes, I do not believe any of them would take part against Athens.

It is clear that Demosthenes did not see the Peace of Philocrates as anything but ephemeral, and his talk of a 'fresh war over Amphipolis' speaks volumes. He also talks of an inevitable future war later in the speech.[3] His take on the situation seems to be that the peace is a bad one for Athens, but that it is necessary to maintain it for now as it will give the people time to regroup financially and militarily against Philip. The speech was successful, and the Athenians took part in the games.

After they were over, Philip attended an Amphictyonic Council meeting and then he and his army returned to Macedonia. At the same time he made sure that his gateway into Greece remained open because he handed over Nicaea, the most important town that guarded Thermopylae, to Thessaly, and arranged the installation of a Thessalian garrison in it.[4] Diodorus tells us that Philip was now anxious to make war on Persia,[5] but while he may have started to think about an expedition there, an invasion was not on the cards yet. In any case, it would be necessary for him to subdue Thrace first so as to maintain a line of communication with Macedonia.[6]

The fragile nature of the Peace of Philocrates had not grown any sturdier by 345. The Thebans, as has been said, were bitter as a result of having been left high and dry in 352, and were even more so now that they knew Philip had shortchanged them – and that feeling would only increase over the next few years.[7] The Spartans were discontented at their further isolation after the king brought an end to the war between Sparta and Megalopolis, which had ravaged that region for almost half a decade. Arcadia and Argos even set up bronze statues of Philip, so Demosthenes says,[8] and by the late 340s only Achaea and Corinth were friendly with Sparta and not allies of Philip. The Thessalians had expected more than Magnesia and Nicaea, and in many cities civil strife took place that led to the emergence of rulers who would defy Philip.

The Athenian attitude to the peace would become polarised in the Macedonian policies of Demosthenes and Aeschines. A year earlier, in 346, Demosthenes had stood shoulder to shoulder with Philocrates in bringing the peace to fruition; Aeschines' role had been incidental. Now Demosthenes was out to sabotage the peace, and Aeschines to keep it alive, believing that, imperfect though it might be, it was the only means of maintaining friendship and alliance with Philip. Ultimately Demosthenes' policy would prevail, but in the process he would misinterpret and even lie about the king's aims and mislead the Athenians. Philip, as we shall see, bent over backwards to accommodate the Athenians – at least until 342 or 341, when he finally realised the alliance was no more.

The Trial of Timarchus: Aeschines vs Demosthenes

The Athenian envoys to Philip had undergone a scrutiny to determine whether they had acted in a corrupt manner. Afterwards Demosthenes charged Aeschines with misconduct on the second embassy, alleging that he deliberately hoodwinked the people about Philip's intentions and took bribes from him.[9] The charge was serious, and Timarchus of Sphettus, one of Demosthenes' political allies (both had been members of the Boule in the previous year), was to prosecute Aeschines. In a swift counter-move, Aeschines prosecuted Timarchus for his scandalous and perverse sex life, including his activities as a male prostitute.[10] Such a lifestyle would debar him from citizenship, and hence he would be unable to continue with his prosecution of Aeschines. Aeschines' speech (which survives) is riddled with references to the political situation: he states he still believes the peace is to Athens' advantage, and the trial throws a vivid light on the people's attitude towards Macedonia.[11] Demosthenes may have had something to do with the defence (as did Hegesippus, one of his political associates), although he did not speak in court. Despite Timarchus' contacts with Demosthenes and Aeschines' diplomatic failure over Phocis (for unsuccessfully trying to divert any punishment from the state), the jury found Timarchus guilty and deprived him of his citizenship.

Then, in the spring of 345, the Assembly elected Aeschines to argue before the Amphictyonic Council (at its spring Pylaea) that Athens should retain ownership of the Temple of Apollo on the island of Delos. The island was Apollo's home before Delphi, and it was also the traditional home of the Ionians, the oldest people in Greece. The Athenians had assumed control of it two centuries earlier during the tyranny of Pisistratus (545–528),[12] but in 346 the people of Delos lobbied the council to end Athenian domination of their island. Delos was not a member of the council, so the Delians were clearly taking advantage of Athens' loss of influence and playing on the dislike of the other members towards it.

Clearly the Athenians were not prepared to let go of Delos, and the Assembly's choice of Aeschines, not Demosthenes, as its representative is interesting. Matters changed dramatically when one of the oldest organs of the Athenian constitution, the Council of the Areopagus,[13] then refused to accept the Assembly's choice, calling Aeschines a 'traitor and public enemy', according to Demosthenes.[14] As a result Hyperides was elected to head the diplomatic mission instead. Demosthenes connects Aeschines' dismissal with his alleged complicity in Antiphon's plot to burn the Piraeus dockyards (see p. 119).[15] However, this incident most likely took place in 343, in which case Demosthenes is distorting the truth.

The real reason may have had something to do with Aeschines' role on the fourth embassy to Philip. He had supported Philip's urging of leniency on the Phocians, and he had gone so far as to argue that only those Phocians who had occupied Delphi should be punished. He would not have won many friends on the council for this, given the sacrilegious nature of the Phocians' act and the eagerness of some states to exact the maximum penalty. The Areopagus may well have considered that his arguments to keep Delos, no matter how sound, were insufficient, and they would thus have fallen on deaf ears. On the other hand, Demosthenes would enjoy favourable relations with the Areopagus until virtually the end of his political career, and it would not be too great a stretch of the imagination to see him at work in Aeschines' rejection.

Since there was little love lost between Athens and the other council members, it comes as a surprise that Hyperides was successful and the council ruled against the Delian appeal. The only possible explanation for this decision has to lie with Philip. The king had no wish to alienate the Athenians, especially if he needed their fleet for his expansionist plans. If the Amphictyonic Council, of which Philip was now a member, ruled against the Athenians, the decision would have strained relations between the two of them. In that situation, the collapse of the Peace of Philocrates was not beyond the bounds of possibility.

Philip in 345: Illyria and Population Transplants in Macedonia

Exactly how Philip spent 345 is unknown. He was preoccupied (in that year or possibly 344)[16] with a shadowy campaign against Pleuratus of the Ardiaioi, a powerful Illyrian tribe by the Rhizon Gulf on the Dalmatian coast of what is now northern Albania. Diodorus implies that his involvement there was inevitable, arising out of the enmity that existed between the Macedonians and Illyrians from the days of Philip's father, Amyntas III.[17] Diodorus may not be far from the truth, given the readiness of the Illyrians to invade Macedonia. However, another explanation may be their expansion southwards following Philip's defeats of the other tribes in that area. The Macedonians defeated Pleuratus and returned home towards the end of the year. They took with them much booty that, like the spoils from Philip's other victories throughout his reign, were added to Macedonia's coffers. During this campaign, 150 Companion Cavalry were hurt, Hippostratus the son of Amyntas was killed, and Philip seems to have broken his right collarbone.[18] The risks he took in battle were serious enough for Isocrates to criticise him for putting his life in danger when he should have been thinking about invading Asia:[19]

For there is no one who has not condemned you for risking yourself more rashly than is appropriate for a king and for being more concerned about winning praise for your courage than about the situation as a whole. It is just as disgraceful not to show your superiority to others when enemies surround you as it is, when there is no pressing need, to throw yourself into the sort of combats where, should you succeed, you would accomplish nothing great but, should you die, you would destroy all the good fortune you currently have.

Philip, though, remained a traditional warrior king *par excellence* to the end, so he was always in the thick of the fighting.

Although the date is controversial, probably after (and perhaps because of) the Illyrian campaign (as opposed to years before it) we have the equally shadowy business of the transfer of population groups from one part of Macedonia to another.[20] Our only source for this transfer is Justin:[21]

Philip returned to his kingdom and, just as shepherds drive their flocks at different times into winter and summer pastures, so he now capriciously transplanted whole peoples and cities as he felt regions needed to be populated or depopulated. Everywhere it was a dismal picture, almost of desolation. True, it was not a scene of panic inspired by an enemy; there was no movement of troops through a city, no armed mêlée, nor the plundering of property and abduction of people; but there was silent, forlorn dejection, as men feared that even their tears might be taken to signify opposition. Grief is actually intensified when repressed, becoming the more deeply rooted the more its expression is denied. The evacuees looked wistfully now at the tombs of their forefathers, now at their ancient family deities, now at the houses in which they had been born and had themselves produced children, sorrowing at one moment for their own fate for having lived to see that day, and at the next for that of their children, for not having been born after it. Some of these peoples Philip settled right on his borders as a bulwark against his enemies, others he set on the remote frontiers of the empire, and some, who were prisoners-of-war, he distributed to supplement the populations of his cities. Doing this he made one kingdom and one people from large numbers of different clans and tribes.

At Opis in 324, Alexander gave a passionate speech to his mutinous army in which he praised his father's achievements (see p. 3). Among other things, he said that his father had brought the Macedonians down from the hills to the plains. He may have been referring to this movement of peoples in 345, although what he says does not help to fix the year. It is obvious from the above passage that the people were not thrilled by such large-scale removals: that hardly comes as a surprise. However, they had little choice in the matter, and it appears that if they had protested they would have faced Philip's wrath. This gives us an interesting insight into how Philip exercised power – apparently through fear – and into how the people saw him.[22]

There was nothing capricious about where Philip moved the people to, as the extract above says. His rationale for the transpopulation was primarily military, hence many groups were settled in specific colonies that would serve as military outposts in case of enemy incursion. For example, some were established in the north-west along the Illyrian frontier, including Astraea, Dobera, Kellion and Melitousa. Others were set up in the region called Kavadarci (Tikvetch) in Paeonia, to act as a barrier against possible Dardanian invasions. Perhaps some Macedonians were now moved to the tracts of land in the Chalcidice that Philip had granted them after Olynthus fell, as a prelude to his further expansion east. The new cities were also training grounds for the military, for local and transplanted boys would be trained in Macedonian tactics and weaponry. They would gain experience from serving on the borders in their local areas, much as Philip had done in Amphaxitis, and so become a valuable pool of first-class soldiers.

Philip also gave orders for swampy terrain to be drained in order to provide more land for agriculture. Some pastureland was switched to arable farming, dykes were built on the rivers and canals, and all-weather roads were constructed to aid communications, especially with the coast. The boost to the Macedonian economy was great, just as it was to the individual wellbeing of those who had previously lived in more remote regions. The army undertook the vast majority of these projects, and in the process became experienced in dealing with engineering and other works when on campaign. Moreover, Philip's foundations generally seem to have had the effect of turning smaller towns into larger urban centres, with their own distinct administrative and social structures and urban planning.[23] The growth in urbanisation was another of the king's means of stimulating the kingdom's economy, maintaining unity and creating national pride.

Final Intervention in Thessaly

In the meantime Thessaly was about to erupt again, forcing another intervention on Philip's part. As we have already noted, the king's arrangements at the end of the Third Sacred War had not gone down well with the Thessalians, who had expected more from him. As a result of civil strife in many cities rulers came to power, supported by mercenaries, who were no friends of Macedonia. It comes as no shock that one such defiant city should have been

Pherae, but so too was Larisa. There, a member of the Aleuadae family, Simus, even began to strike coinage in his own name.

Enough was enough. In the summer of 344 a frustrated Philip marched at speed into Thessaly, expelled the Aleuadae from Larisa and seized Pherae. He no doubt expelled renegade leaders from other cities, though we have next to no information about these – one of them may have been a certain Aristomedes, an exiled leader from Pherae who served with the Persians against Macedonia in 340 and 333.[24] There was to be no diplomatic settlement with Thessaly as in the past. Philip installed Macedonian garrisons in Pherae and in other cities (in all of them if we can believe Demosthenes), and in each he placed power in the hands of a board of ten men (decadarchy).[25]

Even more radical was Philip's revival of the earlier administrative system of the tetrarchies.[26] Now, each of Thessaly's four original tribal areas (Thessaliotis, Pelasgiotis, Hestiaeotis and Phthiotis: see Map 5) was put under the command of a governor, appointed by the king and answerable only to him.[27] Nothing was done overtly to reduce the power of the cities (which might well have led to mass rebellion), but Philip must have ensured that his governors wielded sufficient power to keep them in check. Indeed, one source calls the tetrarch Thrasydaeus a 'tyrant over his peers, a man of small intellect but a master of flattery' because of the power he wielded over his tetrad and his sycophancy to Philip.[28] Demosthenes went so far as to accuse Philip of enslaving the Thessalians, saying that the latter were traitors to the Greek cause of freedom.[29] Yet Isocrates waxed lyrical that Philip's treatment of them was fair and just,[30] and Philip was always careful in his dealings with Thessaly, so Demosthenes' rhetoric should not be taken at face value.[31] Once again, his language is designed to promote the idea of Philip as the destroyer of Greek freedom.[32]

To an extent Philip's manœuvres were part of a longer-standing policy to ensure firmer control over Thessaly, perhaps having its origins in 352 when he became its *archon*. In 349 he had taken measures against various cities in the interests of Thessalian unity. By 346 he had given his supporter Agathocles of Thessaly control of Perrhaebia.[33] An offshoot of this move, given Larisan influence over Perrhaebia, was Philip's removal from power of Eudicus and Simus in Larisa, and his favouring of a democratic faction there.[34] Consequently, after the (re)formation of the tetrarchy, with Philip ultimately at its head, the Thessalian League remained firmly in control of Thessaly. Its coinage, previously struck by the cities themselves, came largely to an end (though Larisa may have continued minting for some time afterwards) and was replaced by Macedonian coinage.

Philip's Proposals to Amend the Peace of Philocrates: Demosthenes' Second *Philippic*

Things were going less well for Philip in Athens, where Demosthenes was bent on swaying popular opinion against Macedonia. He had successfully proposed the dispatch of an embassy to the Peloponnese to counter Philip's growing influence there, and was zealously trying to convince the people that Philip had broken the terms of the Peace of Philocrates. The king may also have been interfering in Euboea by now, which worried the Athenians greatly. Towards the end of 344 (or perhaps early in 343), after he had settled affairs in Thessaly, Philip sent his friend Python of Byzantium on a goodwill embassy to Athens to reassure the people that he was abiding by the terms of the peace and alliance – which in fact he was – for the Peloponnesians and Euboeans had not been part of the peace. Envoys from Argos and Messene in the Peloponnese (Philip's allies) accompanied Python.

Philip ordered Python to challenge the slanders directed against him and to deliver a message that he was willing to change the Peace of Philocrates from a bilateral to a multilateral arrangement. Thus, any state that wished to join the peace would become an ally of both Macedonia and Athens. The new arrangement would be a Common Peace, something that Philip had steadfastly resisted in 346 but that Demosthenes had advocated at the time. Now, however, he had no choice if he wanted to keep Athens as an ally and offset the people's concern over the growth in his power, especially in the Peloponnese.

Python's embassy was not the only foreign one in Athens, for there was also one from the Great King of Persia, Artaxerxes III Ochus. He planned to invade Egypt in the winter of 343 and to that end sought assistance (in the form of troops) from many Greek states. At least Thebes and Argos on the Greek mainland agreed to help him, but the Athenians refused, although they did reaffirm their friendship with the Persians (as did the Spartans).[35] When Python appeared before the Assembly he made it plain that Philip wanted the peace to continue and that he wanted 'to win the friendship of Athens more than that of any other state'.[36] When he delivered Philip's main proposal about making the peace a common one, and said that he was also inviting the Athenians to propose any further amendments they wanted, the Assembly was loud in its appreciation. Led by Aeschines, the people decided to extend the Peace of Philocrates to include any Greek state that wished to join it. Taking Philip at his word, the Assembly further proposed that the members of the treaty should together protect any ally that was threatened by a hostile party. The latter measure was not likely to cause any problems with the king, for it was in accordance with a Common Peace treaty.

So far so good, it would seem, for Philip. Then Demosthenes stood up on the platform and delivered what was probably for him his most important speech to date in his campaign to undo the Peace of Philocrates, the second *Philippic*. He pointed out (quite rightly as it transpired) that under the new arrangement Athens would be separated from its allies, for in the earlier bilateral peace each *hegemon* (Athens and Philip) had sworn on behalf of itself and its allies. Athens, stressed Demosthenes, would be in a far weaker position in Greece. Then he went further and proclaimed that Philip was plotting against Megara and was now out to destroy Athens. He proposed his own amendment, which was that as far as allies and possessions went the original treaty should be amended from 'what each party possessed' to 'what was each party's own', and finished off with an attack on Aeschines. His amendment might have seemed inconsequential, but in reality it had massive implications for it reasserted Athens' claim to Amphipolis, Potidaea and the Thracian fortresses that Cersebleptes and Chares had established in 347.

Hegesippus followed Demosthenes in the debate. He went so far as to propose a decree that Amphipolis and various settlements in Thrace should be returned to Athens. This was absurd, of course, but the people, swayed as they so often were by a combination of oratorical prowess and the emotion of the meeting rather than the content of what was said, passed it. They also requested the return of Halonnesus (off the coast of Thessaly). This tiny island had been an Athenian possession, but they had lost their influence there when Sostratus the pirate seized it in 346 and turned it into a base for his activities. This action did not seem to bother the Athenians at the time, for they made no attempt to regain it, nor did they seem too bothered by Philip's later action in expelling the pirates and establishing a Macedonian garrison there (an indication of his concern about the now rampant problem of piracy). When the nearby island of Peparethus (an Athenian ally) moved against Halonnesus and captured its garrison, Philip immediately retook the island and held onto it. Thus, Philip believed his actions and the Athenians' apathy were sufficient grounds for him to see Halonnesus as his own now.

There is no question that Demosthenes knew that Philip would find these later proposals, especially his own amendment, unacceptable. There is also no question that his ability to persuade the Athenians shows how far Philocrates' influence had dwindled, and it would not be long before he was impeached. It is easy to condemn Demosthenes for the path that he took and the allegations he made in his speeches about Philip's activities and about his being out to reduce Athens. Then again, Philip himself had not shown any consistency in his dealings with the Athenians, and he was clearly prepared to use them for his own benefit. In 346 he had rejected outright the idea of a Common Peace and now, only two years later, the Athenians must have viewed his volte-face with suspicion. Demosthenes' desire to protect his city from perhaps yet another cunning and harmful ruse on Philip's part is understandable.

Moreover, Demosthenes recognised that Athens could not defeat Philip on its own, so he now began working frantically to assemble a coalition of Greek states (including the all-important Thebes) that together could end the threat from Macedonia. Persia might also be an ally against Philip, for it is interesting to note that when the Great King sent for aid to the Greeks he did not approach Philip. Perhaps he saw him even then as a potential threat to Persian power. Unfortunately for Demosthenes, the reality of the situation as far as Philip's power and Athens' role in central Greece were concerned escaped him, and in 340 his policy propelled Athens into a war that it could not win.

Although Python had already left Athens for Pella to take news of the Assembly's decision to Philip, the Athenians sent Hegesippus at the head of a delegation to the king to report its decision formally. This embassy set out probably in late 344. Of course, Philip could not accept anything that would re-establish Athenian influence in the Thracian Chersonese. For one thing, that would pose a threat to his own security, and for another, he was probably by now planning to move eastwards against Thrace and add it to his empire. Nor could he allow the other members of the peace to follow Athens' precedent and demand the return of their possessions: this might mean, for example, that the Chalcidic cities would have to be restored. His temper probably snapped when he offered to give Halonnesus to the Athenians, as per their request, but Hegesippus said he could not 'give' it to them, but only 'give it back', as it was already theirs, not his.[37] This was nonsensical quibbling, and Philip sent Hegesippus packing. In doing so, Demosthenes would have jubilantly told the people that the king had shown his untrustworthiness yet again. Athenian policy was rapidly coming to be dictated by Demosthenes.

The Trial of Philocrates

Nevertheless, Philip made no move against the Athenians, perhaps because of their reaction to the Persian embassy, as we have seen, and his belief that the worsening situation could still be salvaged. It was now early 343, the year that the Phocians began to repay their fine. However, what was really significant about that year were the two trials that took place in Athens, which offer us a vivid contemporary insight into the political feelings of the people. The first was the trial of Philocrates, whom Hyperides – 'foremost of the orators in speaking ability and in his hatred of the Macedonians'[38] – impeached for taking bribes (from Philip) against the common good.[39] The second was that of Aeschines for misconduct during the second embassy to Philip.

At the heart of Philocrates' impeachment was the charge that his proposal in 346, that the Athenians should accept Philip's offer of peace and alliance, was contrary to the common good and the result of bribery. The charge was political in origin, of course, for at the time the Assembly had of its own volition chosen to adopt his proposal. Nor could the allegation of bribery be substantiated. Philip had given gifts to the Athenian envoys (of whom Philocrates was only one) at his court: gifts were part of Greek diplomacy, and refusal would have breached diplomatic protocol. However, there was a fine line between receiving a gift as part of diplomacy and taking one as a bribe to betray the best interests of the state,[40] as Philocrates was now accused of having done.

At his trial Philocrates might have argued that his policy three years earlier had been in the best interests of the people and that they had endorsed it. He might also have pointed out that Demosthenes had supported him, so it was curious that no accusations were being made against him. Finally, he might have countered the bribery allegation by arguing that he had accepted gifts as a normal part of diplomacy. However, he could no longer rely on Demosthenes to defend him, as in 348 when he first proposed an embassy to Philip, and in fact Demosthenes was distancing himself further from the peace, and hence Philocrates, with every passing day.[41] As far as character witnesses went, there was only Aeschines, and his political influence was on the wane. Philocrates saw the writing on the wall and therefore fled into exile before his trial. It was still held, but his flight confirmed his guilt to many at the time,[42] and thanks to Hyperides' prosecution he was sentenced to death *in absentia*.[43] His property was confiscated by the state and sold.

The False Embassy Trial: Demosthenes vs Aeschines

Philocrates' fate came as a nasty blow to Aeschines, who, no doubt worried about guilt by association, had prudently remained on the periphery of events. His low profile would not be enough to save him, however. Demosthenes had been waiting to renew his attack on Aeschines since the latter had successfully deflected it with his prosecution of Timarchus in 345, and in view of the popular reaction against Philocrates he now decided that the time had come. In the autumn of 343 Demosthenes brought the same charges against Aeschines as against Philocrates of misconduct (*parapresbeia*) on the second embassy. By this he meant Aeschines' stance towards Philip and his peace terms at the Assembly meetings of 18 and 19 Elaphebolion and 16 Skirophorion. Further, he alleged that Aeschines had deliberately slowed down the second embassy so that the king was able to campaign in Thrace before he returned to Pella for the oath.

The charges were as political in motivation as those levelled against Philocrates.[44] In prosecuting Aeschines, Demosthenes needed to distance himself completely from the peace, given that he had now settled firmly on a policy of resistance to Macedonia at all costs. He may also have wanted to get rid of Aeschines, who was an effective speaker and who in wanting to maintain the peace with Philip might block Demosthenes in the Assembly. The details of the trial do not concern us here. We have the speeches of both the prosecution and the defence (a rare survival indeed), both titled *On the False Embassy* and both riddled with distortion of the facts, which detrimentally affects their value as historical sources.[45] Demosthenes as prosecutor spoke first, then Aeschines, who was supported by Eubulus and Phocion. A jury of 1,501 men over the age of thirty, selected by an intricate process, then cast their votes as soon as the speeches were finished, with no time for the sort of discussion and legal guidance that is customary today.

Unlike Philocrates, Aeschines stood his ground. He would have been unaware of exactly what Demosthenes would say in court, but he clearly felt confident of being able to refute the allegations against him. Thus, for example, when Demosthenes tried to link Aeschines to Philocrates in the hope that the latter's flight would influence the jury to declare against him too, Aeschines simply outlined Demosthenes' association with Philocrates down to the Assembly of 16 Skirophorion when the two parted political ways. Demosthenes did his best to distance himself from his role in the negotiations that led to the peace, at one point accusing Philocrates of taking bribes against the city, which he said he had spent on fish and prostitutes.[46] It was not enough. The jurors acquitted Aeschines by the narrow margin of thirty votes.[47] Demosthenes failed because he did not have tangible evidence and relied mostly on supposition, namely that Aeschines accepted bribes to the detriment of Athens. However, Aeschines had not been spared by a landslide vote, and his acquittal 'should not be taken as a sign of any significant softening of the people's view of Philip'.[48]

Final Intervention in Epirus

In the meantime Philip was distracted by renewed problems with Arybbas, the Molossian ruler of Epirus.[49] In 350 he had taken Arybbas' stepson (and Philip's brother-in-law) Alexander into a protective custody of sorts at Pella. Alexander was now twenty, and apparently completely loyal to Philip. In 343 Arybbas may have been taking steps to ensure the continuation of his rule, which led him to make overtures to the Athenians, since he, like his father and grandfather, was an Athenian citizen. At the best of times Philip could not allow any form of insurrection to his south-west, but especially not now with the Peace of Philocrates looking shakier every day.

Thus, Philip decided to invade Epirus to secure his south-western border once and for all, and to stall any Athenian military support for Arybbas. He sent an embassy to Athens with a letter addressed to the people that reiterated his intentions for a Common Peace that any state could join. Further, he responded to Athenian claims about the Thracian fortresses and ownership of the island of Halonnesus by offering to submit both matters to arbitration. The latter was completely insignificant compared to the former, and Philip knew this. However, by offering to have outside parties decide the issue he was showing open-mindedness and denying the Athenians any formal grounds on which to complain about his actions. Picking up on one of the terms of the peace, he also proposed a joint expedition, funded by Macedonia and with Athens providing only ships and crews, to rid the Aegean of piracy. About Amphipolis he said nothing, for realistically there was nothing to be said on that matter.

While Philip's proposals were being debated in Athens, the king led an army into Epirus (Map 2). In a bloodless campaign, he expelled Arybbas, who moved to Athens and was offered the same rights of protection as any Athenian citizen.[50] The people thought of restoring him to his throne, but no action was actually taken. Philip's brother-in-law Alexander was made king of Epirus.[51] He would show his loyalty to Macedonia a number of times: most significantly in 337, when his sister Olympias and her son Alexander (the Great) fled from Pella to Epirus and may well have tried to stir up trouble against Philip. Alexander of Epirus seems to have wanted nothing to do with the plan, and shortly after married his niece Cleopatra, daughter of Olympias and Philip. The desire to control Epirus went beyond the question of mere border security, however. The kingdom had good pastureland and timber, and at least part of the proceeds from this must have flowed into the Macedonian treasury.

Philip had promised to secure for the Molossians the southern part of Epirus on the Ambraciote Gulf, then controlled by the Ambracians and Cassiopaeans. In early 342 he set fire to the territory of three small Cassiopaean cities, Pandosia, Bucheta and Elatea, and made them subject to the Molossian Alexander. The Ambracians feared that the king would move against them next, perhaps even with a view to taking over the island of Leucas, the main exporter of timber from eastern Epirus. Hence they sent an urgent appeal for help to Corinth, which in turn asked for Athenian help. Both cities immediately committed troops.[52]

Ambracia's invocation of Corinthian help is not surprising, for Corinth had founded the colony (and Leucas) in about 625. Colonies, while autonomous, maintained sentimental ties with their mother cities for the most part. More unexpected is the Corinthian appeal to Athens and the fact that the latter sent troops, for the two had often been at loggerheads and worse in the past. Corinth is likely to have been worried by a possible threat to its trade route if Philip decided to push further south and perhaps establish a western line of communication from Epirus via the Ambraciote Gulf and the Gulf of Corinth to Achaea.[53] His treaty with the Aetolians, on the northern edge of the entrance to the Gulf of Corinth, would confirm Corinth's suspicions. In the event, Philip withdrew, but Demosthenes would make much of this scare.

The Intensification of the Athenian Opposition to Philip

In Athens the people were weighing the pros and cons of Philip's proposals while he was campaigning in Epirus. The verbal quibbling over whether Philip was 'giving' or 'giving back' Halonnesus was blown out of all proportion and cynically exploited as political ammunition to fire at the king. This represented political oratory at its worst, and Aeschines saw through it by saying that Demosthenes was 'arguing about syllables'.[54] Hegesippus delivered a speech called *On Halonnesus*, which has survived as the seventh speech in the Demosthenic corpus. In it he painted a disturbing portrait of Philip's intentions, pointing to his recent campaigning in Epirus and especially Thrace, which brought with it a threat to the Athenian cleruchs in the Chersonese and to the corn route. His speech, together with Demosthenes' appeals to the Assembly, carried the day, and the people rejected all of the king's proposals.

The rejection of the campaign against piracy is surprising. Piracy was a substantial threat to merchant shipping by this time, and there seem to have been several pirate bases in the Aegean (Halonnesus was clearly one, and perhaps also some of the islands in the north Aegean). Since the Athenians were dependent on imported corn from the Black Sea region as well as on trade for their economy, it made sense for them to combat the danger posed by pirates. Ditto Philip, whose expansion of trade had generated the need for Macedonian ships, which would also be vulnerable to piracy. The Athenians may not have taken measures against piracy before owing to monetary considerations, but now Philip was offering to meet all costs. The reason for their rejection lies in Hegesippus' speech, for he proclaimed that Philip wanted to exploit Athenian naval power in order to win control of the Aegean for himself. That distortion of the truth was all that was needed to sway popular opinion.

Philip is not likely to have wanted control of the seas, and his own navy would always be small compared to that of Athens. However, Hegesippus may have been onto something when he suggested that Philip wanted to limit

Athens' naval power, for it is possible that he was behind a plot at this time to destroy the Piraeus dockyards. According to a story told by Demosthenes in a speech of 330 (and retold by later sources),[55] an Athenian man called Antiphon, who had been struck from the Athenian citizenship roll and forced to leave Athens, returned to the city. He did so, says Demosthenes, because Philip had paid him to set fire to the Piraeus dockyards. He was caught red-handed, but when he was brought to trial Aeschines defended him and he was acquitted. However, Demosthenes brought him before the court of the Areopagus, where he was found guilty. He was then retried in a regular court, convicted and executed.

Although the plot could have taken place in 346,[56] Antiphon was one of the first men to be tried under a legal procedure (*apophasis*) that was only introduced in 343.[57] Besides, it makes little sense for Philip to have resorted to this course of action in 346 as he worked towards ending the war with Athens. A context of 343 is more likely. The fact that we have no reference to this plot in Hegesippus' speech when leading anti-Macedonians were looking for anything that would denigrate Philip means little as the attempt probably came after the Assembly rejected the request for ships. By that time the Athenian attitude to peace and to Philip was obvious, and the king may well have wanted to try to neutralise Athens' naval power if the peace negotiations broke down completely, which would mean further warfare.

When the Corinthian appeal for help was heard in Athens Demosthenes persuaded the Assembly to send a military force to support the Ambracians (it actually went to Acarnania), and at least five embassies (with himself serving on one) to different states of the Peloponnese to encourage them to resist Philip. While the troops achieved little, the embassies met with some success, for at least Argos, Messene, Megalopolis (all three allies of the king), Mantinea and Achaea made alliances with Athens. Philip may have secured Epirus, and he would soon be campaigning successfully in Thrace, but his actions allowed Demosthenes to combat his influence in the Peloponnese and even to unite some states against him.

The success of Demosthenes' rampant anti-Macedonian policy showed Philip that the continued existence of the Peace of Philocrates in any form was impossible and that efforts to maintain peace between Macedonia and Athens by diplomatic means were fruitless. Hence he may have been behind the attack on the Piraeus dockyards; certainly by late 342 or 341 he had closed the door finally on any further negotiations. By then, Thrace was his and the critical issue had become the Athenian settlements in the Thracian Chersonese. Given Demosthenes' political ascendancy in Athens, further conflict loomed frighteningly large on the horizon.

THRACE:
THE DIE IS CAST

Alexander and Aristotle

For the moment Philip turned to other matters, including the education of
Alexander. The heir, now aged fourteen, was a precocious boy who played the
lyre and was an avid reader of Homer and of Greek tragedy (Euripides was his
favourite). In 342 Philip invited the leading philosopher of the day, Aristotle,
then living in Mytilene on Lesbos, to tutor Alexander.[1] Aristotle was from
Stageira in the north-east of the Chalcidice (a town that Philip may have razed
during his campaign there in 349/8); his father had been court physician to
Amyntas III, and after his death (and that of his mother) Aristotle had
maintained social contacts with the Macedonian kings, including Philip.
Aristotle was living in Athens when Philip annexed the Chalcidice, and he
seems to have thought it better to leave (perhaps his Macedonian ties were
making it unsafe for him to stay there). He went to the literary court of a
former student, Hermias, tyrant of Atarneus in the Troad, and spent three
years there before his move to Mytilene.

Philip decided that Aristotle would tutor Alexander not at Pella but in the
Precinct of the Nymphs at Mieza, part of the Gardens of Midas on the slopes
of Mount Vermion (Map 2).[2] Why Philip settled on Mieza rather than the
royal capital is unknown. He may have wanted Alexander to have fewer
distractions than surrounded him in Pella and so be better able to concentrate
on his studies, and hence sent him away to 'boarding school'. However, since
Philip was about to go on campaign in Thrace – for how long and with what
success he could not reasonably predict – he may also have wanted to remove
Alexander from the influence of Olympias. As the mother of the heir to the
throne, Olympias probably enjoyed a superior position among Philip's wives.[3]
At Pella Alexander had more contact with her, given his father's constant and
lengthy absences on campaign. She was quick to criticise her husband to

Alexander from a relatively early age, and the two of them may even be implicated in his assassination in 336.

Alexander's tutoring lasted for three years until 340, when Philip ordered the heir back to Pella and appointed him regent of Macedonia. Exactly what the great philosopher taught Alexander is unknown, but it would have included philosophy, rhetoric, geography, zoology, medicine and geometry. As the years of Alexander's kingship passed, he and Aristotle had a falling-out of sorts. Yet Aristotle's influence was strong enough that when Alexander invaded Asia he took with him an entourage of intellectuals and scientists to record all manner of practical and scientific information about the areas through which he travelled. He also took with him Aristotle's edition of Homer's *Iliad*, which he would keep in a casket (that had belonged to the Persian Great King) under his pillow, along with a dagger.[4]

Athenian Intellectuals and Philip

The hiring of Aristotle would have been common knowledge in many Greek cities, not least in Athens, the cultural and intellectual centre of the Greek world. Philip was certainly a lover of Greek culture, including philosophy. He held a high opinion of Isocrates and also had some regard for Plato – the latter's Academy had received support from several previous Macedonian kings, though not from Philip. When Plato died in 342, another prominent philosopher, Speusippus, succeeded him as head of the Academy. The news of Aristotle's appointment as Alexander's tutor in 342 may well have spurred Speusippus to write to the king seeking his patronage.

His letter to Philip survives in the so-called Socratic letters of the first century AD, which are mostly spurious.[5] It throws an interesting light on the attitude of fourth-century Greek intellectuals (as opposed to the political warmongers) to Macedonia. Speusippus' letter cannot predate 343–342 because of its reference to Ambracia and Philip's activities in that area in its seventh section. It seems that a certain Antipater, a man from Magnesia, had been wronged by another Magnesian and was appealing to Philip, who by then controlled the area. At the time Antipater was living in Athens, where he was writing a history of Greece. The letter includes material ranging from Greek mythology to more recent history, specifically references to the good deeds of Philip's predecessors, and has commonly been seen as a public document written with two aims in mind. The first was practical, to debate Philip's imperialistic policies; the second was intellectual, to discredit the opposing school of rhetoric run by Isocrates. There was a bitter rivalry between the Academy and Isocrates' school, and the letter contains a long attack on Isocrates' *To Philip* of 346.

A recent radical reinterpretation (with which I agree) has argued that the letter is not a public document at all, and hence had nothing to do with political affairs, but a private one.[6] In essence it was an attempt by Speusippus to re-establish the same sort of relationship between the Academy and Philip that it had enjoyed with the king's predecessors, and the wrongs suffered by Antipater gave him a convenient pretext to plead his cause. Thus, Speusippus argued that since previous Macedonian kings had performed good deeds for the Greeks, and Perdiccas III, Philip's immediate predecessor, had supported Plato and the Academy, Philip must do likewise. As noted, one byproduct of Philip's patronage of the Academy would have been some decrease in the influence of Isocrates' school, which Academicians would have been keen to see.

It looks as though Philip was not swayed, perhaps because of the attacks on Isocrates. Nonetheless, the letter shows that among Athenian intellectuals such as Speusippus and Isocrates (and the same may be true of other states) Philip was perceived differently from the way he was portrayed by Demosthenes.[7]

The Reduction of Thrace

By 342 Cersebleptes was causing sufficient trouble again in Thrace, where he had been reducing the Thracian Hellespontine cities to subject status, to demand Philip's serious attention. There was also the possibility of Persian involvement in Greece, which made control of Thrace up to (and perhaps even including) the Hellespont essential for Macedonian security. Since Philip probably intended to extend his empire eastwards anyway, the time for that had come.

In about June 342 he led an army from Pella to subdue Thrace and annex it as part of the Macedonian empire (Map 3).[8] He must have known that the campaign would last for some time, for he engaged in operations not only in European Turkey (against Cersebleptes) but also in the Hebrus valley (the Bulgarian Maritza) and north of the Great Balkan Range. Therefore, it is likely that he appointed Antipater as his deputy in Greece in his absence, for we find him representing the king at the autumn Pythian Festival at Delphi.[9] Alexander was still only fourteen and had just begun to study under Aristotle, and Philip needed someone trustworthy to hold the reins for him back home. Antipater clearly did a good job, and his services were called on again in 334 when Alexander made him 'guardian' (*epitropos*) of Greece when he left for Asia.

To the Thracians fighting was a way of life: they thumbed their noses at farming and preferred to fight for booty. However, Philip's Thracian campaign was executed with the precision that we have come to expect of him and success was soon forthcoming. Diodorus gives the only narrative of it, and what he says is brief, to say the least:[10]

> Philip conceived a plan to win over the Greek cities in Thrace to his side, and marched into that region. Cersobleptes [*sic*], who was king of the Thracians, had been following a policy of reducing the Hellespontine cities bordering on his territory and of ravaging their territories. With the aim of putting a stop to the barbarian attacks Philip moved against them with a large force. He overcame the Thracians in several battles and imposed on the conquered barbarians the payment of a tithe to the Macedonians, and by founding strong cities at key places made it impossible for the Thracians to commit any outrages in the future. So the Greek cities were freed from this fear and gladly joined Philip's alliance.

What these 'several battles' were, where they took place and what cities Cersebleptes had reduced to subject status are all unknown. All that we know for certain is that at the end of this lengthy campaign Philip expelled Cersebleptes, the cities became members of his empire and the Greeks in Thrace eagerly embraced an alliance with him.

What else can we add to shed light on this campaign? Philip's route[11] probably took him first close to Philippi, on the Nestos river, so that he could secure his eastern frontier. There he seized Masteira, which is still to be identified, and then to its west he founded Philippolis (Plovdiv) in the Hebrus valley.[12] This allowed him access to Kabyle in the east, and from there to the Euxine Sea. At the mouth of the Hebrus, in the south, Doriscus fell to him.[13] Then he most probably marched into the kingdoms of Cersebleptes and Teres, conquering both, before moving through Cardia[14] and the Chersonese (making no moves against Athenian settlements there). From there he marched north-eastwards along the coast to Titistasis or Tyrodiza, Serreion Teichos, Myrtenon and Bisanthe, as far as Heraeion Teichos. Control of these locations gave Philip Thrace and also opened up an inland route from Bisanthe to Macedonia.

Philip would most likely have used his regular phalanx infantry and Companion Cavalry as well as lighter-armed and more specialist troops. Demosthenes' third *Philippic* (delivered in 341) tells us that he used 'light troops, cavalry, archers and mercenaries, and this is the kind of army he puts together'.[15] Perhaps these troops constituted only a small portion of the eventual invasion army, for he was later forced to demand reinforcements from Antipater. The men evidently performed superbly, but according to Demosthenes' speech *On the Chersonese* (delivered a few months before the third *Philippic*) Philip suffered an illness. The latter may have contributed to the length of the campaign, and hence some of the fighting might have had to take place during the winter months.

Probably in late 342 Philip turned northwards against the Getae, another Thracian tribe (Map 3). These were a semi-nomadic people who lived in the area between Thrace and the Danube basin by the Schipka Pass. He made an alliance with Cothelas, their king, who was quick to recognise the power of Philip. Cothelas gave him lavish gifts including his daughter Meda (along with a substantial dowry), whom Philip took as his wife (his sixth marriage, after a gap of a decade).[16] This alliance with the neighbouring rulers meant that Thrace would not be able to seek help there in any future revolt, but to be on the safe side Philip still took the precaution of posting Macedonian garrisons and colonists in several towns including his own foundations of Beroi (Stara Zagora) and Philippopolis (Plovdiv). Thus, Macedonia's territory now extended as far north as the Istrus (Danube) river; satisfied for the moment, the king returned to Pella.

The Odrysian kingdom was no more. After less than a year of hard campaigning, Thrace, which had been valued for its economic resources for over a century, was Philip's.[17] Several times larger in size and population than Macedonia, it provided valuable manpower for the Macedonian army, both in Philip's time and later in that of Alexander. Moreover, and this provided an important boost for the Macedonian economy, Philip imposed a tithes tax on Thrace.[18] As far as administration was concerned, he appointed local princes as his vassals, and probably also created at this time the office of General (*strategos*) of Thrace.[19] Although Alexander of Lyncestis (the son-in-law of Antipater) is the first person we know to have held this post (in 336: the year of Philip's assassination and Alexander's succession), its creation was in keeping with Philip's policy towards areas that he had conquered – we might compare Thessaly in 344.[20] One of the general's duties was probably also to oversee the collection of the tithes tax.

Philip's imperialistic ambitions, not to mention the fall-out from his earlier move into Crenides, meant that an extension of Macedonian power eastwards came as no surprise. The eventual timing for such a manœuvre was in part dictated by Cersebleptes' activities, but even more by the way that the Athenians had reacted to Philip's proposal to maintain the peace. Their attitude to the return of Halonnesus hardly endeared them to him either, and it may even have been this issue that was, as has been suggested, the 'final straw'.[21] If Philip had hoped in 344 that changing the Peace of Philocrates to a Common Peace would bind the Greeks together, leaving him free to campaign in the east, by 342 and certainly by 341 that hope had been dashed. He would have known that his campaign in Thrace would worry the Athenians greatly, given their settlements along the Thracian Chersonese and its strategic importance on the corn route. There was potential for confrontation if Athens committed forces to that region. At least one of the Greek towns in the area, Apollonia, made some sort of alliance with Philip,[22] thus setting a precedent for others to follow; this would have given little comfort in Athens. To make matters worse, at roughly the same time Philip led his army into Thrace he exploited tensions in Euboea to divert Athens' attention from his movements.

The Euboean Factor

As we have seen, in 348 Euboea had secured its independence from Athens (apart from Carystus at its southern tip), with Philip perhaps playing a role in its defection. Then in 343 the tyrant of Chalcis, Callias, went to Pella to win Philip's support for a new Euboean League that would resist Athens or Thebes if either city tried to reassert its influence over the island. Some of the other key towns on Euboea, such as Eretria and Oreus (Histiaea), had already expelled pro-Athenian factions or imprisoned their leaders. Callias was unsuccessful, probably because Philip was still optimistic about the continued existence of the Peace of Philocrates and had no wish to antagonise the Athenians. But the Athenians' verbal quibbling over Halonnesus when so much was at stake elsewhere changed his mind dramatically. When rebels overthrew the tyrant Plutarchus at Eretria, seized neighbouring Porthmus (on the southern Euboic Gulf) and appealed for help to Philip, he sent Hipponicus with one thousand mercenaries to assist them. This was probably at about the same time as he set off for Thrace (summer 342). Very soon after, Parmenion and Eurylochus joined Hipponicus.

Hipponicus quickly secured Eretria and set up Cleitarchus as tyrant. Next was Porthmus, where the walls were destroyed and an anti-Macedonian (that is, pro-Athenian) group was expelled. The Macedonians confirmed in power the three tyrants (Hipparchus, Automedon and Cleitarchus) who already ruled there. The people were not impressed with this arrangement, and twice attempted to overturn the triumvirate. On both occasions Macedonian mercenaries expelled their opponents, the first time when they were led by Eurylochus and the second by Parmenion. The latter then installed a pro-Macedonian group headed by Philistides at Oreus. This posed a danger to Athens, for Oreus was on the Euripus straits which narrowly separated Euboea from Attica. Moreover, it was obvious that the tyrants of at least two of the island's most important cities owed their position to Philip, and correspondingly his influence in Euboea can only have increased to the detriment of Athens. Yet Philip made no moves against Carystus, which remained firmly loyal to the Athenians throughout this period.

Armageddon in the Chersonese: Demosthenes Rampant

Matters started to come to a head in spring 341, when Philip became involved in a territorial dispute between the Athenian cleruchs in the Chersonese and their neighbours in Cardia (one of Philip's allies in the Peace of Philocrates). Some time earlier the Athenians had sent a mercenary force under the leadership of Diopeithes of Sunium, a friend of the hawkish Hegesippus, to the Chersonese. Diopeithes (aided and abetted by the Athenian cleruchs there) had encroached greatly into Cardian territory, and had attacked Krobyle and Tiristasis, which were also Philip's allies. He held the inhabitants of these two places hostage, and when Philip sent Amphilochus to petition on his behalf for their release Diopeithes tortured him and held him to ransom as well. Further, Diopeithes resorted to the piratical activity of robbing merchant ships bound for Macedonia. The latter course of action was seemingly to pay for his troops since the Athenians were unable to cover all of his costs.

Eventually the Cardians appealed to Philip for help. He committed only a small force to their assistance, but sent several embassies to the Athenians to complain – justifiably – about Diopeithes' activities.[23] The king had taken great pains not to break the peace; he knew his actions in Thrace would alarm the Athenians, but there is no question that the provocation for war came from them. At the very least Diopeithes ought to have been recalled to stand trial, for his acts were in clear breach of diplomatic protocol. However, Demosthenes was vehement in his support of him, and Hegesippus misled the people by saying that Philip was operating outside Thrace and hence in an area to which he had no right.[24] As such, both orators claimed that Diopeithes was doing nothing wrong in protecting Athenian interests in this region.

Demosthenes answered Philip's letters with his speech *On the Chersonese* (the title literally translated is 'Concerning those living in the Chersonese'), which was followed a few months later by his next *Philippic*.[25] In both speeches to the Assembly he argued emphatically to keep an Athenian force in the Chersonese and not to recall Diopeithes. His opponents of course wanted the opposite, fearing that Diopeithes' continued presence would cause war with Macedonia.

In *On the Chersonese* Demosthenes argued that since Philip was to all intents and purposes at war with Athens, whether this was in Thrace, Epirus or Euboea, Diopeithes should do as he pleased and indeed be sent reinforcements. The speech is a rhetorical masterpiece. Demosthenes set out to worry the Athenians by widening the specific context of the speech to the general struggle between Athens and Philip. Thus, we move from Diopeithes in the Chersonese to the danger posed to the whole of Greece by Philip's expansion in Thrace, and then dramatically to Philip's intention to conquer Greece and then destroy Athens. He also returned to his familiar theme that the Athenians should maintain a standing army and unite their allies against Philip to maintain their freedom. Philip is portrayed as the enemy of democracy and Athens as its supporter; hence those bribed by Philip are his agents, and therefore against democracy and should be beaten to death.

In about May 341 Demosthenes delivered his third and fourth *Philippics*.[26] In them, he continued his attacks on his opponents and called to have them executed as traitors. He encouraged the Athenians to levy an *eisphora* (extraordinary tax) to fund a military expedition against Philip, and said they rather than mercenaries should serve on it. Significantly, he advised the Athenians to appeal to the Persian Great King, Artaxerxes III, for money and even an alliance.

Demosthenes' speeches were wildly successful in the now emotionally charged atmosphere in which the Athenians were living. Although the people did not beat his opponents to death, they did not recall Diopeithes, and did send a support force under Chares to the Chersonese. Their actions merely worsened relations between Athens and Philip, who had been slowly assembling troops in anticipation of further intervention in the Chersonese against Diopeithes (and now Chares). This build-up of course gravely worried the remaining Greek independent cities of the Hellespont, Perinthus (Marmaraereglisi), Selymbria (Silivri) and Byzantium, who saw themselves as Philip's next victims. The Athenians shared their concerns, not so much out of sympathy for the possible fate of these cities should Philip move against them, but owing to the obvious danger to the corn route if he did.

They also sent an embassy to the Persian king.[27] No doubt remembering the rebuff he suffered at the Athenians' hands in 344, Artaxerxes did not make a formal alliance.[28] However, there seems to have been some tacit arrangement, for he gave the Athenian ambassador Ephialtes money to use against Philip, some of which was apparently passed to Demosthenes and Hyperides.[29] Artaxerxes' rejection of a formal alliance must have relieved Philip, for the vast monetary and manpower resources of the Persian empire combined with an aggressive Athens would have presented a nightmarish prospect. The Persian king was evidently keeping an eye on Macedonian activities, though, for in spring 341 he gave orders for Philip's ally Hermeias of Atarneus to be deposed and tortured, presumably to find out whether the king was planning to attack him.[30] Hermeias could tell him nothing, and Philip would not have used him in any invasion anyway. However, on top of the Athenian problem he now had to factor Persia into his thinking.

Philip had finally had enough of diplomatic dealings with the Athenians. They in turn were prepared to engage him in the Chersonese if it came to it.

The die was thus cast when Philip left Pella in the summer of 341 to march back to Cardia.

Euboea Again

In the meantime events on Euboea suddenly began to favour the Athenians. In spring or early summer 341 there came an unexpected overture from Callias of Chalcis for an alliance. In return for Athenian help to establish a Euboean League under his hegemony, he would ensure that the league remained an ally of Athens. Callias was seeking an alliance on equal terms rather than have Chalcis return to the Athenian confederacy as a member state. Nevertheless, a pragmatic Demosthenes persuaded the Athenians that the deal was in their best interests (which indeed it was) if they wanted to regain influence on Euboea. Given Macedonia's own involvement in Euboea, an Athenian intervention could not be ignored by Philip. Demosthenes would have been well aware of this, but he knew that in any showdown with Philip it was essential to have Euboea on Athens' side.

The Athenian involvement in Euboea is complicated and controversial, largely because our contemporary evidence is tucked away in Demosthenes' speeches *On the Chersonese* and the third *Philippic*. His call to liberate Euboea from its Macedonian tyrants[31] was successful, for over the summer the Athenian commanders Cephisophon and Phocion attacked Oreus (helped by some soldiers from Megara) and Eretria on behalf of Callias and expelled their tyrants.[32] Callias also embarked on a series of piratical attacks with ships provided by Athens against towns on the Gulf of Pagasae: these were allies of Philip and also, under the terms of the Peace of Philocrates, Athens. He followed these actions with attacks on merchant shipping to Macedonia as well as the dispatch of embassies to various cities in the Peloponnese to drum up support against Philip. For Callias' activities against Macedonia the Athenians conferred a vote of thanks and citizenship on him. They also supported Demosthenes' motion that a Euboean League be formed, and so Callias' wish was finally granted.[33]

Philip Declares War on Athens

While all of this was going on, Philip was in the Thracian Chersonese area (Map 3). Diopeithes died soon after, and the Athenians placed their future in the entire Hellespont region in the hands of Chares and a fleet of forty ships. They also sent out embassies to various states against the king, and it is in this context that we find Demosthenes and Callias appearing before the Assembly and telling the people that the entire Peloponnese, Acarnania,

Achaea, Megara and Euboea were willing to take part in a campaign against Philip. Moreover, Achaea and Megara would provide 60 talents and the Euboean League 40 towards it. Demosthenes was clearly exaggerating the extent of support for rhetorical effect. A few years later, in 338, when Athens and Thebes led a coalition of Greek states against Philip at Chaeronea, it was hardly the whole of the Peloponnese that fought on the allied side (see pp. 147–9).

Nonetheless, the Athenians in 341 seem to have taken seriously the idea that Philip could be stopped. That was not to be, for Philip himself declared war in that year. It is commonly believed (based on a much later source)[34] that war broke out in 340 after Philip besieged Perinthus and Byzantium and seized the Athenian corn convoy (see below).[35] This is not the case: Philip actually declared war on Athens in 341 while he was defending Cardia, but the Athenians did not realise what had happened until later (after he seized their corn fleet).[36] This version of events is based on an interpretation of the wording of 'Philip's Letter', a document he sent to the Athenians at this time, which has survived as Speech 12 in the Demosthenic corpus. In it, Philip berates the Athenians for their actions since 342, responds to their complaints about his activities in Thrace and in the Chersonese with his support of Cardia (12.2–5, 12.16), and, significantly (at 12.23) threatens that, 'having made the gods witnesses, I shall deal with you about these matters'.[37] The latter is his declaration of war.

The above scenario explains Philip's move towards the Hellespont. His previous campaign in Thrace had taken him very close to Perinthus, Selymbria and Byzantium, which were now his closest independent Greek neighbours in the east. Byzantium was the strongest power in the region, and it was an ally of Philip; however, all three viewed the geographical expansion of his power with anxiety. So also did the Athenians, who sent out embassies to various states soliciting assistance against Philip. Demosthenes went to Byzantium in what must have been the autumn of 341. It was essential for the Athenians to remain on friendly terms with Byzantium, given its strategic location on the Hellespont and its importance on the route taken by Athens' corn convoy.[38] Although Demosthenes claimed to have secured Byzantium's friendship,[39] he probably did not conclude an actual alliance. In the meantime Hyperides visited Chios, Cos and Rhodes on a similar mission, and also met with success.[40]

It is interesting that these places – Chios, Cos, Rhodes and Byzantium – had been the instigators of the Social War in 356. Now they came over to the Athenian side, evidently realising that the danger from Philip was greater than any problems they had experienced with Athenian hegemony in the past. Their realisation came too late.

In April 340 Demosthenes was crowned for his services to the people in the Theatre of Dionysus, during the annual festival in honour of that god.[41] Of course, Philip's recent activities in Thrace would have helped his case immensely, but the crowning was a significant moment in his career. It could not be done without the endorsement of the Assembly and thus showed majority approval for his anti-Macedonian tirades, for 'he allowed no act of Philip's to pass uncriticised, and seized upon every occasion to incite and inflame the Athenians against him'.[42] From the youth who had stammered and lost his nerve in front of Philip in 346, Demosthenes had come a long way indeed: Athens' policy was his.

Alexander's Regency

At some point in spring 340 Philip sent word to Alexander, now aged sixteen, to leave Mieza (where Aristotle was tutoring him) and return to Pella as regent of Macedonia. This was an important position, for a regent performed various civic duties. He carried around the royal seal to use on state documents, and he protected the state's security. He also performed the daily religious sacrifices to Heracles Patrous (Heracles the Father), the ancestor of the Temenids, on behalf of the state. Alexander's new powers clearly demonstrated to all that he was next in line to the throne. Given his distance from Pella at the time, Philip's decision to appoint him regent is best explained by his declaration of war on Athens.

Antipater and Parmenion were also based in Pella, perhaps to act as the young regent's advisers, but Alexander soon showed everyone that he was his own man. When the Maedians, a Paeonian tribe on the upper Strymon river, revolted, Alexander marched north and ended the rebellion (Map 4).[43] He followed up his victory in battle by transplanting people from Macedonia, Greece and Thrace to live in a city (really, a military outpost) that he founded on Maedian territory and that he named after himself, Alexandropolis. After Alexander's triumph, Antipater and Parmenion reduced three other inland Thracian tribes: the Tetrachoritai or Bessoi (on the Hebrus river), the Danthaletai (on the headwaters of the Strymon) and the Melinophagi (on the Pontic coast, north of Byzantium).[44]

It is hard to say whether all three Macedonians were acting under Philip's orders, or whether Antipater and Parmenion took the course they did to prevent trouble from other tribes in light of Alexander's Maedian campaign. Either way, Macedonian rule was now enforced on the inland area from the upper Strymon and Hebrus rivers to the Pontus, which further isolated Perinthus, Selymbria and Byzantium, as Philip no doubt intended. We do not know Philip's reaction to Alexander's actions (especially the naming of

Alexandropolis); however, he was clearly impressed by his son's battle prowess, for two years later he gave him command of the Companion Cavalry at the Battle of Chaeronea.

Philip's Siege of Perinthus

Finally, probably in early summer 340, Philip besieged Perinthus with about thirty thousand infantry and his small navy.[45] He may have moved against Perinthus first as it was geographically closer; Selymbia was about 14 miles (22 km) east of it, and Byzantium about 30 miles (48 km) beyond that. The Perinthians were favouring the Athenians, perhaps even to the extent of making a treaty with them,[46] for they had refused to send Philip assistance in his campaign against Cersebleptes. Since Philip was now at war with Athens, as far as he was concerned he had a legitimate excuse to move against an enemy's ally.

The siege of Perinthus failed thanks to the supplies the city received and – especially – thanks to its setting. It was built up a steep hillside or headland at a height of some 160 feet (50 m); its houses were on terraces running up the side of the hill, akin to tiered seats in a theatre, and were protected behind walls. After arrows and javelins did nothing to breach the city's walls, Philip ordered huge stones to pound them from catapults on siege towers, which were apparently as high as the hillside, and on top of which were archers to fire at the defenders.[47] In some places the walls were breached, but the Perinthians, despite heavy losses, blocked up the narrow roads in front of and in between their houses, and retreated upwards to the next terrace. This meant in effect that the defensive walls of the city grew higher and higher. Although these additions were hastily thrown together, the Macedonians were unable to burrow underneath them or smash them with battering rams and collapse them. The siege continued by day and by night, and as Perinthian losses mounted the city sent an urgent request for help to Byzantium. The latter responded with men and equipment, including catapults, and Philip's army found itself under serious attack.

Byzantium's manpower and supplies helped the Perinthians, as did unexpected support from the Great King, who viewed Philip's growth in power 'with great alarm' (says Diodorus). He ordered his satraps (governors) on the sea coast of Asia Minor to send mercenaries to the besieged city along with food, money and other supplies.[48] Arsites, the satrap of Hellespontine Phrygia, immediately sent a mercenary force, which also appears to have raided Thrace. Philip used his own small navy to transport his siegecraft to Perinthus; however, its size meant that he could not prevent ships from Byzantium ferrying in supplies since the coastline was dominated by Athenian cleruchs. Moreover, the Athenian fleet (commanded by Chares) was based at nearby Elaious, which controlled the entrance to the Hellespont. To have risked a naval encounter with the superior Athenian navy was a gamble the king knew he could not afford to take.

Philip's Siege of Byzantium: Goading the Athenians

The siege of Perinthus had been going on for some months, with no end in sight despite considerable losses on both sides, when Philip suddenly changed tack. Splitting the infantry force in two, he ordered one half to continue the siege of Perinthus while he led the other half to besiege Byzantium itself (this was in August or early September 340).[49]

Philip's shift in tactics has been rightly criticised: if he could not take Perinthus with his entire force, how could he have any hope of taking Byzantium, given the city's thick and massive fortification walls,[50] with only half his men?[51] Perhaps he was relying on the element of surprise. Yet news of his sudden move would have travelled ahead of him to Byzantium, for he probably stopped off at Selymbria on the way and invested that place (most likely it fell to him without too much trouble given its small size). He may also have left a detachment of men to keep Selymbria in check, which would have further reduced his available manpower for Byzantium.[52] Perhaps he thought that Byzantium's resources would be depleted by its support of Perinthus. Wrong again, it would seem, for almost as soon as he arrived there the city received money, manpower, supplies and even missiles from Chios, Cos, Rhodes and Persia.

It is more likely that Philip's primary object was not actually to take Byzantium, given its strongly defensible position and the impossibility of shutting off the Hellespont to deny it supplies – both of which a strategist of Philip's calibre must have known beforehand. Instead, I suggest he used the siege as a means of further provoking the Athenians now that he was at war with them. This rings even more true if they had still not realised the full import of his earlier letter to them, with its subtle declaration of war. Given the vital importance of the Hellespont region (and hence Byzantium's position on it), Philip may have calculated that Byzantium would become for the Athenians another Amphipolis. In other words, the city would dispatch a fleet to join with Chares, and the war of words would turn into fighting against Philip in the Chersonese. Since by now he must have been intent on a more lasting settlement of Greece, which was different from his intention in 346, it was essential to bring this new war to a speedy close. Goading the Athenians to action would help to achieve this aim.

Diodorus gives us a lot of detail about the siege of Perinthus but none about that of Byzantium. It does appear that at one stage the Macedonian army almost breached its walls during a night attack, but barking dogs gave away their position and they were repelled. The siege is also important because it is here that the torsion catapult, developed by Philip's engineering corps, was used for the first time (Figure 2).

Philip would have known that the level of concern in Athens would escalate as soon as news of his siege of Byzantium reached the city. That is exactly what happened. Not long afterwards, Demosthenes' misguided anti-Macedonian policy finally yielded fruit. The Athenians destroyed the *stele* (stone) on which was recorded the Peace of Philocrates, a sign that they finally recognised that they were at war.[53] They called this (their second) war against Philip 'the war over Byzantium' and, as Philip had predicted, immediately sent a fleet north under the command of Cephisophon and Phocion to act in liaison with Chares.[54] Phocion had contacts at Byzantium who let him into the city, and with this renewed support it continued to stand fast against Philip throughout the spring and into the summer of 340.[55] Byzantium, as Philip had gambled, did become the Amphipolis of the east for Athens.

The timeline for these few months is controversial, principally because Demosthenes says that Athens did not declare war on Philip until after he seized the corn fleet.[56] This must be wrong: the Athenians declared war on him before the seizure and during the siege of Byzantium, as is shown by the name they gave to the war which indicates that Byzantium was the issue.[57] They did not realise that Philip had already declared war on them, which is why he called the Athenian vessels 'prizes of war'.[58] It was in this perspective that Philip felt it was within his rights to seize the corn fleet.[59]

Seizing the Corn Fleet: The Writing on the Wall for Athens, and Greece

The corn fleet consisted of probably 230 vessels,[60] which were assembling at Hieron, close to the mouth of the Propontis (Sea of Marmara). The task of protecting it from piracy (and now possible danger from Macedonia) was given to Chares' warships. However, Chares was suddenly called away to a meeting of the satraps who were supporting Perinthus and Byzantium to discuss both sieges and general opposition to Philip. As soon as he left, Philip struck. The Macedonian fleet led by Demetrius captured the entire corn fleet while Philip and his land army seized the crews who were ashore at Hieron. Philip kept 180 ships (those that were actually Athenian) and released the other fifty. He destroyed the Athenian ships, using their timber for his siege engines, and sold off their contents. The sale netted him the huge sum of 700 talents, which was around a year's income for the Athenians.[61] Although Chares retaliated by rushing back and driving Demetrius into the Propontis, the damage had been done. Philip's action caused a corn shortage in Athens, though not a famine; but a far greater effect was the resulting Athenian resolution to resist the king at all costs.[62]

The siege of Byzantium (and of Perinthus) was now a dead issue in Philip's mind. This is shown by his release of the other fifty ships from the corn fleet, for they belonged to Byzantium, Rhodes and Chios. Clearly he was ready to end the sieges, make peace and return to Greece to bring the war with Athens to a close. That Philip's initial aim was not to reduce Byzantium is shown by the further splitting of his force when he sent part of it to attack Athenian settlements in the Chersonese. He could have ordered reinforcements from Macedonia at any time if he had really wanted to take Byzantium (and Perinthus too, for that matter), but he did not. True, the provisions and reinforcements that both received were a thorn in his flesh, but they were obstacles that he could have overcome. That he did not is surprising given his military genius, and hence we have to find an adequate explanation. The obvious one is that ultimately the sieges did not matter to him, as they were only ever part of a broader strategy to coax the Athenians into action, thus opening the door for him to bring about (by military means) a more lasting settlement in Greece.

There was still the matter of the Macedonian fleet, which had been forced into the Propontis. Philip could not risk a naval battle with the Athenians, and so he resorted once more to a ruse involving a letter, this time addressed to Antipater.[63] It contained an appeal to send troops to Thrace immediately because of a massive revolt. Macedonian garrisons in Thracian towns were under attack, and Philip had decided to break off the siege of Byzantium to march to their help at once, he said. The letter never reached Antipater: the Athenians stationed at the Bosphorus intercepted it and, responding to its contents, immediately set sail for the Aegean coast of Thrace to reinforce the Thracians in their revolt.

Of course, the letter's contents were a fabrication, and Philip had deliberately arranged for it to fall into Athenian hands. He knew that the Athenian navy would rush to support any Thracian insurrection, and in its absence his fleet would be able to escape and join him. That is exactly what happened, and as soon as it was through the Propontis Philip left Byzantium. He began the long march west through the Chersonese, travelling along a coastal route so as to support his fleet. In the meantime Phocion, who had been wounded when attacking some Macedonian merchant vessels, returned to Athens.

Although Philip's sieges were technically failures, when peace was finally made with Byzantium, Perinthus and their allies in 339, the king left the area far stronger than when he had entered it. He had extended his influence further geographically (Map 4), he had done real damage to the Athenian fleet and he was in a superior position in the new war with Athens. Also, he had once again benefited the Macedonian trading sphere, which now extended from the Aegean to the Hellespont (and the Black Sea beyond). The danger that Athens could still put together a large coalition of Greek states was enough to warrant his immediate return home. This second war between Athens and Philip would last only two years, though, and it would end very differently for the Athenians (and for all Greeks) from the first.

CHAERONEA AND THE END OF GREEK LIBERTY

While Philip was besieging Byzantium the regular spring meeting of the Amphictyonic Council at Delphi was scheduled to take place under the presidency of the Thessalian Cottyphus of Pharsalus, no friend of Athens. The Athenians were careful to elect experienced delegates – Aeschines, Meidias, Thrasycles and Diognetus – to attend the meeting. It was just as well. When the Athenian delegation arrived at Delphi, it was told that Amphissa, a city of the western Locrians and an ally of Thebes, intended to accuse their city of impiety.[1] The objective was to orchestrate a sacred war against them, thus isolating them in central Greece.

The Fourth Sacred War: Aeschines' Triumphant Diplomacy

The Amphissan charge was flimsy. In 373 the Temple of Apollo at Delphi had burned down. There had been some interruption to the reconstruction works during the Third Sacred War, but by 340 or so the temple had been rebuilt. Before it was formally consecrated, the Athenians had rededicated to Apollo gilded Persian and Theban shields seized at the Battle of Plataea that brought to an end the Persian Wars in Greece in 479. They had also added the caption: 'The Athenians from the Medes and the Thebans, when they fought on the opposite side to the Greeks.'[2] During these wars, the Thebans had medised (adopted a pro-Persian stance), a treacherous action that they could never live down – it was still being brought up against them when Alexander the Great razed the city in 335. The Athenians' action now made them guilty of impiety. It is hard to understand exactly why the Athenians rededicated these shields before the temple was reconsecrated, unless they were trying to provoke or at least offend the Thebans in some way. The Amphissans, allies of Thebes (which may have egged Amphissa on), denounced them to the council. They wanted the Athenians excluded from consulting Apollo and fined (they pressed for 50 talents). They were most probably calculating that the people would refuse to pay, and hence their defiance would escalate into a Sacred War being declared on them.

There is no question that a war of this nature would involve Philip, not least because of the role Thessaly would play in it since he was its *archon*. Whether he had anything to do with the Amphissan charge (by that time he had declared war on the Athenians) is unknown, but it is unlikely in view of his distance from Greece. It most probably originated in local disputes.[3] Given the anti-Athenian sentiment among many members of the council, even the flimsiest of charges would be taken seriously, and so the Athenian delegation found itself in a situation that boded extremely ill for the city.

Diognetus and Meidias did not address the council meeting, allegedly because they were ill with a fever. For some reason Thrasycles did not speak either. The three of them may well have thought that the Amphissans would be successful, and so decided that by not speaking they would suffer less criticism at home than if they did and the city were fined. That left Aeschines, who responded to the Amphissan charge with a withering counterattack. Ignoring the case made against Athens, he accused the Amphissans themselves of impiety for cultivating the sacred Plain of Cirrha (under Delphi) and the nearby harbour, even to the extent of constructing buildings there. His arguments were so convincing that no rebuttal came from the Amphissans. Any support that they expected from Boeotia and the other anti-Athenian states evaporated.

The next day, on the council's orders, an Amphictyonic force was ordered to verify Aeschines' allegations. It found properties set up on the sacred land as he had said and was about to destroy them when Amphissan troops sent it fleeing. This act of defiance led to another meeting of the council the following day. Here, it was resolved that unless the Amphissans made good on their actions the council would hold an extraordinary meeting at Thermopylae, at which it would declare a Sacred War (the fourth) against Amphissa. Thanks to Aeschines, the charge against Athens was brushed aside, never to reappear.

Aeschines thus seemingly played a significant role in diverting attention away from Athens and onto the Locrians. Demosthenes, of course, thought differently. He later claimed that Aeschines had taken bribes from Philip and that the whole episode was a put-up job so that he could become involved in central Greek affairs.[4] As was noted above, it is hard to see Philip's hand in the war's origins, so what Demosthenes says must be taken with a large pinch of salt. Indeed, since the late 350s Demosthenes' bias against Philip had been so great and so persistent that one might be justified in believing the exact opposite of everything he said about the Macedonian king.

Demosthenes and Thebes

Demosthenes was now working hard towards making an alliance with Thebes against Philip, and so Athenian reaction to the council's decision was crucial. If, as seemed likely, Thebes' sympathy lay with the Amphissans, the Thebans would abstain from voting at the extraordinary council meeting. That would mean they would be seen by the other Greeks as siding with the enemy. This scenario suited the Athenians, so Aeschines thought. It meant that if they joined the other council members in voting for the war, they would have to come to terms with Philip. Moreover, they could even unite with the other council members in a move against the defiant Thebans.

Demosthenes, on the other hand, realised that Athens would make an enemy of Thebes for ever if events played out as projected above. He realised, as Aeschines did not, that the Athenians' actions over the past half a dozen years meant there would never be a long-term alliance on equal terms between them and Philip. Moreover, Philip did not need Aeschines or anyone else to engineer an excuse for him to return to central Greece because by 340 he was going to lead an army there anyway. Only by an alliance of Athens and Thebes, given the strength of the Boeotian army, could he plausibly be stopped. Therefore, Demosthenes persuaded the Assembly that Athens should not take part in the extraordinary council meeting, thus gambling that earning the other states' disfavour was better in the long run than earning that of Thebes.

The extraordinary meeting was held in May or June 339, and it was not attended by either Thebes or Athens. A sacred war was declared against the Amphissans, who thus found themselves in the very position in which they had expected to place the Athenians. The council's president, Cottyphus, was given command of an Amphictyonic force that would deliver its decision, which included the imposition of fines and the banishment of those who had taken part in defying the earlier Amphictyonic force, to Amphissa. Significantly, it was decided (perhaps at Cottyphus' suggestion) that Philip would be elected commander of the Amphictyonic troops if the Amphissans refused to comply.[5]

Philip's Campaigns in Scythia

These events were occurring while Philip was in Scythia en route back to Pella. After raising the siege of Byzantium, the king decided to settle a score with the Scythians, who lived south of the Danube (Romanian Dobruja) and were led by Atheas, their ninety-year-old king (Map 3). The Scythians were renowned for their mounted archers, who would retreat before an enemy force, causing it to relax its line as it pursued, and then gallop back and encircle it, firing off volleys of arrows with deadly accuracy. Until recently, Philip had expanded his empire without encroaching on Atheas' domain, and the latter had likewise expanded Scythian influence south of the Danube without threatening Philip. The situation had changed dramatically during Philip's Thracian campaign, however.

Atheas wanted to see the reduction of Byzantian power, and so welcomed Philip's siege of the city. When he was suffering losses in a war against the Histrianoi in Scythia Minor, he sent the people of Apollonia an urgent request to Philip for military support. In return, he said he would adopt Philip as the heir to the Scythian throne.[6] Despite being involved with Byzantium at the time, Philip decided to send a small force of infantry and cavalry to help him. When it arrived, however, it found it was no longer needed, for the king of the Histrianoi had died in the meantime and Atheas had made terms with them. Instead of thanking the Macedonian troops, Atheas abruptly ordered them to leave and refused to pay their expenses. He explained the latter by saying that his kingdom's harsh climate and barren soil provided barely enough to support the locals, let alone to pay Philip's troops as well. Philip viewed this behaviour as hostile, and he also believed that Atheas' expansionist plans would jeopardise any Macedonian settlement of Thrace. Thus it was that, probably in early spring 339 after lifting the siege of Byzantium, he led his army north to deal with the Scythians.

Philip tried to mask his intentions by sending an embassy to Atheas requesting safe passage to the mouth of the Ister (Danube) so that he could dedicate a statue of his ancestor Heracles there.[7] He said he had sworn to do this during the siege of Byzantium, and the statue would be something of a symbol of Macedonian power. Atheas saw through Philip's scheme immediately and refused his request. His response, according to Theopompus, was in keeping with his reputation for bluntness:

> Let Philip send the statue, and it will not only be set up but be safeguarded on my word of honour. I shall not permit an army to enter my territory. Should a statue be set up against the will of the Scythians, I shall remove it on Philip's departure and convert the bronze of the statue into arrow heads.[8]

Atheas' ultimatum, as we might expect, had no effect. When the Macedonian army arrived there was only one battle, during which Atheas was killed. No other details of the campaign are known, and it was all over by early summer. Thus, Philip added Atheas' kingdom, which stretched from south of the Danube to the Sea of Azov, to his realm – whether he got to erect the statue of Heracles at the mouth of the Danube is unknown. If he did, though, no trace of it remains, nor have any traces ever been recorded by Romanian archaeologists.[9]

Finally the Macedonians could head back to Pella. They took with them as plunder some twenty thousand thoroughbred horses for breeding purposes and the same number of Scythian children and women to be used as slaves or sold for profit. Significantly, there was no gold or silver to plunder, and hence the campaign 'was the first time that reports of the poverty of the Scythians were corroborated'.[10]

Battle with the Triballi: Philip's Leg Wound

The Macedonians' route lay north of the Balkan Mountains, through the Isker valley (by Sofia), down the Strymon to the Doberus (Strumitsa), and then west to the Axius river (Map 3). While they were still in the Danube area (probably reached via Pleven),[11] the Triballi, a collection of fierce Thracian tribes (and clearly still independent), barred their way and demanded they hand over some of their Scythian booty.[12] The Macedonian soldiers were not the sort of people to give in easily, and a fierce battle ensued. During the fighting, Philip was badly wounded when (apparently) the sarissa of one of his own men went through his upper leg or thigh and killed his horse under him. He lost consciousness, and his men fled the area to carry him to safety, reaching Pella in probably the late summer of 339. Their hasty departure allowed the Triballi to seize all of the booty. (One of Alexander's earliest campaigns when he became king was to wreak revenge on them for the harm inflicted on his father and the Macedonian army.)

We do not know for sure which leg was hurt, but the wound was almost fatal, and it took Philip several months to recover. He was lame for the rest of his life.[13] His legs required greaves of different shapes. A pair in which the right was 1⅓ inches (3.5 cm) longer than the left was found by the door of what may be his tomb at Vergina. The identity of the occupant of this tomb is disputed, but the peculiarity of the greaves lends some weight to the argument that it was Philip (see Appendix 6).

Philip and the Fourth Sacred War: The Courting of Thebes

The Scythian campaign and the battle with the Triballi took place at about the same time as the extraordinary meeting of the Amphictyonic Council that declared a sacred war against Amphissa. There was little enthusiasm for this Fourth Sacred War. The Greeks may have still been recovering from the costs of the Third Sacred War, but more likely is that they saw this new war for what it really was: the means by which Philip would settle Greek affairs. When

Cottyphus took the decision of the Amphictyonic Council to the people of Amphissa, he was treated with contempt and his force was sent packing, probably because of the lacklustre reaction of the other states. Accordingly, at the autumn Pylaea of 339 the council formally elected Philip as its *hegemon* to settle the war.

At some point before that council meeting Thebes had seized Nicaea, a strategic fortress town that controlled the Pass of Thermopylae, from Thessaly.[14] The latter had received Nicaea from Philip as part of the settlement of the Third Sacred War, and at this time Nicaea had a Macedonian garrison stationed in it. The Thebans now expelled this garrison and installed their own. This action was clearly anti-Macedonian, and may have been an attempt on the Thebans' part to safeguard themselves in case Philip still had the same attitude to them as in 346. Their concern about how the king would deal with them becomes the basis of their policy at this point, which helps to explain why they would soon ally with Athens against him. Thus, Philip now had to plan what to do not only about Athens (which had not yet tried to engage him), but also about Thebes.

Philip would not have decided to enter Greece immediately after the council's decision to appoint him *hegemon* of its troops: the rapidly approaching winter made campaigning in the mountainous regions around Thermopylae practically impossible. Plus, he was still recovering from his leg wound. In 346 he had tried to settle Greek affairs by diplomatic means; now it was inevitable that he would have to settle them more permanently by military force.[15] Thus, in early 338, perhaps even before the advent of spring, he officially joined in the sacred war, and was supported by troops from the Thessalians, Aenianians, Dolopians, Phthiotians and Aetolians. The last were not members of the Amphictyonic Council, but they presumably marched with him as they were enemies of the western Locrians and anticipated some gains from a successful campaign.

Philip's route took him through the rugged terrain of Mount Oeta and Mount Callidromus to Doris, on the road to Amphissa. Doris was a member of the Amphictyonic League, and so an ally. He fortified the town of Cytinium, about 6 miles (10 km) north of the wide Gravia Pass, which opened the route south to Amphissa. The latter was now encircled by a number of his allies, including Delphi.

So far Philip seemed to be advancing towards Amphissa, hence playing his expected role in the sacred war. Then he changed direction literally. Rather than pushing on south to Amphissa, he turned suddenly south-east down the Cephissus valley into Phocis (still recovering from the Third Sacred War and so unable to put up any resistance) and headed towards the Boeotian border. There he seized Elatea, on the eastern side of the valley and on the main road between eastern Phocis and western Boeotia, which linked Nicaea to Thebes, and thence Athens. He now had an easy access route to Amphissa but, more ominously, also to Thebes and Athens, the latter only two to three days' march away. Yet instead of marching immediately into Boeotia and then Attica, a manoeuvre that, given the anxiety and confusion in both states now because of his proximity to them, had every chance of success, Philip reverted to diplomacy once more.

He sent an embassy composed of Amyntas and Clearchus, two Thessalian tetrarchs (Daochus and Thrasydaeus) and representatives from those other states that had marched with him thus far to Thebes.[16] His intention was to persuade the Thebans to continue their alliance with him, at the expense of Athens. To this end the envoys ordered that the Thebans join him or at least allow the Macedonian army safe passage through Boeotia to the Attic border. In return, the Thebans could have whatever booty they seized in Athens when it fell to Philip. If the Thebans refused, they would suffer Philip's wrath. Finally, the embassy requested the surrender of Nicaea, not to Philip but to the Locrians, given that Nicaea lay in their state.[17] The multi-state composition of the embassy was significant, for it showed that if the Thebans refused they would be opposing not only Philip but the Amphictyonic Council too. Even without this strong-arm measure, the Thebans must have been attracted by Philip's offer, for a crippled Athens would boost their influence in central Greece significantly. The situation looked gloomy indeed for the Athenians.

Despair in Athens: Success at Thebes

The news that Philip had seized Elatea and that, to all intents and purposes, Athens was his next target caused panic among the Athenians. Demosthenes, in his speech *On the Crown*, described the reaction in the city when the news broke in one of the greatest passages of Greek oratory to survive:[18]

> It was evening, and a messenger reached the Presiding Officers with news that Elatea had been taken. Immediately they got up from dinner, some to clear the stalls in the marketplace and set the scaffolding alight, others to summon the generals and call out the trumpeter.[19] The city was full of turmoil. At break of dawn the next day, the Presiding Officers called the Council to the Council-house while you proceeded to the Assembly, and before the Council could deliberate and endorse a proposal, the entire citizen body was seated up there. After this, the Council entered and the Presiding Officers announced the news they had received, and they produced the messenger to give his report. Then the herald asked, 'Who wishes to speak?' but no one came forward. The herald asked many times

but to no avail. No one rose, though all the generals were present and all the politicians too, and the country was calling for a speaker to save it. For the voice of the herald lawfully discharging his task is rightly considered the common voice of the country. If those who desired the city's safety were asked to come forward, all of you and all other Athenians would have risen and advanced to the platform, for all of you, I know, desired the city to be safe . . . . But it seems that that moment and that day called for a man who not only was devoted and wealthy but had also followed events from the beginning and figured out correctly what Philip was aiming at and what his intentions were in taking the action he did. Someone who did not know these things and had not studied the situation for a long time, even if he was devoted and even if he was wealthy, would not be better informed about what had to be done or be able to advise you. The one who emerged as the right man on that day was I. I stepped forward and addressed you . . . . I alone of the speakers and politicians did not abandon my post of civic concern at the moment of danger but rather proved to be the one who in the very midst of the horrors both advised and proposed the necessary measures for your sake.

Demosthenes is clearly full of himself here, but his use of language is dazzling. Diodorus' account (obviously based on Demosthenes' description of the Athenians' mood) is equally vivid when it talks about how the city was 'tense with terror', how 'silence and terror gripped the Assembly and none of the usual speakers dared propose a course of action', and how 'again and again the herald called for someone to come forward to speak for the common safety, but no one came forward with a proposal. In utter perplexity and dismay, the crowd kept their eyes on Demosthenes. Finally he came down from his seat' and went on to tell the people what to do. Equally influenced by Demosthenes is Plutarch, who talks in his life of Demosthenes of the Assembly being 'struck dumb' and of Demosthenes alone coming forward.[20]

The picture painted by Demosthenes is not exaggerated. Aeschines' policy towards Philip was now shown to be utterly unrealistic, and with Thebes still something of a wild card the Athenians could not know for sure whether they faced just Philip, only two days' march away, which was a bad enough scenario, or Philip and the Thebans, which was a far worse one. One point that Demosthenes went on to emphasise, though, was that Thebes had not immediately joined Philip, so that should give the people hope.

In addressing his fellow Athenians, Demosthenes' sole purpose was to persuade them to put aside their past differences with the Thebans and to make an alliance against Philip. He proposed that all men of military age should muster immediately in infantry and cavalry ranks and march to

Eleusis, on the road to Thebes. They would remain there, ready to join the Boeotians immediately if need be, while ten envoys and the generals travelled to Thebes with unrestricted authority to negotiate an alliance and to decide the military logistics of blocking Philip. Whether he outlined the lengths to which he suspected the Athenians would have to go in order to secure an alliance, given the traditional enmity that existed between Athens and Thebes, is unclear.

The Assembly enthusiastically supported the proposal, and then the people 'turned to the search for their most eloquent representative. Demosthenes willingly answered the call to service', says Diodorus.[21] This was going to be Demosthenes' finest hour, and it is significant that there is absolutely no mention of Aeschines' involvement in the negotiations.

When the Athenian embassy reached Thebes it found a counterpart from Philip already there. The Macedonians spoke first in the Theban Assembly; then Demosthenes addressed it. The carrot that Philip was dangling, specifically of combining against Athens and giving the Thebans free rein to loot the city, must have shaken Demosthenes. He knew that if his speech failed that day an isolated Athens would be at the mercy of Philip and Thebes. We do not know what he said, but it was enough. Despite Philip and his army being a mere day's march from their gates, the Thebans voted in favour of an alliance with Athens, and hence war with Macedonia.[22] Demosthenes' eloquence, so Theopompus tells us, stirred their courage, kindled their desire to win glory and put every other consideration into the shade. As if transported by his words, they cast off all fear, self-interest or thought of obligation towards Macedonia and chose the path of honour, says Plutarch.[23] The memories of Philip's treatment of the city in the lead-up to the Peace of Philocrates in 346 and now his treatment of Nicaea, as Aeschines observes, may also have helped decide the vote.[24] Whatever the case, there is no question that this was one of Demosthenes' greatest diplomatic triumphs.[25]

It came at great cost, for he had to agree to a number of Theban demands. To begin with, Athens would no longer support the autonomy of any Boeotian city. Indirectly, this meant it would have to recognise Thebes' hegemony of the Boeotian League. As for the war against Philip, the Thebans would pay only one-third of the costs of the land army, and at sea the Athenians were to pay all costs. Worse, the Thebans were to have sole command of the land army, and would share command of the fleet, and the strategic headquarters of the joint force would be at Thebes, not Athens. In his defence speech in the famous Crown trial of 330, Demosthenes glorifies his role in bringing about the alliance, but says nothing about the concessions he was forced to make. He slyly intimates that the jury would find them boring and that as such he was doing it a favour by not going into detail:[26] 'As for what we said in response, I would give my entire life to relate it in detail, but since the moment has passed, and you may feel as if a cataclysm has overtaken the political world, I fear that speeches on this subject would seem pointless and tedious.' Information about the concessions made comes, as we might expect, from Aeschines' prosecution speech at that trial.[27]

The Greeks Rally: Philip Ends the Fourth Sacred War

Philip had cast the martial die in Thrace, and the Thebans now prepared to meet the threat of warfare. His use of the strategic Thermopylae Pass was neutralised by their control of Nicaea. However, Philip controlled the mountain road to Cytinium and the Cephissus valley as far as Elatea, which meant he was within easy march of both Amphissa and Boeotia. Therefore, the Thebans stationed a force a few miles to the north in the Gravia Pass on the route to Amphissa. It included a force of ten thousand Athenian-hired mercenaries under the command of the generals Chares and Proxenus.[28] Another Athenian/Theban force took up position at Parapotamii, on the Boeotian border, and so on the route from Phocis to Boeotia. It may also have fortified some Phocian towns that had been razed at the end of the Third Sacred War, using them as garrison posts in case of a Macedonian attack.[29]

Both of these positions produced strategically useful lines of defence, for they blocked Philip's entrance into Boeotia and, beyond that, Attica. Other states now had to throw in their lot either with Athens or with Philip. To this end, during the winter both Athens and Thebes sent out embassies seeking support against Philip. Few states rallied to their cause. Megara and Corinth promised assistance, as did Achaea (the only state in the Peloponnese to do so), Euboea, Acarnania and some islands; the rest either refused or, like the remainder of the Peloponnesian states, stayed neutral. The reason for their attitude was a dislike, hatred even, of Athens that overrode the potential danger that Philip posed to Greece. Athens had openly exploited its allies in the fifth and fourth centuries, had been an ally of the sacrilegious Phocians in the Third Sacred War, and now it was tacitly supporting Amphissa in the fourth. Enough was enough.

Philip was not meeting with much success either. His request for support from his Peloponnesian allies fell on deaf ears, and only Phocis, which now found itself literally between the Greek and Macedonian camps, showed him any sympathy. Although Athens had been a supporter of Phocis, its new alliance with Phocis' enemy Thebes would have nullified any chance of Phocian support. Moreover, the Phocians very likely felt they were in Philip's debt for the way he had moderated their punishment in 346. As a mark of his gratitude Philip may have restored Phocis, supporting the reconstruction of the towns that were destroyed in 346.

The very alliance that Philip had worked so hard to prevent, both before and after the Peace of Philocrates, was now a reality. However, the widespread alliance of states against the king that the Athenian–Theban coalition might have encouraged had not materialised. After a Macedonian envoy sent to Athens and Thebes asking for peace had been rebuffed, Philip turned to the business of the Fourth Sacred War. He issued a call to arms in support of the Amphictyonic Council against Amphissa. By extension, this meant also the friends of Amphissa, hence Thebes and Athens, but he was unsuccessful in thinking most of Greece would support him against these two cities.

Over the course of the late spring, both sides resorted to guerrilla warfare in and around the Cephisus valley. At one stage the king made a sudden attempt to cross the Cephisus river to undermine both of the allied positions. This is a shadowy business, a situation not helped by Demosthenes, who mentions two battles, one 'by the river' and one (earlier?) 'in winter'.[30] These appear to have been nothing more than skirmishes in which Philip was unsuccessful (if we can believe Demosthenes).

Philip could not allow his position to deteriorate any further as the opposition mounted against him. True, he was *hegemon* of the Amphictyonic army, but that meant nothing in practice, for he knew that the Greeks would lose no sleep if he were to fail in Greece. Therefore, in the spring of 338 he decided that it was time to act. Parapotamii could not be breached because the pass was too narrow and he could not deploy his cavalry. That left the Gravia Pass and Amphissa itself, which meant taking on the mercenary troops commanded by Chares and Proxenus.

As he had previously done to fool the Greek fleet at Byzantium, Philip drafted a letter that he intended his opponents to intercept and by which he hoped to beguile them into relaxing their guard. The letter said that he was withdrawing from Cytinium, and Philip made corresponding moves to do so. The Greeks' gullibility was proved yet again. One dark night, as they relaxed their vigil, Parmenion blasted through the pass, massacred many of the mercenary troops and within three hours had taken Amphissa.[31] Some years later, in 323, Proxenus is called a traitor in a prosecution speech by Dinarchus against Demosthenes,[32] but there is no evidence for this allegation. It may well derive from anti-Theban bias and an attempt to lay the blame for the eventual Greek defeat at Chaeronea at the door of anyone but the Athenians.

At Amphissa, those deemed guilty of sacrilege in the eyes of the Amphictyonic Council were banished, and the city surrendered to Macedonia. Thus ended the Fourth Sacred War, with as much of a whimper as it had begun. Parmenion then continued west to Naupactus, where he put to death the Achaean garrison and its commander. He handed over the town to the Aetolians, in fulfilment of an earlier promise in 341.[33] In the meantime the mercenary force abandoned Parapotamii, for the fall of Amphissa created a dire new military situation. To all intents and purposes Philip had acted on the orders of the Amphictyonic Council against Amphissa. However, the reality was quite different, for the seizure of Amphissa had opened up central Greece to him.

The Battle of Chaeronea: The End of Greek Liberty

In later summer the Greek coalition force decided to fight a pitched battle on the plain of Chaeronea (on the border of Phocis, not far from Thebes). The battle was to decide the fate of Greece: if the Greeks won, they calculated that they would retain their freedom and autonomy, perhaps hoping for another army desertion similar to that following Philip's defeat in 353. If Philip won, Greece was his. It was as simple as that.

The plain of Chaeronea was about 2 miles (3 km) wide, with a number of rivers flowing through it and hills on its northern and southern sides (Map 6). The city of Chaeronea was below the southern hills. Topography and the fact that to the east of the plain there was marshy ground (thanks to the Cephisus river) that limited the amount of available fighting space, hence affecting the deployment of cavalry, made it the only realistic place where Philip might be stopped on the road to Thebes.

Philip moved from Elatea to Parapotamii, and thence to Chaeronea. He did not engage the opposing army immediately, but kept his own men camped close to the plain for a day, perhaps longer, since we are told that his son Alexander pitched his tent by an oak tree by the Cephisus river 'which was known as Alexander's oak' even in Plutarch's time.[34] This was the major river of the plain and flowed from the north-west to the south-east, forming in effect the plain's eastern border. That helps to fix the location of the Macedonian base camp, and suggests that the Macedonians were there for some time if they needed to pitch their tents. The allied base camp was by the Haemon (Lykuressi) stream.

Philip's troops numbered about 30,000 infantry and 2,000 cavalry.[35] Of the infantry, 24,000 were Macedonians, with the rest being drawn from allies, including Thessaly. The latter's job was to protect the flanks of the Macedonian phalanx. (Compare this number to the force Philip inherited in 359, and we note again the success of his military reforms.) The allied side, commanded by the Athenian generals Chares, Lysicles and Stratocles and the Theban general Theagenes, numbered around 30,000 infantry and 3,800 cavalry.[36] Boeotia sent 12,000 hoplites, including the Sacred Band of Thebes,

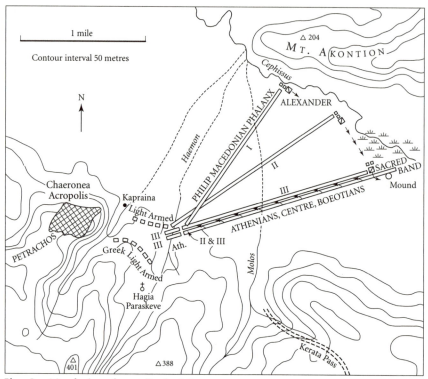

Phase I   Macedonians advance; Greeks stationary

Phase II   Philip retreats, his centre and left advancing; Athenians, Centre and Boeotians advance to left front, but the Sacred Band stands firm

Phase III   Alexander charges, the centres engage, and Philip drives the Athenian wing up the Haemon Valley

Map 6: Chaeronea

an elite 300-strong infantry corps (Theagenes may have been its commander), and some light-armed infantry.[37] Athens mobilised at least 6,000 soldiers up to the age of fifty, and hired about 2,000 mercenaries. Achaea sent 2,000 soldiers, with the remainder coming from Corinth, Megara, Acarnania, Phocis and several islands.[38]

The allied force was in a superior, albeit defensive, position on the plain. The exact location of the armies cannot be determined with absolute certainty, but the following is the most likely scenario (Map 6). The Greeks stretched out their line with each flank next to a river and arranged it by ethnic units. The right wing, headed by the Boeotians (including the Sacred Band on the far right), was by the Cephisus. The left wing, headed by the Athenians under the command of Stratocles, was by the Haemon. The five thousand light-armed infantry were also on the left flank, stretching in a line to the slope of the Acropolis of Chaeronea. The other allies were in the centre of their line, facing the bulk of the Macedonian phalanx. On the Macedonian left flank, facing the Boeotians (and the Sacred Band), were the Companion Cavalry, commanded by Alexander, then aged eighteen, who was probably supported by Parmenion and Antipater.[39] He was stationed by the Cephisus, and hence by the marshy part of the plain. On the right flank, facing the Athenian troops by the Haemon, was Philip, probably with his specialist troops including the hypaspists.

Philip understood instantly his enemy's strategy. This instinct was something Alexander inherited and would use time and again in Asia to the despair of his enemies. In setting up this long line, the Greeks intended to force Philip to extend the Macedonian line and thus reduce the depth of the phalanx. Since both sides were unable to use their cavalry to maximum effect because of the narrowness of the plain, the outcome of the battle would be decided by a frontal charge and the ensuing hand-to-hand fighting. If the Macedonian phalanx's depth were reduced, that would weaken its charge. Further, if the allied line successfully penetrated the Macedonian line, it could then pivot on its right wing and force the Macedonians onto the marshes and even into the Cephisus river. In such circumstances even an allied defeat would carry the advantage that the Greek troops on the left flank and in the centre could flee over the Kerata Pass, through which the cavalry could not ride, and so live to fight again. Philip needed to smash the enemy line and prevent any retreat that might lead to a regrouping of forces.

Shortly after dawn on either 7 or 9 Metageitnion (1 or 4 August) 338, the two sides faced each other in battle.[40] Although their numbers were about the same, there was a chasm of difference in terms of battle experience. The Macedonian army had fought almost every year since Philip became king, and it was superbly trained in terms of its handling of weapons and of its discipline.

On the allied side, the Boeotians were probably the best fighters, but the Athenians en masse had never yet faced the Macedonian army.[41] Moreover, the allied generals were no match for Philip. As Diodorus says: 'on the Athenian side, the best of their generals were dead – Iphicrates, Chabrias and Timotheus too – and the best of those who were left, Chares, was no better than any average soldier in the energy and discretion required of a commander.'[42]

As Map 6 shows, Philip's strategy at Chaeronea was essentially threefold. He began by leading his line at an acute angle towards the allied line rather than facing it straight on, with his right flank closer to the allied line than his left. The allied line held fast as the Macedonian right came into contact with it. Next, Philip's right wing began to retreat at a predetermined time, moving further to the right. This caused the Athenians on the allied left to give pursuit and in the process to shift position further to their left. In doing so, they opened up a gap in the allied line, forcing those in its centre and right to move more to their left to plug it. Only the Theban Sacred Band stood firm, no doubt grasping that if it moved left Alexander could easily penetrate the exposed right flank. No corresponding gap had opened up in the Macedonian line because, knowing his strategy, as Philip moved further to the right, his men in the centre and to the left followed suit.

Philip continued his controlled retreat for perhaps 100 feet (30 m) or so and then stopped by the Lykuressi stream. His strategy had deliberately exploited the Athenians' inexperience and gullibility. Thinking that he was actually retreating and that the battle could be theirs, Stratocles was alleged to have yelled to his men to continue the attack and to shut Philip up in Macedonia.[43] He gave little thought to the consequences of the Athenians' impetuous action. With the allied line in disarray and a gap opening up in it because the Sacred Band on the far right flank had not moved left to keep up with the others, the third part of Philip's plan now came into play.

From the Macedonian left flank Alexander headed a charge against the opening in the allied line. Some of the cavalry contingents veered right to penetrate the gap and wheel behind the Thebans at that point, while Alexander led the Royal Squadron and veered left to encircle the Sacred Band. That Alexander would choose to take on this renowned fighting unit first comes as no surprise. At eighteen he was eager to win battle glory and to prove his father's trust in him. He annihilated the Sacred Band, which, despite the over-whelming odds, was said to have fought to the last man.[44] After that he turned to the other Boeotians and defeated them in fierce fighting. In the meantime Philip's phalanx had suddenly halted its feigned retreat and engaged in brutal fighting. Against such an onslaught, and armed with weapons that could get nowhere near the Macedonian soldiers with their sarissas, the allies stood no chance. Philip drove the Athenians back into the river valley. There, one thousand were killed and another two thousand taken prisoner. It was said that the Haemon ran red with their blood. The battle was over.[45]

The Boeotian losses overall were great, as were those of the Achaeans who were stationed next to them in the line. The Acarnanians fought bravely in the allied centre,[46] but as the battle turned into a rout the remainder lost heart and broke ranks. The survivors, who included Demosthenes, struggled over the Kerata Pass to Lebadea (Levadhia) in Boeotia. Later court speeches would accuse Demosthenes of cowardice,[47] an indictable offence leading to loss of citizen rights. However, in an effort to win their case his accusers deliberately conflated the flight after the battle with his behaviour during it. The anecdote in Plutarch that when Demosthenes' cloak caught on a bramble bush he thought he had been captured and appealed for his life is pure invention.[48]

Luck or Fortune, on which Demosthenes fixed most of his hopes (the shield that he carried into the battle bore the motto 'good luck' in gold letters),[49] had deserted the Greeks. In Athens the general Lysicles was put on trial for the defeat, the prosecutor referring to him as 'a living monument of our country's shame and disgrace', and was condemned to death.[50] Years later the Athenians would try to excuse their loss on grounds of bad luck or treachery. Perhaps the most miserable example of this occurs in Dinarchus' prosecution speech of Demosthenes of 323. In it, Theagenes, who commanded the Theban phalanx at the battle and was most likely the commander of the Sacred Band,[51] is described as 'a man of misfortune and open to bribery'.[52] As we have seen, the Thebans held firm, with the Sacred Band refusing to budge and being annihilated for its trouble. Its commander was hardly corrupt, and another ancient writer compares Theagenes' moral decency to that of Epaminondas and Pelopidas.[53]

The Battle of Chaeronea changed Greece for ever.[54] It made Philip master of a Greece that used to be composed of autonomous states, each of which believed in its freedom at all costs. 'For the whole of Greece this day marked the end of its glorious supremacy and of its ancient independence.'[55] It now became part of the Macedonian empire, and subject to Macedonian hegemony.

From Philip's perspective, defeating the Greeks had been the easy part of his work. Now he had to turn to the future, and to the challenge of maintaining Macedonian rule there and even of trying to reconcile the Greeks to it.

FROM MASTER OF GREECE TO CONQUEROR OF PERSIA?

The Aftermath of Chaeronea

Philip knew that setting up garrisons and pro-Macedonian oligarchies in the Greek cities would produce the opposite effect to the one he intended: namely, to keep Greece passive. During the fifth and early fourth centuries, cities such as Athens, Sparta and Thebes had expelled existing governments from enemy states and set up new regimes supported by garrisons, only to find themselves faced with civil insurrection and even more trouble.

Philip was therefore determined to enforce a Common Peace on the Greek states: in other words, a general agreement with all Greeks. He believed (rightly) that this arrangement was the only way to keep all of the states, especially Athens, in check and subservient to Macedonia. In 346 he had no such intention, but by 344, when he proposed to change the Peace of Philocrates to a Common Peace, he was beginning to see the merits of this structure. It was also the only way to maintain peace without a large-scale Macedonian presence in Greece, which he could ill afford with his eyes now turning to Asia. But before he could consider a new campaign, he had to deal with the aftermath of Chaeronea, and especially to settle matters with various central and Peloponnesian states, including those that had so recently opposed him, not least of which was Athens.[1]

Philip first honoured the Macedonian battle dead by cremating their remains (as was the Macedonian practice), which were then placed under a burial mound (*polyandreion*) around 23 feet (7 m) high located in the eastern part of the plain. A parade in their honour and sacrifices to the gods followed. A mound on the plain was excavated in 1913. It contained pottery from the period, coinage, bones, teeth and weaponry, including long, 15-inch (38 cm) spearheads presumably from sarissas – so was found the *polyandreion*.

The story goes that as Philip walked across the battlefield he saw the Theban Sacred Band lying dead together and burst into tears.[2] As a tribute to its bravery, he had a statue of a lion erected over the spot where the band fell.[3] This was on the western border of the battlefield. The restored Lion of Chaeronea (the original was smashed during the Greek War of Independence) could well mark this spot today, for under it the bones of 254 men in seven rows have been discovered (Plate 16). They were clearly not Macedonians, for they were not cremated. The identification is not certain, however, for the band numbered three hundred and was supposed to have fought to the last man.[4]

A less flattering story has it that Philip and his friends celebrated their victory with copious drinking.[5] They imbibed so much alcohol that they lost their self-control and paraded in a drunken revel (*komos*) through the prisoners, mocking them and Demosthenes (who had fled) as they did so. One of the Athenian prisoners, an orator named Demades, who 'when he used his natural gifts was invincible as an orator, and ... when he spoke on the spur of the moment ... far excelled Demosthenes' carefully prepared efforts',[6] chided the king for the way he was behaving. According to Diodorus, he said to him: 'O King, when Fortune has cast you in the role of Agamemnon, are you not ashamed to act the part of Thersites?' Philip immediately came to his senses and regretted the way he had behaved, freeing Demades for daring to speak as he had before him.

The origins of this tale lie in what Theopompus critically says about the period after the battle:[7]

After the Athenian ambassadors had departed, Philip immediately summoned certain of his companions, and he bade them bring in the flute-girls and Aristonicus the cithara-player and Dorion the flute-player and the others who were accustomed to drink with him. Philip used to take such people around with him everywhere and he was equipped with many accoutrements for a drinking-bout and a party; for being fond of drink and intemperate by nature, he used to keep about himself many buffoons, both musicians and jesters. After drinking all night and becoming very drunk and much jesting, he dismissed all of the others and when it was already near dawn he went on a revel to the Athenian ambassadors.

Theopompus saw Philip as an immoral drunkard, and the story is probably an invention, manufactured to show what louts Philip and his men were. For it to have any impact, though, it had to contain a kernel of truth, and it was no doubt anchored in the real drinking habits of the Macedonians, who were famous for quaffing unmixed wine in excess. Philip must have been euphoric after his victory, and no doubt had a drink or two, but he knew that at this crucial time any celebratory parties needed to be put on hold while he dealt with the Greek states.

Support for this view is seen in the normally hostile Justin, who says that after the battle Philip:[8]

> concealed his joy at this victory. He did not offer the customary sacrifices that day nor did he laugh at dinner; he permitted no games during the feasting, used no garlands or perfume. As far as he could, he conquered without making anyone feel that he was a conqueror. He issued orders that he be addressed not as 'king of Greece' but as 'general'. He showed such restraint, concealing his joy and respecting his enemies' distress, that he avoided the impression of either gloating amongst his own countrymen or of being insulting toward the vanquished.

Settlements with Individual States

After honouring the Macedonians who had fallen and seeing to arrangements for the prisoners, the king turned to deal with the states that had opposed him. He began with the Thebans, perhaps relishing the opportunity to exact revenge for what may have been hostile memories of his forced stay in that city as a youngster. Like Olynthus in 348, which had also broken its oath of allegiance, Thebes was treated harshly: this represented the culmination of Philip's dealings with that city during his reign.[9] The Thebans had to pay a ransom for those killed at the battle (excluding the Sacred Band) and Philip sold the Thebans taken prisoner there as slaves. Although the Boeotian League continued in existence, the Thebans lost their hegemony of it. The cities destroyed by Thebes in the past, such as Plataea and Thespiae in 373 and Orchomenus in 371, were now to be rebuilt; the native inhabitants who had been exiled at the time, or as many as possible, were to be brought back to live in them. These people had long memories, for in 335 it was the citizens of these three places, representing the League of Corinth, who gave Alexander the go-ahead to raze Thebes to the ground when it defied him. Thus, Philip now returned the Boeotian League to what it was originally supposed to be, a federal body, which Thebes could no longer dominate. Even worse, Philip stationed a Macedonian garrison in Thebes and recalled the city's political exiles, from whose numbers he set up a pro-Macedonian oligarchy of three hundred men.[10]

Philip, as was noted before, probably now gave formal approval to the Phocians to begin rebuilding the cities that had been demolished in 346. He could not simply waive the money that they had to repay to Apollo, otherwise he would risk flying too far in the face of the Amphictyonic Council; however, they did not make any repayments in 338.[11] In the west, he now controlled the main north–south trade route from Naupactus on the Gulf of Corinth to

Epirus, although to be on the safe side he stationed a garrison in Ambracia (one of Corinth's colonies), and in Acarnania, which had fought so hard at Chaeronea, a pro-Macedonian faction expelled the ruling regime and took over the reins of power.[12]

Other cities were in a state of panic. Athens and Corinth both expected Philip to besiege them. After Chaeronea, overall command of what was left of Athens' military forces had been given to the mercenary leader Charidemus, one of the generals at Chaeronea, who in 357/6 had been granted citizenship for his services to the state. Demosthenes and Hyperides had proposed a series of emergency measures, which included adding to the city's fortifications, evacuating the countryside, and sending the women, children and sacred objects to the Piraeus. In an effort to boost manpower, further measures were passed that included preventing anyone from leaving the city, calling to arms all men up to the age of sixty, restoring the rights of the *atimoi* (those who had lost their civic rights for offences), granting citizenship to metics (resident aliens) and freeing the slaves who worked in the mines and in the country-side.[13] Leaving Athens at this time was evidently seen as an act of treachery, for in 330 Lycurgus prosecuted a certain Leocrates for doing just that.[14]

In the event these measures were never implemented, for the Athenians' worst fears were not realised. Philip did not invade Attica, and treated the Athenians leniently.[15] He sent Demades to the city with an offer of peace; in this period Demades played no small role in the diplomatic exchanges between Philip and Athens.[16] The king followed this with an official embassy headed by no less than Alexander, Antipater and Alcimachus. They formed something of a guard of honour, for they took with them the ashes of the Athenian dead (bodies of fallen soldiers were always burned after battle) and the prisoners (all two thousand of them) from Chaeronea, for whose return they demanded no payment. Their only request was that the Athenians send an embassy to the king to discuss peace and so end the Athenians' war against him. Why Philip did not himself go to Athens is unknown. Despite facing Athenian opposition almost every year of his reign, and genuinely appre-ciating Athenian culture, he never visited the city, and Alexander visited it only once.

The treatment of Athens was in sharp contrast to that meted out to Thebes. Philip had always shown a different attitude to the Athenians from the other Greeks.[17] We saw this before in the terms of the Peace of Philocrates and we see it now in his settlements after Chaeronea. The reason for his benevolent attitude to the Athenians is hard to fathom, especially in view of their treatment of him. Explanations such as their naval strength and his love of their culture may have played a role, but surely not a major one. Indeed, if he did not plan to invade Asia until the late 340s, the Athenian navy (crucial for any such invasion) cannot have played any significant part in the negotiations that led to the Peace of Philocrates.

A more likely reason for his attitude to Athens, at least in the post-Chaeronea period, concerns his twofold plans to invade Asia and to block Theban influence in central Greece. During the Persian Wars Athens had been looted by Persian troops. Philip could hardly punish Athens, and then state a few months later at Corinth that one of the reasons for invading Asia was to seek revenge for what Athens had suffered (see below). He would be acting no differently from the Persians, and the anti-Persian propaganda that he concocted at Corinth would be patently transparent.

Second, in order to keep Thebes cowed in central Greece, Philip needed an independent Athens that was on good terms with him, for the Athenians could never be underestimated. Athens was still the most powerful Greek *polis* and the one most likely to rouse support against Macedonia – a dozen years or so later, in 324, Alexander's corrupt treasurer Harpalus fled to Athens in the hope of persuading the people to unite Greece against the king. The defeat at Chaeronea had been catastrophic, but the Athenians were resilient: they had been defeated before and had managed to bounce back within a matter of years. Indeed, it has been argued that in the mid- to later fourth century the people had a sound strategic foreign policy that could, and at times did, block Philip militarily and diplomatically.[18]

Demosthenes' anti-Macedonian policy was now in tatters. He was clearly not the man to be sent to treat with Philip, and in any case he thought it prudent to leave Athens for the time being – he acquired a commission to obtain corn supplies from elsewhere.[19] In two later trials against him, he was accused of running away, and there is more than an element of truth to this allegation.[20] Since Demades seems to have been trusted by Philip and the Athenians,[21] he, Aeschines and Phocion were now sent by the Assembly to hear Philip's peace terms. Not many in Athens would have slept well until the embassy returned with its news.

In an atmosphere of what must have been genuine relief, the embassy reported what were favourable terms indeed.[22] The city would escape a Macedonian garrison or oligarchy. The democratic institutions of Athens were to be left untouched, meaning that the city was to remain free and autonomous. No demand would be made for the surrender of anti-Macedonian politicians, nor would any steps be taken to reduce the city's position or influence in the Amphictyonic Council. The Athenian navy would also be left untouched, and Philip would restore to Athens the border town of Oropus, seized by Thebes in 366.[23] However, the Second Athenian Naval Confederacy was to be disbanded, and the cleruchs in the Chersonese, so long the point of tension between the city and Philip, were ordered back to Athens.

As recompense, Philip would allow the city to retain ownership of its 'traditional' islands, Lemnos, Imbros, Scyros and Salamis, to which he added Delos and Samos.[24] Phocion advised the Assembly to accept the king's terms,[25] and a treaty of friendship and alliance was officially concluded.[26] We may even have a fragment of the inscription that recorded this treaty (see p. 162). Thus ended the second war (340–338) between these two powers.

The Athenians conferred citizenship on Philip and Alexander and set up an equestrian statue of Philip in the Agora.[27] Such gestures should not be taken as evidence of a real change of heart towards Macedonia – as Philip must have recognised. For one thing, citizenship or at least shelter was granted to any refugee who fled to Athens in the wake of Philip's purges elsewhere. These included Theban exiles, democratic exiles from Acarnania, and the tyrants Callias and Taurosthenes of Chalcis. The last presumably indicates that Philip severed Athens' alliance with the Euboean League. Hypereides was indicted for his emergency proposals after Chaeronea, but he was not found guilty. At his defence he said that 'it was not I that proposed the decree, but the battle of Chaeronea'.[28]

More revealing of Athenian attitudes to Macedonia are the activities of Demosthenes. When he returned to Athens, he was allegedly indicted 'every day' in the courts and needed someone else to move decrees for him in the Assembly.[29] Yet he still managed to serve on a board of ten that oversaw the city's fortifications, and was elected Treasurer of the Theoric Fund for the following year.[30] Moreover, he was chosen to deliver the funeral oration (*epitaphios*) to honour the Athenian dead at Chaeronea.[31] Athens was the only *polis* in Greece to honour those who had died in battle with a public oration,[32] and this solemn ceremony, attended by foreigners as well as citizens, followed a rigid procedure. It is described by Thucydides and, as he tells us (and there is no reason to think that the process had changed by the later fourth century), the man 'who is regarded as best endowed with wisdom and is foremost in public esteem' was selected by the state to deliver this type of speech.[33] That Philip's arch-enemy was selected to deliver this solemn oration speaks volumes about popular feelings towards Philip, especially as Aeschines had also been a candidate to give the speech.[34]

In either late September or October, Philip entered the Peloponnese.[35] He would still remember the rebuff he suffered at Peloponnesian hands over his call to arms before Chaeronea, and so it was necessary for him to deal with every state, some his allies, others his foes. Moreover, there was always Sparta, which had taken a neutral stance towards Macedonia. Although it had been something of a spent force since its defeat at the hands of the Thebans in 371, phoenixes do rise from ashes. As such, Philip was concerned to arrange a settlement that would ensure Sparta and any anti-Macedonian sympathisers were held firmly in check. The last thing Philip wanted was trouble that would require his attention again as far south as the Peloponnese.

The Corinthians, like the Athenians, had expected the king to besiege them, but they and the Megarians had forestalled this by surrendering. A pro-Macedonian government and garrison were installed in Corinth and perhaps also in Megara.[36] The town of Aigeiroussa was taken from Corinth and given to Megara, further denuding Corinth of power. Philip next travelled to Argos (from which his Argead family claimed descent), an ally that had stayed neutral in the war. That left Sparta, and Philip now put in motion a plan to neutralise any resurgence of its influence.

The Spartans had been engaged in territorial conflicts with many states in the Peloponnese: this was the principal reason why so many of them had allied with Philip in the first place. The king could not allow this situation to continue. Thus, he issued demands to the Spartans to surrender all disputed territories.[37] Apparently, he had asked whether they would like him to go into Laconia (where Sparta was located) as their friend or as their foe, and they had responded 'neither'.[38] This answer would hardly discourage him, and he devastated and burned their land. He did not march on Sparta itself, probably because he had no desire to destroy it once and for all, believing that if he did the other states, now rid of their greatest enemy, might try to remove the Macedonian presence. The campaign had the desired result. Arcadia, Argos, Megalopolis, Tegea and Messenia were satisfied by the areas they recovered, and a circle of Macedonian allies now ringed Sparta. The troublesome Peloponnese remained passive for some time as a result.

The Greek Settlement: Common Peace

It was now the winter of 338/7. Since Philip had made it his headquarters for the campaign in the Peloponnese, it was to Corinth that he summoned deputations from all of the Greek states.[39] The summons was the archetypal invitation that could not be refused. The Spartans did stay away, however, stubbornly asserting that 'what was imposed by a conqueror was not peace but servitude'.[40] Philip left them alone; ringed in as they were by his allies, they no longer presented any threat to him or to other Greeks. Apparently Phocion advised the Athenians against going until they knew exactly what Philip intended to do.[41] For once the Assembly did the right thing, and Phocion's advice was rejected.

Philip was anxious not to be seen as a despot, despite the power he now obviously wielded. Once the envoys had gathered at Corinth, he treated all of them kindly, both in private and in public.[42] Then he announced his intention of establishing a Common Peace among the Greeks. The idea was not a new one, for there had been such peaces before, with in one case the Great King of Persia acting (oddly, it seems to us) as the guarantor of the peace.[43] The previous ones had all proved ephemeral. This time, however, Philip did not intend the settlement to lapse, nor was it to involve the Persian ruler, so he constructed a different way of maintaining it. Intent as he was by now on campaigning in Asia, it was essential for Philip to establish a constitutional mechanism that would keep the Greeks passive and under the rule of Macedonia in his absence. Thus was born what the Greeks were to call the Community of the Greeks (*to koinon tōn Hellēnōn*),[44] but which usually goes by the name given to it by modern scholars: the League of Corinth.[45]

Each state was to swear an oath of allegiance not to harm any other member of the Common Peace or Philip and his descendants. No member state was to interfere in the domestic or foreign policies of any other member state, nor was it to ally with any foreign power that might want to do harm to any other member state. No state was to do anything in its own territory that might lead to civil unrest or the overthrow of its constitution. For example, there were to be no unlawful executions or exiles or confiscations of property, no cancellation of debts, and no manumission of slaves in any politically subversive situations.

There was to be a council (*synedrion*) of the allies to maintain the peace, headed by a *hegemon* (somewhat reminiscent of the allied *synedrion* in the Second Athenian Naval Confederacy). Each state would send a number of council members (called *synedroi*), elected by its own political organs, to the *synedrion*'s meetings. Macedonia was not a member of this council. How many members each Greek state had (and thus how many votes each had on the council) was perhaps determined by its military capacity as well as its size (see below). The council would decide all league matters (military, financial, domestic and foreign policy issues) by a majority vote, and its decrees were binding on all members. It would be the final authority for settling disputes that arose between individuals or member states, and it could exile offenders. How often it met is unknown, but since Philip wanted the Greeks to appear to be in charge of their own affairs, it was probably at regular intervals.

The envoys then left for their home states, taking with them the king's blueprint for Greek peace and unity. The next move was for the states to endorse the settlement and elect their *synedroi*, and for the latter to return to Corinth to attend the first actual meeting of the council. There was nothing voluntary about joining, of course, and it is no surprise that the Greeks (again with the exception of Sparta) voted in favour of Philip's settlement.

Philip's Plan to Invade Asia

In spring 337 a second meeting was held with Philip at Corinth at which he was officially elected *hegemon* of the league. Once some other constitutional matters had been dealt with (including perhaps the creation of a standing body of *proedroi* to organise league meetings and liaise with the *hegemon*), Philip presented his next (and, as it turned out, final) grand plan: a panhellenic war of liberation and revenge against the Persians.[46] This was a variation on the scheme advanced by Isocrates in his *Panegyricus* of 380,[47] and especially in *To Philip*, written shortly after the conclusion of the Peace of Philocrates in 346.

The invasion had two objectives. First, Philip was going to liberate the Greek cities of Asia Minor from Persian rule and the burden of paying a tribute to the Great King. They had been reduced to this status in 386 by the Spartans in return for concessions from the Great King, including his support in re-establishing their hegemony in Greece. Second, Philip was going to punish the Persians for their sacrilegious acts, which included defiling sanctuaries and sacking Athens, during the Persian Wars of 480–479. There was no statute of limitations for acts that offended the gods. Although Greeks and Persians had had diplomatic ties since the King's Peace of 386, the Persians' actions in the earlier wars had never been forgotten, and calls to liberate the Asiatic Greeks and exact revenge had surfaced from time to time. For example, in 388 the orator Lysias had urged such a campaign at an Olympic festival,[48] and Jason of Pherae had toyed with the idea. Hence, no Greek would have thought it unusual for Philip to propose this mission 150 years after the events in question.

Philip singled out the Athenians for special mention in outlining his project, not so much because of what they had suffered but because he knew that with them on his side the rest of the Greeks would be less inclined to query the campaign. Athens' treatment at the hands of the Persians continued to be intimately linked to the Asian campaign: in 326, as Alexander was campaigning against the Indian prince Porus and struggling to cross the Hydaspes river, he is said to have cried out, 'O Athenians, can you possibly believe what perils I am suffering to win glory in your eyes?'[49] But in reality Philip's reasons for the invasion had little to do with what he told the Greeks. He may well have been in dire straits financially and needing the wealth of Asia (see pp. 168–9). Of course, the Greeks would not support his campaign on such grounds – therefore he sold it to them as a war of liberation and revenge. Polybius also confirms that the panhellenic aspect was merely a pretext.[50]

The Macedonian Hegemony of Greece

Philip's settlement thus assured peace among all member states; future civil strife and internecine wars in Greece were (in theory) constitutionally prevented, and the members' constitutions, citizens and possessions as of 337 were recognised and protected for the future. The glue that held the settlement together was not so much Philip's military strength as the deterrent of risking isolation. If one state attacked another member, thus breaching the Common Peace, it would find itself facing an eager coalition of the other states bearing down on it. It was the xenophobia of the Greek states towards one another and the weakness of the *polis* system that allowed Philip to overcome them. He knew his history and the Greeks well.

There were some major differences between his Common Peace of 337 and previous ones. First, it was an enforced peace (thanks to Macedonia's military power) and the Persian king was not a party to it. More significantly, the Macedonian king would be the *hegemon* of the league.[51] Hence, behind the façade of the Greeks seemingly making their own decisions in an allied *synedrion* without Macedonian involvement, it was the Macedonian king who was pulling the strings. His role as *hegemon* of the *synedrion* gave him all the power. For Philip, all Greeks were equal, but some Greeks were more equal than others.

Philip's Common Peace was thus revolutionary: arguably the most significant event in Greek history given what it brought about. Yet our sources have frustratingly little to say about it. Diodorus is concerned mostly with the second meeting at Corinth and the plans to invade Persia. He does not refer to the Common Peace as such, merely saying that after Chaeronea Philip 'conceived of the ambition to become the leader (*hegemon*) of all Greece', that he 'wished to discuss with [the envoys] matters of common advantage' and that he was 'installed as leader (*hegemon*) by the Greeks'.[52] Justin does refer to the first meeting and Philip's various conditions, but he devotes most of his account to the plan to invade Persia and the troops that the king requested.[53] Most information about the league comes from a speech of the later 330s attributed to Demosthenes called *On the Treaty with Alexander*.[54] It deals with Alexander's apparent later breaches of the peace and calls the Greeks to arms against Macedonia. It is from this speech that we learn the Greeks in Philip's settlement were to swear oaths (2, 6), were to be free and autonomous (8), were to have an allied council or *synedrion* (15), had to help other members who were attacked (6, 8, 19) and were forbidden to receive support from foreign powers (10, 15–16), and that there were to be reprisals for anyone breaking the Common Peace (6, 10).

Some of these conditions cannot be true. Macedonian garrisons were established in cities such as Corinth, Chalcis, Thebes and Ambracia as part of the individual settlements made by Philip after Chaeronea. These hardly align with what the speech has to say about the Greeks' freedom and autonomy.

We also have a contemporary inscription that is thought to be the Athenian copy of the peace since it contains an oath and apparently echoes the terms of the settlement.[55] It consists of two pieces of stone, both badly fragmented. This state is not unusual, for the stones on which many public inscriptions recording laws, decrees, alliances and so forth were written broke over the course of time and the pieces became scattered, or they were deliberately broken so that the stone could be used in later building projects. The inscription has been heavily restored to read:[56]

> Oath. I swear by Zeus, Earth, Sun, Poseidon,
> Athena, Ares, all the gods and goddesses; I shall
> abide by the peace (?); and I shall neither break
> the agreement with Philip (?) nor take up arms for
> harm against any of those who abide by the oaths (?),
> neither by land nor by sea; nor shall I take any
> city or guard-post nor harbour, for war, of any of
> those participating in the peace, by any craft or
> contrivance, nor shall I overthrow the kingdom
> of Philip or his descendants, nor the constitutions
> existing in each state when they swore the
> oaths concerning the peace; nor shall I myself do
> anything contrary to these agreements, nor shall I
> allow any one else as far as possible.
> If any one does commit any breach of treaty
> concerning the agreements, I shall go in support
> as called on by those who are wronged (?), and I
> shall make war against the one who transgresses
> the common peace (?), as decided by the common
> council (*synedrion*) and called on by the *hegemon*; and
> I shall not abandon——

It is not an open and shut case that this fragment refers to the Common Peace settlement. While the context might indicate as much, it can also be argued that it refers to the treaty between Philip and Athens that concluded their second war of 340–338.[57]

Another fragment lists what are commonly thought to be the states that swore to uphold the Common Peace, followed by a series of numerals. What we have today are mostly the names of states in northern and central Greece:

————Thessalians: 10.

—ans: 2.

—iots: 1.

————(?) Samothracians and] Thasians: 2.

—ans: 2.   Ambraciots: [1 (?).

————from Thrace and

————Phocians: 3. Locrians: 3.

————Oet]aeans and Malians and

[Aenianians ———— Ag]raeans and Dolopians: 5.

————Pe]rrhaebians: 2.

————Zacynthu]s and Cephallenia: 3.

The numbers are puzzling. Most probably they denote the votes that each state had on the council, perhaps indicating that votes were assigned on the basis of proportional representation. This is not certain, though, for why should the small island of Cephallenia need three envoys and not just one? Alternatively, the numbers could refer to the troop levies that each state was expected to furnish. The *hegemon* was asking for (or could ask for) several thousand soldiers – Justin talks of '200,000 infantry and 15,000 cavalry, in addition to which there were also the armies of Macedonia and the subject barbarian tribes on the borders'.[58] Since some states could furnish more men than others, the numerals may represent the numbers of units (each containing a fixed number of soldiers, for example) that were required.[59] Against this possibility, however, is the fact that nowhere in our source material are we told anything about units of men, and furthermore there seems to be no differentiation between infantry and cavalry, or specialist troops that might be peculiar to a state.

At the end of the second meeting at Corinth (technically, the first formal meeting), the representatives from the Greek states returned home, as did Philip to Pella. The next meeting of the league was set for the following autumn at Argos, in conjunction with the Nemean festival there. Philip could afford to celebrate, for he had finally defeated the Athenians, rendered the Thebans impotent, stabilised the Peloponnese, neutralised the Spartans and crafted a Common Peace that because of several new conditions made Greece subservient to Macedonia for the long term. He had established an empire, and in doing so he had created the first national state in the history of Europe.

The Philippeion

An overt symbol of Philip's power was the splendid Philippeion ('Philip's building'), which Pausanias says the king commissioned in the sanctuary of Zeus at Olympia after the Battle of Chaeronea (Figure 3).[60] It was a large, circular building (*tholos*), which had an external row of eighteen Ionic columns and an internal row of nine Doric columns. It housed statues of Philip, his mother and father (Eurydice and Amyntas), his son Alexander, and Olympias (Alexander's mother and Philip's fourth wife). The statue of Philip was placed in the centre.[61] Its architect was one of the foremost artists of the day, Leochares of Athens, who had worked on the Mausoleum at Halicarnassus.[62]

The building borrows from several different regional styles, including Athenian. However, matters of architecture are not as important for our purposes here as the question of why Philip had it built at Olympia, although we must acknowledge that features and purpose are intertwined since architecture is a form of cultural communication.[63] Hence the features communicate to the viewer the 'message' of any building, something that is as true of the Philippeion as of any other building. It was located in the sacred

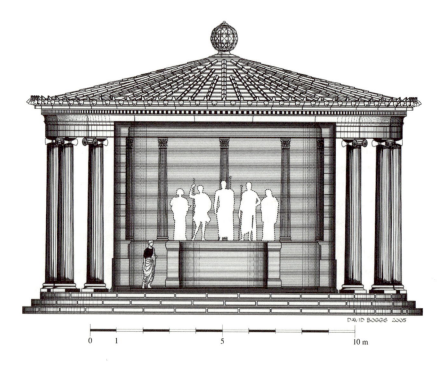

Fig. 3 Cut-away elevation of the Philippeion at Olympia

temenos, the area of the sanctuary in which statues and buildings in honour of gods and heroes were erected and to which every visitor went. Its location and especially its circular shape (making it like no other monument in this area) would have rendered it eye-catching. While it may have been seen as a thank-offering to Zeus for Philip's recent victory at Chaeronea, its ultimate purpose was to proclaim the power of Philip – and his heir – in Greece.

Nonetheless, there is controversy associated with the Philippeion. For example, there is a suggestion that when Philip died in 336 it was unfinished, and that Alexander oversaw its completion. This might explain why Olympias' statue was included in the family group, for she harboured ill feelings towards her husband, which he presumably reciprocated: he may therefore have had little wish to set up her statue in such a prominent building. However, it has been persuasively argued that the building could have been put up within the twenty-two months or so from the time of Chaeronea to Philip's assassination.[64] Further, based on an autopsy of the cuttings for the statues found in the semicircular stone on which they stood, it has been shown that all five statues were planned at the same time, hence Olympias was always intended to be part of the family group.[65] We may also mention the apparent family group of five ivory heads (Philip, Alexander, Olympias and an unknown male and female, probably Amyntas and Eurydice) that was discovered in what is believed to be Philip's tomb at Vergina (see Appendix 6). This would also indicate that – strained relations or not – Olympias was included in family groups, presumably because she was the mother of the heir to the throne.

It is sometimes thought that the building was intended to be a temple and that the statues were chryselephantine (gold and ivory), which was used for cult statues, hence that Philip had come to see himself as divine. However, close analysis of the mountings of the statues reveals they could not have been chryselephantine but probably heavily gilded stone. This was a practice that is found elsewhere, and so Pausanias (our source for their being chryselephantine) was mistaken (perhaps because he did not see the building himself but went on hearsay).[66] Moreover, Philip had no pretensions to personal divinity (for arguments in support of this, see Appendix 5). Hence, the Philippeion was conceived as a secular building to show off the king as the *hegemon* of Greece. With that in mind, the suggestion that the inclusion of women in so public a structure was meant to start a trend of royal females being publicly acknowledged as part of the monarchy, and hence as having a greater say in political affairs,[67] is suspect. While Olympias meddled in political affairs at Pella after Alexander left for Asia in 334, it is clear that Philip had no plans for elevating her role in political life in 337 or 336.

If Macedonia's hegemonic power was somewhat masked by the façade of a Common Peace, which on the surface seemingly allowed the Greeks freedom and autonomy, the Philippeion at Olympia made no such pretence. Since visitors and pilgrims came from all over Greece to attend and take part in the games as well as simply to visit the site – the statue of Zeus there was one of the Seven Wonders of the ancient world – everyone would understand immediately the function of this unique Macedonian building.[68] The deliberately eye-catching shape of the exterior and the fact that the five statues inside were set on a semicircular stone encouraged people to walk round both its outside and the statues inside it. They would marvel at the design and execution – and by extension feel something of the power of Macedonia. It would have been analogous to the feelings that visitors have when viewing the Crown Jewels in the Tower of London.

The Invasion of Asia: Military and Economic Factors

With Greece cowed, Philip could now turn his attention to more distant shores. Exactly when he set his sights on Asia is unknown. Artabazus (the rebel satrap of Hellespontine Phrygia) and his family fled to Pella in either 353 or 352 at the start of the western satraps' revolt, which for a time had challenged the power of the Persian king. They were given asylum at court for a number of years before Artabazus was recalled to Asia.[69] He was not the first Persian to flee to Macedonia, for Curtius tells us of one Amminaspes who did the same thing and was later made satrap of Hyrcania by Alexander.[70] Offering refuge does not mean that Philip was already preparing for war, but his contact with these men at this time may well have made him look more closely at Persia.

It is of interest to the reign of Alexander that one of Artabazus' daughters, Barsine, befriended the young heir while at court in Pella before returning with her father to Persia. However, in 333, not long after Alexander's victory over the Persians at the Battle of Issus, she was captured by Parmenion at Damascus and sent to Alexander. She became his mistress and even bore him a son, Heracles. It was a small world even in those days. Further, the story goes he lost his virginity to her, for he 'did not know any woman before he married other than Barsine'.[71]

Diodorus has the earliest mention of the idea of an Asian campaign at the conclusion of the Peace of Philocrates and Third Sacred War in 346, when he says that Philip 'was ambitious to be designated general of Hellas in supreme command and as such to prosecute the war against the Persians'.[72] Diodorus may be confused here since Philip was only elected to this position in 337. On the other hand, he may be making assumptions based on the fact that 346 was the year in which Isocrates wrote his *To Philip*. This treatise urged the king to reconcile Athens, Thebes, Sparta and Argos,[73] and then to lead a joint Greek expedition against the Persians both for revenge and to liberate the Greek

1 The face of Philip II, showing the right eye blinded by a wound received during the siege of Methone, reconstructed from the remains of the skull found in what is believed to be his tomb at Vergina.

2a and b Aegae (Vergina), in the northern foothills of Pieria, founded by King Perdiccas I, was the original capital of Macedonia until 399.

3a, b and c Pella, on a branch of the Loudias river, became the capital of Macedonia in 399 when it was founded by King Archelaus.

4 Mount Olympus, the home of the gods and the frontier between Greece and Macedonia in antiquity.

5 A portrait commonly thought to be of Philip II on a gold medallion from Tarsus.

6 Philip II on horseback wearing the *kausia* or Macedonian cap on a silver tetradrachm that bears his name.

7 Small ivory head of Philip II found in what is believed to be his tomb at Vergina.

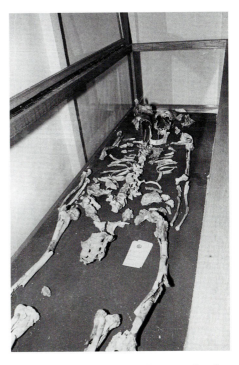

8 The male skeletal remains that were placed in the gold *larnax* found in what is believed to be Philip II's tomb at Vergina.

9 The modern display on the promenade at Thessaloniki of the deadly Macedonian sarissas next to a statue of Alexander the Great.

10 A portrait commonly thought to be of Olympias, Philip II's fourth wife and mother of Alexander the Great, on a gold medallion from Aboukir.

11a View from the Acropolis in Athens of the rocky outcrop called the Pnyx, the meeting place of the Assembly, where matters of domestic and foreign policy were debated and decided by the people.

11b The Pnyx, looking back to the Acropolis. To the right is the stepped rostrum, from which speakers addressed the people.

11c The Pnyx. View over the Agora from the rostrum. The columned building in the foreground is the reconstructed Stoa of Attalus in the Agora.

12 Roman copy of the bronze statue cast by Polyeuctus of Demosthenes of Athens, Philip II's greatest opponent.

13 A silver tetradrachm coin bearing the name of Philip II and depicting a victorious jockey to commemorate his Olympic victory in 356.

14 Dium, the main Macedonian religious sanctuary in the foothills of Mount Olympus.

15 A gold stater coin bearing the name of Philip II with the head of Apollo to commemorate his liberation of the Delphic oracle in 346.

16 The lion of Chaeronea, a monument set up by Philip II to commemorate the fallen Theban Sacred Band at the Battle of Chaeronea in 338.

17 The theatre at Aegae, where Philip II was assassinated in 336.

18 The tumulus at Vergina, under which are believed to be the tombs of Philip II and other royal persons.

19a A mosaic at Pella from the early Hellenistic period of the god Dionysus riding on a panther.

19b A mosaic at Pella from the early Hellenistic period of a lion hunt. One of the figures is supposedly a young Alexander the Great.

20 A portrait of Alexander the Great from the early Hellenistic period found at Pella.

21 A model of the ante-chamber and main chamber of Tomb II at Vergina, believed to be the tomb of Philip II and one of his wives.

22 The façade of Tomb II at Vergina with a modern reconstruction of the frieze depicting a hunting scene.

23a The gold *larnax*, which held male skeletal remains, from the main chamber of Tomb II.

23b Simple yet beautiful silver drinking vessel from the main chamber of Tomb II.

23c An iron cuirass with goldwork from the main chamber of Tomb II.

23d Five miniature ivory heads, believed to be of Philip II and members of his family, from the main chamber of Tomb II.

24 Modern line drawing of the hunting frieze on the façade of Tomb II at Vergina.

cities of Asia Minor. Isocrates had first advanced this theme in his *Panegyricus* of 380, believing that an expedition of this type would give the Greeks the chance to combat their civil disturbances and disunity, which he saw were damaging to both security and prosperity.[74] Philip was not swayed by Isocrates' plea – at the time, at least.[75] Isocrates did not let the idea drop, though – aged ninety-eight, he discussed it with Antipater during the latter's visit to Athens after Chaeronea. After the departure of the Macedonian embassy, he again wrote to Philip urging a campaign against Persia. This time there was no call to unite the major cities and lead a joint campaign as Philip had already imposed his authority on the Greeks.

It has been argued that since Greece was poor compared to the vast wealth of Asia Philip's settlement in 346 was really just a prelude to an invasion of Asia. Hence, the Peace of Philocrates had been intended as an exit policy from Greece but had not gone according to the king's plan.[76] The flaw in this theory is that Philip was in no position to invade Asia in 346 or in any year before Thrace had been properly secured and while relations with Athens and Thebes were so precarious. Hence his plans for Greece were always longer term.[77] His Thracian campaign of 342–340 may well have been to lay the groundwork for a move into Asia, which of necessity meant he had to settle affairs with Athens and Thebes, indeed Greece in general, before he could cross the Hellespont. This further explains his declaration of war on Athens and his manipulation of the siege of Byzantium to goad it into action so he could finish the city off.

The Persian king seems to have viewed Philip with alarm at this time. In 341 he ordered his coastal satraps to support Perinthus when Philip besieged it, and it might even have been at this time that Philip decided on a campaign to Asia to seek revenge for this assistance.[78] In 336 Philip sent an advance force to Asia as a prelude to the crossing of the main army, his plans now aided by events in Persia. In 338 Artaxerxes III and other members of the royal family were murdered. The state of uncertainty in Persia caused by this, coming in the same year that Chaeronea gave him mastery of Greece, presented Philip with a golden opportunity. He was busy in 337 setting up the League of Corinth and working on plans for Asia, but then in 336 Artaxerxes' successor, his youngest son, Arses, was also murdered. That led to a peripheral member of the royal family becoming Great King as Darius III (the same Darius who would later face Alexander).

Two crucial questions remain: first, why did Philip plan to invade Asia, and second, how far did he intend to go?

To begin with the first question. There are several reasons why Philip may have turned to Asia. It has been argued that he intended to defeat the Great King, add the entire empire to his own, and use it as a stepping stone to establishing an absolute monarchy and promoting his own deification.[79] This view is incorrect, and is better treated in relation to the second question. More plausible reasons for the invasion involve Persian aggression towards Macedonia and the need for money.

In the wider military perspective, Persian satrapal assistance to Perinthus meant that the Great King himself was attacking Philip as the besieger. We should not underestimate Persian assistance here as a motive for an invasion of Asia, for in 333 Alexander the Great brought it up in a letter to Darius III, in which he wrote: 'for you gave help to the people of Perinthus, who wronged my father, and Ochus sent troops into Thrace, which we controlled.'[80] Philip was also aware of the presence of a Persian embassy in Athens and the danger that an alliance between these two powers, as Demosthenes had advocated,[81] would pose for him. To some extent it had been Persia's involvement in the Peloponnesian War (431–404) on the side of Sparta that had spelled Athens' doom in that conflict, and Philip had no desire for the same thing to happen to him. The Persian king evidently viewed Philip's intention to invade Asia as a serious threat, for he had earlier tortured Hermeias of Atarneus for information (see p. 127). Moreover, after Philip's assassination in 336 he gave 300 talents to support a Greek revolt against Macedonia, hoping this would keep the new king (Alexander) out of Asia.

Other motives may have included the opportunity to unite the Greeks, as Isocrates had urged, especially if Philip believed his central Greek settlement was failing and needed a cause to shore it up.[82] The downside of this theory is that it fits better with the situation in 346 or the years immediately following than it does with the period after 338. The Greeks did revolt on Philip's death, but that was because of his assassination. It is a testament to how well Philip had crafted the League of Corinth that Alexander was able to resurrect it so quickly and effortlessly.

There is also the motive of greater personal glory. Whether Philip intended to campaign in Asia or just Asia Minor (see pp. 169–71), successes there would add to his reputation. News was probably reaching Greece now of Timoleon of Corinth, who with numerically smaller numbers had beaten numerous Greek tyrants and even the powerful Carthaginians in Sicily. These achievements earned him universal praise and the reputation of being the greatest Greek of his era.[83] Philip might well want the same recognition, especially as there was now nothing left for him to win in Greece. An offshoot of this was the need to keep the army on campaign, given his dependency on it: sustained military action was patently no longer possible if he remained on the Greek mainland.

But one reason that might have the edge over the others was the need to increase state revenue. Philip exploited the natural resources of Macedonia to a far greater extent than any previous king (Map 4).[84] Macedonia was an economic power to be envied, and its currency was the strongest in Europe. The mines gave the king a vast income – over 1,000 talents per annum from those at Philippi alone. The annual income of the Athenians had sunk to 137 talents at one stage and even in the mid-350s it was still only 400 talents.[85] However, throughout his reign Philip frittered away vast sums of money on his army and navy and on maintaining his court at Pella as well as on bribes to influential statesmen or to ensure the betrayal of cities to him (such as Mecyberna, Olynthus and Torone).[86] Awarding huge building contracts for temples, fortifications and the like as the reign progressed was also very costly.[87] Diodorus' comment that Philip used gold more than arms to enlarge his kingdom is not too far off the mark;[88] Theopompus and Justin were also critical of Philip's spendthrift ways.[89]

Philip practised a rolling economy, using money from one campaign to fund another, and he was almost always successful in this. By the end of the 340s he had concluded a lengthy and costly Thracian campaign. The new revenues that this campaign would generate would not be immediate, and his defeat at the hands of the Triballi on his return march to Pella had lost him a great deal of much-needed booty that could have been turned into liquid capital. He was also now gearing up for involvement in the Fourth Sacred War and of course was at war with Athens again, both of which would involve no small military presence in central Greece. There is even the possibility that the Mount Pangaeum mines may have started to run dry. Hence, Philip needed money. It was said that when Alexander invaded Persia in 334 he had no more than 70 talents in the treasury, maintenance for only thirty days, owed 200 talents and had to borrow 800.[90] This was a debt that he had clearly inherited from his father. Since the wealth of Persia was legendary, Philip's major reason for the invasion may therefore have been to generate extra revenue.

The second question is how far Philip intended to go in Asia. No contemporary source tells us what his exact goals were. Isocrates wanted him to conquer the whole Persian empire, but that was impractical in many respects, not least because with the League of Corinth in its infancy an invasion seems too ambitious a project even for Philip to have contemplated. There was always the danger of something going wrong: the famous march of the Ten Thousand as recounted by Xenophon (in the *Anabasis*) had shown the problems facing a force struggling to return to Greece. If something were to happen to Philip with the army far from home, the future of the Macedonian empire and its hegemony of Greece would be put in jeopardy. Nor, as was noted earlier, did Philip want to defeat the Great King, set up an absolute monarchy and establish his own divinity.[91]

The story goes that Philip consulted the Delphic oracle to ask about his invasion, and received the reply: 'Wreathed is the bull. All is done. There is also the one who will smite him.'[92] Apollo here was at his enigmatic best: did the oracle refer to the Persian king, who was like the sacrificial bull, ready to be toppled by Philip? Or did it refer to Philip? The king believed the former, but perhaps to his own detriment, for he died at the hands of an assassin a year later. There is a parallel with Croesus of Lydia, who wanted to end Persian rule in the sixth century. When he consulted the oracle he was told a great kingdom would fall. It did: Croesus' own.

More likely, then, is that Philip intended to operate principally in Asia Minor, which in effect was Isocrates' second choice (the aim was to establish agrarian colonies to which to send the disreputable elements on the Greek mainland). Some support for this may be inferred from an offer the Great King Darius III made to Alexander in 332. By that stage Alexander controlled all of Asia Minor, the coastline south to Egypt and Egypt itself, and had twice defeated the Persian army (at Granicus and Issus). As he returned from Egypt, our sources tell us that a letter (or several letters written over a period of time) came to him from Darius offering to buy back his family (captured after Issus) and to give all lands west of the Euphrates as far as 'the Greek Sea' to Alexander.[93] The Companions urged the king to accept. It was now that the famous exchange occurred when Parmenion said, 'If I were Alexander I would accept', to which Alexander replied, 'If I were Parmenion, I would.' Alexander continued fighting, of course. There are problems with the handling of the various diplomatic exchanges between Alexander and Darius in the sources, but the plea to ransom his family and offer of territory seem fairly secure. The readiness of the senior generals (who had served under Philip and knew his plans; Parmenion had been one of the commanders of the advance force in 336) to accept Darius' offer may indicate that it aligned with Philip's original territorial intentions.

Philip's projected campaign would involve liberating the Greek cities, and thus the expansion of his empire and an influx of new wealth. Although some sources say that he intended to overthrow the Persian king, they are problematic and/or later,[94] and could be interpreted as merely meaning that he intended to overthrow the Great King's rule in Asia Minor. Even the oracle quoted above does not specifically state the overthrow of the entire Persian empire, and it is only Diodorus who infers after citing it that Philip was planning to take on all of Asia.[95] More significant, however, is that when Alexander invaded in 334, he threw a spear into Asian soil before he landed to signify that he was taking Asia from the gods as spear-won territory.[96] His act was more than symbolic: it was to show that his invasion of Asia was very different – and more extensive – than the one his father had envisaged. That is perhaps another reason why he rejected Darius' offer of territory: precisely because it *did* refer to the territories on which Philip had set his sights.

Philip's campaign and its outcome would have brought him into conflict with the Great King of course. However, Persia was still in chaos in 338 after Artaxerxes' assassination, and his successor, Arses, was still busy trying to establish himself securely on the throne. Philip may well have calculated that Arses would be more concerned with his own position than with worrying about the Macedonian king's activities far away in Asia Minor. When Arses was murdered in 336, Philip's interpretation of Apollo's oracle seemed correct.

Thanks to Philip, the Macedonian hegemony of Greece was now a reality, anchored in the League of Corinth. Apart from a brief interruption on Philip's death in 336, when the states revolted, the settlement endured until Alexander's death in June 323. Philip never campaigned in Asia, for in July 336 he was assassinated. His invasion plan would live on, however – though Alexander deviated far from his father's original intentions as he brought it to spectacular fruition.

ASSASSINATION

Another New Queen: Philip's Marriages as Policy

Meanwhile in Pella preparations were being made for Philip's seventh (and as it turned out final) marriage to a Macedonian noblewoman, Cleopatra.[1] Still in her teens, she was a good many years Philip's junior. It seems her father and brother were both dead, and that her guardian, Attalus, a Macedonian nobleman, had at some point adopted her as his niece. Philip's previous six marriages had been military or diplomatic in motivation, as we have seen, but this one was different: with Cleopatra, so we are told, Philip was marrying for love. This break in the pattern is wont to raise eyebrows and warrants consideration of the reasons for his other marriages.

The only source that names Philip's seven wives and gives his reasons for marrying them is a fragment from a biography of the king written by the third-century BC Peripatetic biographer Satyrus, which is quoted in a much later writer, Athenaeus (second century AD). It says:[2]

> Philip of Macedon did not, like Darius (the one overthrown by Alexander, who, though fighting for the survival of his whole empire, took 360 concubines around with him, as Dicaearchus recounts in the third book of the History of Greece), take women along to war: Philip rather on each occasion used to contract marriages to do with (?according to) (the) war (currently in hand). At any rate, 'in the twenty-two years he was king', as Satyrus says in his biography of him, 'he married Audata the Illyrian and had from her a daughter Cynna. And then he married Phila, the sister of Derdas and Machatas. Then, as he wanted to appropriate the Thessalian people as well, on grounds of kingship, he fathered children by two Thessalian women, one of whom was Nikesipolis of Pherae, who bore him Thessalonike, and the other, Philinna of Larisa, by whom he fathered Arrhidaeus. Then he acquired the kingdom of the Molossians as well, by marrying Olympias. Then, in addition to all these, he married Cleopatra,

the sister of Hippostratus and niece of Attalus, having fallen in love with her. And when he brought her into household beside Olympias, he threw his whole life into confusion. For immediately, during the actual wedding celebrations, Attalus said, 'Now surely there will be born for us true-bred (i.e. legitimate) kings, and not bastards'. Now Alexander, when he heard this, threw the cup, which he was holding in his hands, at Attalus; thereupon he too threw his goblet at Alexander. After this, Olympias fled (or: went into exile) to the Molossians and Alexander (fled) to the Illyrians. And Cleopatra bore Philip the daughter named Europa.

As we know, Philip was polygamous and did not divorce one wife in order to marry another.[3] Of his first six marriages, four were to Greek-speaking women (Phila, Olympias, Philinna and Nicesipolis) and two to non-Greek-speakers (Audata and Meda), and they were all made at a time when he was either protecting or expanding Macedonia and securing his borders. In fact, his first five marriages took place quickly in the earlier part of his reign, before 352 (the sixth was a decade later in 342). Some of the wives we hear hardly anything about and they may have been nothing more than concubines (perhaps Philinna and Meda). Nicesipolis apparently died twenty days after giving birth to their daughter Thessalonike (presumably from birthing complications?), and some of the others may also have died while Philip was king. If so, that information is lost to us.

The extract above presents some problems of interpretation (as can be seen in the bracketed alternatives), and the order of Philip's wives is erroneous. That for the Thessalian wives is incorrect, probably owing to an oversight on Satyrus' part, although so much happened so quickly in the early years of Philip's reign that the details were murky.[4] What is significant is the statement that all of Philip's marriages had something 'to do with (?according to) (the) war' (the Greek phrase is *kata polemon*) apart from the last one.[5] Hence, it is commonly accepted that Philip's first six marriages were for political/military reasons and the seventh was an exception.

The accuracy of the phrase about Philip's marrying *kata polemon* has been questioned. The extract from Satyrus appears as part of an encomium on married women in the larger framework of Athenaeus' literary work.[6] The encomium dealt with Spartan promiscuity, Athenian monogamy, Socrates' alleged bigamy, and then polygamy. Thus, in citing Satyrus, Athenaeus is showing us something of the problems caused by multiple wives: Philip (who took no wives on campaign) vs Darius with his 360 concubines,[7] and especially the rift created in Philip's household when he introduced his seventh wife, Cleopatra, into it. In order to achieve his aim, Athenaeus may have adapted and 'edited' much of the actual passage from Satyrus to fit the aims of his own work, and thus – significantly – it may have been he (not Satyrus) who attributed Philip's marriages to war.[8] If this is the case, Philip's first six marriages may have had nothing to do with military affairs. But this is not so as the 'pattern' to Philip's marriages indicates they are connected to military policy.

Border security, unification and economic vitality were Philip's priorities; expansion *per se* followed on from these three. To achieve these ends, he had married five of his seven wives by 352, the year in which he was elected *archon* of Thessaly and had begun to play a more decisive role in central Greek affairs. From then on he was secure in his kingdom, his borders were protected, and his influence in Greek politics was on the rise. That may explain why he chose not to marry again for a decade (to the Thracian Meda in 342), by which time he was heavily involved in his Thracian campaign, his central Greek settlement of 346 was in a shambles, and further warfare with Athens was inevitable. The evidence is irrefutable that his first six wives came from areas that bordered Macedonia, and that the majority of his marriages occurred at a significantly early stage in his reign *kata polemon* as he fought to centralise the kingship and secure his borders.

His successes in Thrace and then over the Greeks at Chaeronea, leading to the establishment of the League of Corinth, explain the pause in his marrying cycle until 337. Since in that year he was not faced by any threats to Macedonian security, the marriage to Cleopatra seems to have had nothing to do with military matters. But is this really true? An important suggestion has recently been made that Philip had a pragmatic reason for the marriage, and that was the need for more heirs, especially as he was about to leave for Asia.[9] His other wives were perhaps now beyond safe child-bearing age. Philip had only two sons, Alexander and the mentally deficient Arrhidaeus. If something were to happen to the former, Arrhidaeus' succession might be challenged because of his mental state.

That Philip was attracted to the young Cleopatra seems beyond doubt, but more likely it is with the aforementioned practical thoughts in mind that he decided to break his *kata polemon* 'marrying pattern' and take her as his wife. Given her age, she would be expected to bear him another heir (or two) fairly quickly, although he would not anticipate that any son of theirs would displace Alexander. However, the plan, if such it was, may not have been seen in that light by everyone – and this is perhaps at the heart of the Satyrus extract about how the seventh marriage caused a rift with Olympias.

Marital Disharmony: Implications for Alexander

Olympias (Plate 10) had married Philip in 357 and given birth to Alexander in 356. She may have enjoyed some sort of seniority over the other wives because she was the mother of the heir to the throne.[10] She disliked Philip intensely, was a woman of 'bad temper', 'jealous and sullen', and apparently wasted no opportunity to criticise her husband to her son.[11] Since Philip was on campaign almost every year of his reign, there was little in the way of father–son bonding. The distance between the two of them is illustrated by the way that Alexander referred to Leonidas, his physical fitness tutor, as his foster father.[12] Alexander spent more time with his mother, and was much influenced by her. Perhaps this was one of the reasons why Philip sent him away from Pella to study under Aristotle on the eve of his campaign to Thrace.

Olympias took great pains to extend Alexander's position at court. Plutarch says that she poisoned Arrhidaeus (perhaps causing his condition) so that Alexander would become heir,[13] and sensationalist though this story is we cannot discount its veracity given Olympias' later behaviour. Justin tells us that Philip had many children, of whom some died in battle and others by accident or of natural causes,[14] but it is most odd that we do not have more information about them, not even their names. The only two sons we know about are Arrhidacus (son of Philinna of Larisa) and Alexander, and since Arrhidaeus was the oldest he was first in line to the throne. At some point he was diagnosed with a serious mental and physical disease.[15] What this was is unknown: epilepsy perhaps, or he may have suffered an accident that incapacitated him mentally – or Olympias may have poisoned him.

When Alexander's new status was bestowed on him is unknown, but it had happened by the time he turned fourteen, in 342, for in that year Isocrates wrote to him in terms that indicate he was already the heir.[16] That year would also tie in with Philip's hiring of Aristotle as his son's tutor. At no time does Amyntas, the son of Perdiccas III, whom the Assembly had set aside in 359 in favour of Philip, ever appear to have been considered as a future king. No action was ever taken against him, and he is said to have lived a privileged life at court.[17] In fact, Philip arranged for him to marry his daughter Cynnane. (One commentator has taken this to indicate that he was making Amyntas next in line behind Alexander.[18] This is highly unlikely, however, for Cynnane was the daughter of Audata of Illyria. The Macedonians' suspicion of Illyrians would hardly endear the pair, and their offspring, to the people, something Philip would have known.) Amyntas' days were numbered when Alexander succeeded his father, for the new king had him executed, and he promised Cynnane as wife to Langarus, the king of the Agrianians.[19]

Philip's seventh marriage apparently widened the already existing rift between him and Olympias, for the latter now had another person to hate: the new queen, Cleopatra.[20] This appears to have had nothing to do with any jealousy arising out of the Macedonian practice of polygamy: we certainly do not know of any similar feelings she may have harboured towards the other wives. Presumably they all lived in different areas or wings of the palace compound and may not have been around each other a lot of the time, although Plutarch does talk of 'quarrels which took place in the women's apartments' because of Philip's marriages and love affairs.[21] The main reason for her feelings towards Cleopatra, though, lies in the ethnicity of the two women and the succession, for Olympias, albeit the mother of the heir, was from Epirus, while Cleopatra was a full-blood Macedonian, perhaps from Lower Macedonia.

Philip and Alexander: The Estrangement Begins

The significance of this ethnic difference is well illustrated at the wedding of Philip and Cleopatra. As the wine flowed in abundance, the marriage feast began to turn into a typical Macedonian symposium. The women left, as was the custom, and the men continued drinking. At some point a very drunk Attalus (now Philip's father-in-law) stood up to propose a toast to the king and his new wife. There was nothing unusual in this, but he went on to pray that Macedonia might at last have a legitimate heir.[22] The implication is that he saw Alexander as illegitimate, because his mother was not Macedonian but from Epirus, and a son from the marriage of Philip and the Macedonian Cleopatra as legitimate. Further, that he expected any son from the marriage of Philip and Cleopatra to leapfrog over Alexander as heir.

The young heir was infuriated, and the two men got into a bitter argument. Alexander hurled a drinking cup at Attalus' face and called on his father to reprimand him. The already ugly situation got even worse when Philip refused. Perhaps fuelled by copious amounts of alcohol, Philip took Attalus' side and ordered Alexander to apologise. Needless to say, Alexander refused, at which point Philip drew his sword and lurched towards his son, but fell over a table in a drunken stupor. Alexander is supposed to have said contemptuously: 'Here is the man who was making ready to cross from Europe to Asia, and who cannot even cross from one table to another without losing his balance.'[23]

At that point Alexander walked out of the room, collected his mother and left the court for Epirus. We can see how strained relations were between father and son because while Olympias remained with her brother in Epirus Alexander journeyed on to Macedonia's old enemy Illyria.[24] Justin says Olympias tried to persuade her brother Alexander of Epirus to make war on Philip;[25] perhaps Alexander was trying to persuade the Illyrians to do the same.

Philip soon recalled his son Alexander to Pella, apparently swayed by the intervention of Demaratus of Corinth,[26] but bad blood continued to exist between them.[27] Olympias was still at large. Since it was Philip who had installed his brother-in-law Alexander on the throne of Epirus, he expected to be able to count on his loyalty. Then again, Philip had not got where he was by relying on such assumptions and expectations. To be on the safe side, he offered the Epirote king his daughter Cleopatra (by Olympias) in marriage – in other words, Alexander of Epirus' niece.[28] The union would tie the two ruling houses even more closely together. This plan, says Justin, neatly countered any influence Olympias may have had with her brother. Her uncle accepted, and the marriage was scheduled at Aegae (the former capital, which continued to be the venue for royal marriages and burials) for the following summer of 336.

This sudden arrangement may have prompted Olympias to return to Pella; she seems to have suffered no reprisals, and Philip did not divorce her as is sometimes thought.[29] Nonetheless, resentment continued to run high in Alexander and Olympias,[30] for Attalus had not been punished for his remark. To make matters worse, a short while later he married the daughter of Parmenion, thereby further enhancing his own status at court. The marriage of Cleopatra to Philip would have done wonders for his social and political standing anyway: he may even have adopted her as his daughter (rather than keeping her as his ward) precisely because he knew Philip had decided to make her his wife.

The reaction of Alexander and Olympias to Attalus' taunt at the wedding is significant in the deteriorating relations between both of them (especially Alexander) and the king. Alexander had suffered a personal insult at the hands of both Attalus and his father, and we can understand his angry and hurt reaction. Olympias' concerns are more surprising. It is hard to believe she really thought that a son born to Philip and Cleopatra would pose a threat to her son's succession. Alexander was almost twenty years old and the recognised heir to the throne. That had been shown in 340 when Philip made him regent, and again in 338 when he gave him a critical command on the left flank at Chaeronea (Map 6). That appointment was closely followed by his diplomatic mission to Athens as the official representative of Macedonia. Now, in 337, as plans for the invasion of Asia were taking shape and with the Greeks having just had the League of Corinth imposed on them, the last thing Philip needed was to create doubt in the mind of his son and heir about the succession. In any case, any son born to Philip and Cleopatra would always be far younger than Alexander, and so not be in a position to usurp the latter.

In reality, too much has been made of Attalus' drunken comment. His slur on Alexander's mother was probably meant as a taunt and nothing more. More than likely, given that the Macedonians liked to tell stories about themselves at their symposia, Alexander had been showing off, boasting of his role at Chaeronea, at which his annihilation of the Sacred Band would have brought him much repute. The older and distinguished Attalus might have wanted to take him down a peg or two. Since Alexander was close to his mother, any taunt that denigrated her would affect the heir. Attalus knew that Philip would hardly go to her defence given their troubled relationship, and he may have thought that, as Philip's father-in-law, he could get away with a joke in doubtful taste anyway.

Cleopatra gave birth some months after the wedding to a daughter (Europa), but this does not seem to have had any impact on Olympias and Alexander. Rather, what the two of them saw, and according to Justin led to them plotting to kill Philip, was that the marriage had brought Philip and Attalus closer together. Attalus and another general, Coenus, were married to the daughters of Parmenion, and Attalus and Parmenion would soon be named as part of the joint command of the advance force to Asia.[31] In other words, Philip and his generals were binding themselves closer together while Alexander remained on the periphery. True, he was still heir to the throne, but he was not part of that powerful inner circle. At no time was that better illustrated than at the wedding feast when Philip took the side of his relative by marriage Attalus over his son. Alexander might live at Pella as heir, but he did not share in his father's power.[32]

Attalus' taunt, incidentally, goes some way to determining whether Philip's mother, Eurydice, was Lyncestian or Illyrian.[33] If she had been the latter, then Attalus' remark would, by implication, make Philip also 'illegitimate'. It is hard to accept that Attalus did not realise this or that he thought Philip would have guffawed at being called a bastard. Hence Philip's mother was probably Lyncestian.

The Pixodarus Affair

It was probably about the winter of 337 by now, and father and son were heading for another showdown. This time the cause was Pixodarus, the Satrap of Caria, which had its capital at Halicarnassus (Bodrum) in southern Anatolia. Pixodarus was the youngest of the three sons of Mausolus, who had supported the revolting allies in the Social War of 356–355. He had become ruler of Caria in about 340 when he expelled his sister Ada, the widow (and sister) of the previous ruler, Idreus. When Bagoas murdered Artaxerxes III in 338, Pixodarus took advantage of the confusion and planned to revolt from the Great King, to whom he paid a tribute. To this end he sought an alliance with Philip.

It made sense for Pixodarus to ally himself with the Macedonian king, and the alliance was to Philip's advantage as well, for Caria would be a useful base for his manœuvres into Asia Minor. However, this was to be more than a mere agreement between the two powers: Pixodarus wanted a marriage pact with the Macedonian royal house, and he offered his oldest daughter, Ada. Marriages for political reasons were certainly not unknown to Philip, and he proposed Arrhidaeus as the would-be husband; Pixodarus accepted. At this point Alexander surprisingly became furious that Philip had overlooked him. With a complete disregard for his father the king's wishes, he ordered Thessalus, a tragic actor and close friend, to take word to Pixodarus that he was putting himself forward as husband to Ada. This union suited Pixodarus even better.[34]

The king immediately scotched Alexander's plan, not least because he wanted a better marital tie for the heir to the Macedonian empire. Negotiations with Pixodarus were now abandoned, and the alliance never took place. According to Plutarch, Philip and Philotas, the son of Parmenion, visited Alexander and the king 'angrily reproached him for behaving so ignobly and so unworthily of his position as to wish to marry the daughter of a mere Carian, who was no more than a slave of a barbarian king'.[35]

Philip exiled several of Alexander's closest friends from Pella as a warning to his son not to interfere in his plans again.[36] These friends were Harpalus, later Alexander's imperial treasurer; Nearchus, who was to sail along the Makran coast of the Indian Ocean in an epic voyage; the general Ptolemy, whose eyewitness account of Alexander's exploits is the basis of at least Arrian's narrative history of Alexander; and the brothers Erigyius and Laomedon, who would become army commanders. (Thus, we see how Alexander later rewarded his boyhood friends for their loyalty.) Philip also ordered the extradition in chains of Thessalus, who had fled to Corinth when he heard about Philip's reaction.

There is a possibility that the Pixodarus episode is an invention, given the tight chronology for the years 337 and 336,[37] but the case for dismissing it is no stronger than the case for accepting it, and it provides the most reasonable explanation for Philip's expulsion of his son's friends at this time. (The only other possible occasion for the expulsion might be after Alexander and Olympias left the court following Attalus' comment, but no source supports that.) Philip's moves against Alexander's friends perhaps indicate that they had something to do with Alexander's decision to offer himself to Pixodarus, perhaps even egging him on to put himself forward. Alexander used to say to his friends that his father would be the first to do everything and leave him with nothing great to do.[38] If this comment is true, we can see in it evidence of a growing resentment against his father, who he thought was holding him back. Presumably, his friends would have echoed his sentiments, and Philip was not the sort of man to listen idly to a chorus of criticism. What is also interesting about the whole incident is that Alexander had not merely acted out of turn, but had done so for emotional rather than rational reasons. He seems to have believed that his father was marginalising him, excluding him from the inner circle of power. The feeling grew into paranoia: something that characterises his reign. As king, Alexander personally killed or arranged to be killed Attalus, Philotas, Parmenion, Cleitus and Coenus as he replaced Philip's Old Guard with his own men.[39]

Thus ended 337, which had had its fair share of ups and downs for the royal family.

The Advance into Asia

In spring 336 Philip sent an advance guard of ten thousand Macedonians and mercenaries (the latter probably making up the bulk of this force) under the command of Parmenion, Attalus and Amyntas, son of Arrabaeus of Lyncestis, across the Hellespont to Abydus.[40] As noted before, that Attalus was appointed one of the three commanders further increased the animosity between Alexander and Philip. The advance force had an important job to do, namely to win the Asiatic Greeks' support for their liberation since no Greeks from Asia Minor had been present at Corinth when Philip announced his grand plan. If some of the mainland states were suspicious of Philip's motives, an enthusiastic response from the Asiatic Greeks might allay their concerns. Moreover, if Philip's coffers were drying up these Greeks would help his cash flow by contributing to the costs of the expedition. The advance force could hardly take on the entire Persian army on its own, and was meant to pave the way for the larger, panhellenic army that would leave after the wedding of Cleopatra to Alexander of Epirus in July, after the Etesian Winds had abated.

After reaching Asia Minor the Macedonians marched southwards down the coast. As they did so, cities as far south as Ephesus as well as several islands (such as Tenedos, Lesbos and Chios) revolted from Persian control. These places most likely now became members of the League of Corinth. Eresus (on Lesbos) erected an altar to Zeus Philippios in Philip's honour,[41] and the people of Ephesus put up a statue of him in the Temple of Artemis.[42] Both were acts of gratitude as opposed to recognitions of Philip as a god, as has been sometimes thought (see Appendix 5). Then it appears that the Macedonians suffered a defeat at the hands of the mercenary general Memnon close to Magnesia.[43] The details are sketchy, but by the following year (335) the Macedonians had suffered more reversals.[44] In 336, nonetheless, the news from Asia Minor would have been encouraging to the mainland Greeks.

Then came the thunderbolt of Philip's assassination in July.[45] Although Alexander was quickly acclaimed king, almost immediately he faced trouble from the Illyrians, a major revolt by the Greeks and competition from other possible contenders for the throne. News of Philip's murder and its worrying aftermath would probably have reached Parmenion within a matter of weeks, when the advance force had been in Asia Minor for about four or five months. Alexander would continue with his father's invasion plan, but it was obvious that nothing was going to happen until he had re-established Macedonia's control over Greece, and so Parmenion made no further advances.

Philip's Assassination: The Circumstances

How was Philip assassinated, and (especially) why? The first question is the easiest to answer. In July 336 the wedding of the king's daughter Cleopatra (by Olympias) to her uncle, Alexander of Epirus, took place in Aegae.[46] Many Macedonian nobles, together with envoys from all of the Greek states and members of the ordinary Macedonian populace, attended the wedding. It was meant to be a grand affair, with Philip planning 'brilliant musical contests and lavish banquets for his friends and guests'; the king also wanted to use the occasion to 'show himself to the Greeks as an amiable person and to respond to the honours conferred when he was appointed to the supreme command with appropriate entertainment'.[47] The Greek envoys brought with them all manner of gifts including gold crowns, and the Athenians went so far as to promise that they would never give refuge to anyone who conspired against him.

The lavish wedding was meant to celebrate a number of things. There was most obviously the marriage to bind Epirus closer to Macedonia. The League of Corinth was running smoothly, an advance army was now operating in Asia and the main army would shortly join it. Philip was about forty-six years old and, despite the injuries he had picked up over the years, had every reason to be looking forward to the new campaign. Finally, Cleopatra (Philip's wife) had only a few days before borne him a new daughter, Europa.[48]

The day after the marriage was set aside for athletic games, before which a grand procession would take place in the theatre of Aegae, which was one of the largest theatres in Greece (Plate 17). The spectators packed the theatre before dawn, and at sunrise the procession was arranged. First, statues of the twelve Olympian gods, 'wrought with great artistry and adorned with a dazzling show of wealth to strike awe in the beholder', were carried in from a side entrance. These were followed by a statue of Philip, similar to the others before it, which apparently was meant to show him 'enthroned among the twelve gods'.[49] That Philip thought himself divine, hence a thirteenth god on Olympus, is most unlikely, however (see Appendix 5).

After the statues, most likely at the same side entrance to the theatre, Philip, Alexander the heir, and Alexander the king of Epirus then appeared. Justin talks of Philip hurrying into the theatre flanked by the two Alexanders.[50] If this is true, as opposed to the two Alexanders entering first and taking their seats, they quickly moved away from the king, since Philip dismissed his royal bodyguards and walked by himself before the spectators. The idea behind this gesture was to 'show publicly that he was protected by the goodwill of the Greeks, and had no need of a guard of spearmen. Such was the pinnacle of success that he had attained.'[51] When he reached the middle of the theatre's large orchestra (the performance area, some 93 feet [28.4 m] in diameter), he stopped to face the seated crowd and receive its applause.

The cheers of the people were the last sounds that Philip ever heard. Suddenly, one of his royal bodyguards, Pausanias of Orestis (in western Macedonia), rushed forward and stabbed him in the chest.[52] The horrified onlookers watched Philip die within minutes, if not immediately, his white cloak stained red with his blood. Some of the king's bodyguards, and presumably Alexander too, rushed to his side. Where Olympias was, we do not know. The assassin tried to escape, but he slipped when his foot became caught in a vine and three of the other bodyguards speared him to death with their javelins on the spot.[53] His corpse was later crucified (to show he was a traitor). Philip II was dead at the age of forty-six.[54]

Philip's Assassination: The Motives

Why Philip was assassinated is much harder to answer. The sources give us various reasons,[55] and plenty of ink has been used up trying to explain them.[56] We shall probably never know the true story. Two explanations are usually advanced: one entirely personal, whereby Pausanias acted alone in a fit of jealous anger (this was the 'official' reason that Alexander later circulated to explain Pausanias' action); and the other more broadly political, involving a conspiracy that may well have revolved around Olympias and Alexander.

To begin with the personal reason, which is at the core of the accounts of Aristotle and Diodorus. Pausanias had had a homosexual relationship with Philip. At some point, perhaps some years earlier, the king ended the affair and took up with another man, coincidentally of the same name. Pausanias the assassin naturally felt jilted; he began to mock the new lover, calling him a hermaphrodite, and the lover complained to his friend Attalus, who had adopted Cleopatra, later Philip's seventh wife. When the new lover was killed in battle against the Illyrians while saving the king's life, Attalus (for some reason) decided to avenge him. Apparently, he lured Pausanias to his house where he and several others gang-raped him, before kicking him outside where his muleteers (who were slaves, to make matters worse) did the same thing. A furious Pausanias complained to the king. Philip sympathised, but chose to do nothing against Attalus 'because of their relationship, and because Attalus' services were needed urgently' (for the upcoming Asian expedition).[57]

In an effort to appease Pausanias, Philip promoted him within his private guard and gave him gifts. His efforts did not work; still feeling that justice had not been served, and even more angry when Attalus was made one of the commanders of the advance force to Asia Minor, Pausanias decided to kill both of them. He posted horses at the gates of the city, hid a Celtic dagger under his clothing, and when he saw Philip was alone and unguarded in the theatre stabbed him in the chest. Thus, he acted from personal reasons, and alone.

Justin gives much the same details as above, although he says that when Pausanias complained to Philip, the king fobbed him off with excuses and even ridiculed him.[58] Justin's account takes a dramatic turn when he then introduces a political motive for the assassination. He tells us that 'it was also believed that Pausanias had been suborned by Olympias, mother of Alexander, and that Alexander was not unaware of the plot to murder his father'.[59] Olympias, continues Justin, was aggrieved by her 'repudiation' and Philip's attentions to Cleopatra; Alexander was afraid that a son born of Cleopatra and Philip would rival him for the throne, and so Olympias and Alexander left the court for Epirus and Illyria, respectively. After their return (he does not mention the circumstances of this), the two of them incited Pausanias to kill Philip, and Olympias prepared the horses for his getaway. When he murdered Philip she showed her pleasure openly by putting a gold wreath on the head of the crucified Pausanias, buried him in a tomb close by that of Philip and ordered funerary offerings to be made to him every year. Plutarch also tells us that 'it was Olympias who was chiefly blamed for the assassination, because she was believed to have encouraged the young man and incited him to take his revenge, but a certain amount of accusation was also attached to Alexander'.[60]

Both reasons, personal and political, have their problems. For one thing, after Pausanias murdered Philip we are told that he tried to run to waiting horses (plural) that he had prepared for his escape.[61] If he had acted alone he would have needed only one horse. The suggestion that Olympias and Alexander were implicated in the plot comes from Justin, a much later source who puts a premium on sensationalism (as the conclusion of his account shows) and gets facts like the relationship of Cleopatra to Attalus (he says she is his sister) wrong.

Significant, though, is the inclusion of Attalus in the accounts. At the time of Philip's death he was in Asia Minor as co-commander of the advance force.

Afterwards Alexander embarked on a series of purges to rid himself of opponents, and one of those killed was Attalus (in 335). He had never forgotten his taunt at his father's marriage to Cleopatra, and doubtless nor had Olympias. It is more than likely that Attalus was included in the account of Philip's assassination to blacken his name. After all, if Pausanias had wanted to kill both Philip and Attalus, a good time to do so would have been before Attalus left for Asia!

As has been said, the real reason for the assassination may never be known. The personal explanation is sometimes preferred because it was advanced by Aristotle (himself in Pella at the time), a source usually regarded as having nothing to gain by embellishment or sensationalism. At the same time, as Alexander's former tutor, he may perhaps have been unwilling to believe that his student could conspire in so heinous a deed as patricide. That casts some doubt on his explanation. So too does the absurdly bad timing of Pausanias, sacrificing all for a private grudge. Thus, we return to a conspiracy involving Alexander and his mother, and in view of her later murderous actions it seems reasonable to conclude that she would not think twice about arranging the death of her husband.[62]

We know that Pausanias killed Philip, but why did he do so at that particular time and in full view of everyone? As the assassin of the most powerful man in the Greek world, he would hardly have been able to slip quietly into obscurity. He seems to have been swayed somewhat by his teacher, Hermocrates the sophist. The story goes that when Pausanias asked him 'how one might become most famous, the sophist replied that it would be by killing the one who had accomplished the most, for just as long as he was remembered, so long his slayer would be remembered also'.[63] But did Pausanias crave fame that much? Perhaps he thought he could flee to Persia and enlist in the service of a satrap. Yet there seems little doubt that Alexander would have hunted him down, or that sooner or later someone would have handed him over for a price. The time to kill the king (and also Attalus if he really was a target) was when he was mistreated, not months after Attalus had left for Asia Minor.

Were Alexander and Olympias Involved in the Assassination?

Both Alexander and Olympias had concerns about Philip that affected their attitude towards him. Alexander's late-teenage years were marred by his sense of being disregarded and belittled. A sixteen-year-old who is entrusted with the regency of Macedonia, and who goes on to defeat a tough enemy in battle and name a city after himself, is not the type of person who readily accepts being overlooked. Nor is the person who at eighteen played a key role in the

Battle of Chaeronea and was responsible for defeating the famed Sacred Band of Thebes. The Pixodarus incident showed Alexander who was king and who was heir. Attalus' taunt and his father's reaction showed him how seriously Philip the father and king took the hurt feelings of his son and heir. And if Cleopatra did give birth to a son, Alexander presumably thought he had cause for worry. This child might well become king on his father's death, but was it really implausible that the powerful Attalus would try to proclaim his new grandson king and even put himself forward as regent? Macedonia's history included instances of rival kings (cf. Appendix 3), and such a situation would undo the stability that Philip had achieved, as well as undermine Alexander's kingship.

Finally, and perhaps most important for Alexander at that time, Philip seems to have decided that his son would not march with him to Asia, but would stay behind as regent of Macedonia and deputy *hegemon* of the League of Corinth. Coming on top of Attalus' appointment to the advance force, this was the straw that broke the camel's back. There is no question that the job Philip picked out for Alexander was enormously important, and he clearly needed someone who had proved his worth and whom he could trust to maintain Macedonia's hegemony of Greece in his absence. Philip would also have been well aware of the danger to the Macedonian empire if both of them went to Asia and came to grief. In connection with this, he may well have been remembering the grim prophecy of Apollo at Delphi, whom he had consulted after his victory at Chaeronea. When Philip asked the god what would become of him, the reply was:

> Let me fly far from the battle at Thermodon (Chaeronea), let me take
>   refuge
> Watching from high in the clouds, as I soar with the wings of an eagle.
> Tears are for the loser, but death for the victor.[64]

The last line must have given him nightmares, and he had no wish to have both himself and his son die in Asia.

Of course, Philip probably did not mean to marginalise Alexander, but that meant little to his son, who was always quick to overreact (as the Pixodarus affair shows). He was out to establish his own military reputation, and now he was to be denied a valuable new opportunity for glory, while his father would go on to conquer new territories. We are told that:

> Whenever he heard that Philip had captured some famous city or won an
> overwhelming victory, Alexander would show no pleasure at the news, but
> would declare to his friends, 'Boys, my father will forestall me in everything.

There will be nothing great or spectacular for you and me to show the world.' He cared nothing for pleasure or wealth but only for deeds of valour and glory, and this was why he believed that the more he received from his father, the less would be left for him to conquer. And so every success that was gained by Macedonia inspired in Alexander the dread that another opportunity for action had been squandered on his father.

Alexander's earlier admiration of his father changed to resentment, with deadly consequences.[65]

When we remember that Alexander had taken refuge in Illyria and that Pausanias the assassin came from Orestis in western Macedonia, the idea of Alexander's (and his mother's) involvement in a plot that used a willing Pausanias does not seem so far-fetched.[66] Is it merely a coincidence that Philip was murdered the day after the wedding of his daughter to Alexander of Epirus as part of a plan to limit Olympias' influence at the Epirote court? Or that his son Alexander had found out so recently that Philip was going to march to Asia without him?

Even more significantly, is it mere coincidence that, in 331, when Alexander visited the oracle of Zeus Ammon at the Oasis of Siwah in Egypt, he apparently asked whether all of those implicated in his father's murder had been punished?[67] Patricide was a heinous crime. He visited this oracle for a number of reasons, but why would he ask about his father's murder, five years after the event, unless some suspicion was still attached to him? Mud sticks, and if any were sticking to him it would be completely washed off when the god responded that all those implicated in his father's murder had indeed been punished.

AFTER PHILIP

Reactions

The assassination of Philip had widespread repercussions, not least being the Greeks' revolt from the League of Corinth. According to Aeschines,[1] scouts of the Athenian general Charidemus were the first people to send news of Philip II's death to Athens, and Charidemus may at that time have been involved in covert military activities in Thrace. An ecstatic Demosthenes persuaded the Boule to make a public sacrifice of thanksgiving and to vote a crown for Pausanias (the assassin), and then he 'appeared in public dressed in magnificent attire and wearing a garland on his head, although his daughter had died only six days before'.[2] The incident shows us the level of his hatred for Philip since he doted on his daughter and the normal mourning period was one month.

In Macedonia, Philip's death was met with chaos and anxiety:

In Philip's army, reactions to his death varied with the different nationalities of which it was composed. Some renewed their hopes of liberty believing they were held in unjust servitude; others, tired of service far from home, were happy to have been spared the expedition [to Asia]; a number grieved that a torch lit for a daughter's marriage had been put to her father's funeral pyre. The sudden turn of events had also caused the late king's friends no little trepidation as their thoughts turned to Asia, which had been challenged to fight; then to Europe, which was still not totally subdued; then to the Illyrians, the Thracians, the Dardanians and the other barbarian tribes of dubious loyalty and unstable character – a simultaneous uprising by all these peoples would be impossible to check.[3]

At the capital we are told that Alexander's friends armed themselves in case of trouble, and that 'all of Macedonia was ablaze with discontent, and was looking to Amyntas and the sons of Aeropus'.[4] Friends arming themselves in case of trouble may simply indicate that it was not immediately clear whether Alexander's life was also in danger – after all, Pausanias might have had an accomplice whose job was to kill the heir to the throne. The 'looking to' the individuals named perhaps indicates that Alexander's succession was not set in stone. Amyntas was Perdiccas III's son and Philip's nephew (the true heir to the throne in 359). The three sons of Aeropus of Lyncestis (who had been exiled by Philip),[5] were Arrhabaeus, Heromenes and Alexander (Antipater's son-in-law). If they were taking advantage of Philip's sudden death, then the king's campaigns to secure his western frontier early in his reign and subsequent founding of colonies might not have kept the area in check as he had hoped.[6]

Alexander Becomes King

In the event no trouble came for Alexander, probably because of Antipater's swift action in leading him before the people and proclaiming him king.[7] The people assented, and from Asia Minor Parmenion also proclaimed his loyalty. In the meantime Alexander had called a formal Assembly to allay fears and offer encouragement.[8] So it was that in these circumstances Alexander III succeeded to the throne of Macedonia.

The new king's first duty was the funeral of his father, which was to take place at Aegae. While busying himself with this task as well as the Greek revolt, he conducted a series of purges to eliminate his opponents.[9] These continued for the remainder of the year and into the next (335). Alexander immediately executed the three sons of his father's assassin, Pausanias (under Macedonian law, traitors and their families could be executed), followed by Arrhabaeus and Heromenes (Alexander was spared for a while), and Amyntas son of Perdiccas. Later, he sent a letter to Parmenion in Asia ordering him to kill his old enemy Attalus.[10] In the meantime Olympias killed Philip's seventh wife, Cleopatra, and her baby daughter Europa.[11] Alexander's half-brother Arrhidaeus was spared, an indication perhaps of a closer familial bond with him.

Philip's Burial

While the first round of executions was under way, Philip's funeral took place. The dead king's body, along with his arms and armour, was placed on a great pyre, past which marched the entire Macedonian army. Arrhabaeus and Heromenes were executed next to it, as were the horses to which Pausanias the assassin had tried to flee. The corpses and harnesses of the horses were then also thrown onto the pyre. After the flames had died down, Philip's bones were taken down, washed in wine, wrapped in a purple robe and placed in a gold *larnax* or box, emblazoned on its lid with the Macedonian starburst (a sixteen-point star), the emblem of the royal house, and rosettes.

The *larnax* was put inside a stone sarcophagus. It was to be buried in a tomb (constructed by Alexander), along with various funerary goods, such as gold and silver vessels, other pieces of the king's arms and armour, and a series of small ivory heads of the royal family that were placed on a wooden couch. The tomb was later covered with earth to form a large tumulus, 43 feet (13 m) high and 328 feet (100 m) in diameter. In its fill were thrown various objects from the royal burial including the corpses of Arrhabaeus and Heromenes and the horse paraphernalia. Over two millennia later, in the modern village of Vergina (ancient Aegae), a tumulus was excavated (Plate 18). Inside it were found four tombs, one of which (Tomb II) may well hold the remains of Philip and one of his wives: for detailed discussion, see Appendix 6.

The Revolt of Greece

The Greek revolt was a serious one. Some states lent only vocal support while others resorted to actual military action. The Ambracians and Thebans expelled the Macedonian garrisons and oligarchies that Philip had set up as part of his settlement of Greece after Chaeronea. The Thessalians seized the Tempe Pass and were ready to defy Alexander if he marched on them. Alexander could not allow the Macedonian hegemony of Greece to be undone, given his eagerness to invade Asia, so he marched south at speed. He ended the revolt almost as quickly as it had begun. We are told that he won over some cities by diplomacy, others by striking fear into them, and others again by actual force.[12] First, in Thessaly he re-established his position in the Amphictyonic Council, and it was perhaps at this time that he became, like his father, lifelong *archon* of Thessaly.[13] Second, at Corinth he called together representatives from the Greek states, as his father had first done a little over a year previously, and resurrected the League of Corinth. He was now its *hegemon*, and the Greeks (with the exception of Sparta) swore an oath of allegiance to him.[14] Alexander had faced no trouble from Epirus, so the marriage that Philip had arranged between Alexander of Epirus and Cleopatra was working well. Some five years later Alexander of Epirus misguidedly invaded Italy and was killed in fighting.

Alexander's Early Campaigns: The Destruction of Thebes

The Macedonian hegemony of Greece was now a fact again, but to the north there appeared to be trouble from the Triballi and the Illyrians. In 335 Alexander led an army against both of them – perhaps his motive in the case of the former was to avenge what Philip had suffered at their hands on his way home from Thrace. Some three thousand of the Triballi were killed, while Alexander's army was reputed to have lost a mere eleven cavalry and forty-one infantry. Alexander was gaining the upper hand in Illyria when he learned that Thebes had defied him again. In addition to calling the other Greeks to arms, the Thebans may have been offering political asylum to Amyntas, even with a view to establishing him on the throne.[15] Alexander marched south at such speed that the Thebans at first did not believe it was him because of the distance he would have had to travel.[16] He gave the people one chance to surrender; when they refused, he besieged the city. It fell soon after, and as an example to the other Greeks of how resistance to Macedonia would be punished he had the city razed to the ground and its people either killed or enslaved.[17]

Philip and Alexander admired enemies who fought resolutely and conducted themselves nobly against them. Philip's reaction to the dead Sacred Band at Chaeronea is an example of this, as is Alexander's order to give Darius a royal burial in Asia. Another example dates from the sack of Thebes. A Macedonian soldier had raped a noble lady by the name of Timocleia, the sister of Theagenes who had fought at Chaeronea (and had perhaps even commanded the Sacred Band). Afterwards she had lured the soldier down a well on her property, saying she had thrown her silver bowls, gold and money into it, and had then stoned him to death. She did not beg for mercy when brought before Alexander, but looked him in the eyes and said:

> Theagenes was my brother, who was a general at Chaeronea. He died fighting against you while defending the freedom of Greece so that we might not suffer an outrage like this. Since I have suffered an outrage that is unworthy of my status, I am ready to die. It is better to die than to experience another night like the last one, which is what will happen to me unless you forbid it.[18]

Alexander was so impressed by her demeanour that he gave orders that she was not to be harmed.

Alexander Invades Asia

It was late 335 when Alexander returned to Pella to hone the plans for the invasion of Asia in the following spring. The last of his opponents, real or potential, was dead, Greece was again passive, and Alexander could finally set his sights on the military glory he was so anxious to win for himself. He had decided that Antipater should remain behind as guardian (*epitropos*) of

Greece and Macedonia and to act as deputy *hegemon* of the League of Corinth. At some stage he had recalled Parmenion from Asia Minor to Pella to help with his preparations. That recall gave the Persians the opportunity to recapture many of the cities won over by the advance force the previous year. When Alexander invaded in 334, however, he would quickly reverse those Persian gains, after which the liberated cities of Asia Minor most likely became members of the League of Corinth again.

In spring 334 the young king (he was at that time only twenty-two) crossed the Hellespont and invaded Asia. He took with him a force of 48,100 soldiers and 6,100 cavalry, together with a fleet of 120 warships and transport vessels with a total complement of about 38,000.[19] While he was away, Greece remained quiescent, apart from an attempt to unite the Greeks against Macedonian rule led by Agis III of Sparta in 331. This met with no success, and the following year Agis was defeated and killed by Antipater.[20] Alexander would never return to Greece, but would die in Babylon in 323. His dazzling exploits in Asia, where in his short reign of only thirteen years he would conquer the entire Persian empire, including Egypt, extend Macedonia's empire from Greece in the west to what the Greeks called India (today, Pakistan) in the east, and open up a new world to the mainland Greeks, are another story.

Demosthenes: Later Career and Death

Greece as a whole prospered under the Macedonian hegemony,[21] although this does not mean that the Greeks were happy about the arrangement. In Athens, for example, Demosthenes and Hyperides refused Alexander's demand for Athenian ships in 335,[22] but after this time Demosthenes' opposition to Macedonia was far more muted. None of his speeches from the reign of Alexander is extant, but we know that he made some and for a while hoped that Alexander 'would be trampled underfoot by the Persian cavalry'.[23]

He continued to clash with Aeschines, who in 330 attempted to discredit him completely in the famous Crown trial. Its origins lie in 336, in which year Ctesiphon proposed that Demosthenes be awarded a gold crown in recognition of his services to Athens.[24] Aeschines had prevented this at the time by arguing at an Assembly that a magistrate could not receive an award like this while he was still in office (which was true) and, further, that Demosthenes had never advised the best policies for Athens and so never acted in the city's best interests. The matter fell by the wayside until 330, when Aeschines decided the time was ripe to attack Demosthenes in court. He was ultimately unsuccessful.[25]

Aeschines brought a charge against Ctesiphon for the illegality of his proposal in 336; his speech is called *Against Ctesiphon*. Since Aeschines had

Demosthenes in his cross hairs, Ctesiphon gave only a short defence speech before Demosthenes stood up to rebut Aeschines' case in his speech *On the Crown.* We have the speeches of Aeschines and Demosthenes from this trial (just as we do from the false embassy trial of 343), which is unusual in forensic oratory and shows the importance of the case as both speeches were revised for posterity. Both are valuable historical sources for the period, although they are full of rhetorical embellishments and tricks.[26] Demosthenes' speech deals with his entire political career, and is a massive justification for his policies towards Macedonia. In the end the jurors at the trial were convinced; so much so, in fact, that Aeschines did not even win one-fifth of their votes.[27] Afterwards he retired to Rhodes, where he established a school of rhetoric. There is a story that he would recite his losing speech to his students, and when they expressed surprise that he had lost he would tell them that if they had heard Demosthenes' speech they would understand why.[28]

After the trial Demosthenes finally got his crown for services to the city. He then remained out of the limelight until 324, when the disgraced imperial treasurer Harpalus fled to Athens to try to stir up a revolt against Macedonia. Demosthenes did not support Harpalus; in fact, he arranged for his incarceration, but at some later stage Harpalus escaped. It was believed that Demosthenes and several other politicians and generals had taken bribes from the former treasurer. So serious was the matter that the Areopagus conducted a special investigation into the affair and alleged that Demosthenes had received a bribe of 20 talents (an enormous sum). He was put on trial in 323; although no actual evidence was brought against him, he was found guilty and fled into exile. The fact that no evidence could be produced and that some of the others accused of taking bribes were exculpated (when no evidence existed against them either) suggests that this was a political trial designed to remove Demosthenes from political life once and for all.[29]

When Alexander died in June 323, the Greeks revolted once more against Macedonian rule in what is commonly called the Lamian War.[30] Demosthenes, still in exile, played no small role in persuading other states to join the revolt, and he was officially pardoned by Athens in the first year of the conflict. The Lamian War was short-lived; despite some early Greek successes against Antipater, the Greek fleet was destroyed in the summer of 322, and not long after Antipater defeated a Greek army at the Battle of Crannon (in Thessaly). The Athenians' fate was inglorious. They were ordered to surrender the anti-Macedonian leaders to Antipater; a Macedonian garrison was stationed at Munychia (a hill in the Piraeus, the port of Athens); and Athenian citizenship was henceforth to be based on wealth alone. Although the numbers are not certain, up to twelve thousand Athenians may have been disfranchised by this last measure, with only nine thousand citizens (i.e., those above the wealth limit of 2,000 drachmas) being allowed to remain in the city.[31] Demosthenes was condemned to death but fled to Calauria (modern Poros). When Antipater's men tracked him down, he committed suicide by drinking poison.[32]

Thus ended the life of the greatest of all Greek orators, whose anti-Macedonian policy may well have destroyed Greece's independence, but whose steadfast defiance of Philip's imperialism and oratorical prowess, passion and patriotism influenced many who came after him. For example, Cicero titled his famous speeches against Mark Antony the *Philippics*,[33] and Cicero, Horace and Juvenal echoed Demosthenes in relating how Philip had bribed his way to his successes.[34] The ideals of the ancient world are frequently taken up in the modern. Thus, in London during World War I, parts of Pericles' funeral oration in Thucydides (of 430) on the value of democracy were displayed on public buses.[35] A similar use was made of Demosthenes, for in the 1930s Winston Churchill likened himself to Demosthenes and Hitler to Philip. To earlier scholars Demosthenes was a hero and Greece's staunchest patriot.[36] In more recent years Demosthenes' policy has rightly been questioned,[37] but it is worth bearing in mind that, given the weaknesses of the *polis* system, no state could have effectively opposed Philip II.

PHILIP IN RETROSPECT:
KING, MAN – AND GOD?

King and Man

This book began with Philip's victory at Chaeronea, the culmination of the career of a remarkable king who transformed Macedonia into an imperial power, but who died before he could go on to accomplish greater deeds. It is impossible not to praise Philip or to call his legacy anything but brilliant. We need only compare Macedonia in 359 (see Appendix 3) when he became king to its standing in 336 at the time of his death to note the very obvious differences in both kingdom and kingship. By the time he died, after a reign of only twenty-four years, his empire stretched from southern Greece to the Danube. His military reforms revolutionised both army and state, and he left Alexander with the best army in the Greek world, an empire, a centralised monarchy, no external threats, a stable and growing economy, no dynastic upheavals and general prosperity. What had led to many of his accomplishments was his enforced stay as a teenager in Thebes, where he saw how a state could fuse together military and diplomatic prowess to achieve power. Yet Philip was careful not to have his state suffer the same fate as Thebes, and the marriage of his daughter Cleopatra to Alexander of Epirus in 336 was the 'mass-media event' in today's parlance that showed how successful he had been in this respect.

Moreover, it is not just us today who can speak highly of Philip; the evaluations of our two narrative sources for his reign, Diodorus and Justin (from Trogus), are very fitting.[1] Diodorus has this to say in his concluding comments about Philip:

Such was the end of Philip, who had made himself the greatest of the kings in Europe in his time, and because of the extent of his kingdom had made himself a throned companion of the twelve gods. He had ruled twenty-four years. He is known to fame as one who with but the slenderest resources to support his claim to a throne won for himself the greatest empire in the Greek world, while the growth of his position was not due so much to his prowess in arms as to his adroitness and cordiality in diplomacy. Philip himself is said to have been prouder of his grasp of strategy and his diplomatic successes than of his valour in actual battle. Every member of his army shared in the successes which were won in the field, but he alone got credit for victories won through negotiations.

Justin is likewise laudatory, bringing into his summation an interesting comparison between Philip and Alexander:

(4) [Philip] . . . was a king with more enthusiasm for the military than the convivial sphere; (5) in his view his greatest treasures were the tools of warfare. (6) He had a greater talent for acquiring wealth than keeping it, and thus despite his daily pillaging he was always short of funds. (7) His compassion and his duplicity were qualities which he prized equally, and no means of gaining a victory would he consider dishonourable. (8) He was charming and treacherous at the same time, the type to promise more in conversation than he would deliver, and whether the discussion was serious or lighthearted he was an artful performer. (9) He cultivated friendships with a view to expediency rather than from genuine feelings. His usual practice was to feign warm feelings when he hated someone, to sow discord between parties that were in agreement and then try to win the favour of both. (10) Besides this he was possessed of eloquence and a remarkable oratorical talent, full of subtlety and ingenuity, so that his elegant style was not lacking fluency, nor his fluency lacking stylistic elegance. (11) Philip was succeeded by his son Alexander, who surpassed his father both in good qualities and bad. (12) Each had his own method of gaining victory, Alexander making war openly and Philip using trickery; the latter took pleasure in duping the enemy, the former in putting them to flight in the open. (13) Philip was the more prudent strategist, Alexander had the greater vision. (14) The father could hide, and sometimes even suppress, his anger; when Alexander's had flared up, his retaliation could be neither delayed nor kept in check. (15) Both were excessively fond of drink, but intoxication brought out different shortcomings. It was the father's habit to rush from the dinner party straight at the enemy, engage him in combat and recklessly expose himself to danger; Alexander's violence was directed not against the enemy but against his own comrades. (16) As a result Philip was often brought back from his battles wounded while the other often left a dinner with his friends' blood on his hands. (17) Philip was unwilling to share the royal power with his friends; Alexander wielded it over his. The

father preferred to be loved, the son to be feared. (18) They had a comparable interest in literature. The father had greater shrewdness, the son was truer to his word. (19) Philip was more restrained in his language and discourse, Alexander in his actions. (20) When it came to showing mercy to the defeated, the son was temperamentally more amenable and more magnanimous. The father was more disposed to thrift, the son to extravagance. (21) With such qualities did the father lay the basis for a worldwide empire and the son bring to completion the glorious enterprise.

Philip's achievements and character certainly live up to the contents of these passages. He turned Macedonia from a near-feudal, tribal society into the first nation-state in Europe, in the process doubling its size and population. The systematic reduction of previous enemies within Upper Macedonia and elsewhere on his frontiers, especially Illyria, Paeonia, Thrace and the Chalcidice, plus the removal of foreign influences from towns on Macedonian soil, such as Pydna and Methone, and a new centralised government at Pella, created border security and a unified Upper and Lower Macedonian kingdom for the first time in its history. Philip's ultimate accomplishment has been succinctly summed up as his 'systematic improvement of the security of the state firmly rooted in the monarchy'.[2]

In place of the poorly trained and equipped conscript army that was gathered together hastily to defend, never to attack, he left a first-class professional army. In addition to new tactics, training and weaponry (especially the sarissa, Plate 9), Philip created an engineering corps, whose developments in siegecraft laid the groundwork for Alexander's famous sieges, especially with the development of the torsion catapult (Figure 2). Among the army's ranks were (importantly and cleverly) provincial regiments and commanders from Upper Macedonia, who had previously been the king's enemies and were now part of a larger whole. Grants of land to individuals as the reign progressed (for example, in the Chalcidice) also fostered loyalty to the king. The integration of foreigners did pose problems that had to be monitored, but the dangers they presented were ultimately outweighed by the successes of the army.

The military reforms that were at the heart of Philip's policy to unite Macedonia also fed its economic development.[3] He was intent on exploiting Macedonia's natural resources and promoting trade and the economy to an unprecedented degree. It is interesting to see that even in his earliest campaigns (of 358 against the Paeonians and Illyrians) he had one eye on established trade routes, and as he expanded the kingdom southwards and eastwards he was careful to take advantage of such routes. There was already agricultural land in abundance in Macedonia, and Philip added substantially to this by his conquests, and by other improvements such as land reclamation and irrigation practices. Trade and communications were improved by the building of new roads and towns, and urban centres developed as small towns became organised cities, as is shown by progress in urban planning, administration and social structures.[4] Income in the form of taxes, harbour dues and the like from places that became part of the Macedonian empire (such as the Thessalian League and Thrace), not to mention booty from defeated enemies (such as the twenty thousand Scythian horses), also flowed into state coffers.

The areas in which Philip stimulated the economy most significantly were mining and coinage. He revised the state's weights and minted new, standard coinage.[5] His new silver tetradrachms (Plates 6 and 13) weighed ½ oz (14.5 g) like those of the Chalcidian League and Amphipolis, the major silver coins in the region until the mid-340s. His new gold staters (Plate 15) weighed (⅓ oz (9.5 g) and replaced the Persian daric, which until his time was the main gold coin. There was also a new, large bronze coin to replace the smaller denominations of the silver coins. All of these were minted at Pella (the main mint), Amphipolis and Philippi (silver until 348, then gold), and circulated widely. This immediately took Macedonia into the international market. Regardless of the state of the Macedonian treasury when Philip died, the success of his economic reforms is obvious, and Macedonian coinage became the strongest in Europe.

Relations between the Greeks and Macedonians underwent radical change thanks to Philip. When he became king his goal was to secure – by diplomacy, deceit and military force when and where needed – his borders and to try to end foreign involvement in domestic and regal affairs. Machiavelli would have approved of the way he achieved this, given that Justin says Philip was 'charming and treacherous at the same time' and the 'type to promise more in conversation than he would deliver'. Would we not expect a king fighting to unite his kingdom, to protect its borders from invasion and to defy interference on the part of hostile Greek powers to 'cultivate friendships with a view to expediency rather than from genuine feelings'? While we might indeed describe Philip as Machiavellian, we cannot go so far as to say with Churchill that he was a classical Hitler.[6]

Yet Philip's successes at home embroiled him in Greek politics. His first war with the Athenians did not see him marching south; it was his alliance with Thessaly and the latter's appeals for assistance during the Third Sacred War that first brought him physically into central Greece. Not that this implies any intention on his part to conquer Greece: he might still help to defeat Phocis, make peace and an alliance with Athens, and go home.

That was not to be. His defeat at the hands of Onomarchus, followed by the desertion of the army, proved a turning point. He restored his military leadership with some difficulty, but for his own sake and that of Macedonian security he could not allow a similar situation to arise again, especially if it involved discontent in Upper Macedonia. Keeping his army active in Macedonia clearly would not be enough, hence he resolved to play a more integral role in Greek affairs. This may be seen in the dramatic manner of his return, his men wearing laurel wreaths and he styled as Apollo's Saviour. Such involvement also gave him the chance to turn the tables on Thebes, which had a history of interfering in Macedonian domestic politics and in which city he had lived as a hostage as a youngster. Revenge was sweet. When Philip brought the Third Sacred War to an end and concluded peace with Athens in 346, he was a power to be reckoned with in Greece, something that he, and certainly the Greeks, could hardly have foreseen in the chaos of his accession.

Still hoping that he could maintain amicable relations with the Greeks, Philip kept up diplomatic contacts with them, even when Demosthenes was rousing his former allies the Athenians against him. When diplomacy failed, he declared war in 341, which culminated in the last stand, and Greek defeat, at Chaeronea in 338. After his establishment of the League of Corinth, the constitutional machinery by which Macedonian hegemony over Greece was assured, the Greeks could no longer sneer at their northern neighbours. The propaganda of the new coins promoted Macedonia and Philip and empha- sised their power (as the inscription *Philippou* proclaimed) wherever they circulated in the ancient world. In 337 that power was sufficiently great and secure for the king to turn to his next imperial venture, the invasion of Asia.

None of Philip's achievements happened by chance: his calculated combination of diplomacy and military action systematically defeated his enemies.[7] Apart from military intervention in the Chalcidice, in the Sacred Wars and at Chaeronea, he achieved his positions in Greece (*archon* of Thessaly, member of the Amphictyonic Council, President of the Pythian Games, Commander of the Amphictyonic army in the Fourth Sacred War and *hegemon* of the League of Corinth) by diplomacy, and even ancient writers commended him for this.[8]

Central to his policy of border security was his use of political marriages. Six of his seven wives came from areas that bordered Macedonia, and five of his marriages occurred in the earlier part of his reign (by 352) as he consolidated power. A decade later, involved in Thrace and with war with Athens looming, he married again (Meda of Thrace). Thus, we see him marrying, as Satyrus would say, for reasons to do with war, *kata polemon* (see p. 173). The break in the marrying cycle seems to come with Cleopatra in 337, at a time when he was not faced by any threats to Macedonian security, having defeated the Greeks at Chaeronea and established the League of Corinth. Perhaps, then, his marriage to Cleopatra was for love, or, on the eve of his Asian expedition, contracted with a view to producing another heir – or both. Regardless, we can see a pattern to Philip's marriages, and presumably if he had lived to invade Asia, there would have been an eighth wife.

As a man, he must have been engaging, a lover of life and probably a great raconteur. He needed to be, for if the reconstructed face is accurate in its detail, he would not have endeared himself to people with his looks (Plate 1). He was certainly afraid of no one and nothing, and never shirked his responsibilities, remaining the traditional Macedonian warrior king to the end.[9] He treated embassies to him lavishly – better than the Athenians looked after embassies to them, apparently – and a large colonnaded area of his palace complex was reserved for greeting foreign ambassadors. At the same time, he did not think twice of using bribery or deceit to achieve his goals, and he was ruthless with his enemies when he needed to be. In these regards he was no different from the Greeks, and he resorted to such measures in the best interests of his state.

There are other downsides to Philip's reign, especially the character of his rule. It is significant that in his description of the king's transpopulation of peoples (probably in 345), Justin (from Trogus) talks of the people's 'silent, forlorn dejection, as men feared that even their tears might be taken to signify opposition', of how the evacuees looked wistfully at all they were leaving, and that 'everywhere it was a dismal picture, almost of desolation' (see p. 109 for the full description).[10] One cannot expect people to be happy at being forced to relocate to other parts of the kingdom, especially on the dangerous western frontier. However, the passage suggests more than grumpiness at having to move home. If the people refused to go, what would Philip do to them? Their reluctance to show opposition even with their tears indicates that if they did they knew they were letting themselves in for harsh treatment at his hands. They must have suffered this before and had no wish for it to be repeated. Perhaps one occasion was after the army deserted when Onomarchus defeated it in 353; hence, it was not just Philip's oratorical prowess that persuaded his men to continue the fight.

Moreover, in the context of the amount of money Philip was spending on various public works, Justin says that Philip invited contractors to his kingdom. 'When these contractors arrived in Macedonia, however, they were put off by various excuses, and so they left without complaint out of fear of the violent character of his rule.'[11] What these illuminating passages portray is a rule of fear, of people staying loyal to their king out of fear rather than out of admiration, despite his achievements. This is in stark contrast to the adulation of the crowd for Philip at Aegae in 336, the day of his assassination.

The surprising desertions that followed his defeat (hardly an annihilation) in 353, taking place as they did after Philip had been king for six years and had more than proved himself, led to his rethinking relations with his army, the body in which the kingdom's unity was anchored.[12] That defeat had repercussions elsewhere, with both Cersebleptes in Thrace and the Olynthians turning their backs on him and – again – threats of invasion from the Paeonians and Illyrians, all of which spelled trouble for Macedonian security. This is the time when Philip realised the extent to which his kingship was dependent on the army despite his accomplishments elsewhere.

Philip was quick to reverse the defeat with a crushing victory some months later over Onomarchus at the Battle of the Crocus Field. Now it became imperative to keep the army on campaign, and winning. He had, after all, come to power in extraordinary circumstances, and the real heir to the throne (Amyntas) was still alive. Philip campaigned in every year of his reign; while the army was victorious his position was secure, and the Macedonian people enjoyed the prosperity that came from his victories. After he had subdued Greece and established the League of Corinth in 337, one motive for the upcoming invasion of Persia was to keep the army deployed. Hence, the army was both a source of power for Philip and a weakness. The same is true for Alexander, who was faced by two mutinies. The first (in India) forced him to turn back from marching further east, and the second (at Opis) was a reaction to the unpopularity of his policies and his pretensions to divinity.[13]

Another criticism of Philip, echoed by the sources, concerns his inability to manage money.[14] The cost of maintaining his army, navy (albeit a small one) and court would have been enormous. There was also the near-constant and substantial outlay in bribes to Greeks, and lesser costs for such things as awarding building contracts for temples, fortifications and the like.[15] Even so, Macedonian kings owned all of the state's natural resources such as mines and farmland, and as such received income from them. Philip had added dramatically to Macedonia's holdings, and hence to the state's and to personal incomes. Yet he seems to have been running short of the finances towards the end of his reign if money really was a reason for invading Asia. Then again, as has been noted, Philip practised a rolling economy, using money from one campaign to fund another or income from one area to develop another.[16] We should also make the distinction between liquid capital (which Philip may well have needed after the lengthy campaign in Thrace followed so quickly by renewed involvement in central Greece) as opposed to possessions.

Philip's Divinity?

Macedonian kings were likely regarded as semi-divine while alive, and deified on death. However, a number of ancient sources (literary and material) indicate that towards the end of his life Philip thought he was divine or deserved divine recognition. For example, Diodorus tells us that in the procession at Aegae in 336 (the day of Philip's murder) statues of the twelve gods were carried along with a thirteenth statue, 'suitable for a god', of Philip himself, so that he 'exhibited himself enthroned among (*sunthronon*) the twelve gods'.[17] The statues of the royal family in the Philippeion at Olympia may indicate a royal cult, and we are told that there was a cult to Philip at Amphipolis, a statue of him in the Temple of Artemis at Ephesus, altars to Zeus Philippios at Eresus (on the island of Lesbos), and that even the Athenians worshipped him.

If Philip did seek divine honours, the implications are far-reaching. They obviously affect his rule and his goals, and it has been argued that by 336 his aim was to establish an autocratic rule, along the lines of the Great King of Persia, over his European and Asian empire, and that divine honours were a sign of this.[18] They also affect Alexander's belief in his own divinity and the aims of his invasion of Asia – whether he inherited a plan to invade Asia Minor only and extended it as his reign progressed, as is most often thought,[19] or whether he adopted the grand designs of his father from the outset. We will return to Alexander in Chapter 16.

A close examination of the ancient evidence, however, reveals no compelling grounds for believing that Philip sought divine honours in 336. For example, Diodorus does not refer to Philip's statue as an *agalma* (the Greek word for a cult statue) but as an *eikon*, which was simply a statue of a person, with no religious connotations. The Philippeion was a secular, not a religious, building; Philip's statue at Ephesus was an honorary, not a religious, one; and at Eresus the link to Zeus shows the people were worshipping Zeus in his role as Philip's protector. In the case of the Athenians, the evidence is later and is perhaps influenced by a proposal made towards the end of Alexander's reign to recognise him as a thirteenth god. All of the evidence (which includes more than that cited here) is discussed in detail in Appendix 5, to which the reader is directed.

It is plausible that our sources imposed the later Hellenistic and Roman practice of carrying statues of rulers into a theatre as part of a ruler-cult onto the procession at Aegae, and hence Philip was made to appear to have divine aspirations when nothing was further from his pragmatic mind.

Conclusions

The fourth century is arguably the most important in Greek history, for thanks to Philip we see the end of Greek autonomy, the failure of the city-state (*polis*) system, and the rise of the first nation-state under Philip.[20] Theopompus and Demosthenes were wrong to say that Philip owed his successes in Greece to his use of bribery;[21] his triumphs were certainly helped considerably by the Greeks themselves, or rather by their *polis* system. Greek inter-state xenophobia was a breeding ground for social and military instability and subversion, and for much of the fifth and fourth centuries many of the Greek states were at war with each other: 'for all their attempts to impose their rule on each other, they only succeeded in losing their ability to rule themselves. With no restraint they rushed into mutual destruction, and realised only in subjection that what they forfeited individually constituted a loss for them all.'[22]

Contemporary writers acknowledged the problems. Aristophanes used the plot of his comedy *Lysistrata* (produced in 411) to call for change after the Athenians were massively defeated in Sicily, losing most of their fleet and much manpower. Plato had gone on record that only philosopher kings could properly govern states and restore stability.[23] In 346 Isocrates urged Philip to head a panhellenic invasion of Asia, but it is clear that he did so not so much for Philip's sake but rather as a means of ending the civil disunity in Greece as he saw it.[24]

The truth is that the *polis* system was outdated and worked against the Greeks' common interests, but they did nothing about it, hence 'perhaps the end of Greek liberty was inevitable.'[25] Philip might indeed have superiority in the field, but he campaigned little in Greece compared to Upper Macedonia and Thrace, for example, because he was able to exploit the weaknesses of the *poleis* and achieve what he wanted through diplomacy and bribery. Demosthenes is not far off the mark when he says that Philip was aware of Greek disunity and resorted to bribery to stir up further animosity between the states.[26] Indeed, if he had resorted to a military conquest of Greece earlier in his reign, the sheer number of the Greek states would have forced him to maintain an army in Greece permanently. Hence, he might have bitten off more than he could chew given the recurring problems on Macedonia's borders and to its east. Recognising this, he turned to other methods.

The only state that might have resisted him was Athens, which to an extent explains his careful dealings with the city (more careful than with any other state),[27] although keeping Thebes in check was at the heart of his policy too. Nevertheless, Athens had its weaknesses. Demosthenes was right to criticise the people for their sloth in resisting Philip II, and for their reliance on mercenaries and not citizen soldiers. He even contrasted Philip's willingness to sacrifice his own body and the injuries he received (his blinded eye, broken collarbone and maimed leg) in the pursuit of power, honour and glory with the Athenians' apathy.[28] Yet ultimately it was the Athenian form of democracy that was at fault, for it could not run a war, often indicted its generals, and was slow and cumbersome. If Philip had been born in Athens, he could not even have been a member of the Boule or served on a jury until he was thirty – by which age, he had had secured all of Macedonia's borders and started to make serious inroads into Thrace and central Greece – and he would always have been held in check by the democracy.[29] That democracy and some of its demagogic leaders had failed spectacularly during the Peloponnesian War and ultimately cost the city victory, yet the Athenians failed to draw any lessons from this. Multiple meetings of the Assembly, in which the people were all too easily swayed by the rhetoric of a few individuals, were no match for the single-minded purposefulness of a king like Philip and his army.

Philip was a charismatic leader whose merits far outweighed his faults, though the latter were plentiful. It has been the fashion to think of the fourth century as the age of Alexander the Great, given his spectacular achievements in battle. In view of Philip's great deeds, and not just in battle, and especially of his legacy, it is fairer to see it as the age of Philip *and* Alexander. Ancient writers did not merely put Philip on a par with Alexander but (it can be argued) spoke more highly of him. For example, at the end of his narrative of Alexander the Great's reign Diodorus says that he 'accomplished greater deeds than anyone, not only of the kings who had lived before him but also of those who were to come later down to our time'.[30] But Diodorus is referring to Alexander's military exploits only, for no one came close to matching what he did on the battlefield, including Philip, who laid the foundations for the invasion of Asia but did not himself invade because he was assassinated. However, as the extracts quoted at the start of this chapter show, Diodorus' closing commentary on Philip's reign is lengthier and offers more praise than that on Alexander, and even to the critical Justin Alexander's bad qualities far outweigh his good qualities – as well as the bad aspects of his father. We will consider why these writers felt this way when we compare and contrast father and son in the next chapter.

There is no question that Philip was one of the greatest Macedonian kings and that he deserves to live beyond the shadow of his more famous son. Perhaps he also deserves for history to know him as 'the Great', for he was indeed the king behind Alexander the Great's achievements

PHILIP AND ALEXANDER:
LIKE FATHER, LIKE SON?

It is inevitable that in a book about Philip mention should be made of his more famous son, Alexander the Great, and a comparison made between the two. In their actions and characters they had much in common, but there were also some profound differences, as Diodorus and Justin quoted at the start of Chapter 15 suggested. Certainly, the empire Alexander forged was greater in extent and vision than anything his father achieved. Yet without Philip's achievements for Macedonia, Alexander could not have created that empire, and he owed much to his father. He himself was aware of this, as the testimonial to Philip in the speech he gave to his mutinous troops at Opis indicates (see p. 3). The opening of this speech, with its reference to how Philip had transformed the people, has been taken to indicate that the speech is merely rhetorical.[1] Then again, if the opening refers just to the people of Upper Macedonia (and geographically the tribes mentioned support this), we have some support that the speech is historical, given what we have seen of Philip's activities in these regions.[2]

Alexander's words, while offering glowing praise, are simply an acknowledgement of what his father had done for Macedonia as opposed to what he (Alexander) was now doing, for he goes on to say that Philip's deeds were small compared to his own.[3] Children who outgrow and outdo their parents are not unusual, but with Alexander it was different. We expect Philip to have influenced his son's life, yet it appears that after death his impact hardly diminished. Philip's 'ghost', to call it that, continued to have an influence on Alexander's life, or rather on his personality, and may have ultimately motivated him to do what he did.[4]

Alexander's relationship with Philip was complex; it deteriorated sharply after he had been regent when emulation, which characterised much of his earlier years, changed to resentment. We have already traced the reasons for this in Chapter 13: his feelings of marginalisation after his treatment at Philip's wedding banquet in 337 and in the Pixodarus affair, the shock of not going to

Asia despite having proved himself on the battlefield of Chaeronea, Olympias' incessant criticisms of her husband, and the implications of his father's last marriage for his succession. All of these may have led to his possible involvement in patricide.

When Alexander became king, he inherited everything his father had produced, including the blueprint for his invasion of Asia. This was not a grandiose scheme for the complete overthrow of the Persian king and the creation of an absolutist monarchy, but merely for operations in Asia Minor. Yet Alexander seems not to have been content to follow in his father's footsteps but wanted rather to eclipse his deeds, to do the great things that he used to tell his friends he would be unable to achieve while Philip lived. This became the motivation for the vast majority of his actions. We can see it in Alexander's grandiose plan to conquer the Persian empire, symbolically casting a spear into Asian soil before he landed on it in 334 and saying, 'I accept Asia from the gods.'[5] From the outset he was making it clear that he intended to go further than his father, and to keep going. This was a significant deviation from the mandate bestowed on Philip by the League of Corinth. That was why Alexander made the journey to Gordium in 333, where it was said that anyone who could undo the famous Gordian knot would conquer Asia.[6] Alexander, so we are told, severed it with his sword. By the time of his death in 323 he had plans to launch an invasion of Arabia from Babylon, with the likelihood of a foray into Carthage and the western Mediterranean after that.

The paranoia that grew from his feelings of marginalisation in the later years of Philip's reign developed into something else. Military conquest was not enough because his father had already done that, albeit on a smaller scale. One area in which Alexander could outdo – not just match – his father was in his pursuit of apotheosis while alive (proof that Philip was not declared divine while alive – if he had been, Alexander would not have pursued it so relentlessly). The turning point in his pretensions to personal divinity came in 331 when he visited the Oracle of Zeus Ammon in the Oasis of Siwah (in the Libyan Desert of Egypt).[7] This was a Greek oracle, and the main sanctuary of the god in the Greek world. There, the priest answered many of Alexander's questions, including one regarding whether the murderers of Philip had all been punished. This is an indication, perhaps, that Alexander was still under a cloud of suspicion for his father's murder, but the oracle cleared him.

The priest also told Alexander that Philip was not his mortal father: his real father was Zeus. Or at least Alexander says he did, for the meeting between the two took place in private, and we have only Alexander's account of the occasion. It was the answer Alexander always planned to report, as one source states: he went to Siwah to learn 'his own origins more exactly, or at least to say that he had learned them'.[8] The apparent confirmation of divine parentage aligns with the various stories of Alexander's divine conception and birth that he may have been responsible for circulating himself to promote his 'divine pedigree'. One such story was that the night before Olympias and Philip married she dreamed that during a violent thunderstorm a thunderbolt fell from the sky and landed in her womb.[9] It was Zeus impregnating her. Another has it that Zeus came to earth disguised as a snake and had sex with her. Philip spied on the two of them, and because of his voyeurism the god got his own back by having him blinded during the siege of Methone in 354.

After Siwah, Alexander openly called himself 'Son of Zeus' as opposed to a mere descendant of the god, a distinction that was not lost on his men. At various times on the march his army expressed its dissatisfaction with the way he was changing, becoming less Macedonian and more like a Persian monarch.[10] Nowhere is this better illustrated than at the mutiny at Opis in 324, when the men sarcastically said that if Alexander wanted to invade Arabia he could so with his father Zeus.[11] This is on a par with the comments made, in a similarly contemptuous vein, by Demosthenes, that 'Alexander could be the son of Zeus and of Poseidon if he wanted to be', and by the Spartan king Damis, that 'we concede to Alexander that, if this is what he wants, he may be called a god'.[12] Contempt for Alexander from Macedonia's former enemies we might expect, but not from his own army.

There is the famous question that Alexander asked of several Indian philosophers: 'How can a man become a god?' The answer was: 'By doing something a man cannot do.'[13] Therein lay his motivation – and thus how he saw himself. Everything else in his reign became subordinated to his drive towards self-deification. From that came his eventual belief in his own divinity – at the end of his life, one of his reasons for invading Arabia was his desire to have the Arabs worship him as their third god alongside Dionysus and Uranus,[14] and his identification with Dionysus during the famous march through Carmania in 324 is an overt sign of his self-proclaimed divinity.[15] The genesis of this drive was his attempt to excel Philip at all costs. Like the ghost of Julius Caesar that dominates Shakespeare's play long after Caesar is assassinated, so Philip's ghost dominated Alexander's life to the end. It was essential for Alexander to glorify himself over Philip at all costs, as is seen in the juxtaposition he makes of his own deeds with those of Philip in his Opis speech. That need had repercussions for those around him, as is seen in his murder of Cleitus at Maracanda in 328. The two men had got into a fierce argument, fuelled by excessive alcohol, but Alexander's emotions got the better of him when Cleitus praised Philip over Alexander.[16] After more shouting Alexander ran Cleitus through with a pike. Alexander's excessive drinking was also subject to criticism,[17] and his contemporary Ephippus referred to life at court as being dominated by fear, for the king 'was a very violent man, and he had no consideration for human life'.[18]

Alexander's legacy could hardly have been more different from that of his father. At the end of his reign, in 323, when the Macedonian empire was at its greatest extent geographically, national pride at home was probably at its lowest ebb and dissatisfaction with its king at its highest level. We can see this most plainly in the coinage. This continued to be minted at Pella, Amphipolis, Philippi and Damastium, as during Philip's reign, but the designs did not change. We would expect the people to want to exploit the propaganda of Alexander's enormous successes in Asia, but the reverse seems to have been the case: the only coinage that featured Alexander was produced at his own mint in Babylon.

Worse than his claim to personal divinity was Alexander's failure to produce an heir in his lifetime, for his wife Roxanne of Bactria (another visit from Philip's ghost, for the marriage was political) was still pregnant when he died in June 323. Before he left for Asia in 334, Parmenion and Antipater advised him to marry, but he ignored them.[19] Then again, choosing a royal bride at that turbulent time would perhaps not have been the easiest of jobs. When Alexander, on his deathbed, was asked to whom he was leaving his empire, his perversely enigmatic reply was 'to the best'.[20] He did give his signet ring to his second-in-command, Perdiccas,[21] which perhaps indicates that he intended him to be his successor, but the other generals, each one thinking he was the best, had no wish to follow Perdiccas. Roxanne gave birth to a boy (Alexander IV) in about August, and a joint kingship of him and Alexander's half-brother Philip Arrhidaeus (still living in Pella, and then about thirty-five years old) was established. Little loyalty was felt for these kings, and with no undisputed heir to succeed Alexander the dynasty established by Philip came to an end.

The Macedonian throne became a symbolic bone of contention in the subsequent wars and power struggles waged by Alexander's generals. The two kings were nothing more than pawns in the struggles, and both were murdered, Philip III in 317 and Alexander IV in 311. By the end of the century, the Macedonian empire of Philip and Alexander had ceased to exist. In its place arose the Hellenistic kingdoms, in which Macedonia played a significantly weaker role than, say, Egypt or Syria. On the positive side, one can argue that Alexander aided and abetted the economic development and intellectual and cultural output of the Hellenistic era.[22] However, does that outweigh his failings as a king and the sacrifice of his empire for his own personal reasons – that is, to eclipse his father at all costs and have pretensions to personal divinity?

It is the legacies of Philip and Alexander that drive the summations of Diodorus and Justin on Philip's reign, as quoted at the start of Chapter 15.

Their assessments of the reigns and characters of these two kings revolve around their interpretations of the nature of kingship and what a good king should be. They are bound up not so much with what each king did, but with how each acted and especially with the legacy of each. And when we look at the legacies of these two kings, we see a chasm between Philip and Alexander. Diodorus waxes lyrical about Alexander because of his military successes and the extent of the empire he forged. Thus, he accomplished 'greater deeds than anyone, not only of the kings who had lived before him but also of those who were to come later down to our time'. However, his overall record as a king is a very different matter, as the words of Justin reveal. Does Alexander even deserve to be called Great?[23] His greatness, if such it is, is surely further proof of the success, sensibility and indeed greatness of Philip II.

APPENDICES

Appendix 1

THE SOURCES OF INFORMATION

We have no accounts of Macedonia – and of Macedonia's dealings with the Greeks – written from the Macedonian viewpoint, apart from fragments of a work by Marsyas of Pella (*FGrH* 135/56). This is in stark contrast to the wealth of sources that exists for the history of Greece. For example, we have Herodotus' history of the Persian Wars (of 480–479), which deals with far more than just the period of these wars, Thucydides' history of the Peloponnesian War for events until 411, and Xenophon's *Hellenica*, which picks up where Thucydides leaves off and takes us up to 362. So for Macedonia we have to rely on Greek (especially Athenian) sources, which are often sparing in their treatment of affairs north of Mount Olympus, and written from the perspective of Greece's dealings with Macedonia, not the other way around.[1]

It is also frustrating that in the cases of Philip II and Alexander, kings who transformed the Greek world, our contemporary literary sources are mostly oratorical, do not give us a proper account of their reigns, and are biased. The last is understandable, for these writers did not see the changes brought about by the kings as good, involving as they did the subjugation of Greece. The sources that give us a continuous narrative of both kings' reigns have similar pitfalls, for they were written centuries later (in the Roman period) and were often influenced by their own political times and social backgrounds.

There are a number of historians who wrote histories of Philip (and Alexander) or of the period in which they ruled, and lived either contemporaneously or a generation or two following their deaths. Their works survive today only in fragmentary form, quoted by later writers as source material for their own accounts. Principal among these early writers are Theopompus of Chios (*FGrH* 115), Ephorus of Cyme (*FGrH* 70), Callisthenes of Olynthus (*FGrH* 124) and, to a lesser extent, Anaximenes of Lampsacus (*FGrH* 72). We do not know how much they said about Macedonia. Philip also gets less attention than Alexander because of the latter's spectacular successes in Asia, and ancient writers seem to view Philip's reign as a preamble to Alexander's.

The one exception (as noted above) is Marsyas of Pella, who may have been a royal page.[2] He wrote a *Makedonika* in ten books in the later fourth century BC, beginning with the reign of the first of the Macedonian kings and continuing down to 331 – a significant part of his work dealt with Philip.[3] Also, Theagenes' *Makedonika* is important for Macedonian toponyms and urban settlements, especially in Lower Macedonia, but that work also exists today only as fragments.[4]

Fortunately, we have a large number of fragments (over two hundred) of a huge *Philippica* (*History of Philip*) in fifty-eight books, written by Theopompus of Chios (a student of the Athenian orator Isocrates) most likely in the late 330s and early 320s.[5] Copies of the *Philippica* were in existence in Constantinople as late as the ninth century AD, but at some point it disappears from view in its complete state. The *Philippica* begins with the famous line in the proem that Europe had never produced such a man as Philip, which at first sight is nothing short of eulogistic.[6] However, Theopompus then goes on to discuss Philip's ruthlessness and various other character flaws, such as his penchant for excessive drinking, his voracious sexual appetite for women, men and boys, his incontinence, his disregard for friends and allies, his inability to manage money, and his destruction of Greek cities. He also states that Philip's successes owed more to luck than to anything else, and expounds on the dangers of life at the Macedonian court.

Theopompus visited Philip in Macedonia, and what he says appears to be true, for it is supported by other sources. Demosthenes talks of the dangers of life at court and says that Philip owed his successes to a crop of traitors throughout Greece.[7] Justin also says that Philip was better at getting money than hanging on to it and was unable to keep tabs on his income and expenditure,[8] and both Diodorus and Justin say that he was a womaniser and a pederast (giving only one, rather dubious example: his brother-in-law, Alexander of Epirus, when a young boy), and that nothing was too shameful for him.[9] Satyrus, who wrote a biography of Philip, blamed his seventh marriage for creating a rift between him and Olympias,[10] and according to Plutarch the domestic strife 'that resulted from Philip's various marriages and love-affairs caused the quarrels which took place in the women's apartments to infect the whole kingdom, and led to bitter clashes and accusations between father and son'.[11]

Theopompus' criticisms are surprising to say the least after his gushing opening. It is most probable that the opening line, so often quoted as praise for Philip, has been misinterpreted: that it is deliberately ambiguous, and means that Europe produced a man like Philip, who changed the course of its history at this time for better or worse.[12] Another translation, also in a negative sense, could be: 'Europe had never endured such a man at all as Philip, the son of Amyntas.'[13] Theopompus is swayed more by his own moral preconceptions than by historical methodology. Hence he attributes Philip's success to luck and especially to the decline in morality among the Greeks, which allowed the king to bribe his way to victory. That is also why he has little time (surprisingly) for Philip's principal opponent, Demosthenes.[14] Nevertheless, Theopompus is a crucial source for the period, and as we shall see his evaluation of Philip (based presumably on the observations he made during his visit to the Macedonian court) is not wrong on all counts.

Also of great importance is a fragment from a biography of the king written by the third-century BC Peripatetic biographer Satyrus, which is our only source for the names of Philip's seven wives, the order in which he married them, the reasons why, and the problems his seventh and final marriage created. This fragment is found in the work of the later writer Athenaeus of Naucratis (Egypt), of the second century AD, but it presents problems. These are discussed on pp. 172–4.[15]

The first continuous narrative of Philip's reign is that of Diodorus Siculus (of Sicily), who was working in Rome from 30 to 8 BC.[16] His *Universal History* consisted of forty books (only fifteen are extant) and stretched from mythical times to Caesar's campaigns in Gaul in 54 BC. Philip's reign is the focus of Book 16, but because Diodorus was writing a universal history no small part of it deals with events elsewhere in the Greek world, especially Sicily. Diodorus does not name his sources consistently, but for Philip he drew principally on Ephorus (whose account of the Third Sacred War was augmented by Ephorus' son Demophilus' work) until 340 when Ephorus' account ends. For events after this time, Diodorus most likely used Diyllus (who began with the Third Sacred War),[17] and even Theopompus.[18] His account of events after 340 is sketchier, (surprisingly) omitting the details of Philip's settlement of Greece in 337 by which Macedonian hegemony was established.

Despite these weaknesses, along with some chronological errors and telescoping of events (hardly surprising in such a vast work), Diodorus is generally accepted as a credible source. This view really stems from his reliance on earlier sources such as Ephorus, whose critical approach to history was well regarded, Theopompus, who knew of life at court and Philip from his time there, and Marsyas, who was from Pella and, having been born in about 356, would have known Philip. Diodorus thought highly of Philip, saying that he was a man who created the greatest kingdom despite his humble beginnings, and that he did so more by diplomacy than by warfare.[19]

Justin's account is an epitome of an earlier work, the *Historiae Philippicae* by Pompeius Trogus of the first century BC (which has not survived).[20] We do not have a specific date for Justin, and estimates range from the second to the fourth century AD.[21] His treatment of Philip runs from the end of Book 7 to the end of Book 9. Since we cannot compare Justin's work with its source, we are not in a proper position to judge its value. His work has often been criticised for errors and telescoping of events, but more recent research suggests a different perspective. Justin gives a generally hostile view of Philip, whom he regards as a cruel person. For example, he says that Philip had no hesitation in plundering and selling into slavery the women and children of allied cities and he characterises him as deceitful and beyond shame in his actions.[22]

Away from history, we have Plutarch of Chaeronea, who in the second century AD wrote a number of biographies of prominent Greeks and Romans down to the end of the Roman Republic.[23] Of these, the lives of Demosthenes, Alexander and Phocion are of relevance to Philip's reign. Plutarch used a number of earlier sources, but it is important to remember that biography is not history. While these biographies give us details that we can use to construct our picture of relations between Greece and Macedonia, Plutarch is less interested in historical accuracy than in showing the moral character of his subjects and in retailing any gossip that could be attached to them to make them more interesting and appealing.

Our main contemporary sources for the reign of Philip are speeches by several Athenian orators. The most important of these are Demosthenes' *Philippics, Olynthiacs, On the Peace, On the Chersonese, On the False Embassy* and *On the Crown*, Aeschines' *On the False Embassy* and *Against Ctesiphon*, Isocrates' *Peace, Areopagiticus, Antidosis, Panthenaicus, To Philip* and two letters to the king, and some speeches ascribed to Demosthenes but not actually by him, such as *Philip's Letter* and a speech by the orator Hegesippus.[24]

The Athenian orators are biased against any non-Athenians, as we might expect, but also against each other. Demosthenes and Aeschines played crucial roles in the political history of Athens during Philip's reign, often pitting themselves against each other. The information that they give in their speeches is open to question, especially that of Demosthenes, who may well have cynically used the threat from Philip as a means to his own political ascendancy in Athens.[25] His hatred of Philip caused him to lie and to malign the king's person and aims in an effort to resist the peace and alliance with Macedonia in which Aeschines believed. Their different takes on Philip quickly escalated into an intense personal enmity that saw Demosthenes prosecuting Aeschines in 343 and vice versa in 330. Both personal enmity and their differing views of Philip's aims fuelled their animosity, and by extension affect their value as sources.[26]

In addition to the problems posed by the individual orators, there is the difficulty offered by the genre of oratory itself. As with biography, it is important to remember that oratory is not history, and that the orators were not historians but rhetoricians. They wrote to persuade an audience at either an Assembly or in a lawcourt, and so the emphasis was on performance, not veracity.[27] To achieve their aims, they used rhetorical tricks that today would be disallowed in court and that would cause the speaker to be fined for contempt. When they dealt with history, they manipulated their portrayal of facts, people and events.[28] To make matters worse, speeches were revised after delivery. Hence the orators may well have used material differently in the oral version of a speech, especially as their audience had a working knowledge of current affairs as a result of their involvement in the democracy,[29] and so would have reacted against obvious lies and embellishments. This process of revision explains the historical inaccuracies in speeches, even those to do with events that had taken place only a few years earlier. The speeches of Demosthenes and Aeschines from the trial of the latter in 343 are an excellent example as far as the roles both played in the Peace of Philocrates of 346 are concerned.[30] Demosthenes, for example, is suspect as a credible source; in addition to misrepresenting Philip's motives and actions at any given time, he may have revised his speeches with the benefit of hindsight, elevating his own role in affairs.[31]

There are references to Philip in other sources, such as the geographer Strabo (first century BC–first century AD), Polybius (second century BC) and our most reliable narrative source for Alexander, Arrian (first century AD), who, along with the less reliable Quintus Curtius Rufus (first century AD), provides us with the text of Alexander's speech at Opis and its detailing of Philip's achievements (see p. 3). Since Diodorus and Justin are our two major narrative sources for Philip, I cite them more often than other sources in my notes. I also make regular references to the speeches of the orators since they are contemporary sources, although their shortcomings as outlined above should always be remembered.

Numismatic and epigraphic evidence is also crucial. The numismatic evidence tells us how relatively poor Macedonia was before Philip and how much wealthier (and hence more developed economically) it was by the end of his reign, given the silver and gold coins he minted and their value as currency in Greece and abroad.[32] As far as epigraphic evidence is concerned, we have next to no inscriptions from Macedonia itself and precious few from the Greeks that have anything to do with Philip's kingship. Those that do exist are conveniently collected together in M.N. Tod, *Greek Historical Inscriptions 2* (Oxford: 1948), which has a Greek text and English commentary. Some of these are translated in P.E. Harding, *From the End of the Peloponnesian War to the Battle of Ipsus* (Cambridge: 1985). More recently, there is P.J. Rhodes and R. Osborne, *Greek Historical Inscriptions, 404–323 BC* (Oxford: 2003), which includes some of the inscriptions in Tod as well as others. The texts are in

Greek but they have a facing English translation and commentary. In Athens, the Research Centre for Greek and Roman Antiquity, part of the National Hellenic Research Foundation, has for a number of years been collecting epigraphic (and other) evidence from all over ancient Macedonia; its results appear in its publication *Meletemata*.

Finally, the archaeological evidence that has appeared in the past three or four decades thanks to a burst of excavating activity at many sites, both urban and rural, is of the utmost significance.[33] All of the artefacts found at these sites are of course exciting and illuminating, bringing as they do the people of that time back to life. The most staggering include the sanctuary to Zeus at Dium,[34] the pit graves at Pieria, the tombs at Derveni and the royal tombs at Vergina (Aegae).[35] The last in particular plays a role in the history of Philip II (or the Argead ruling dynasty), and is discussed more fully in Appendix 6.

Appendix 2

THE QUESTION OF MACEDONIAN ETHNICITY

There is no consensus on the issue of Macedonian ethnicity: whether the Macedonians were of Greek or mixed descent; for example, a Slavic people who later adopted Greek culture. This confusion is a consequence of the nature of the ancient source material[1] and the influence of modern politics, especially after 1991 when the 'new state' of the Republic of Macedonia was formed.[2] One theory is that the Macedonians were a Balkan people, hence members of a different ethnic group that only gradually became influenced by Greek culture through contact (cultural and otherwise) with the Greeks. However, this is flawed, for it fails to explain the Greek words (especially the names of towns) common to both Greek and Macedonian cultures well before the Greeks began to have dealings with their neighbours. Moreover, almost all of the literary sources and archaeological evidence, spanning several centuries, point to the Macedonians speaking Greek, hence (importantly) being Greek, as the following survey shows.

The epic poet Hesiod of Boeotia (eighth century) gives us the genealogy of the Macedonians' ancestors. He tells us that Deucalion had a son, Hellen, from whom the Greeks derived the name they used for themselves, 'Hellenes'. Hellen had three sons and a daughter, Thyia. The latter was impregnated by Zeus and gave birth to two sons, Macedon and Magnes. Macedon and his descendants lived in Pieria and around Mount Olympus (giving the name of Macedonia to the region), and Magnes and his descendants lived in Thessaly (to the south). Macedon and Magnes were thus nephews of Hellen's sons and grandsons of Hellen, and so part of the same family. Since Hellen's three sons were supposed to represent three dialect groups of Greece (Doric, Ionic and Aeolic) and Magnes settled in Thessaly, which was Greek-speaking, it follows that Macedon (and hence the Macedonians) must also have been Greek-speaking.

In the mid-fifth century, Herodotus, the 'father of history', who visited Macedonia, traced the ethnicity of the Macedonians to Perdiccas.[3] The latter was a member of the royal house of the Temenidae at Argos in the north-eastern Peloponnese; he came to Macedonia in the seventh century.[4] The house was descended from Temenus, whose ancestor was Heracles (son of Zeus), and who founded Argos in the twelfth century. Hence Perdiccas and his people would have spoken the Doric dialect of Greek. Thus was established the Temenid dynasty, taking its name from Temenus. Herodotus also tells us that Alexander I, who was the king at the time of the Persian Wars (of 480–479), took part in the Olympic Games, finishing equal first in the 200-yard (185 m) race.[5] (Herodotus may well have learned this information from Alexander himself since the two of them likely met.)[6] Now, only Greeks could compete at these games, and apparently Alexander was able to do so because he successfully argued that the ruling house of Macedonia came originally from Argos.

Other writers followed suit. Thucydides, writing in the later fifth century, and often critical of his predecessors, especially Herodotus, also accepts the arrival of the new dynasty led by Perdiccas from Argos. Under that king, the newcomers pushed back Illyrian influence in many areas of Macedonia and settled in places such as Pieria, Bottia, the Axius valley and even Aegae. All together, goes on Thucydides, the places were called Macedonia.[7] The Athenian orator Isocrates, who repeatedly urged Philip to invade Asia, had no trouble in accepting that the king was a descendant of Argos: 'Argos, for one, is your ancestral home, and it is right that you have as much regard for it as you would for your own ancestors.'[8] And even later Strabo, writing around the time of Christ, said succinctly that 'Macedonia is Greece'.[9]

Of course, literature is not history. Hesiod's genealogy has been accused of indulging in make-believe, and mythical descendants are common among Greek nobility. Herodotus and Thucydides also have their shortcomings when it comes to factual accuracy, and the grounds for Alexander I's eligibility to compete in the Olympic Games are anchored only in a tradition that at some time a new dynasty of the Macedonian royal house came from Argos. Moreover, Alexander's name does not appear on the list of victors kept at Olympia. However, in 408 we know that Archelaus was victorious in the four-horse chariot race (*tethrippon*),[10] and Philip II's chariot teams won races there in 356, 352 and 348 (after the first triumph he issued commemorative coinage).[11] Moreover, in 346 Philip was elected President of the Pythian Games at Delphi, another Olympic festival, for which he minted a commemorative gold stater (Plate 15). Thus, even if we discount the opposing arguments, what is common to all accounts is the arrival of the new ruling dynasty from Argos in the Peloponnese and participation in the Olympic Games, both of which facts point to the 'Greekness' of the Macedonians.

In terms of language, the proper name for the Macedonians was 'Makedones', a Greek word meaning 'highlanders'.[12] The names of the months, the names of the people and (especially significant) the names of the towns were all Greek.[13] Thus, the first known king (in the mid-seventh century) was Perdiccas, a Greek word that may have something to do with justice (*peridikaios*). While we are told that the Greeks could not understand the Illyrians without an interpreter,[14] no source says that Athenian envoys to the Macedonian court needed them, and Aeschines indicates that Macedonian ambassadors spoke before the Athenians without interpreters: '[Demosthenes] called Antipater to the platform and put a question to him (having told him in advance what he would say and coached him in the reply he must give against the interests of the city).'[15]

Archaeological evidence, such as inscriptions in Greek, has been found at Dium (the main religious sanctuary), Vergina, Pella and Amphipolis, and Greek was used widely on Macedonian coins. Also, the style of Macedonian theatres was Greek (that at Dium has the only underground access tunnel between the centre of the *orchestra*, or performance area, and buildings at the rear). It would also have made little sense for the late fourth-century king Archelaus to invite Euripides and Socrates from Athens to his court if no one could understand them. Socrates declined the invitation, but Euripides wrote at least two plays at Pella and died there (he was buried at Arethousa). He was granted citizenship, for the Macedonians refused to hand over his corpse to the Athenians.

If the Greeks called non-Greek-speaking people 'barbarians', it is important to note that so also did the Macedonians. In 324 Alexander the Great was faced with a mutiny at Opis. He delivered a passionate speech to his men that included a eulogy of his father Philip. In it, Alexander says that Philip 'made you [the Macedonians] a match in battle for the barbarians on your borders'.[16] He is talking here of tribes such as the Illyrians and Paeonians, who had had a habit of expanding their territories and invading Macedonia before Philip put an end to the practice.[17] The content of the speech may be questioned, although its general context must be accepted, and it is hard to accept that Alexander's use of the word 'barbarian' is make-believe. Hence, if 'barbarian' refers to someone who does not speak Greek, the person using the word must by definition be Greek-speaking.

Religion also shows many commonalities. Macedonia was home to the twelve Olympian gods and the nine Olympian Muses, the daughters of Zeus and the goddess Memory (who gave birth to them not far from Olympus' peak), as well as to Dionysus and Orpheus, all deities found in Greece, Asia Minor, Crete and Thrace. The Thracian poet Orpheus, the god of poetry and music, gave his name to the Orphic religion (whose initiates believed in life after death). The Macedonians were said to have killed him and buried him at Dium, and the earliest Orphic hymn was found in a fourth-century tomb at Derveni (central Macedonia). Like Zeus and Heracles, Dionysus (god of fertility, vegetation and wine) enjoyed a special place in the Macedonian pantheon, and there was a cult to him. Towards the end of his reign, Alexander the Great came to identify himself more with Dionysus than with his heroes Heracles (an ancestor on his father's side) and Achilles (an ancestor on his mother's). During a procession through Carmania in 324, Alexander, who by then most likely believed in his own divinity, dressed as the god.[18]

The gods whom the Makedones worshipped were all members of the Greek pantheon. These included Zeus, Athena (as protectress of cattle), Heracles Patrous (Heracles the Father – that is, of the royal family), Artemis, Hermes, Poseidon, Pluto, Persephone and Apollo – it was not just for the political leverage in central Greece that Philip II involved himself in the Third Sacred War (355–346) when Phocis seized Delphi, home of the oracle of Apollo (see Chapter 6). At Aegae, for example, there was a cult of the Mother of the Gods and of Eucleia, and at Pella of Aphrodite and Cybele. One of the king's daily duties was to perform religious sacrifices to Heracles Patrous. He was the ancestor of the Temenids, for Temenus was one of the sons of Heracles, himself a son of Zeus and a mortal woman, who had been deified on death. The Temenids were replaced by the Argead dynasty (of which Philip and Alexander were members) in about 540, when Amyntas I became king. Thus, the Macedonian kings could trace their lineage back to Zeus, who was the Macedonians' principal god.

We have nothing today that was written in what might be called 'ancient Macedonian', and it is implausible that if these people did write in another language every example of it has been lost. Thus, the Macedonians probably did not have an entirely different language (as the Persians did, for example), but, just as their material culture had local or regional styles, they probably had a local dialect, most likely a version of Aeolic Greek.[19] We know, for example, that names beginning with Bil- and Bilist- are the Macedonian equivalent of the more widespread and common Greek Phil- and Philist-.[20] Also, in 330, for example, Philotas, the commander of Alexander's Companion Cavalry, was put on trial for treason and reprimanded by Alexander for not speaking Macedonian in his defence. Alexander also resorted to what is referred to as Macedonian to prompt a quick response from his guards during his drunken and fatal exchange with Cleitus at Maracanda in 328.[21] The existence of the dialect hardly comes as a surprise: there were different dialects south of Mount Olympus as well. However, Macedonia's separation from the Greeks by Mount Olympus and the numerous tribes living on its borders probably contributed to its development. Greeks presumably could not understand it and so called the people there 'barbarians' (non-Greek-speakers). Therefore, there is enough evidence and reasoned theory to indicate that the Macedonians were Greek.

Appendix 3

MACEDONIA BEFORE PHILIP II

The Traditional Enemies

During the eighth and seventh centuries much of what would become Macedonia was in the hands of the Illyrians, who lived to the north-west of the territory (Map 2). There was no single political entity that was Illyria; various tribes (Dardanians, Taulantii and Grabaeans) competed for power, and the Greeks referred to these tribes as simply Illyrians. From the ninth century they expanded their own territories significantly,[1] but the arrival of the Temenid family from Argos in about 650 or 640 changed all that. Under Perdiccas I, the Macedonians encroached into many areas subject to Illyrian influence,[2] including Pieria, Bottia and Aegae (Vergina), which became their capital. Nonetheless, incursions from the Illyrians (even during Philip's reign) posed the most relentless threat to Macedonia's borders, with that represented by the Paeonians (who occupied the Axius valley to the north) running them a close second.

The imperialistic designs of cities such as Athens and Thebes had been a constant thorn in Macedonia's side since the fifth century.[3] The Athenians had made an alliance with Amyntas I (c. 540–498) and were keen to expand their influence in Macedonia. They were especially eager to regain their former colony of Amphipolis on the lower Strymon river, which they had lost in 424, and many of their policies in the north after this time were designed to achieve this aim. The Greek cities on the Thermaic Gulf (on the plain of Lower Macedonia) paid a tribute to Athens for membership of its empire. As such they had some independence from the Macedonian capital, and they allowed the Athenians to use them as bases in that area.

To Macedonia's east was the Chalcidice (Map 2). This promontory was a prosperous and well-populated region because of its harbours, natural resources (timber, gold, silver, copper and lead mines) and fertile land, on which corn was grown. Since Macedonia's ports were on the Thermaic Gulf, and so were far removed from the principal shipping lanes that ran from the

Black Sea through the Thracian Chersonese (Gallipoli peninsula) to the island
of Euboea in the Aegean Sea and beyond, the Chalcidian ports were used
primarily for Macedonia's imports and exports. In 432 Olynthus, a little over
a mile from the head of the Gulf of Torone, became the principal city of the
Chalcidice, and later established itself as head of a federal Chalcidian League.
It minted its own gold and silver coinage, with the head of Apollo on the
obverse and a tripod on the reverse. In 379 the Spartans and King Amyntas III
of Macedonia forced the league to disband. However, it re-established itself
two years later and became an Athenian ally.[4]

Early Attempts to Impose Stability

Two kings of the fifth century, Alexander I 'the Philhellene' (485–454) and
Perdiccas II (454–413), tried to bring some stability to the state.[5] One of them
(probably Alexander, perhaps taking advantage of the Persian invasion of
Greece in 480–479) made some incursions into western areas, including
Lyncestis, besides extending Macedonia's borders eastwards as far as the
Strymon. Alexander was also the first king to put his name on his coins,
thereby starting the trend of royal coinage, and there may even have been a
marital tie between Elimeia and the Argead ruling house. The amount of
additional control he secured in Upper Macedonia is not known, but
ultimately the attempts of both kings came to nothing, and Perdiccas II's later
involvement in the Peloponnesian War led only to further distrust of the
Macedonians on the part of many Greeks. Perdiccas made a treaty with Athens
in 425 and at some point tried to oust the king of the Lyncestians, Arrhabaeus.
However, he was beaten back thanks to Illyrian support for Arrhabaeus, and
his own power was weakened considerably. He died of natural causes in 413.[6]

Archelaus: A Time of Advancement

A turning point came with Archelaus, who ruled from 413 to 399.[7] He usurped
the throne by murdering his uncle (Perdiccas' brother) and his son
(Archelaus' cousin), and at some later point killed Archelaus' younger brother
too, all because of their claims to the throne. From these brutal beginnings
Archelaus set out to centralise the monarchy, to increase the size and efficiency
of the army, and to stimulate trade. His economic and military reforms
included selling timber to Athens, which may have led to the introduction of
a new standard weight (along with a new coin, the didrachm),[8] building
military roads to aid communications, constructing fortresses and making
various changes to the army. The cavalry was generally in good shape, but
Archelaus provided the infantry with some extra sort of training and

weaponry. He also divided Lower Macedonia into a number of cantons, each dominated by a central town, which had responsibility for military recruitment. There was clearly a conscious effort to develop the fighting potential of the infantry, echoed in Thucydides' words that Archelaus 'organised his country for war by providing cavalry, arms, and other equipment beyond anything achieved by all of the eight kings who preceded him'.[9]

In 399 Archelaus moved Macedonia's capital from Aegae (Plates 2a–b) to Pella, north-west of the Thermaic Gulf and on a branch of the Loudias river (Plates 3a–d).[10] Aegae continued to be the traditional venue for royal weddings and burials, but Pella became the largest city in Macedonia. It was situated close to the gulf (and beyond that the Aegean), which was reachable via the Loudias river – in antiquity Pella was coastal; today, because of the silting of the sea, it is about 22 miles (35 km) inland. However, Macedonia did not have a fleet, nor did Archelaus build one (even when Philip II had one built, it was small and never became a formidable force). The reason for its site may have had something to do with the Greek cities on the shores of the Thermaic Gulf, especially Methone and Pydna, against which Archelaus was campaigning at the start of his reign. For more details about Pella and the great palace there, see Appendix 4.

Philip II was keen to promote his capital as a cultural centre, and to this end he may have taken a few pages out of Archelaus' book. The latter was a philhellene, that is, someone who loved Greek culture, but perhaps Philip also had a political agenda in the sense that he wanted to make his own people look to Pella as the capital (and thus to him as king), and not to the Argead-dominated Aegae. Prominent literary figures and thinkers of the day were invited to Archelaus' court. These included the Athenian tragic playwrights Agathon and Euripides, the musician Timotheus, and Socrates (who declined).[11] At the court Euripides wrote the *Bacchae*, a play about the power of Dionysus, which may well reflect the 'wild west' lifestyle of Macedonia. He also wrote the *Archelaus* (on the Argive connections of the king as the son of Temenus; only fragments survive), and he supposedly died in Macedonia in 406. According to Diodorus,[12] Archelaus instituted a festival to Zeus at Dium that included a drama competition.[13] Whether this was meant to compete with the games of the Greek Olympic cycle is unknown.

Art and artwork were exquisite and of the highest standard, including silver drinking vessels and containers, gold artefacts and jewellery, busts, and bronze and iron arms and armour. Zeuxis, the leading fresco painter of his day, came from Italy to decorate Archelaus' palace with ornate frescos. He established a school whose designs influenced painters in the Hellenistic and Roman periods. Indeed, he may even have introduced an appreciation of mosaics, for magnificent examples from the early Hellenistic period have been found at some of the large and wealthy houses in Pella, testaments to the skill of the Macedonian artists (Plates 19a–b). Thanks to the impetus provided by Archelaus, Pella would become a leading centre of culture in the Greek world.[14] More generally, Macedonia, as its paintwork, goldwork, architecture and especially mosaics attest, played an important part in the development of Greek culture.

Archelaus had his dark side, as we have seen from the manner in which he seized power. This influenced Plato's description of him as 'the greatest criminal in Macedonia, the most wretched of all the Macedonians, and not the happiest'.[15] It is perhaps fitting, then, that Archelaus was murdered in 399 by a son-in-law, who was seemingly disappointed by his marriage to one of the king's daughters. Nevertheless, Archelaus left Macedonia sufficiently powerful to take part in affairs in Thessaly (Map 5). There, the Macedonian kings already had a tie with the people of Larisa, which headed a Thessalian League that would play a valuable role in Philip II's dealings with the Greeks. Archelaus had also taken very real steps to attempt to stimulate Macedonia's economy, reform its army and expand its cultural clout. Thucydides' remark that he was better than the eight kings before him is not an overstatement.

Macedonia in Chaos

However, Archelaus' legacy had two crucial weaknesses: Upper and Lower Macedonia had not been united, and his dynasty was still not securely established. In the half-dozen or so years following his murder, no fewer than five or six kings came to power, and their brief reigns coupled with a succession of Illyrian invasions, proved disastrous for the kingdom.[16] Then in 393/2 Amyntas III, the father of Philip II, came to power (393/2–369), although like Archelaus he did so only after a murderous campaign against his opponents.[17] Almost immediately he was faced with an invasion of the powerful Dardanians led by Bardylis, who had ruled over them for forty years. Amyntas secured an alliance with Olynthus, the chief city in the Chalcidian League, but Bardylis marched so quickly into central Macedonia that any Olynthian help that was forthcoming did not arrive in time. Amyntas was forced to abandon Pella and to entrust parts of eastern Macedonia to his new ally, Olynthus.

The Dardanians now had an open road to Pella, but instead of taking it they ravaged the land, and after about three months Amyntas struck a deal with them: in return for paying them an annual tribute, they would leave Macedonia. Although this deal was to Macedonia's disadvantage, at least Amyntas was able to return to Pella to resume the kingship. However, Olynthus refused to return the parts of eastern Macedonia that he had placed in its hands. Worse was to come. The Olynthians had set their eyes on Pella and, although the chronology is uncertain, the capital probably fell to them in the mid to late 380s. Whether Amyntas fled again is unknown, but this time the Olynthians installed their own ruler on the throne, Argaeus.[18]

In desperation Amyntas appealed for help to Sparta, then the most powerful state in Greece, and his call was answered. The Spartans expelled Argaeus, and Amyntas III again found himself sole king, but still in the debt of the Illyrians and now beholden to the Spartans. By the mid-370s, however, the power of Sparta in Greece was diminishing and that of Athens, which had founded a naval confederacy in 378, was on the rise. The Athenians had been especially active in trying to regain their former colony of Amphipolis, which had opened its gates to the Spartan general Brasidas in 424. Although the Spartans abandoned the city in 421, it remained independent, and its strategic location and proximity to timber resources made its recovery a priority. Amyntas thus broke with Sparta at some point in the mid-370s to ally with Athens. His timing could not have been better, for in 371 a Theban army defeated the Spartans at the Battle of Leuctra. Unfortunately for Amyntas, the Athenians and the Thebans were so intent on increasing their influence in the North Aegean that he was plagued by their interventions for the rest of his reign.[19]

Amyntas' successor was his eldest son, Alexander II (369–368/7).[20] Faced with a threat from his brother-in-law Ptolemy of Alorus (a city close to the mouth of the Haliacmon), he appealed to the Thebans for assistance. In return for their help, Alexander had to surrender fifty sons of noble Macedonians as hostages, including his youngest brother, Philip (later Philip II).[21]

Perhaps only a few weeks later Alexander II was murdered while watching a dancing performance at a symposium.[22] There is some disagreement in the sources about the identity of his murderer, but it was either Ptolemy or perhaps a supporter of his named Apollophanes of Pydna, who was later executed on the orders of the Assembly. Since the lawful heir, Alexander's brother Perdiccas, was only a minor, the Assembly appointed Ptolemy as regent.[23]

Further chaos ensued for a number of years, during which time the Chalcidian League supported a certain Pausanias, perhaps a member of a rival royal house, or even a son of Archelaus,[24] for the throne. The regent Ptolemy immediately called on the Athenians for help, and Iphicrates, who was then conducting a campaign against Amphipolis, expelled the pretender from the kingdom. Needless to say, the Thebans were unhappy with this Athenian intervention, and in 367 they again intervened in Macedonia to keep Ptolemy in line. Ptolemy was ordered to support the people of Amphipolis against the Athenians, thus robbing him of future Athenian support, but any escalation of hostilities ended when Ptolemy died in 365 and Perdiccas III (who was now of age) ascended the throne.[25]

Perdiccas III

Perdiccas immediately reaffirmed the alliance with Thebes and sent troops to the aid of Amphipolis, which was being attacked by Athenian troops, and seems to have installed a garrison there. When Amphipolis made a treaty with Perdiccas, the Athenians declared war on him. Their general Timotheus besieged and won over a number of places, including the important port towns of Methone and Pydna, followed by Potidaea and Torone in the Chalcidice, while another Athenian general, Callisthenes, invaded Macedonia. A first wave of Athenian settlers was sent to Potidaea, followed by a second in 361. Given the close proximity of Potidaea to Olynthus, the latter viewed the Athenian presence as a serious concern, and the Athenians at Potidaea were soon at odds with the Olynthians.

In response to Perdiccas' actions, the Thebans released his brother Philip, who was about seventeen at the time. Then, in the summer of 360 or 359, Bardylis (now aged ninety) massed his Dardanians for yet another invasion. The reason for this mobilisation is unknown, but perhaps Perdiccas had refused to pay the tribute agreed on by Amyntas III. Perdiccas led out a Macedonian army, and he and four thousand Macedonian soldiers were killed in a pitched battle. Since his son and heir, Amyntas, was only a minor, the Assembly elected his uncle Philip as king.

Appendix 4

PELLA

See Plates 3a–d. Founded by Archelaus in 399, Pella's rate of expansion after Philip's accession was probably faster than that of Athens.[1] It was especially prosperous in the Hellenistic period following Alexander's death in 323. The Romans sacked it in 168, when their general Aemilius Paullus defeated the last Macedonian king, Perseus (Thessaloniki became the capital of the new Roman province). Pella was largely destroyed by an earthquake in the 90s.[2]

Archaeological excavation began at Pella in 1914, resumed between 1957 and 1963, and has been ongoing since 1977. It has revealed a strongly fortified city, which was built to a strict urban gridplan, with regular-sized building plots (each containing two or more houses) and roadways. Those that ran east–west were 30 feet (9 m) wide, and those north-south were 20 feet (6 m) wide. Two of the wider roads stretched from the harbour to the Agora (in the city's centre), through which ran a larger, ornamental road, 49 feet (15 m) wide. There was also a water supply, with wells, fountains, a reservoir and baths, and a drainage system. The private houses varied in size, with some equivalent to modern mansions, having courtyards surrounded by colonnades. The 'House of Dionysus', in which were found the famous Dionysus on the panther and lion-hunt mosaics (Plates 19a–b), is 3,588 sq yards (3,000 sq m) in area and has two courtyards. The walls were built of stone to the height of 3 feet (1 m) or so, and then finished in brick. The murals on walls and (from the later fourth century) mosaics on floors that decorated the wealthier houses, as well as portraits, such as a marvellous early Hellenistic one of Alexander (Plate 20), are a testimony to the affluence of Pella, not to mention providing fodder for Roman copyists.

The Agora (marketplace), also built to a gridplan, took up 17 acres (7 ha) in the centre of the city. It was surrounded by large stoas (20 feet [6 m] wide) housing various administrative offices, shops selling all types of products (food, pottery, lamps, metalwork, precious objects) and workshops. In addition to locals, traders and merchants from all over Greece came to the Agora to buy and sell their goods. All the gods in the Macedonian pantheon were worshipped in Pella. To the north of the Agora was a sanctuary with a small temple to Aphrodite and the Mother of the Gods, and there were other sanctuaries in different parts of the city, including to the south one to Darron (a local god of healing). To the east, south-east and west of the Agora were cemeteries, the earliest dating back to the reign of Archelaus and the latest to Roman times (the west cemetery). The Macedonians did not cremate their dead but buried them by inhumation. Several hundred tombs, containing a vast number of skeletal remains of all ages, as well as four double-chamber and two single-chamber Macedonian tombs (these from Hellenistic times) have been discovered to date.[3]

The palace was built on the middle of three hills north of the city, still within easy reach but at a comfortable distance from its noise and bustle (Plate 3d). Its location provided an excellent view of the plain, Lake Loudias and the mountains in the background. It grew substantially in size from what Archelaus had first planned, and by the Hellenistic period it occupied 15 acres (6 ha), almost as much as the entire Agora area. It was not a single structure but rather five complexes, each consisting of two or more buildings, hence a compound, with living quarters, storerooms, rooms for entertaining, guardrooms, and even a swimming pool and a training/exercise yard. These complexes were built up the slopes of the hill and were linked to each other by corridors and stairs. The living quarters of the royal family were situated in four large buildings, with big, open courtyards, in the centre of the compound. The palace was the heart of all aspects of the Macedonian government (financial, military, economic, administrative), hence a structure of this size was needed given the large royal family, the number of courtiers who by necessity lived there, and the need to entertain foreign ambassadors and the like, all of which increased under Philip. Today the site of ancient Pella is among the most impressive in Greece.

Appendix 5

PHILIP'S APPARENT DIVINITY

Some ancient sources indicate that Philip sought divine recognition towards the end of his life. Now, while Macedonian kings were probably deified on their deaths, did Philip really break with tradition and come to see himself (as his son Alexander was to do) as a god while he was still alive?

Much is made of a passage in Diodorus about the royal procession held on the day he was assassinated in 336 in the theatre at Aegae (Plate 17). That occasion was designed to celebrate both the wedding of his daughter to Alexander of Epirus and his new status in Greece. Diodorus tells us that a procession entered the theatre which included 'statues of the twelve gods wrought with great artistry and adorned with a dazzling show of wealth to strike awe in the beholder, and along with these was conducted a thirteenth statue, suitable for a god, that of Philip himself, so that the king exhibited himself enthroned among (*sunthronon*) the twelve gods'.[1] Later, in the aftermath of the assassination, Diodorus says: 'such was the end of Philip, who had made himself the greatest of the kings in Europe in his time, and because of the extent of his kingdom had made himself a throned companion of the twelve gods.'[2] In other words, according to Diodorus, Philip had set himself up as a thirteenth god.

In support of Diodorus' assertion we have a variety of other evidence.[3] For example, it is believed that the statues of the royal family in the Philippeion indicate a cult. Further, Isocrates wrote to Philip and said that, if he defeated the Persians, 'there would be nothing left to do except become a god'.[4] Then there is the statement that at the Battle of the Crocus Field in 352 Philip's soldiers wore laurel wreaths 'as though the god were going before'.[5] Also, a cult to the king apparently existed at Amphipolis before it fell to him in 357,[6] as well as one to him at Philippi,[7] and there was a statue of him in the Temple of Artemis at Ephesus,[8] and altars to Zeus Philippios at Eresus on the island of Lesbos. We are also told that the Athenians worshipped Philip in the sanctuary of Heracles by the Acropolis.[9] All of this (and other) evidence seems conclusive. However, a closer examination reveals nothing to support the view that Philip was seeking divine recognition in 336.

Let us begin with his processional statue. Two matters connected to Diodorus' use of language must be addressed immediately. First, he refers to the statue as an *eikon*, not an *agalma*, the Greek word for a cult statue. An *eikon* did not designate the object of a cult, and we have evidence of *eikones* of mortal men where the distinction between *eikon* and *agalma* is carefully made.[10] Second, *sunthronos* ('enthroned among') need not mean anything other than that Philip was seeking divine support for his forthcoming Asian campaign, another of the reasons for the celebrations that day. Alexander did the same when he invaded Asia. Before he crossed the Hellespont, he sacrificed at the tomb of the hero Protesilaus, who gave his life so that the Greeks would defeat the Trojans, and then when he landed in Asia he made a detour to Troy to sacrifice at the tomb of Achilles.

Furthermore, the first passage in Diodorus really connects Philip's statue with the cost and adornment of the others. That it was 'suitable for a god' so that the king became 'enthroned among the twelve gods' is Diodorus' inference, and he is not averse to imposing his views on his narrative and getting things wrong.[11] Philip used the procession at Aegae to show off: his statue was just as expensively made and adorned as the others, deliberately part of the 'dazzling show of wealth to strike awe in the beholder'. Just the day before the procession, the wedding Philip had arranged for his daughter Cleopatra to Alexander of Epirus was also brilliant and lavish, with the foremost actor of the day (Neoptolemus) speaking at it. The procession and games were meant to be a great political event, with lots of hype, to show off the king as *hegemon* of Greece. Moreover, if he was running short of funds by this time, this ostentatious display may have been cunningly meant to mask his need for money. Thus, Diodorus misunderstood what Philip's statue was meant to symbolise. We can understand how this may have happened if we remember he was writing far later than Philip's reign, after the end of the Hellenistic period, during which (significantly) statues of rulers were carried in processions as indications of their cult.

There is also the image we have built up of Philip over his years as king, which runs counter to pretensions of divinity. For one thing, to the Greeks worship of a living man was blasphemous. Some men had received divine honours while alive, the first being the Spartan general Lysander (who had a cult, altar and festival in his honour on Samos).[12] However, these were isolated instances, and usually represented extraordinary grants bestowed on individuals for founding cities or doing great deeds. The practice (to call it that) had stopped early in the fourth century and remained dormant until Alexander the Great.[13] Philip was a pious and realistic individual. While the implications of his statue that day at Aegae might have resonated less with the Macedonians than the Greeks (it was after all part of a procession in a Macedonian city), at this early stage of his campaign against Persia he would not want to provoke a hostile reaction from his Greek subjects. It has been suggested that the statue was designed to introduce the idea of his divinity into people's minds, so that at a later date, probably when Philip had concluded his campaign in Persia, all that would be left would be his apotheosis (cf. Isocrates' letter cited above).[14] However, any such agenda on Philip's part seems unlikely and rather too much of a gamble, not only because of what we know about him but also if he were defeated in Asia, he would have no grounds then for claiming divinity.

Philip's manner of dressing that day, I suggest, gives us a clue as to how he saw himself. When he fought in the Third Sacred War he did so as the Saviour of Apollo: he and his men wore white wreaths in their hair to show that they were fighting for the god. That war was a major turning point in the formal expansion of Philip's power into Greece. At the end of it he was awarded the Phocian votes on the Amphictyonic Council and elected President of the Pythian Games. His statue coming next to those of the gods in the Aegae procession emphasised both his power and his piety. The white cloak he wore to the theatre has interesting affinities with the white wreath he wore when fighting for Apollo in the Third Sacred War. So too does Justin's comment in connection with that war: 'the man who had championed the majesty of the gods deserved to be regarded as second only to the gods.'[15]

Philip's statue showed his power as *hegemon* of Greece and as the man 'second only to the gods'. If he had arranged for the statue himself, he may well have been influenced by the people of Ephesus, who had set up a statue of him in the Temple of Artemis in gratitude for the great changes he had brought about there. The suggestion has been made that the Macedonian Assembly or a 'large body of Macedonian citizenry' ordered his statue.[16] This theory is based on the detail that the ambassadors from the Greek states (including Athens) gave Philip gold crowns, which are normally associated with honouring a god. Thus, if the Greeks recognised Philip's exalted status it follows that the Macedonians would follow suit. This is possible, but again it is hard to believe that Philip would deliberately fly in the face of the religious principles of the Greeks when it came to declaring the divinity of living mortals. In fact, we can alter the suggestion and say instead that his own people may well have arranged for the statue to honour their king as the benefactor of Macedonia and bringer of prosperity.[17] That was what the celebration in the theatre at Aegae was all about, after all: the wedding had taken place the previous day, and this was supposed to be Philip's day. Hence, a statue of the king was a fitting tribute.

Now we turn to the Philippeion (Figure 3), whose historical context and purpose were discussed on pp. 164–6. Was this building really meant to be a symbol of Philip's divinity, and did the statues in it represent a dynastic cult of him and his family?[18] The answer is no. We are told that the statues were *eikones*, not *agalmata*,[19] which is crucial. Also, as has been astutely pointed out,[20] the building itself tells us its function was not religious. It was a *tholos*, and *tholoi* were generally not religious in function. Moreover, it faced south whereas a *heroon* (if it was one of the royal family) should have faced west, and it contained no cult statue (*agalma*), no altar (*bomos*) and no hearth (*eschara*). Finally, the recent examination by P. Schultz of the remains of the building has shown conclusively that the statues were not chryselephantine, which was normally reserved for cult statues,[21] but made of heavily gilded stone (marble).[22]

Schultz's careful study and persuasive arguments cast new and important light on the form and function of this building. However, his discussion of the public image that Philip was trying to project of himself leans towards a 'divinising' agenda on the part of the king. In truth, we do not know exactly what the Philippeion was meant to represent, but the political interpretation is the more plausible. Located as it was in the *temenos*, the Philippeion was meant to show Philip for what he was: the most important person in Greece, the *hegemon*.[23] This is not over the top when we think of his background and of the Greeks' attitude to Macedonians, which must have had no small effect on him. The location of the statue in the *temenos* perhaps suggests another motivation that can be traced back to the Greek attitude to their 'barbarian' neighbours. If Archelaus had created a counter-games because the Greeks blocked Macedonians competing in the Olympics, how fitting that there was now so overt a Macedonian presence in the home of those games! Even more so, in fact, given that the Philippeion was planned for completion by the Olympic Games of 336.[24]

As for the 'worship' of Philip elsewhere, at Ephesus the statue erected in the temple was an *eikon*, not an *agalma* or cult statue. Hence it was an honorary one, set up by the locals in gratitude for their liberation from Persian rule by Parmenion's advance force in 336. The altars of Zeus Philippios on Eresus are not to Philip alone. The link with Zeus is important, indicating the people were worshipping not Philip as Zeus but Zeus in his role as Philip's protector. We have no idea why the altars were set up or when (340 or 339 are perhaps the more plausible dates),[25] but they seem to be a token of gratitude by the locals for something Philip ordered (or financed), not to accord him divine recognition.[26] Demosthenes tells us that Arcadia and Argos set up bronze statues of the king,[27] but we have no way of knowing whether this is true or rhetorical embellishment. If true, we should note they were bronze, not chryselephantine, which would indicate that they had nothing to do with a cult. Then again, the *agalma* of Artemis in Icarus was made of wood, and that of Hera Cithaeronia in Thespia was merely a roughly hewn tree stump.[28]

Whether there was a cult of Philip in Amphipolis before it fell to him in 357 is open to doubt. After 357 Philip hardly treated the people harshly, so there would appear to be no need to abandon the cult after this date as our source says. Given his treatment of other cities that he took by force (think of Methone and Potidaea in particular), it was in the Amphipolitans' best interests to maintain the cult, and so remain in his good books. His cult at Philippi also has its problems. The evidence is inscriptional and it refers to *temene* (sacred lands) belonging to various gods and heroes. Named are Ares, Poseidon and 'the heroes' as well as at least two *temene* of Philip. The implication of the king's being grouped with various gods and heroes who possess sacred land is that he was divine like them. However, the inscription cannot be dated with greater precision than to the period 350–300. Hence, any cult of Philip could postdate his reign. More importantly, it was Greek practice to worship the founder of a city (*ktistes*). Since Philip founded Philippi (when he renamed it from Crenides) a local cult to him would have been merely following this tradition, and thus cannot be said to have implications for any pretensions to divinity on his part.

The Athenians did not vote to worship Philip. The (much later) account of Clement of Alexandria has been justly criticised,[29] but even more important is the fact that Demades, who had proposed recognising Alexander as a thirteenth god, was fined for his suggestion after Alexander's death.[30] We would expect the person who proposed divine honours for Philip to have been punished too, but we hear nothing about this. While contemporary evidence exists that there was a cult of Alexander in Athens,[31] there is absolutely no mention of one of Philip. Since the Athenians conferred citizenship on Philip and Alexander after Chaeronea, why did they not introduce a sycophantic cult of the king at that time as well?

Isocrates might write to Philip and talk about his becoming a god after his Asian expedition, but this is clearly a rhetorical device, not least because Isocrates had been badgering Philip for years to invade Asia and would use any means of persuasion to get him to go. Philip's soldiers did wear laurel wreaths at the Battle of the Crocus Field, but this merely reflects the king's new role in the Third Sacred War. He was now championing the cause of Apollo, intent on liberating Delphi and freeing the god's oracle. For that he needed to defeat the Phocians. To all intents and purposes, therefore, the god was leading his troops that day.

The idea that Philip thought of himself as divine springs from a later time, specifically the Hellenistic and Roman periods when statues of rulers were carried into theatres and sacrifices were made before them. Although no sacrifice was made before Philip's statue, our later sources mistakenly connected his statue at Aegae that day (and perhaps also the other ones erected to him) to the Hellenistic practice of ruler-cult, which was influenced by Alexander, not by his father.[32] As a result, Philip was mistakenly thought to have been seeking his own divinity.

Appendix 6

THE VERGINA ROYAL TOMBS

Philip II was buried at ancient Aegae, which remained the site for royal weddings and burials after Pella had become the official capital of Macedonia (Map 2). The circumstances of his assassination and burial have already been related in Chapters 13 and 14. Alexander had to bury his father hastily because of the problems he faced from the Greeks and possible contenders to the throne. He seems to have intended to revisit his father's resting place, for one of his (alleged) plans was to build a tomb to rival the greatest pyramid. He was not able to do so since he died in Babylon in June 323 and all of his plans were scrapped.

When the Galatians invaded Macedonia in the mid-270s BC they looted various temples and tombs. At that time the tombs of Philip and others at Aegae were covered with earth to form a large tumulus, 43 feet (13 m) high and 328 feet (100 m) in diameter, to protect them from robbers. Over the centuries the location of these tombs and indeed of Aegae itself was forgotten. Then the former royal capital was identified with the small village of Vergina, close to Thessaloniki, by N.G.L. Hammond,[1] who also suspected that a tumulus there might be the one covering Philip's tomb. The latter was not excavated until 1997 by a team of Greek archaeologists led by Manolis Andronikos. Within the tumulus Andronikos discovered four tombs of varying sizes, two of which had not been plundered, and the foundations of a *heroon* (a small shrine at which to worship the deceased) in front of Tomb II (the largest). The Vergina royal tombs, containing spectacular, precious and beautiful artefacts, are among the most important archaeological discoveries of the twentieth century, as is vividly illustrated by Andronikos' account of the excavations (written in the first person, which creates a sense of dramatic immediacy).[2] The finds are now displayed on site within a modern shelter that is meant to resemble the size and shape of the original tumulus, and which allows access to the façades of the tombs themselves (Plate 18).

Tomb II has excited the most interest and raised the most controversy. It is rectangular in shape, of barrel-vault construction, and has two chambers, a main one and a smaller antechamber (Plate 21). Its façade has columns and a large painted frieze (of a hunting scene) to give it the look of a Doric building (Plate 22). In the main chamber were discovered a stone sarcophagus that had inside it a gold *larnax* (box) on which was the Macedonian starburst (a sixteen-point star), the emblem of the royal house, and rosettes (Plate 23a). Inside the *larnax* were the bones of a middle-aged man and the remains of strands of purple cloth in which they had been wrapped. Forensic testing revealed the bones had been fired and washed in wine, hence were in keeping with the manner of Philip's final send-off.

The tomb also contained many precious and beautiful grave goods, including personal items such as silver drinking vessels and containers (Plate 23b); a silver strainer for decanting wine; armour, including an iron cuirass with goldwork (Plate 23c); a pectoral; a helmet and a magnificent ceremonial shield of gold, ivory, glass and wood; weaponry; an exquisite gold wreath of myrtle leaves and flowers; a silver diadem; and five carved ivory heads, each about the size of an adult thumb (Plate 23d). These had originally been placed on a chryselephantine (gold and ivory) wooden couch. This had deteriorated over the years, so they were lying scattered on the floor when Andronikos entered the tomb. Surprisingly, given all the rich goods inside the tomb, the walls were not decorated but had been left in their rough stucco.

The antechamber contained another stone sarcophagus, inside which was a smaller gold *larnax* containing the skeletal remains, wrapped in a gold and purple cloth, of a young woman in her twenties. Lying against the outside of the sealed door of the main chamber was a pair of gilded greaves of different size and shape (the right one is 1⅓ inches [3.5 cm] longer than the left one), and close by them a magnificent gilded and decorated Scythian *gorytos*, which contained the remains of seventy-four arrows.

Over the front entrance to the tomb was a wide frieze (18 feet 4 inches [5.6 m] in length and about 3 feet 3 inches [1 m] high) depicting a hunting scene (Plate 22). This shows three men on horseback and seven on foot hunting various animals including deer and a lion. One of the horsemen, who is set centre, is about to spear the lion. The frieze is badly decomposed, not so much by the ravages of time but because the earth that had become stuck to it over the centuries took off much of the paint during excavation. It took three years to clean and secure the frieze, but even so any attempt to re-create what it portrays cannot boast 100 per cent accuracy, as the line drawing based on the state of the original when cleaned shows (Plate 24).

Andronikos believed that the occupants of Tomb II were Philip and his last wife, Cleopatra, who was murdered by Olympias a little time after his assassination.[3] Other scholars followed suit.[4] Then came a wave of scepticism as Philip III Arrhidaeus (Alexander's half-brother) and his wife Eurydice were put forward as the tomb's occupants.[5] Arrhidaeus was killed on Olympias' orders in 317 and Eurydice was forced to hang herself; they were then buried, but about six months later the bodies were removed and given a royal burial at Aegae in 316.[6]

The arguments for Arrhidaeus and Eurydice and against Philip II are based on several important factors. To begin with, there are the chronological problems posed by some of the grave goods, such as pottery that is similar to some found in tombs at Derveni dating to the last quarter of the fourth century, hence after the time of Philip II. The same holds true for four black-glazed saltcellars: similar finds in wells in the Athenians Agora are dated to around 315 (hence, roughly the time of the burial of Arrhidaeus and Eurydice).[7] The skeletal remains have also been the focus of much scrutiny, especially the skull. Among other things, macrophotography has been used on its bones, and from the bone pathology based on the close-up photos the argument was made that the trauma around the right eye and cheek (which would be consistent with Philip's wound at Methone in 354) was most likely the result of the cremation or of poor facial reconstruction.[8] Hence, Arrhidaeus is the more probable fit. There is also the hunting frieze on the façade of the tomb (Plate 22; cf. Plate 24). Based on the style and iconography of other hunting scenes, it has been argued that this belongs to the age of Cassander (the son of Antipater, who came to power in the later fourth century during the power struggles of Alexander's successors). Further, it has been suggested that the lion-hunt theme came from the east (where Persian kings apparently hunted lions frequently), and that it was exploited by Alexander's successors to help establish their rule since he enjoyed hunting and had ordered lion-hunt scenes on Hephaestion's funerary monument.[9] We are told that Philoxenus painted such a picture for Cassander,[10] and that this could be the frieze on Tomb II. The armour in the antechamber is thought to belong to the female occupant, and Eurydice rather than Cleopatra is the more likely candidate here: hence it must be her husband who is buried in the main chamber.[11] Finally, some of the grave goods of the main chamber of Tomb II, specifically the cuirass (Plate 23c), helmet and ceremonial shield, and perhaps also the diadem, may well have belonged to Alexander the Great and ended up in the hands of Arrhidaeus and then Cassander. The latter buried these with Arrhidaeus in a symbolic gesture to show the end of the old regime and the beginning of the new one.[12]

If Tomb II housed Philip III Arrhidaeus and Eurydice, where was Philip II buried? One possibility is Tomb I, a cist-tomb that had been plundered but still contained the scattered bones of three people, a mature male, a younger female, and a baby or infant. We know that Olympias had Cleopatra and her baby daughter killed, so the remains would seem to tie in with that murderous deed. Also in this tomb is a magnificent wall painting depicting Pluto's abduction and rape of Persephone, probably by Nichomachus; this could indicate a date of the third quarter of the fourth century, and hence tie in with Philip II.[13]

However, there are serious problems with associating Philip II and Tomb I. To begin with, the remains of the three people inside it were not cremated but inhumed, and as we know Philip was burned on a funeral pyre and Cleopatra and her daughter were also cremated. Next, the baby bones belonged to a 'late fetus of 38–39 intrauterine weeks. It could also have been a viable neonate.'[14] The daughter of Philip and Cleopatra was born before her father's death;[15] she would have been several months old, even a year, when she and her mother were killed on Olympias' orders.

Moreover, the arguments for Tomb II not being that of Philip II are far from watertight. To begin with, it has been argued that the barrel-vault construction was imported from Asia as a result of Alexander's campaigns there, hence it must postdate 336. However, the chronology of the structural developments of Macedonian tombs is a contentious issue. Equally good arguments have been advanced that the barrel-vaulted tomb grew out of the Macedonian cist-tombs of the early fourth century, hence were being built on the Greek mainland well before Alexander's invasion of Asia. Furthermore, there is also a significant difference between the Greek and Asian versions in that the Macedonian tombs used wedge-shaped stones to fill in the gaps whereas the eastern ones used square bricks and stones.[16]

More importantly, the antechamber was added on to the main chamber, hence we have a two-stage period of construction (cf. Plate 21). Philip III Arrhidaeus and Eurydice were put to death at the same time and inhumed in a planned double burial, hence the main chamber and antechamber to house them would have been built at the same time. The later construction of the antechamber of Tomb II can be explained by the fact that Cleopatra and her daughter were put to death on Olympias' orders while Alexander was absent from court putting down the Greek revolt: when he returned and discovered what had happened he was angry with her.[17] Hence, there was a need for a new burial chamber.

However, no baby remains have been found in the *larnax* of the ante-chamber.[18] This implies either that the little girl was not buried with her mother or that the female is not Cleopatra. The former is possible because the intense heat from the cremation of Cleopatra and her daughter may well have reduced delicate baby bones to nothing: hence their absence from the *larnax* does not rule out Cleopatra.[19] The latter possibility is perhaps more likely, however, for it is hard to believe (human nature being what it is, and especially that of Olympias) that Olympias would have allowed Cleopatra, whom she disliked intensely, to be buried with Philip. The same is true of Alexander, for it was his father's marriage to Cleopatra that led to him fleeing from the court after the wedding feast in 337, his ears still ringing with Attalus' taunt and his eyes still seeing his father drawing his sword against him. Thus, Cleopatra being laid to rest beside her husband is open to doubt.[20] The other possibility is that the remains are those of Meda, Philip's sixth wife, the daughter of Cothelas of the Getae (see p. 124), who may well have committed ritual suicide (*suttee*) when her husband was assassinated.[21] The Thracian tribes were tough, warrior people, women included. The military weaponry in the antechamber, especially the *gorytos* (a unique find in Greek tombs but not in Scythian ones), could well belong to Meda rather than Eurydice. More important is the estimated age of the female skeletal remains.[22] As has been shown, the bones are of a mature young woman of about twenty-five years of age. This would rule out Eurydice (who was about twenty when she died), and even Cleopatra (who was perhaps no older than twenty-two), whereas Meda was about twenty-five when Philip was assassinated in 336.

The frieze, on which so much attention has rightly been focused, is so badly worn that parts of it are invisible, and reconstruction of what it was originally like is fraught with difficulty (Plate 24). Hence, the hunting scene becomes a matter of interpretation. It could indeed belong to the age of Cassander when its lion-hunt theme was exploited by Alexander's successors for political reasons, as has been argued. However, given the state of the frieze, this interpretation can hardly be called 'definitive',[23] because it could just as easily depict Philip II on horseback about to kill a lion, with Alexander in the centre galloping to help him, attended by the Royal Pages, the youths who served the king from fourteen to eighteen.[24] The Macedonians loved to hunt, and this is something Philip and Alexander would have done together. Hence, a hunting scene would be a fitting choice to go on the façade of Philip II's tomb. All we can say with certainty amidst all the controversy is that the painting in its original glory must have been stunning.

The evidence of the saltcellars can now be reconsidered, for other objects from the Agora wells have been dated earlier, making it possible that the Vergina saltcellars could date to about 340.[25] Then there is the matter of the specially shaped greaves, the ivory heads and the skeletal remains, which link to Philip's funeral pyre and burial. The right greave is 1⅓ inches (3.5 cm) longer than the left one, which would be consistent with the greaves that Philip would have needed after he was maimed in the thigh while fighting against the Triballi in 339 (see p. 140). One ancient source (Didymus) says that Philip was wounded in the right leg, which would cast doubt on the greaves being Philip's,[26] but the veracity of that source has been questioned and in truth we do not know which leg it was.[27] The explanation as to why they were lying outside the main chamber is that in the haste of burying the king they were accidentally left outside it. The same goes for the *gorytos*: if it did not belong to the female occupant, it could have been part of the booty Philip seized after his defeat of Ateas and the Scythians in 339, and it too may have been inadvertently left out of the king's chamber.

Two of the five ivory heads bear a striking resemblance to other images of Philip II and Alexander; that of Philip portrays him as wounded in the right eye (Plate 23d; cf. Plate 7). A third seems to be of Olympias (Plate 23d; cf. Plate 10). The identities of the other two heads (one male and one female) are unknown. It may be going too far to connect the five heads with the five statues in the Philippeion at Olympia of Philip, his mother and father (Eurydice and Amyntas), his son Alexander, and Olympias (Figure 3). However, the coincidence of the number of sculptures in each location is worth considering, and we would expect the heads to represent prominent members of Philip's family and to be buried with him. It is hard to understand why Olympias' head would be part of any family ensemble buried with Philip III if he were the occupant of Tomb II, since it was Olympias who had him and his wife put to death.

The forensic analysis of the skeletal remains in the *larnax* (Plate 8) showed that they had been washed in wine and wrapped in purple cloth, consistent with the burning of Philip's corpse on the funeral pyre and the way his bones were treated afterwards. Then there is the skull. An initial examination surprisingly revealed that it was not damaged: in other words, it showed no indication of the terrible eye wound that the king received during the siege of Methone in 355/4 (see p. 49).[28] Later, a British anatomist disagreed, finding severe trauma around the right eye and cheekbone, and with the assistance of scholars and other forensic and medical professionals methodically and scientifically rebuilt the skull and reconstructed the face (Plate 1).[29] As can be seen from the reconstruction, there is severe damage in and around the right eye that would be consistent with Philip's wound at Methone. Moreover, as has been noted, the ivory head of Philip II also shows damage to the right eye (Plate 7).

The skull reconstruction has been criticised, not least because bone can suffer damage from intense heat (as with a funeral pyre).[30] However, Bartsiokas' conclusions drawn from the macrophotography which identify the skull with Arrhidaeus have been recently and compellingly challenged, not only on historical grounds but also (more importantly) on forensic ones.[31] In particular, his argument that the occupants of Tomb II were Arrhidaeus and Eurydice because their skeletal remains were degreased (i.e., dry, with no flesh on them) when they were cremated before the royal (second) burial is shown as flawed. Both were buried for six months before being removed and reburied. Based on similar cases from more recent history (including expert testimony of hospital and forensic pathologists), bodies buried for this short length of time would still be greased.

The obvious signs of haste in closing the main tomb (including leaving some of Philip's burial goods in the antechamber) and the lack of decoration on its walls tie in with the situation in the aftermath of Philip's assassination. As has been said, Alexander had to bury his father quickly because of the problems he was facing. His intention to revisit the tomb is shown by his plan to construct a large and elaborate resting place for his father in the future, hence there seemed little point in finishing it properly in the chaotic months of 336. Indeed, whether Alexander intended to enhance the already existing tomb or move his father's remains to another burial place in Aegae is unknown. After Alexander's death, of course, Philip's tomb was left as it was.

Finally, the discovery of royal paraphernalia belonging to Alexander the Great in the tomb can also be disputed. I do not doubt that when Alexander died in 323 his generals and his royal secretary Eumenes took some of his personal effects. However, just because, for example, Alexander was wearing a similar cuirass in the so-called 'Alexander Mosaic' at Pompeii (modelled on a painting of the Battle of Issus in 333) to the one in Tomb II does not mean that it is the same one. Likewise, just because Alexander had a ceremonial shield and Eumenes had Alexander's diadem does not mean they are the same as those found in the tomb. It is hard to imagine that a warrior king as powerful and wealthy as Philip II would not have had a ceremonial shield, for example, and we know that Alexander only got his from the Temple of Athena at Troy after he had crossed into Asia in 334.

What would help to date the tomb would be numismatic evidence, but (significantly) no coins have been found in any of the burials at Vergina. Perhaps (and only perhaps) the absence of coins in Tomb II ties in with Alexander's need for all the money he could lay hands on because of his father's cash shortages.[32]

Overall, the nature of some of the grave goods, especially the armour, the skeletal remains and the hasty closure of the main chamber point more towards Philip II being the occupant of Tomb II rather than away from him. So too does the *heroon* by its side, for it is probable that he was deified on death.

As for the other tombs, Tomb III (discovered in 1978), which lay next to Tomb II, was unlooted. It had in it expensive grave goods and weapons, a wall painting of a chariot race that ran around the entire antechamber, and in the main chamber a silver burial urn with an elaborate gold wreath on its neck that contained the remains of a teenage male. The most likely occupant is Alexander IV, son of Alexander the Great and Roxanne, who was murdered by

Cassander in 311 or 310.[33] It is impossible to say who was buried in Tomb IV, which was looted, although Antigonas II Gonatas is a likely candidate.

In conclusion, it is far more unlikely than likely that the remains of the three people in Tomb I are Philip, Cleopatra and their baby daughter. Who these three people were is anyone's guess, but we need not necessarily limit ourselves to the fourth century and the first half of the third in trying to identify them. The pendulum thus swings thankfully back towards Philip II being the occupant of the main chamber of Tomb II and one of his wives (most likely Meda, although we cannot completely exclude Cleopatra) being the occupant of the antechamber, and perhaps this controversial issue may now be laid to rest.

NOTES

Chapter 1: Preamble: 'The Greatest of the Kings in Europe'?

1. The ethnicity of the Macedonians remains a controversial topic, which I deal with in Appendix 2. I believe that they were Greek and spoke Greek. However, for the sake of convenience, in this book when I refer to 'Greeks' I mean the people who lived south of Mount Olympus, and when I refer to 'Macedonians' I mean those living to its north. I do not mean to suggest any difference from this designation other than the geographical one.
2. Justin 9.3.11. On the battle and its aftermath in more detail, see Chapter 11.
3. Movies: *Alexander the Great*, directed by Robert Rossen in 1956, and *Alexander*, directed by Oliver Stone in 2004 (cf. my review of the latter in *AHR* 110 [2005], pp. 533–4). The room is the Alexander the Great Suite at the Trump Taj Mahal Hotel and Casino in Atlantic City, New Jersey. The song is 'Alexander the Great', to be found on the album *Somewhere in Time* by Iron Maiden.
4. Diodorus 16.95.1–2.
5. Aeschines 2.41.
6. Theopompus, *FGrH* 115 F 27. This statement is open to a different interpretation, however: see below, and especially Appendix 1.
7. Arrian 7.9.2–5; cf. the similarity to Alexander's speech (also highly rhetorical) in Curtius 10.2.23–4.3. On the background to the Opis mutiny, see A.B. Bosworth, *Conquest and Empire: The Reign of Alexander the Great* (Cambridge: 1988), pp. 159–61 and Ian Worthington, *Alexander the Great, Man and God*, rev. and enl. edn (London: 2004), pp. 248–52.
8. The translation is that of P.A. Brunt, *Arrian, History of Alexander*, Loeb Classical Library, Vol. 2 (Cambridge, MA: 1983), *ad loc.*
9. Demosthenes 18.295–96.
10. Cf. Diodorus 16.93.3–4, Justin 8.6.5–8, 9.8.6–7.
11. Arrian 7.9.6–10.7.
12. See A.B. Bosworth, *From Arrian to Alexander* (Oxford: 1988), pp. 101–13.
13. If the opening is a reference just to the people of Upper Macedonia (and the geographical proximity of the tribes mentioned supports this), it is not far off the mark in light of what Philip did for the people in these areas.
14. See especially T.T.B. Ryder, 'The Diplomatic Skills of Philip II', in Ian Worthington (ed.), *Ventures into Greek History: Essays in Honour of N.G.L. Hammond* (Oxford: 1994), pp. 228–57, on Philip's first intentions always being to use diplomacy and his success in doing so; cf. G.L. Cawkwell, 'The End of Greek Liberty', in R.W. Wallace and E.M. Harris (eds), *Transitions to Empire: Essays in Honor of E. Badian* (Norman, OK: 1996), pp. 98–121, setting Philip's diplomatic skills next to his military ones.
15. Athenaeus 13.557b–e for Philip's marriages; see further Chapter 13.

16. Note the extreme view of A. Adams, 'Philip *Alias* Hitler', *G&R* 10 (1941), pp. 105–13: the title and year of publication speak for themselves.

17. For a more detailed consideration of Philip's influence on Alexander, see Chapter 16.

Chapter 2: Philip's Macedonia

1. The Haliacmon is Greece's longest river at 186 miles (297 km). Although the Axius is longer at 235 miles (376 km), only 48 (76 km) of these are in Greece, and the remainder in the former Yugoslavia.

2. Cf. Herodotus 8.137.1 for the longevity of these names.

3. N.G.L. Hammond, 'The Western Frontier in the Reign of Philip II', in H.J. Dell (ed.), *Ancient Macedonian Studies in Honour of C.F. Edson* (Institute for Balkan Studies, Thessaloniki: 1981), p. 199; see also Hammond, *Macedonia* 2, pp. 22–31.

4. Diodorus 7.16. On Perdiccas, see Hammond, *Macedonia* 2, pp. 6–11. For the identification of Vergina as the ancient Aegae (which has been unconvincingly challenged), see N.G.L. Hammond, *A History of Macedonia* 1 (Oxford: 1972), pp. 156–57 and 'The Location of Aegae', *JHS* 117 (1997), pp. 177–9.

5. See further P.B. Faklaris, 'Aegae: Determining the Site of the First Capital of the Macedonians', *AJA* 98 (1994), pp. 609–16.

6. Ellis, *Philip II*, p. 34; cf. Hammond, *History of Macedonia* 1, pp. 12–18.

7. See further E.N. Borza, 'Some Observations on Malaria and the Ecology of Central Macedonia in Antiquity', *AJAH* 4 (1979), pp. 102–24; cf. his 'The Natural Resources of Early Macedonia', in W.L. Adams and E.N. Borza (eds), *Philip II, Alexander the Great, and the Macedonian Heritage* (Lanham, MD: 1982), pp. 17–18.

8. On natural resources, see Borza, 'Natural Resources of Early Macedonia', pp. 1–20 and his *Shadow of Olympus*, pp. 50–7, Errington, *History of Macedonia*, pp. 7–9, Ellis, *Philip II*, pp. 28–34, Hammond, *History of Macedonia* 1, Part 1.

9. See E.N. Borza, 'Timber and Politics in the Ancient World: Macedon and the Greeks', *Proceedings of the American Philosophical Society* 131 (1987), pp. 32–52. The standard treatment of timber in antiquity is still R. Meiggs, *Trees and Timber in the Ancient Mediterranean World* (Oxford: 1962).

10. The best geographical descriptions of ancient Macedonia are still those of Hammond, *History of Macedonia* 1, Part 1, 'The Historical Geography of Macedonia', pp. 3–211, which are all based on extensive personal observations made over the course of visits across many years. See also Borza, *Shadow of Olympus*, pp. 28–50 and M. Sivignon, 'The Geographical Setting of Macedonia', in M.B. Sakellariou (ed.), *Macedonia, 4000 Years of Greek History and Civilization* (Athens: 1983), pp. 12–26 (with some excellent pictures).

11. In detail, see Hammond, *Macedonia* 2, pp. 69–91.

12. Cf. Thucydides 2.80.5, Isocrates 4.3, Demosthenes 15.15. On the origins of the word, cf. Strabo 142.28.

13. Dinarchus 1.24. On the Greeks' perceptions of Macedonians as barbarians from the fifth century to the age of Alexander the Great, see E. Badian, 'Greeks and Macedonians', in B. Barr-Sharrar and E.N. Borza (eds), *Macedonia and Greece in Late Classical and Early Hellenistic Times: Studies in the History of Art* 10 (Washington, DC: 1982), pp. 33–51. Badian has to deal with the Greeks' viewpoint as we have no Macedonian sources to determine what the Macedonians thought of themselves.

14. See further M. Andronikos, 'Art during the Archaic and Classical Periods' and J. Touratsoglou, 'Art in the Hellenistic Period', in Sakellariou (ed.), *Macedonia, 4000 Years of Greek History and Civilization*, pp. 92–110 and 170–91, respectively; cf. D. Pandermalis, 'Monuments and Art in the Roman Period', in Sakellariou, *Macedonia*, pp. 208–21. On mosaics, with discussion of those at Pella, see M. Robertson, 'Early Greek Mosaics', in Barr-Sharrar and E.N. Borza (eds), *Macedonia and Greece in Late*

Classical and Early Hellenistic Times: Studies in the History of Art 10, pp. 241–9. On tomb designs, see S.G. Miller, 'Macedonian Tombs: Their Architecture and Architectural Decoration', in Borza, *Macedonia and Greece,* pp. 153–71. See Plates 19a–b for some Hellenistic mosaics and Plate 20 for a Hellenistic head of Alexander.

15. On this, see C.G. Thomas, *Alexander and his World* (Oxford: 2006); see too G.T. Griffith, 'The Macedonian Background', *G&R*² 12 (1965), pp. 125–39 and Ian Worthington, 'Alexander, Philip, and the Macedonian Background', in J. Roisman (ed.), *Brill's Companion to Alexander the Great* (Leiden: 2003), pp. 69–98.

16. Demosthenes 2.18–19. Theopompus, *FGrH* 115 F 163 and 236 makes heavy drinking part and parcel of Macedonian society. It is interesting that Demosthenes uses the epithet 'water-drinker' critically of a person (6.30 and 19.46).

17. Theopompus, *FGrH* 115 F 282.

18. J. Davidson, *Courtesans and Fishcakes* (London: 1997), p. 40.

19. Herodotus 6.84.

20. On taverns, see Davidson, *Courtesans and Fishcakes*, pp. 53–61.

21. See further R.A. Tomlinson, 'Ancient Macedonian Symposia', *Ancient Macedonia* 1 (Institute for Balkan Studies, Thessaloniki: 1970), pp. 308–15; cf. E.N. Borza, 'The Symposium at Alexander's Court', *Ancient Macedonia* 3 (Institute for Balkan Studies, Thessaloniki: 1983), pp. 45–55.

22. Ephippus, *FGrH* 126 F 1 = Athenaeus 3.120e.

23. On the misuse of the modern term 'alcoholism', cf. Davidson, *Courtesans and Fishcakes*, pp. 147–8; on drinking in the ancient world, see *ibid.*, pp. 36–69.

24. *Ephemerides, FGrH* 117 F 2b = Athenaeus 10.434b.

25. See E. Carney, *Women and Monarchy in Macedonia* (Norman, OK: 2000), pp. 23–27 and 29–31; cf. Hammond, *Macedonian State*, pp. 31–6.

26. Cf. W.S. Greenwalt, 'Polygamy and Succession in Argead Macedonia', *Arethusa* 22 (1989), pp. 19–45.

27. Although focusing on women who married kings, Carney, *Women and Monarchy*, has much to say along the way about social customs, including polygamy, in general. On society and social structure, cf. Hammond, *Macedonia* 2, pp. 162–5.

28. J.M. Hall, 'Contested Ethnicities: Perceptions of Macedonia within Evolving Definitions of Greek Identity', in I. Malkin (ed.), *Ancient Perceptions of Greek Ethnicity* (Cambridge, MA: 2001), pp. 159–86. Badian, 'Greeks and Macedonians', pp. 42–3, rightly says that we have no idea how Macedonians viewed themselves because of lack of the Macedonian sources.

29. On political institutions, see further Hammond, *Macedonian State*, especially Chapters 2, 4, 7 and 8, M.B. Hatzopoulos, *Macedonian Institutions under the Kings*, 1 and 2, *Meletemata* 22 (Athens: 1996), though using later evidence than the reign of Philip II, and Borza, *Shadow of Olympus*, pp. 231–52 (in the time of Philip and Alexander).

30. Hammond, *History of Macedonia* 1, pp. 427–9.

31. The first king to use that title was Alexander the Great: see Hatzopoulos, *Macedonian Institutions under the Kings* 2, no. 62. On the 'royal style', cf. Griffith, *Macedonia* 2, pp. 387–9, and especially M. Errington, 'Macedonian Royal Style and its Historical Significance', *JHS* 94 (1974), pp. 20–37.

32. See Hammond, *Macedonia* 2, pp. 152–8 and W.L. Adams, 'Macedonian Kingship and the Right of Petition', in *Ancient Macedonia* 4 (Institute for Balkan Studies, Thessaloniki: 1986), pp. 43–52. See also next note.

33. On the duties of the king and his relationship to the people, see further Griffith, *Macedonia* 2, pp. 383–404, Hammond, *Macedonian State*, pp. 21–4, 60–70 and 166–70.

34. C. Habicht, *Gottmenschentum und griechische Städte* (Munich: 1970), pp. 11–17 on sources.

35. Ellis, *Philip II*, p. 307 n. 57. On Philip's divinity, see especially Appendix 5.
36. See Hammond, *Macedonia* 2, pp. 158–60.
37. On which, see Hammond, *Macedonia* 2, pp. 160–62 and his *Macedonian State*, pp. 60–4.
38. A good overview of these problems is given by Hammond, *Macedonian State*, pp. 89–99.
39. Cf. Thucydides 4.108.1, Livy 45.30.3. On Pella, see Appendix 4.
40. Xenophon, *Hellenica* 5.2.13; it was also praised as late as 168 by the victorious Roman general Aemilius Paullus (Livy 44.46.4–11).
41. Xenophon, *Hellenica* 7.5.27, Diodorus 15.71.1, 15.77.5, 16.2.4–5.
42. Cawkwell, *Philip*, p. 26.

Chapter 3: Philip's Youth and Accession

1. On Eurydice, see E. Carney, *Women and Monarchy in Macedonia* (Norman, OK: 2000), pp. 40–6. Her ethnicity is disputed, for her father Sirras may have been Illyrian (see the bibliography cited by Carney). However, this is unlikely in light of a comment that Attalus made at the wedding of Philip in 337, intended as a slur on Alexander's legitimacy, for his mother (Olympias) was from Epirus. Attalus presumably would not have wanted to draw attention to Philip's illegitimacy if his mother were non-Macedonian: see further p. 178.
2. Strabo 326c.
3. Pausanias 8.7.6, Justin 9.8.1.
4. Diodorus 16.1.3.
5. Griffith, *Macedonia* 2, pp. 699–701, J.R. Ellis, 'The Stepbrothers of Philip II', *Historia* 22 (1973), pp. 350–4.
6. For example, his lopsided head, watery eyes, round chin, long, thin nose, forehead that bulged above his eyes, and red patches that later mottled his face and chest: see further Ian Worthington, *Alexander the Great, Man and God*, rev. and enl. edn (London: 2004), pp. 31–2.
7. See further G.M.A. Richter, *The Portraits of the Greeks* (Ithaca, NY: 1984), p. 224, for discussion and sources.
8. On the traditional hat, cf. E.A. Fredricksmeyer, 'The Kausia: Macedonian or Indian?', in Ian Worthington (ed.), *Ventures into Greek History: Essays in Honour of N.G.L. Hammond* (Oxford: 1994), pp. 135–58.
9. See A.J.N.W. Prag, J.H. Musgrave and R.A. Neave, 'Twenty-First Century Philippic', in G.J. Oliver and Z. Archibald (eds), *The Power of the Individual in Ancient Greece: Essays in Honour of J.K. Davies* (Stuttgart: 2008).
10. On Alexander, see Worthington, *Alexander*, pp. 33–6.
11. Plutarch, *Alexander* 2.2; see Carney, *Women and Monarchy*, p. 63.
12. Plutarch, *Alexander* 2.9; cf. Athenaeus 14.659f.
13. Diodorus 15.61, 15.67.4, 16.2.2–3, Plutarch, *Pelopidas* 26.4–5, Justin 6.9.7, 7.5.1–3.
14. Justin 6.9.7, 7.5.3.
15. On this period, see in detail J. Buckler, *The Theban Hegemony* (Cambridge, MA: 1980); cf. his *Aegean Greece*, pp. 296–350, 359–66. The period 371–362 is usually referred to as the Theban hegemony, but ascendancy is a better term (cf. Buckler) as the city was never a leader of Greeks in that strict sense.
16. The view of Cawkwell, *Philip*, pp. 155–7, and see further G.L. Cawkwell, 'Epaminondas and Thebes', CQ^2 22 (1978), pp. 254–78.
17. Justin 7.5.2; cf. Plutarch, *Pelopidas* 26.5. Griffith, *Macedonia* 2, pp. 205–6 and 424–5, Buckler, *Theban Hegemony*, pp. 116–19, cf. pp. 245–9.
18. Plutarch, *Pelopidas* 26.5.
19. Diodorus 15.67, Justin 6.9.7, 7.5.2; cf. Plutarch, *Pelopidas* 26.5.

20. See further Plutarch, *Pelopidas* 18.
21. Ellis, *Philip II*, pp. 43–4, does not believe that Philip learned about all this.
22. Cf. Diodorus 16.2.3.
23. Diodorus 15.78, Hammond, *Macedonia* 2, p. 186.
24. Athenaeus 11.506f.
25. Athenaeus 13.557c (from Satyrus). On Phila, see Carney, *Women and Monarchy*, pp. 59–60.
26. See A.D. Tronson, 'Satyrus the Peripatetic and the Marriages of Philip II', *JHS* 104 (1984), pp. 116–26; on Philip's marriages, especially his seventh, which seems to have caused him much trouble, see also Chapter 13.
27. So Ellis, *Philip II*, p. 38; *contra* Hammond, *Philip*, p. 28, that Phila was the second wife, married after he defeated the Illyrians in 358.
28. Diodorus 16.2.5–6, 3.3–4.
29. Justin 7.5.8.
30. Ellis, *Philip II*, p. 47.
31. Discussion at Griffith, *Macedonia* 2, pp. 208–10.
32. Justin 7.5.9–10; see further M.B. Hatzopoulos, 'The Oleveni Inscription and the Dates of Philip II's Reign', in W.L. Adams and E.N. Borza (eds), *Philip II, Alexander the Great, and the Macedonian Heritage* (Lanham, MD: 1982), p. 42.
33. Satyrus in Athenaeus 13. 557b, with Tronson, 'Satyrus the Peripatetic', pp. 120–1.
34. For arguments, see J.R. Ellis, 'The Security of the Macedonian Throne under Philip II', *Ancient Macedonia* 1 (Institute for Balkan Studies, Thessaloniki: 1970), pp. 68–75; cf. Ellis, *Philip II*, pp. 46–7, Griffith, *Macedonia* 2, pp. 208–9 and 702–4, Cawkwell, *Philip*, pp. 27–8, Buckler, *Aegean Greece*, p. 387 n. 3. It is still accepted by some scholars, for example Hammond, *Philip*, pp. 23–4 and Tronson, 'Satyrus the Peripatetic', pp. 120–1.
35. Diodorus 16.1.3.
36. He confuses the order of Philip's wives (see pp. 172–3, with a translation of the Satyrus passage), and A.S. Riginos, 'The Wounding of Philip II of Macedon: Fact and Fabrication', *JHS* 114 (1994), pp. 103–19, argues that Philip's various wounds were embellished by later biographers (including Satyrus) and others for dramatic and comic effect. On the sources on Philip in general, see Appendix 1.
37. See further M.B. Hatzopoulos, 'Succession and Regency in Classical Macedonia', in *Ancient Macedonia* 4 (Institute for Balkan Studies, Thessaloniki: 1986), pp. 279–92.
38. Justin 7.4.5, 8.3.10.
39. See Ellis, 'Stepbrothers of Philip II', pp. 350–4, Griffith, *Macedonia* 2, pp. 699–701.
40. He may have made a bid for the throne when Philip was assassinated in 336: see Chapter 14.
41. The relevant lines of the inscription are 11–16: see Hatzopoulos, 'Oleveni Inscription and the Dates of Philip II's Reign', pp. 21–42 and his 'La lettre royale d'Oleveni', *Chiron* 25 (1995), pp. 163–85. The date of 360 is, however, accepted by many scholars.
42. Diodorus 16.1.3, 16.2.1, 16.95.1, 17.1.1.
43. Justin 9.8.1.
44. Diodorus 16.3.1–2.
45. The phraseology is that of Buckler, *Aegean Greece*, p. 387.

Chapter 4: The New Army and the Unification of Macedonia

1. Diodorus 16.3.1.
2. Diodorus 16.8.7; cf. Demosthenes 9.49 (not necessarily referring only to later in Philip's reign).
3. Justin 7.6.4–5.

4.   Athenaeus 13.557c; see further E. Carney, *Women and Monarchy in Macedonia* (Norman, OK: 2000), pp. 57–8.

5.   Diodorus 16.3.4.

6.   Diodorus 16.3.4, Justin 7.6.1–4.

7.   See further J. Heskel, 'Philip II and Argaios: A Pretender's Story', in R.W. Wallace and E.M. Harris (eds), *Transitions to Empire: Essays in Honor of E. Badian* (Norman, OK: 1996), pp. 37–56.

8.   On this, see T.T.B. Ryder, 'The Diplomatic Skills of Philip II', in Ian Worthington (ed.), *Ventures into Greek History: Essays in Honour of N.G.L. Hammond* (Oxford: 1994), pp. 251–7.

9.   Diodorus 16.3.4.

10. Diodorus 16.3.3, based on Ephorus.

11. Diodorus 16.3.5; cf. Demosthenes 23.121.

12. Cf. Heskel, 'Philip II and Argaios', pp. 50–1; but Griffith, *Macedonia* 2, pp. 211–12, thinks it was a 'small affair in itself, and in its military details merits small attention'.

13. See Ryder, 'Diplomatic Skills of Philip II', pp. 228–57 and G.L. Cawkwell, 'The End of Greek Liberty', in R.W. Wallace and E.M. Harris (eds), *Transitions to Empire: Essays in Honor of E. Badian* (Norman, OK: 1996), pp. 98–121.

14. Theopompus, *FGrH* 115 F 42; cf. Demosthenes 1.8–9.

15. Cf. J.R. Ellis, 'The Dynamics of Fourth-Century Macedonian Imperialism', *Ancient Macedonia* 2 (Institute for Balkan Studies, Thessaloniki: 1977), pp. 103–14.

16. Diodorus 16.4.3.

17. Diodorus 16.35.4–5.

18. Diodorus 17.17.5.

19. Diodorus 16.1.5; the translation is that of Hammond, *Macedonian State*, p. 198.

20. Cf. Griffith, *Macedonia* 2, pp. 406–8.

21. Diodorus 16.3.1–2; cf. Polyaenus 4.1.10. On the military reforms, see in detail Griffith, *Macedonia* 2, pp. 405–49; cf. Hammond, *Macedonian State*, pp. 100–6.

22. See Hammond, *Macedonian State*, pp. 148–9, Griffith, *Macedonia* 2, pp. 705–9; cf. A. Erskine, 'The *Pezêtairoi* of Philip II and Alexander III', *Historia* 38 (1989), pp. 385–94.

23. Diodorus 17.57.2–4.

24. The most exhaustive discussion of the sarissa, with references to pikes and their usage in later periods of military history, is now that of N.V. Sekunda, 'The Sarissa', *Acta Universitatis Lodziensis, Folia Archaeologica* 23 (2001), pp. 13–41. See also N.G.L. Hammond, 'Training in the Use of the Sarissa and its Effect in Battle 359–333 BC', *Antichthon* 14 (1980), pp. 53–63.

25. Polyaenus 4.2.10.

26. A. Tronson, 'The Relevance of *IG* II² 329 to the Hellenic League of Alexander the Great', *Anc. World* 12 (1985), pp. 17–18.

27. *IG* ii² 329 = M.N. Tod, *Greek Historical Inscriptions* 2 (Oxford: 1948), no. 183; cf. Arrian 7.23.3, and see further Hammond, *Macedonian State*, p. 151.

28. On the cavalry spear, see Sekunda, 'The Sarissa', pp. 37–40.

29. Cf. Hammond, *Macedonian State*, pp. 148–50.

30. Cf. Griffith, *Macedonia* 2, pp. 709–13.

31. Justin 11.1.1–6.

32. Plutarch, *Alexander* 15.4–6.

33. Diodorus 16.34.5.

34. Arrian 4.13.1 (who says the institution went back to Philip's time), Curtius 8.6.2 (who talks of the institution as 'customary'); cf. Curtius 5.1.42, 8.6.6.

35. Cf. Hammond, *Macedonian State*, p. 192.

36. On ancient siegecraft in general, see D.B. Campbell, *Ancient Siege Warfare: Persians, Greeks, Carthaginians and Romans, 576–146 BC* (London: 2005), E.W. Marsden,

Greek and Roman Artillery (Oxford: 1969), and most recently D. Whitehead and P.H. Blyth, *Athenaeus Mechanicus, On Machines* (Stuttgart: 2004).

37. See further Y. Garlan, *Recherches de poliorcétique grecque* (Paris: 1974), pp. 202–44 and E.W. Marsden, 'Macedonian Military Machinery and its Designers under Philip and Alexander', *Ancient Macedonia* 2 (Institute for Balkan Studies, Thessaloniki: 1977), pp. 211–23 (p. 212 for the date).

38. Marsden, 'Macedonian Military Machinery', pp. 213–15.

39. See P.T. Keyser, 'The Use of Artillery by Philip II and Alexander the Great', *Anc. World* 15 (1994), pp. 27–49.

40. On this poliorcetic writer, with a translation of his work, see Whitehead and Blyth, *Athenaeus Mechanicus, On Machines*.

41. See G.T. Griffith, 'Philip as a General and the Macedonian Army', in M.B. Hatzopoulos and L.D. Loukopoulos (eds), *Philip of Macedon* (Athens: 1980), pp. 58–77; cf. the very good discussion (including comparison to Alexander) by Cawkwell, *Philip*, pp. 150–65 and his 'End of Greek Liberty,' pp. 108–12.

42. For the details, see Diodorus 16.4.2–7, 16.8.1.

43. Ellis, *Philip II*, p. 58; see also N.G.L. Hammond, 'The Battle between Philip and Bardylis', *Antichthon* 23 (1989), pp. 1–9.

44. Diodorus 16.8.1.

45. On this point, and generally on the western frontier, see H.J. Dell, 'The Western Frontier of the Macedonian Monarchy', *Ancient Macedonia* 1 (Institute for Balkan Studies, Thessaloniki: 1970), pp. 115–26 and N.G.L. Hammond, 'The Western Frontier in the Reign of Philip II', in H.J. Dell (ed.), *Ancient Macedonian Studies in Honour of C.F. Edson* (Institute for Balkan Studies, Thessaloniki: 1981), pp. 199–217.

46. Cf. Errington, *History of Macedonia*, pp. 41–3. See further J.R. Ellis, 'The Unification of Macedonia', in M.B. Hatzopoulos and L.D. Loukopoulos (eds), *Philip of Macedon* (Athens: 1980), pp. 36–47.

47. Philip's economic reforms will be mentioned throughout the book, but on them see further Hammond, *Macedonia* 2, pp. 657–71, Hammond, *Macedonian State*, pp. 177–87 and his 'Philip's Innovations in Macedonian Economy', *SO* 70 (1995), pp. 22–9, in answer to H. Montgomery 'The Economic Revolution of Philip II – Myth or Reality', *SO* 60 (1985), pp. 37–47, who argues against any relationship between Philip's military and diplomatic victories and his economic reforms, and claims that there was no economic revolution.

48. Cf. the caution of A.B. Bosworth, 'Philip II and Upper Macedonia', *CQ*² 21 (1971), pp. 93–105, who argues that Lyncestis is for one was an area that was never completely part of the new unified Macedonia.

49. Carney, *Women and Monarchy in Macedonia*, pp. 58 and 69–70.

50. On Thessaly in the fourth century, see the classic study of H.D. Westlake, *Thessaly in the Fourth Century BC* (London: 1935; repr. Chicago: 1993) and also M. Sordi, *La Lega Thessala fino ad Alessandro* (Rome: 1958). On Philip's first involvement there, cf. G.T. Griffith, 'Philip of Macedon's Early Intervention in Thessaly (358–352 B.C.)', *CQ*² 20 (1970), pp. 67–80, and C. Ehrhardt, 'Two Notes on Philip of Macedon's First Interventions in Thessaly', *CQ*² 17 (1967), pp. 296–301.

51. On the role of Thessaly in Philip's dealings with Greece, see further S. Sprawski, 'All the King's Men: Thessalians and Philip II's Designs on Greece', in D. Musial (ed.), *Society and Religions: Studies in Greek and Roman History* (Torun: 2005), pp. 31–49; see too Ryder, 'Diplomatic Skills of Philip II', pp. 247–50.

52. Xenophon, *Hellenica* 6.4.28.

53. On the introduction of this office and the power of Lycophron and Jason, see S. Sprawski, *Jason of Pherai* (Krakow: 1999), idem, 'Were Lycophron and Jason Tyrants of Pherae? Xenophon on the History of Thessaly', in C. Tuplin (ed.), *Xenophon and his World* (Stuttgart: 2004), pp. 437–52, idem, 'Philip II and the Freedom of the

Thessalians', *Electrum* 9 (2003), pp. 61–4, and E. Badian, 'Philip II and the Last of the Thessalians', *Ancient Macedonia* 6 (Institute for Balkan Studies, Thessaloniki: 1999), pp. 109–22.

54. Xenophon, *Hellenica* 6.1.11–12, 6.1.18, 4.28, Isocrates 5.119–20, Pausanias 6.17.9.

55. Diodorus 15.59.2.

56. See Buckler, *Aegean Greece*, pp. 392–3.

57. Athenaeus 13.557c, Justin 9.8.2, 13.2.11, and cf. Athenaeus 13.578a. For the case for Philinna's more noble status, see Carney, *Women and Monarchy*, pp. 61–2; cf. Ellis, *Philip II*, p. 61 and Griffith, *Macedonia* 2, p. 225.

58. Much archaeological work has been undertaken in Epirus in recent years, but for a convenient if somewhat outdated history, see N.G.L. Hammond, *Epirus* (Oxford: 1967).

59. Athenaeus 13.557c, Justin 7.6.10–12; cf. Diodorus 19.51.1. See Carney, *Women and Monarchy*, pp. 62–7 and 79–81 (Olympias in Philip's reign), and especially her *Olympias, Mother of Alexander the Great* (London: 2006). Carney (correctly) disputes that Philip changed her name to mask her Epirote status: on this, cf. W. Heckel, 'Polyxena the Mother of Alexander the Great', *Chiron* 11 (1981), pp. 79–96. On Olympias and Philip, see also Chapter 13.

Chapter 5: The War over Amphipolis

1. On the war, see most conveniently the one-volume history of D. Kagan, *The Peloponnesian War* (London: 2003) and L. Tritle, *The Peloponnesian War* (Westport, CT: 2004).

2. For an overview of this period, see Buckler, *Aegean Greece*, pp. 12–295; see too P. Cartledge, *Agesilaos and the Crisis of Sparta* (Baltimore, MD: 1987) and C.D. Hamilton, *Agesilaus and the Failure of Spartan Hegemony* (Ithaca, NY: 1991).

3. See further J. Cargill, *The Second Athenian League* (Berkeley: 1981) and R. Sealey, *Demosthenes and his Time: A Study in Defeat* (Oxford: 1993), pp. 50–73; cf. G.T. Griffith, 'Athens in the Fourth Century', in P.D.A. Garnsey and C.R. Whittaker (eds), *Imperialism in the Ancient World* (Cambridge: 1978), pp. 127–44. The charter of the Second Athenian Naval Confederacy, known as the Decree of Aristoteles, survives: see P.J. Rhodes and R. Osborne (eds), *Greek Historical Inscriptions, 404–323 BC* (Oxford: 2003), no. 22.

4. The best book on Athenian democracy is M.H. Hansen, *The Athenian Democracy in the Age of Demosthenes* (Oxford: 1991).

5. See M.H. Hansen, *The Athenian Assembly in the Age of Demosthenes* (Oxford: 1987).

6. On the Boule, see in detail P.J. Rhodes, *The Athenian Boule* (Oxford: 1972).

7. See further Ian Worthington, 'Rhetoric and Politics in Classical Greece: Rise of the *Rhêtores*', in Ian Worthington (ed.), *Blackwell Companion to Greek Rhetoric* (Oxford: 2006), pp. 255–71; on political oratory in general, see S. Usher, 'Symbouleutic Oratory', in Worthington, *Blackwell Companion*, pp. 220–35.

8. Cf. Thucydides 2.65.8–9 on Pericles' domination of political affairs: 'in what was nominally a democracy power was in the hands of one man.' Thucydides was writing about the fifth century, but the same largely holds true for the fourth.

9. On both of these aspects, see the essays in Ian Worthington (ed.), *Demosthenes: Statesman and Orator* (London: 2000). See also, on Demosthenes' excellence in oratory, S. Usher, *Greek Oratory* (Oxford: 1999), pp. 171–278 and, on his political career, Sealey, *Demosthenes and his Time*, *passim*.

10. On the statue, see G.M.A. Richter, *The Portraits of the Greeks* (Ithaca, NY: 1984), pp. 108–13 with various plates.

11. The speeches against Aphobus and Onetor (nos 27–31) have survived in the Demosthenic corpus, although there are doubts as to their authenticity.

12. See further J. Heskel, *The North Aegean Wars, 371–60 BC* (Stuttgart: 1997), P.E. Harding, 'Athenian Foreign Policy in the Fourth Century', *Klio* 77 (1995), pp. 105–25, and cf. E. Badian, 'The Ghost of Empire: Reflections on Athenian Foreign Policy in the Fourth Century', in W. Eder (ed.), *Die athenische Demokratie im 4. Jahrhundert v. Chr.* (Stuttgart: 1995), pp. 79–106.

13. Ellis, *Philip II*, pp. 64–5, T.T.B. Ryder, 'The Diplomatic Skills of Philip II', in Ian Worthington (ed.), *Ventures into Greek History: Essays in Honour of N.G.L. Hammond* (Oxford: 1994), pp. 256–7.

14. On which, see Hammond, *Macedonia* 2, pp. 657–71, idem, *Macedonian State*, pp. 177–87; cf. N.G.L. Hammond, 'Philip's Innovations in Macedonian Economy', *SO* 70 (1995), pp. 22–9.

15. Demosthenes 1.8; cf. Theopompus, *FGrH* 115 F 42.

16. [Demosthenes] 7.27, Demosthenes 23.116.

17. Theopompus, *FGrH* 115 F 30; cf. Demosthenes 2.6.

18. Theopompus, *FGrH* 115 F 30a–b, Demosthenes 2.6.

19. On the pitfalls of oratory as source material, see Appendix 1.

20. See in detail G.E.M. de Ste. Croix, 'The Alleged Secret Pact between Athens and Philip II Concerning Amphipolis and Pydna', *CQ*² 13 (1963), pp. 110–19; cf. Ellis, *Philip II*, pp. 63–7, Cawkwell, *Philip*, pp. 73–5, Griffith, *Macedonia*, pp. 236–43 and Ryder, 'Diplomatic Skills of Philip II', pp. 256–7.

21. On ancient siegecraft and siege warfare, see especially D.B Campbell, *Ancient Siege Warfare: Persians, Greeks, Carthaginians and Romans, 576–146 BC* (London: 2005) and E.W. Marsden, *Greek and Roman Artillery* (Oxford: 1969). See also P.T. Keyser, 'The Use of Artillery by Philip II and Alexander the Great', *Anc. World* 15 (1994), pp. 27–49; cf. Y. Garlan, *Recherches de poliorcétique grecque* (Paris: 1974), pp. 202–44.

22. Demosthenes 1.5.

23. Diodorus 16.8.2.

24. Stratocles and Philon are named in a decree expelling anti-Macedonians from Olynthus: Rhodes and Osborne, *Greek Historical Inscriptions*, no. 49. Errington, *History of Macedonia*, pp. 272–3 n. 3, suggests that the decree could be before then.

25. Theopompus, *FGrH* 115 F 30a–b, Diodorus 16.8.3.

26. Aeschines 2.70, 3.54, Isocrates 5.2, Diodorus 16.8.2–3.

27. Diodorus 16.8.4.

28. Rhodes and Osborne, *Greek Historical Inscriptions*, no. 53.

29. *Ibid.*, no. 50; cf. Diodorus 16.8.5.

30. Diodorus 16.7.2, Rhodes and Osborne, *Greek Historical Inscriptions*, no. 48.

31. Demosthenes 15.3.

32. Diodorus 16.7.3.

33. *IG* ii² 1611, 9 and 1613, 302 record that the Athenians had 283 ships in 357/6. By 353/2 they had 349 according to *IG* ii² 1613, 302. See further G.L. Cawkwell, 'Athenian Naval Power in the Fourth Century', *CQ*² 34 (1984), pp. 334–45.

34. Rhodes-Osborne, *Greek Historical Inscriptions*, no. 47.

35. Plutarch, *Alexander* 3.8.

36. Diodorus 16.22.3.

37. Diodorus 16.8.5.

38. Cf. Griffith, *Macedonia* 2, pp. 358–61, Borza, *Shadow of Olympus*, p. 214.

39. Theophrastus, *Nature of Plants* 5.14.5–6.

40. Cf. G. le Rider, 'The Coinage of Philip and the Pangaion Mines', in M.B. Hatzopoulos and L.D. Loukopoulos (eds), *Philip of Macedon* (Athens: 1980), pp. 48–57; cf. C.M. Kraay, *Archaic and Classical Greek Coins* (Berkeley and Los Angeles, CA: 1976), pp. 138–47.

41. Cf. Hammond, *Macedonia* 2, pp. 662–6. For Philip's coinage in general, see G. le

Rider, *Le monnayage d'argent et d'or de Philippe II frappé en Macédoine de 359 à 294* (Paris: 1977) and V. Poulios, 'Macedonian Coinage from the 6th Century to 148 BC', in J. Vokotopoulou (ed.), *Greek Civilization: Macedonia, Kingdom of Alexander the Great* (Athens: 1993), pp. 83–103.

42. Diodorus 16.8.6.
43. Plutarch, *Alexander* 3.8.
44. Hegesias, *FGrH* 142 F 3 = Plutarch, *Alexander* 3.6–7.
45. Diodorus 16.34.4.
46. See Diodorus 16.31.4, 16.35.5–6, Justin 7.6.13–14.
47. Duris, *FGrH* 76 F 36, though he says the weapon was a javelin.
48. Duris, *FGrH* 76 F 36, Theopompus, *FGrH* 115 F 52, Demosthenes 18.67, Justin 7.6.14–15.
49. Plutarch, *Alexander* 3.2; for the story of Olympias' impregnation, see Plutarch, *Alexander* 2.6. On the eye injury and the role it plays in later variant traditions concerning Philip, see A.S. Riginos, 'The Wounding of Philip II of Macedon: Fact and Fabrication', *JHS* 114 (1994), pp. 106–14.
50. *IG* ii^2 1, 130.
51. On chronology, see J. Buckler, *Philip II and the Sacred War* (Leiden: 1989), pp. 181–5.
52. Demosthenes 4.35.
53. Justin 7.6.16.
54. Buckler, *Aegean Greece*, p. 413 with n. 33, based on his personal observations in July 1996.
55. Diodorus 16.34.5. This was perhaps the only grant Philip made to the ordinary Macedonian people as opposed to senior individuals to whom he gave land: see Griffith, *Macedonia* 2, pp. 361–2.
56. Griffith, *Macedonia* 2, p. 257.
57. Demosthenes 10.37.
58. Demosthenes 10.38.
59. Demosthenes 39.17.
60. On whom, see G.L. Cawkwell, 'Eubulus', *JHS* 83 (1963), pp. 47–67.
61. [Plutarch], *Moralia* 1011b.
62. Dinarchus 1.96.
63. See further E. Badian, 'The Road to Prominence', in Ian Worthington (ed.), *Demosthenes: Statesman and Orator* (London: 2000), pp. 9–44.

Chapter 6: Apollo's Saviour: Philip and the Sacred War

1. Cf. H.W. Parke, *A History of the Delphic Oracle* (Oxford: 1939), J.E. Fontenrose, *The Delphic Oracle, its Responses and Operations, with a Catalogue of Responses* (Berkeley and Los Angeles, CA: 1978).
2. Griffith, *Macedonia* 2, p. 451.
3. There is a belief that this war did not take place, but this is unlikely. The council probably acted as cynically as it did because the power of the Delphic oracle was greater than that of Demeter at Anthela. See further H.W. Parke and J. Boardman, 'The Struggle for the Tripod and the First Sacred War', *JHS* 77 (1957), pp. 276–82 and especially J.K. Davies, 'The Tradition about the First Sacred War', in S. Hornblower (ed.), *Greek Historiography* (Oxford: 1994), pp. 193–212, citing bibliography for and against it.
4. The Second Sacred War, in the mid-fifth century, is also a shadowy affair. It appears that Phocis had gained control of the Delphic oracle, since that state had an ancient claim to it, but eventually the Spartans wrested control from it and restored Delphi to the Delphians.

5. On the war in detail, see J. Buckler, *Philip II and the Sacred War* (Leiden: 1989); cf. his *Aegean Greece*, pp. 397–429 and 442–52.

6. Diodorus 16.23.

7. Cf. Justin 8.1.4–6.

8. Xenophon, *Hellenica* 5.2.28–31, Diodorus 15.20.

9. Homer, *Iliad* 2.517–19.

10. Diodorus 16.24.2, Justin 8.1.4–7. On the role of Sparta in the Sacred War and the attitude of Archidamus to Macedonia, see especially C.D. Hamilton, 'Philip II and Archidamus', in W.L. Adams and E.N. Borza (eds), *Philip II, Alexander the Great, and the Macedonian Heritage* (Lanham, MD: 1982), pp. 61–77.

11. Diodorus 15.14.3–4, Pausanias 10.2.3.

12. Diodorus 16.27.1–2.

13. On mercenaries, see in detail M. Trundle, *Greek Mercenaries from the Late Archaic Period to Alexander* (London: 2004).

14. Diodorus 16.25.1, 16.30.1.

15. Diodorus 16.28.3–29.1.

16. Diodorus 16.30.1–2.

17. Diodorus 16.27.3, 16.28.2.

18. Cf. Thucydides 1.121.3, 2.13.4, Xenophon, *Hellenica* 6.4.30.

19. See P.J. Rhodes and R. Osborne (eds), *Greek Historical Inscriptions, 404–323 BC* (Oxford: 2003), no. 57.

20. The same man with whom Philip had stayed when he was a hostage in Thebes.

21. Justin 8.1.13; see too Diodorus 16.30.3–31.4, Pausanias 10.2.4.

22. Diodorus 16.21.1–3, Pausanias 10.2.5, Justin 8.1.14.

23. Diodorus 16.33.2.

24. Demosthenes 23.183, Diodorus 16.34.1, Polyaenus 4.2.22.

25. Diodorus 16.33.3.

26. On the importance of Thessaly, see S. Sprawski, 'All the King's Men: Thessalians and Philip II's Designs on Greece', in D. Musial (ed.), *Society and Religions: Studies in Greek and Roman History* (Torun: 2005), pp. 31–49; cf. T.T.B. Ryder, 'The Diplomatic Skills of Philip II', in Ian Worthington (ed.), *Ventures into Greek History: Essays in Honour of N.G.L. Hammond* (Oxford: 1994), pp. 247–50 and E. Badian, 'Philip II and the Last of the Thessalians', *Ancient Macedonia* 6 (Institute for Balkan Studies, Thessaloniki: 1999), pp. 109–21.

27. Diodorus 16.35.2, Polyaenus 2.38.2.

28. Buckler, *Sacred War*, pp. 67–9 and his *Aegean Greece*, p. 416.

29. Diodorus 16.35.2. See generally E. Carney, 'Macedonians and Mutiny: Discipline and Indiscipline in the Army of Philip and Alexander', *CP* 91 (1996), pp. 19–44.

30. Diodorus 16.35.2–3, Polyaenus 2.38.2.

31. Ephorus, *FGrH* 70 F 94, Diodorus 16.33.3–4, 16.35.1–3, Justin 8.2.1–2.

32. *IG* ii² 1613, 297–8, Diodorus 16.34.3–4; cf. Demosthenes 23.103, 23.181.

33. Justin 8.2.1.

34. Justin 8.2.3, Diodorus 16.35.5.

35. Justin 8.2.3; cf. Hammond, *Macedonian State*, p. 114, for example. Griffith, *Macedonia* 2, pp. 274–5, sees the wreaths as merely a ruse to restore army morale, but this is unlikely.

36. See Ian Worthington, 'Alexander, Philip, and the Macedonian Background', in J. Roisman (ed.), *Alexander the Great* (Leiden: 2003), pp. 94–6; the following is adapted and extended from this essay.

37. A.B. Bosworth, 'Philip II and Upper Macedonia', *CQ²* 21 (1971), pp. 93–105.

38. Justin 11.1.1–6.

39. Cf. J.R. Ellis, 'The Dynamics of Fourth-Century Macedonian Imperialism', *Ancient Macedonia* 2 (Institute for Balkan Studies, Thessaloniki: 1977), pp. 103–14.

40. J. Buckler, 'Philip II's Designs on Greece', in W.R. Wallace and E.M. Harris (eds), *Transitions to Empire: Essays in Honor of E. Badian* (Norman, OK: 1996), pp. 77–97, argues that Philip was an opportunist who set his sights on expanding into central and southern Greece early in his reign but waited until later before invading. I do not agree with Buckler's view on Philip's focusing on actual interference in Greece so early, but I do agree with him that Philip only turned to military force as a last resort and hence delayed until as late as possible, when there was no other option.

41. Diodorus 16.35.4–5, 16.38.1, Justin 8.2.1–4.

42. Justin 8.2.4.

43. Diodorus 16.35.5.

44. Diodorus 16.36.1.

45. See further Buckler, *Sacred War*, pp. 86–114; cf. his *Aegean Greece*, pp. 421–9.

46. Diodorus 16.35.3–36.1, 16.37–38.2, Justin 8.2.3–12.

47. See further G.T. Griffith, 'Philip as a General and the Macedonian Army', in M.B. Hatzopoulos and L.D. Loukopoulos (eds), *Philip of Macedon* (Athens: 1980), pp. 48–57.

48. Athenaeus 13.557c, [Plutarch], *Moralia* 141b–c.

49. Ellis, *Philip II*, p. 212; see too E. Carney, *Women and Monarchy in Macedonia* (Norman, OK: 2000), pp. 60–1. On the order of the wives, see A.D. Tronson, 'Satyrus the Peripatetic and the Marriages of Philip II', *JHS* 104 (1984), pp. 121–6, and cf. Chapter 13.

50. Cf. Tronson, 'Satyrus the Peripatetic', p. 122, maintaining that the name could refer to 'an earlier (undocumented) Thessalian triumph', which is possible.

51. The chronology is not certain, but 352 is probably to be preferred over 344–342, when Philip was involved more seriously again in Thessaly; for a summary of the arguments, see Griffith, *Macedonia* 2, pp. 220–1.

52. Diodorus 17.4.1, Justin 11.3.2.

53. On the office, cf. S. Sprawski, 'Philip II and the Freedom of the Thessalians', *Electrum* 9 (2003), pp. 61–4.

54. Demosthenes 1.22.

55. Cf. Errington, *History of Macedonia*, p. 62 n. 9.

56. This is the suggestion of E. Badian, 'Philip II and the Last of the Thessalians', *Ancient Macedonia* 6 (Institute for Balkan Studies, Thessaloniki: 2000), p. 115.

57. Ryder, 'Diplomatic Skills of Philip II', p. 248.

58. The view of S. Hornblower, *The Greek World, 479–323 BC* (London: 1983), p. 251.

59. See Sprawski, 'Philip II and the Freedom of the Thessalians', pp. 55–66.

60. On that occasion he divided Thessaly into four areas (tetrarchy), appointing a governor over each one; Buckler, *Aegean Greece*, p. 420, wrongly attributes this division to Philip's involvement in Thrace in 352.

61. Cf. Ryder, 'Diplomatic Skills of Philip II', pp. 252–7, Buckler, 'Philip II's Designs on Greece', pp. 91–2, for example.

62. Herodotus 7.201–28 and, for example, N.G.L. Hammond, *A History of Greece*[3] (Oxford: 1986), pp. 228–36. On the Persian Wars, see for example A.R. Burn, *Persia and the Greeks*[2] (London: 1984) and P. Green, *The Greco-Persian Wars* (Berkeley and Los Angeles, CA: 1996).

63. Diodorus 16.37.3.

64. Diodorus 16.73.3, 16.38.1, Demosthenes 19.84, 19.319.

65. Ellis, *Philip II*, pp. 86–7, Griffith, *Macedonia* 2, p. 280, Ryder, 'Diplomatic Skills of Philip II', p. 243; *contra* Buckler, 'Philip II's Designs on Greece', p. 83.

66. I am unsure why Buckler, *Aegean Greece*, p. 431, says that after the blocking of Thermopylae 'the two sides considered themselves at war', for they had been in this situation since 357.

67. Demosthenes 3.4.

68. Demosthenes 3.5; cf. 1.13, 4.10–11.
69. Theopompus, *FGrH* 115 F 101.
70. Demosthenes 1.12–13.
71. Theopompus, *FGrH* 115 F 127.
72. Demosthenes 8.40, 9.56–66, [Demosthenes] 59.90.
73. See Bosworth, 'Philip II and Upper Macedonia', pp. 93–105, that areas such as Lyncestis were never fully integrated into the Macedonian kingdom.
74. Demosthenes 1.13, Isocrates 5.21.
75. See further M. Errington, 'Arybbas the Molossian', *GRBS* 16 (1975), pp. 41–50.
76. Justin, 8.6.4–8.
77. N.G.L. Hammond, *Epirus* (Oxford: 1967), pp. 542–9.
78. Justin 8.6.6–8.
79. On Demosthenes' earlier political career, see E. Badian, 'The Road to Prominence', in Ian Worthington (ed.), *Demosthenes: Statesman and Orator* (London: 2000), pp. 9–44; on the speech, cf. T.T.B. Ryder, 'Demosthenes and Philip II', in Worthington, *Demosthenes*, pp. 50–2 and 54; cf., for example, G.O. Rowe, 'Demosthenes' First Philippic: The Satiric Mode', *TAPA* 99 (1968), pp. 361–74 and A.M. Prestianni Gialombardo, '*Philippika* I: Sul "Culto" di Filippo II di Macedonia', *Siculorum Gymnasium* 28 (1975), pp. 1–57.
80. Demosthenes 23.107–9, 23.111–13.
81. See most recently Ryder, 'Demosthenes and Philip II', pp. 45–89, whose examination of Demosthenes' anti-Macedonian policy reveals that he was cynical yet politically astute and switched policy as and when needed; his scare-tactic rhetoric was meant not only to excite public alarm but also to give him the edge over rival leaders.
82. Demosthenes 4.4–8.
83. Demosthenes 4.40.

Chapter 7: The Fall of Olynthus

1. See in detail J.R. Ellis, 'The Stepbrothers of Philip II', *Historia* 22 (1973), pp. 350–4; cf. Griffith, *Macedonia* 2, pp. 699–701. Justin 8.3.10 says that Philip had murdered one of the three half-brothers.
2. Cf. Athenaeus 436c.
3. Cf. Justin 8.3.10: he saw them 'as potential claimants to the throne'. It is not going too far to say that the presence of his half-brothers in Olynthus was the reason for Philip's invasion, but note the caution of Borza, *Shadow of Olympus*, p. 217.
4. Justin 8.3.10, perhaps using Theopompus as his source: Hammond, *Philip*, p. 51. On the sources, see Appendix 1.
5. Philochorus, *FGrH* 328 F 49 and 132, Demosthenes 19.266, Diodorus 16.52.9: the place may have been Geira or Zeira, which sources confused with the more famous Stageira; cf. Griffith, *Macedonia* 2, p. 317 n. 1, Buckler, *Aegean Greece*, p. 436.
6. Philochorus, *FGrH* 328 F 49–61.
7. See in more detail C. Tuplin, 'Demosthenes' *Olynthiacs* and the Character of the Demegoric Corpus', *Historia* 47 (1998), pp. 276–320; see too T.T.B. Ryder, 'Demosthenes and Philip II', in Ian Worthington (ed.), *Demosthenes: Statesman and Orator* (London: 2000), pp. 49–50 and 54–7.
8. [Demosthenes] 59.3–5, 59.8; see too M.H. Hansen, 'The Theoric Fund and the *Graphe Paranomon* against Apollodorus', *GRBS* 17 (1976), pp. 235–46.
9. On the suggestion of using Theoric monies, cf. R. Sealey, *Demosthenes and his Time* (Oxford: 1993), pp. 137–43.
10. It may even have preceded the first and been wrongly placed in the corpus of Demosthenes' surviving works: see J.R. Ellis, 'The Order of the *Olynthiacs*', *Historia* 16 (1967), pp. 108–11.

11. Philochorus, *FGrH* 328 F 49, Diodorus 16.52.9.

12. Demosthenes 1.22, 2.11; cf. Diodorus 16.52.9. See too E. Badian, 'Philip II and the Last of the Thessalians', *Ancient Macedonia* 6 (Institute for Balkan Studies, Thessaloniki: 1999), pp. 117–20.

13. *Contra* Ellis, *Philip II*, p. 96.

14. Philochorus, *FGrH* 328 F 50, Diodorus 16.52.9.

15. Diodorus 16.53.2.

16. Demosthenes 9.11.

17. Philochorus, *FGrH* 328 F 51, Diodorus 16.52.9.

18. On the fall of Olynthus in detail, see Ellis, *Philip II*, pp. 98–9 and Griffith, *Macedonia* 2, pp. 321–8.

19. Ellis, *Philip II*, p. 99, G.L. Cawkwell, 'The Defence of Olynthus', *CQ*[2] 12 (1962), p. 132.

20. Demosthenes 8.40, 19.265, 19.342, 18.48, Diodorus 16.53.2.

21. A.M. Snodgrass, *Arms and Armour of the Greeks* (London: 1967), pp. 116–17; cf. Borza, *Shadow of Olympus*, p. 299. On the bolt-heads and Philip's siegecraft at Olynthus, see E.W. Marsden, 'Macedonian Military Machinery and its Designers under Philip and Alexander', *Ancient Macedonia* 2 (Institute for Balkan Studies, Thessaloniki: 1977), pp. 213–15.

22. See especially T.T.B. Ryder, 'The Diplomatic Skills of Philip II', in Ian Worthington (ed.), *Ventures into Greek History: Essays in Honour of N.G.L. Hammond* (Oxford: 1994), pp. 231–2.

23. Philochorus, *FGrH* 328 F 50–1 and 156, Diodorus 16.53.2–3, 16.55.1; cf. Demosthenes 9.26.

24. See further, Griffith, *Macedonia* 2, pp. 365–79.

25. Justin 8.3.11.

26. Demosthenes 9.26; cf. Diodorus 16.53.3.

27. Diodorus 16.53.3, Justin 8.3.11.

28. But see the cautionary comments of Griffith, *Macedonia* 2, pp. 365–6.

29. Six thousand were killed and thirty thousand were enslaved (Diodorus 17.14.1, Plutarch, *Alexander* 11.12). See further A.B. Bosworth, *Conquest and Empire: The Reign of Alexander the Great* (Cambridge: 1988), pp. 194–6 and Ian Worthington, *Alexander the Great, Man and God*, rev. and enl. edn (London: 2004), pp. 58–63.

30. Hegesias of Magnesia, *FGrH* 142 T 3. The translation is that of C.A. Robinson, *The History of Alexander the Great* 1 (Providence, RI: 1953), p. 249.

31. Diodorus 17.14.4, Plutarch, *Alexander* 11.11.

32. See Ian Worthington, 'Alexander's Destruction of Thebes', in W. Heckel and L.A. Tritle (eds), *Crossroads of History: The Age of Alexander the Great* (Claremont, CA: 2003), pp. 65–86.

33. See in more detail Cawkwell, 'Defence of Olynthus', pp. 122–40, P.A. Brunt, 'Euboea in the Time of Philip II', *CQ*[2] 19 (1969), pp. 245–65, J.M. Carter, 'Athens, Euboea and Olynthus', *Historia* 20 (1971), pp. 418–29.

34. See Ryder, 'Diplomatic Skills of Philip II', pp. 235–8.

35. It is worth noting that no source states that Plutarchus was a tyrant, but he probably did hold this position given Demosthenes' reference to him at *Philippic* 3.57: see Ryder, 'Diplomatic Skills of Philip II', p. 236.

36. Cf. Demosthenes 21.110, 21.200, Plutarch, *Phocion* 12.1.

37. He was later charged with desertion: Aeschines 2.148.

38. Plutarch, *Phocion* 12–13.

39. Demosthenes 21.161–4.

40. Aeschines 3.87.

41. For a discussion, see for example Griffith, *Macedonia* 2, p. 318 (for Philip's involvement), Ellis, *Philip II*, p. 263 n. 28 (against it).

42. V. Poulios, 'Macedonian Coinage from the 6th Century to 148 BC', in J. Vokotopoulou (ed.), *Greek Civilization: Macedonia, Kingdom of Alexander the Great* (Athens: 1993), p. 88.
43. Aeschines 2.13.
44. Suggested by Ellis, *Philip II*, p. 100.
45. Aeschines 2.14; cf. 3.62. The penalty when a litigant received less than one–fifth of the votes cast by the jurors at the trial: see D.M. MacDowell, *The Law in Classical Athens* (London: 1978), p. 64.
46. Demosthenes 19.10–11, Aeschines 2.57; cf. 2.79.
47. Demosthenes 18.257–66; on Aeschines, see further E.M. Harris, *Aeschines and Athenian Politics* (Oxford: 1995).
48. Demosthenes 19.303–6, Aeschines 2.79.

Chapter 8: Apollo Rescued, and the Peace of Philocrates

1. Diodorus 16.64.3; cf. J. Buckler, 'Demosthenes and Aeschines', in Ian Worthington (ed.), *Demosthenes: Statesman and Orator* (London: 2000), pp. 117–19.
2. An indication of the Phocians' favourable attitude to their ally Athens may be seen in their incursions into Boeotia.
3. The point is argued more fully in J.R. Ellis, 'Philip and the Peace of Philokrates', in W.L. Adams and E.N. Borza (eds), *Philip II, Alexander the Great, and the Macedonian Heritage* (Lanham, MD: 1982), pp. 43–59. See also N. Sawada, 'A Reconsideration of the Peace of Philocrates', *Kodai* 4 (1993), pp. 21–50.
4. Justin 8.1.4.
5. Justin 8.4.7–8.
6. Cf. Ellis, *Philip II*, pp. 101–2; *contra* Griffith, *Macedonia* 2, p. 345, Cawkwell, *Philip*, pp. 108–10, T.T.B. Ryder, 'The Diplomatic Skills of Philip II', in Ian Worthington (ed.), *Ventures into Greek History: Essays in Honour of N.G.L. Hammond* (Oxford: 1994), p. 244, that Philip intended to allow the Phocians to be punished and to promote Thebes over Athens.
7. Cf. Ryder, 'Diplomatic Skills of Philip II', pp. 244–8, Buckler, 'Demosthenes and Aeschines', pp. 119–23.
8. On Sparta, see C.D. Hamilton, 'Philip II and Archidamus', in W.L. Adams and E.N. Borza (eds), *Philip II, Alexander the Great, and the Macedonian Heritage* (Lanham, MD: 1982), pp. 61–77.
9. Diodorus 16.38.4.
10. Diodorus 16.56.1–2.
11. Aeschines 2.132.
12. Diodorus 16.56.3–57.1, Pausanias 10.2.7.
13. Diodorus 16.58.3.
14. Diodorus 16.58.6.
15. Diodorus 16.61 and 16.64.
16. Aeschines 2.16–17.
17. Diodorus 16.59.2; cf. Aeschines 2.135.
18. Cf. Justin 8.5.3: 'victims of necessity, (the Phocians) struck a bargain for their lives and capitulated.'
19. Demosthenes 19.12–13, Aeschines 2.18.
20. Aeschines 2.17.
21. On the sources in general, and especially the limitations of oratory as source material, see Appendix 1.
22. For example, Aeschines 3.58–78, Demosthenes 18.17–52, 18.79–94, 18.160–87, 18.211–26.
23. On their veracity, see Buckler, 'Demosthenes and Aeschines', pp. 148–54, and pp.

121–32 on the background to the peace. Buckler argues (there and elsewhere in his chapter) that, despite personal animosities, what really divided these two orators was their view of Philip's real aims; cf. T.T.B. Ryder, 'Demosthenes and Philip II', in Ian Worthington (ed.), *Demosthenes: Statesman and Orator* (London: 2000), pp. 58–72, on Demosthenes' ability to switch policy around the Peace of Philocrates and its aftermath. On Demosthenes' false embassy speech (19) see also D.M. MacDowell, *Demosthenes: On the False Embassy* (Oxford: 2000), pp. 1–30.

24. Aeschines 2.18.
25. Aeschines 2.34–5; cf. 2.38.
26. In his account of the meeting with the king, Plutarch, *Demosthenes* 16, has nothing to say of Demosthenes' loss of nerve but suggests that Philip 'was the most careful to answer his speech' (16.2).
27. Aeschines 2.25–33.
28. The following chronology is that of Ellis, *Philip II*, pp. 110–11.
29. Aeschines 2.81 says he saw them personally at Philip's court.
30. Aeschines 2.111; cf. 2.55, 3.76, Demosthenes 19.234–5, 18.28. This was part of normal diplomacy: see F.E. Adcock and D.J. Mosley, *Diplomacy in Ancient Greece* (London: 1975), p. 164.
31. On the Assembly meeting, see the account of E.M. Harris, *Aeschines and Athenian Politics* (Oxford: 1995), pp. 70–7.
32. Theopompus, *FGrH* 115 F 164; the translation is that of Hammond, *Philip*, p. 99.
33. Aeschines 3.69–70.
34. Demosthenes 19.144, Aeschines 3.71.
35. Demosthenes 19.14–16, 19.144, 19.321; cf. Aeschines 2.63–8.
36. Theopompus, *FGrH* 115 F 166; the translation is that of Hammond, *Philip*, p. 99.
37. Cf. Demosthenes 19.291.
38. Demosthenes 19.155–7.
39. Aeschines 2.112.
40. Ellis, *Philip II*, p. 115.
41. Cf. Hamilton, 'Philip II and Archidamus', pp. 75–6.
42. Aeschines 2.101–5, 2.113–19.
43. Cf. Buckler, *Aegean Greece*, pp. 446–7.
44. Justin 8.4.11.
45. Cf. the critical comments of Demosthenes at 19.44, 19.174, 19.278.
46. Demosthenes 19.167–8. Gifts were part of normal diplomatic protocol, although there was (and is) a fine line between the receipt of gifts for diplomatic purposes and as a bribe: see further F.D. Harvey, '*Dona Ferentes*: Some Aspects of Bribery in Greek Politics', in P.A. Cartledge and F.D. Harvey (eds), *Crux: Essays in Greek History Presented to G.E.M. de Ste. Croix on his 75th Birthday* (London: 1985), pp. 76–117; cf. Adcock and Mosley, *Diplomacy in Ancient Greece*, pp. 164–5.
47. Cf. Demosthenes 18.32.
48. Demosthenes 19.158.
49. Demosthenes 5.25.
50. See Ellis' comments, *Philip II*, pp. 125–7.
51. See G.L. Cawkwell, 'Philip and Athens', in M.B. Hatzopoulos and L.D. Loukopoulos (eds), *Philip of Macedon* (Athens: 1980), pp. 100–10 and Ryder, 'Diplomatic Skills of Philip II', pp. 251–7.
52. On naval power, see G.L. Cawkwell, 'Athenian Naval Power in the Fourth Century', *CQ*^{2} 34 (1984), pp. 334–45.
53. Demosthenes 5.14–15, 5.25–6; cf. Ryder, 'Demosthenes and Philip II', pp. 56–69.
54. Cf. Cawkwell, *Philip*, p. 109.
55. Demosthenes 19.167–9.
56. Demosthenes 19.31–50.

57. Demosthenes 6.14.
58. Demosthenes 19.122.
59. For Phalaecus' later adventures and death, see Diodorus 16.61.3–63.
60. Demosthenes 19.61, Aeschines 2.130, Justin 8.6.1.
61. Aeschines 2.139.
62. Diodorus 16.60.1–3, Pausanias 10.3.1–3, and in detail see J. Buckler, *Philip II and the Sacred War* (Leiden, 1989), pp. 138–42.
63. Cf. J. Buckler, 'Philip II's Designs on Greece', in R.W. Wallace and E.M. Harris (eds), *Transitions to Empire: Essays in Honor of E. Badian* (Norman, OK: 1996), pp. 84–5.
64. M. Trundle, *Greek Mercenaries from the Late Archaic Period to Alexander* (London: 2004), pp. 95–6.
65. Theopompus, *FGrH* 115 F 248.
66. Diodorus 16.64.
67. P.J. Rhodes and R. Osborne (eds), *Greek Historical Inscriptions, 404–323 BC* (Oxford: 2003), no. 67; cf. Ellis, *Philip II*, p. 123.
68. Diodorus 16.59.4–60, Justin 8.5.4–6.
69. Aeschines 2.120. See the valid remarks of Errington, *History of Macedonia*, pp. 72–3, on the dangers of viewing Philip's actions (and unpopularity) purely from the Athenian viewpoint.
70. On Philip and the Peloponnese, see Ryder, 'Diplomatic Skills of Philip II', pp. 238–42.

Chapter 9: The Hostile Aftermath

1. On which, cf. T.T.B. Ryder, 'Demosthenes and Philip II', in Ian Worthington (ed.), *Demosthenes: Statesman and Orator* (London: 2000), pp. 71–2.
2. Demosthenes 5.13–14.
3. Demosthenes 5.17.
4. Demosthenes 6.22; see further T.T.B. Ryder, 'The Diplomatic Skills of Philip II', in Ian Worthington (ed.), *Ventures into Greek History: Essays in Honour of N.G.L. Hammond* (Oxford: 1994), pp. 248–9.
5. Diodorus 16.60.5.
6. On why and when Philip planned to invade Asia, see pp. 166–9.
7. Cf. Ryder, 'Diplomatic Skills of Philip II', pp. 244–7.
8. Demosthenes 19.261.
9. Demosthenes 19.8.
10. Demosthenes 19.257, 19.284–6; cf. 19.2.
11. Aeschines 1, *Against Timarchus*. See now N. Fisher, *Aeschines, Against Timarchos* (Oxford: 2001); cf. E.M. Harris, *Aeschines and Athenian Politics* (Oxford: 1995), pp. 101–6, J. Buckler, 'Demosthenes and Aeschines', in Ian Worthington (ed.), *Demosthenes: Statesman and Orator* (London: 2000), pp. 133–4; on the odium attached to male prostitutes, see also J. Davidson, *Courtesans and Fishcakes* (London: 1997), pp. 113–16, 252–7, 260–3 and 265–74.
12. On which period, see most conveniently A. Andrewes, *The Greek Tyrants* (London: 1974), pp. 110–15.
13. On which, see in detail R.W. Wallace, *The Areopagos Council, to 307 B.C.* (Baltimore, MD: 1989).
14. Demosthenes 18.134–5, [Plutarch], *Moralia* 850a.
15. Demosthenes 18.134–5.
16. Griffith, *Macedonia* 2, p. 471.
17. Diodorus 16.69.7; cf. Justin 8.6.3.
18. On the wound and its context, see A.S. Riginos, 'The Wounding of Philip II of Macedon: Fact and Fabrication', *JHS* 114 (1994), pp. 115–16, arguing that the wound

was later embellished by biographers and the like to 'enrich the tradition' regarding Philip.

19. *Letter* 2.3; the translation is that of T.L. Papillon, *Isocrates* 2 (Austin, TX: 2004), *ad loc.*

20. See further J.R. Ellis, 'Population-Transplants by Philip II', *Makedonika* 9 (1969), pp. 9–17.

21. Justin 8.5.7–6.2; cf. Demosthenes 19.89.

22. Cf. Justin 8.3.9: the contractors for the various public building projects were not paid, and they left 'without complaint out of fear of the violent character of his rule'.

23. F. Papazoglou, *Les villes de Macédoine à l'époque romaine* (Paris 1988); cf. M. Siganidou, 'Urban Centres in Macedonia', in J. Vokotopoulou (ed.), *Greek Civilization: Macedonia, Kingdom of Alexander the Great* (Athens: 1993), pp. 29–31.

24. Theopompus, *FGrH* 115 F 222, Curtius 3.9.3.

25. [Demosthenes] 7.32, Demosthenes 6.22, 8.59, 9.12, 18.48. Diodorus 16.69.8 has little to say about the Thessalian campaign; for a detailed discussion, see S. Sprawski, 'Philip II and the Freedom of the Thessalians', *Electrum* 9 (2003), pp. 55–66.

26. Theopompus, *FGrH* 115 F 208 and 209, Demosthenes 6.22, 9.26; *contra* Buckler, *Aegean Greece*, p. 420, who says that Philip made this division in 352.

27. Theopompus, *FGrH* 115 F 208.

28. Theopompus, *FGrH* 115 F 209.

29. Demosthenes 18.295; cf. 19.260, 6.22, 9.26.

30. *Letter* 2.20.

31. On Philip's attitude to Thessaly, see S. Sprawski, 'All the King's Men: Thessalians and Philip II's Designs on Greece', in D. Musial (ed.), *Society and Religions: Studies in Greek and Roman History* (Torun: 2005), pp. 31–49.

32. There is some similarity between how Demosthenes describes the Thessalians and the status of the Greeks after the establishment of the League of Corinth in 338/7 (see Chapter 12). Although the Greeks on the surface had freedom and autonomy, they were subservient to Macedonian hegemony as created by Philip. It is plausible that Demosthenes revised his speeches after Macedonian rule was enforced, and hence referred to the Thessalians in 344 as enslaved because of the similarity of their status to that of the Greeks. On revision of speeches, see Appendix 1.

33. Theopompus, *FGrH* 115 F 81.

34. Demosthenes 18.48, Polyaenus 4.2.19.

35. Philochorus, *FGrH* 328 F 157.

36. [Demosthenes] 7.21.

37. Cf. Aeschines 3.83.

38. Diodorus 18.13.5.

39. Demosthenes 19.116–19, Aeschines 2.6, Hyperides 4.29–30.

40. On this, see F.E. Adcock and D.J. Mosley, *Diplomacy in Ancient Greece* (London: 1974), pp. 164–5, and F.D. Harvey, '*Dona Ferentes*: Some Aspects of Bribery in Greek Politics', in P.A. Cartledge and F.D. Harvey (eds), *Crux: Essays in Greek History Presented to G.E.M. de Ste. Croix on his 75th Birthday* (London: 1985), pp. 76–117.

41. For Demosthenes' relations with Philocrates, see Aeschines 3.58–75; cf. Ellis, *Philip II*, pp. 100 and 148–50.

42. Cf. Griffith, *Macedonia* 2, p. 337, who believes the flight indicates his guilt, though this does not follow. It was common in Athenian law for prosecutors to resort to an argument based on probability (*eikota*), hence we would expect that the others accused at the same time of taking bribes would have been found guilty based on Philocrates' action (i.e., if he took bribes, then probably so did the others), but they were acquitted.

43. Aeschines 2.6, 3.79.

44. See further on the background and charges: Ellis, *Philip II*, pp. 151–3, Harris,

Aeschines, pp. 115–20, Ryder, 'Demosthenes and Philip II', pp. 58–72, R. Sealey, *Demosthenes and his Time* (Oxford: 1993), pp. 175–6, and in detail Buckler, 'Demosthenes and Aeschines', pp. 121–32 and 134–40.

45. See Buckler, 'Demosthenes and Aeschines', pp. 148–54; cf. Ryder, 'Demosthenes and Philip II', pp. 58–72.
46. Demosthenes 19.229.
47. Plutarch, *Demosthenes* 15.5, [Plutarch], *Moralia* 840c.
48. Ryder, 'Demosthenes and Philip II', p. 76.
49. On whom, see M. Errington, 'Arybbas the Molossian', *GRBS* 16 (1975), pp. 41–50.
50. P.J. Rhodes and R. Osborne (eds), *Greek Historical Inscriptions, 404–323 BC* (Oxford: 2003), no. 70; see too Theopompus, *FGrH* 115 F 206–7, [Demosthenes] 7.32, Diodorus 16.72.1, Justin 8.6.4–7.
51. Diodorus 16.72.1.
52. Demosthenes 9.34, 9.72, Aeschines 3.97–108.
53. Cf. Ellis, *Philip II*, p. 158.
54. Aeschines 3.83.
55. Demosthenes 18.132–3; cf. Dinarchus 1.63, Plutarch, *Demosthenes* 14.5.
56. Ellis, *Philip II*, p. 128.
57. Cf. Demosthenes 18.133; see Wallace, *Areopagos Council*, pp. 113–19.

Chapter 10: Thrace: The Die Is Cast

1. Plutarch, *Alexander* 7.2–5; cf. 8.1–2.
2. On Alexander's boyhood (including education) see further Ian Worthington, *Alexander the Great, Man and God*, rev. and enl. edn (London: 2004), pp. 30–43.
3. On Olympias, see E. Carney, *Olympias, Mother of Alexander the Great* (London: 2006).
4. Plutarch, *Alexander* 8.2.
5. The letter is *FGrH* 115 T 7 = no. 30 in the so-called *Socratic Letters*.
6. A.F. Natoli, *The Letter of Speusippus to Philip II* (Stuttgart: 2004).
7. See further M.M. Markle, 'Support of Athenian Intellectuals for Philip: A Study of Isocrates' *Philippus* and Speusippus' *Letter to Philip*', *JHS* 96 (1976), pp. 80–99.
8. On Philip and Thrace generally, see E. Badian, 'Philip II and Thrace', *Pulpudeva* 4 (1983), pp. 51–71.
9. Demosthenes 9.32, presumably referring to Antipater.
10. Diodorus 16.71.1–2; cf. [Demosthenes] 12.8–10.
11. The following reconstruction is based on that of Buckler, *Aegean Greece*, pp. 464–6.
12. Theopompus, *FGrH* 115 F 110, Dexippus, *FGrH* 100 F 22 and 26–7, [Plutarch], *Moralia* 520b.
13. Demosthenes 8.64, 9.15, 19.156, Aeschines 3.82.
14. 'The greatest city in the Chersonese': Demosthenes 9.35.
15. Demosthenes 9.49.
16. Athenaeus 13.557d; on Meda, see E. Carney, *Women and Monarchy in Macedonia* (Norman, OK: 2000), pp. 67–8.
17. The campaign lasted eleven months according to Demosthenes 8.2, 8.35, 18.69.
18. Diodorus 16.71.2.
19. This office is referred to at Diodorus 17.62.5; cf. Arrian 1.25.2, who says that Alexander (at the beginning of his reign) 'sent Alexander the son of Aeropus as general to Thrace', which implies an already existing office.
20. Cf. Ellis, *Philip II*, pp. 170–1, Cawkwell, *Philip*, p. 117.
21. Griffith, *Macedonia* 2, pp. 510–16 (his section on the Halonnesus affair).
22. Justin 9.2.1.
23. Demosthenes 9.17–18, 9.20–1, 9.30–1, 9.71–2, 18.136, [Demosthenes] 12.3–4.

24. Demosthenes 8.8–9, 8.14, 8.28, 8.43, 9.15.
25. Cf. T.T.B. Ryder, 'Demosthenes and Philip II', in Ian Worthington (ed.), *Demosthenes: Statesman and Orator* (London: 2000), pp. 76–8.
26. There is a belief that the fourth *Philippic* is spurious; in favour of its authenticity, see Ian Worthington, 'The Authenticity of Demosthenes' Fourth *Philippic*', *Mnemosyne* 44 (1991), pp. 425–8. See also S.G. Daitz, 'The Relationship of the *De Chersoneso* and the *Philippika quarta* of Demosthenes', *CP* 52 (1957), pp. 145–62.
27. For example, Demosthenes 10.32.
28. Philochorus, *FGrH* 328 F 157, Diodorus 16.40.3–53.8.
29. Dinarchus 1.33, [Plutarch], *Moralia* 847f, 848e.
30. Demosthenes 10.32, Diodorus 16.52.5–8; in detail, see Griffith, *Macedonia* 2, pp. 518–22.
31. For example, Demosthenes 8.36.
32. Diodorus 16.74.1.
33. Aeschines 3.89–105.
34. Dionysius of Halicarnassus, *ad Amm.* 1.11.
35. For example, Griffith, *Macedonia* 2, pp. 567–8, Errington, *History of Macedonia*, p. 81, Ellis, *Philip II*, pp. 179–80, Hammond, *Philip*, p. 132.
36. See Cawkwell, *Philip*, p. 137, and in more detail J. Buckler, 'Philip II's Designs on Greece', in R.W. Wallace and E.M. Harris (eds), *Transitions to Empire: Essays in Honor of E. Badian* (Norman, OK: 1996), pp. 87–9; cf. Buckler, *Aegean Greece*, p. 474.
37. The translation is that of Buckler, 'Philip II's Designs on Greece', p. 88.
38. Lysias 28.6.
39. Demosthenes 18.244, 18.302; cf. Aeschines 3.256.
40. Diodorus 16.77.2; cf. Demosthenes 9.71, [Plutarch], *Moralia* 847f–850a.
41. Demosthenes 18.223–4.
42. Plutarch, *Demosthenes* 16.1.
43. Plutarch, *Alexander* 9.1, Justin 9.1.8.
44. Theopompus, *FGrH* 115 F 217, 221 and 223, Strabo 7.5.12, Livy 44.7.5.
45. For the siege, see Diodorus 16.74.2–76.4, Justin 9.1.1–7; cf. Plutarch, *Alexander* 70.5.
46. Philochorus, *FGrH* 328 F 54.
47. On catapults, cf. E.W. Marsden, *Greek and Roman Artillery* (Oxford: 1969), pp. 60 and 100–1, Griffith, *Macedonia* 2, pp. 572–3. See also Figure 2.
48. Diodorus 16.75.1–2, Arrian 2.14.5, Polybius 1.29.10; cf. Demosthenes 11.5.
49. Siege of Byzantium: Diodorus 16.76.3–4, Justin 9.1.2–4.
50. Cf. Pausanias 4.31.5 (writing in the third century AD).
51. Buckler, *Aegean Greece*, pp. 482–3.
52. Cf. Ellis, *Philip II*, pp. 178 and 288 n. 9, Griffith, *Macedonia* 2, p. 574.
53. Theopompus, *FGrH* 115 F 292, Demosthenes 18.72, 18.87–94, 18.139, 18.240–3, Diodorus 16.77.2, Justin 9.1.5–8.
54. Plutarch, *Phocion* 14; cf. Diodorus 16.77.2.
55. Demosthenes 8.14, 18.80, 18.88–92, 18.244, Diodorus 16.77.2, Plutarch, *Phocion* 14.3–7.
56. Demosthenes 18.73, 18.139.
57. Diodorus 16.77.2; cf. Cawkwell, *Philip*, p. 138.
58. Philochorus, *FGrH* 328 F 162.
59. Theopompus, *FGrH* 115 F 292, Philochorus, *FGrH* 328 F 162; cf. Demosthenes 18.73.
60. On the number, see Ellis, *Philip II*, pp. 179 and 288 n. 101, Griffith, *Macedonia* 2, pp. 575–7.
61. Theopompus, *FGrH* 115 F 292.

62.   Cf. Ellis, *Philip II*, pp. 179–80, R. Sealey, *Demosthenes and his Time* (Oxford: 1993), pp. 188–90.

63.   Theopompus, *FGrH* 115 F 217, Justin 9.2.1.

Chapter 11: Chaeronea and the End of Greek Liberty

1.   Background: Aeschines 3.115–21, Demosthenes 18.140–55.

2.   Aeschines 3.116.

3.   The view of P.D. Londey, 'The Outbreak of the Fourth Sacred War', *Chiron* 20 (1990), pp. 239–60; *contra*, for example, Griffith, *Macedonia* 2, p. 586, that Philip persuaded the Amphissans to act as they did at the meeting.

4.   Demosthenes 18.143–55. On Aeschines' role at the meeting and his potential exploitation by Philip, see E.M. Harris, *Aeschines and Athenian Politics* (Oxford: 1995), pp. 126–30; cf. T.T.B. Ryder, 'Demosthenes and Philip II', in Ian Worthington (ed.), *Demosthenes: Statesman and Orator* (London: 2000), pp. 80–1 and J. Buckler, 'Demosthenes and Aeschines', in Worthington, *Demosthenes*, pp. 142–3.

5.   Demosthenes 18.151–2; see further Ellis, *Philip II*, pp. 186–8, Harris, *Aeschines*, pp. 127–30.

6.   Justin 9.2.1; cf. Diodorus 16.1.5. On the Scythian campaign in full, see Justin 9.2.

7.   Justin 9.2.10 from Theopompus.

8.   Theopompus, *FGrH* 115 F 162; cf. Justin 9.2.12–13. The translation is that of Hammond, *Philip*, p. 136.

9.   I thank my colleague Professor L. Okamura for his search of the modern archaeological material on this area.

10.   Justin 9.2.15–16.

11.   Hammond, *Philip*, p. 136.

12.   Philochorus, *FGrH* 328 F 54, Marsyas, *FGrH* 135/136 F 17, Justin 9.3.1–3; cf. Demosthenes 18.67, Diodorus 16.1.5.

13.   [Plutarch], *Moralia* 331b. On the wound, see A.S. Riginos, 'The Wounding of Philip II of Macedon: Fact and Fabrication', *JHS* 114 (1994), pp. 116–18, who argues that the only source to identify which leg was wounded, Didymus, was wrong to specify the right one, and that Philip's lameness was later embellished by biographers (such as Satyrus) for dramatic effect. Thus, he suggests, the passage in Pseudo-Plutarch (331b) when Alexander comforts and encourages his father who is depressed about his affliction is part of the author's agenda to show a side to Alexander's character that may not actually have existed.

14.   Philochorus, *FGrH* 328 F 56.

15.   Cf. J. Buckler, 'Philip II's Designs on Greece', in W.R. Wallace and E.M. Harris (eds), *Transitions to Empire: Essays in Honor of E. Badian* (Norman, OK: 1996), pp. 77–97.

16.   Plutarch, *Demosthenes* 18.2.

17.   Theopompus, *FGrH* 115 F 328, Demosthenes 18.152–8, 18.168, 18.174–5, 18.178, 18.211–15, Diodorus 16.84.3–85.1, Justin 9.3.6.

18.   Demosthenes 18.169–73; on the background, see too Diodorus 16.84.2–5, Plutarch, *Demosthenes* 18.1.

19.   These were the signals to call the people to an emergency Assembly at dawn the next day.

20.   Plutarch, *Demosthenes* 18.1.

21.   Diodorus 16.85.1.

22.   Aeschines 3.137–51, Demosthenes 18.168–88, 18.211–17; cf. Dinarchus 1.12, Diodorus 16.85.1–4, Plutarch, *Demosthenes* 18.1–2, *Phocion* 16.3, Justin 9.3.4–6, and see Ellis, *Philip II*, pp. 191–3, Cawkwell, *Philip*, pp. 142–4, R. Sealey, *Demosthenes and his Time* (Oxford: 1993), pp. 194–6.

23.   Plutarch, *Demosthenes* 18.2.

24. Aeschines 3.140.
25. Cf. Cawkwell, *Philip*, pp. 143–4, Griffith, *Macedonia* 2, pp. 589–96; more critically, see Ellis, *Philip II*, pp. 191–3.
26. Demosthenes 18.214; cf. Plutarch, *Demosthenes* 18.
27. Aeschines 3.142–6.
28. Proxenus the Athenian, not the Theban: cf. Dinarchus 1.74 (*contra* Ellis, *Philip II*, p. 193).
29. For example, Ambrysus and probably Lilaea: Pausanias 10.36.2–3; cf. 4.31.5.
30. Demosthenes 18.216.
31. Aeschines 3.146–7, Polyaenus 4.2.8; and see Ellis, *Philip II*, pp. 193–7 and Griffith, *Macedonia* 2, pp. 590–5.
32. Dinarchus 1.74.
33. Demosthenes 9.34.
34. Plutarch, *Alexander* 9.3.
35. Diodorus 16.85.5.
36. Diodorus 16.85.2, 16.85.5, 16.86.1, Plutarch, *Demosthenes* 17.3, *Alexander* 12.5, Justin 9.3.9.
37. On the Sacred Band, see Plutarch, *Pelopidas* 18.
38. For the allies, see Demosthenes 18.237.
39. Diodorus 16.86.1 says that Alexander was stationed next to Philip's 'most seasoned generals'.
40. On the date, see Plutarch, *Camillus* 19.5, 19.8. On the battle, see Diodorus 16.86, Plutarch, *Alexander* 9, *Pelopidas* 18.7, Justin 9.3.4–11, Polyaenus 4.2.2, 4.2.7, and for modern discussions, see especially Griffith, *Macedonia* 2, pp. 596–603 and Hammond, *Macedonian State*, pp. 115–19.
41. There is a very useful discussion of both sides' fighting capabilities at Hammond, *Philip*, pp. 149–51.
42. Diodorus 16.85.7.
43. The remark is cited by Polyaenus 4.2.2 (second century AD), but it is doubtful.
44. Diodorus 16.85.5–87, Plutarch, *Alexander* 9.2; see P.A. Rahe, 'The Annihilation of the Sacred Band at Chaeronea', *AJA* 85 (1981), pp. 84–7.
45. Diodorus 16.85.5–86.6, Plutarch, *Alexander* 9.2–3.
46. Cf. P.J. Rhodes and R. Osborne (eds), *Greek Historical Inscriptions, 404–323 BC* (Oxford: 2003), no. 77.
47. Aeschines 3.152, 3.159, 3.175, 3.181, 3.187, 3.244, 3.253, Dinarchus 1.12, 1.71, 1.81; cf. Plutarch, *Demosthenes* 20.2, [Plutarch], *Moralia* 845f.
48. This probably had its origins in the speeches against Demosthenes. Forensic oratory was not known for its veracity: on this, see further Appendix 1. Compare a similar case in 348 when Nicodemus of Aphidna charged Demosthenes with desertion during the Euboean campaign (Aeschines 2.148). Demosthenes had gone to Euboea, but he returned as he was due to provide a chorus at the Great Dionysia festival, hence he did not desert.
49. Plutarch, *Demosthenes* 20.2.
50. Diodorus 16.88.1–2.
51. [Plutarch], *Moralia* 259d; cf. Plutarch, *Alexander* 12.5.
52. Dinarchus 1.74; cf. Demosthenes 60.22.
53. [Plutarch], *Moralia* 259d, 260c.
54. See the discussion of G.L. Cawkwell, 'The End of Greek Liberty', in W.R. Wallace and E.M. Harris (eds), *Transitions to Empire: Essays in Honor of E. Badian* (Norman, OK: 1996), pp. 98–121.
55. Justin 9.3.11.

Chapter 12: From Master of Greece to Conqueror of Persia?

1. On his arrangements, see in detail C. Roebuck, 'The Settlement of Philip II with the Greek States in 338 B.C.', *CP* 43 (1948), pp. 73–92, Ellis, *Philip II*, pp. 199–204 and Griffith, *Macedonia* 2, pp. 604–23.
2. Plutarch, *Pelopidas* 18.5.
3. Pausanias 9.40.10.
4. See P.A. Rahe, 'The Annihilation of the Sacred Band at Chaeronea', *AJA* 85 (1981), pp. 84–7.
5. Diodorus 16.87.1–2, Plutarch, *Demosthenes* 20.3, [Plutarch], *Moralia* 715c.
6. Plutarch, *Demosthenes* 10.1.
7. Theopompus *FGrH* 115 F 236 = Athenaeus 435b–c. Note that Theopompus F 282 says that Philip had a tendency to rush into battle drunk, but this is a view stemming from a bias against the king. The following translation is that of M.A. Flower, *Theopompus of Chios* (Oxford: 1994), p. 105.
8. Justin 9.4.1–3.
9. Diodorus 16.87.3, Pausanias 4.27.9–10, 9.1.8, 9.6.5, 9.37.8, Justin 9.4.6–10, 11.3.8; see too Roebuck, 'Settlement of Philip II', pp. 77–80; cf. Griffith, *Macedonia* 2, pp. 610–12, T.T.B. Ryder, 'The Diplomatic Skills of Philip II', in Ian Worthington (ed.), *Ventures into Greek History: Essays in Honour of N.G.L. Hammond* (Oxford: 1994), pp. 244–7.
10. Diodorus 16.87.3, 17.13.5, Justin 9.4.7–8.
11. Pausanias 10.3.3–4.
12. Diodorus 17.3.3, Plutarch, *Aratus* 23.4, respectively.
13. Lycurgus 1.16, 1.36–7, 1.41, Demosthenes 18.248, [Demosthenes] 26.11, [Plutarch], *Moralia* 848f–849a.
14. The speech is the only extant one we have by Lycurgus.
15. Diodorus 16.56.6–7, 16.87–88.2, Pausanias 7.10.5, Justin 9.4.4–5.
16. Cf. [Demades] 1.9.
17. Cf. G.L. Cawkwell, 'Philip and Athens', in M.B. Hatzopoulos and L.D. Loukopoulos (eds), *Philip of Macedon* (Athens: 1980), pp. 100–10 and Ryder, 'Diplomatic Skills of Philip II', pp. 228–57 (Philip and Athens: pp. 251–7).
18. See P.E. Harding, 'Athenian Foreign Policy in the Fourth Century', *Klio* 77 (1995), pp. 105–25; cf. E. Badian, 'The Ghost of Empire: Reflections on Athenian Foreign Policy in the Fourth Century', in W. Eder (ed.), *Die athenische Demokratie im 4. Jahrhundert v. Chr.* (Stuttgart: 1995), pp. 79–106.
19. Aeschines 3.159, Demosthenes 18.248.
20. Aeschines at the Crown trial of 330 and Dinarchus (1.78, 1.80–1) at Demosthenes' trial in 323.
21. Cf. Ellis, *Philip II*, pp. 198–9, Griffith, *Macedonia* 2, pp. 605–6, Ryder, 'Diplomatic Skills of Philip II', pp. 241–3.
22. Diodorus 16.87–88.2, 18.56.7, Pausanias 1.25.3, 1.34.1, 7.10.5, Justin 9.4.1–5.
23. [Demades] 1.9, Diodorus 18.56.7, Pausanias 1.34.1, P.J. Rhodes and R. Osborne (eds), *Greek Historical Inscriptions, 404–323 BC* (Oxford: 2003), no. 75.
24. Isocrates 15.111–12, Demosthenes 15.9, Diodorus 18.56.7, Nepos, *Timotheus* 1.2, Diogenes Laertius 10.l, Strabo 14.4.18.
25. Plutarch, *Phocion* 16.4.
26. Diodorus 16.87.3.
27. M.N. Tod, *Greek Historical Inscriptions* 2 (Oxford: 1948), no. 180, Plutarch, *Demosthenes* 22.4, Pausanias 1.10.4; cf. [Demades] 1.9; see further Griffith, *Macedonia* 2, pp. 606–9.
28. Hyperides, fragment 18.
29. Aeschines 3.159, Demosthenes 18.249; see too Demosthenes 25.37, Plutarch, *Demosthenes* 21.1, 21.3, [Plutarch], *Moralia* 845f.

30. Aeschines 3.17, 3.24, 3.31, Demosthenes 18.113.
31. Demosthenes 18.285, Plutarch, *Demosthenes* 21.2. This speech survives as Number 60 in the Demosthenic corpus and is probably authentic; for discussion and a new translation, see Ian Worthington, *Demosthenes: Speeches 60 and 61, Prologues, Letters* (Austin, TX: 2006), pp. 21–37.
32. Demosthenes 20.141.
33. Thucydides 2.34.
34. Demosthenes 18.285; cf. Plutarch, *Demosthenes* 21.2.
35. Diodorus 16.89.3 wrongly dates this to 337/6. On the Peloponnesian settlement, see Roebuck, 'Settlement of Philip', pp. 83–9, Ryder, 'Diplomatic Skills of Philip II', pp. 241–2; cf. C.D. Hamilton, 'Philip II and Archidamus', in W.L. Adams and E.N. Borza (eds), *Philip II, Alexander the Great, and the Macedonian Heritage* (Lanham, MD: 1982), pp. 81–3.
36. Diodorus 17.3.4–5, Polybius 9.8.3, 38.3.3.
37. See further Polybius 9.28.6–7, 9.33.8, Pausanias 7.10.3, [Plutarch], *Moralia* 219f.
38. [Plutarch], *Moralia* 216b, 235a–b, 513a.
39. Diodorus 16.89.1–2, Justin 9.5.1; cf. [Demosthenes] 17.1.
40. Justin 9.5.3.
41. Plutarch, *Phocion* 16.5.
42. Diodorus 16.89.2.
43. The best (I think) discussion of Common Peace in Greece is still T.T.B. Ryder, *Koine Eirene* (Oxford: 1965); on the differences between Philip's and earlier peaces, see *ibid.*, pp. 102–06, and cf. his 'Demosthenes and Philip's Peace of 338/7 B.C.', *CQ²* 26 (1976), pp. 85–7 and S. Perlman, 'Fourth Century Treaties and the League of Corinth of Philip of Macedon', in *Ancient Macedonia* 4 (Institute for Balkan Studies, Thessaloniki: 1986), pp. 437–42; cf. his 'Greek Diplomatic Tradition and the Corinthian League of Philip of Macedon', *Historia* 34 (1985), pp. 153–74.
44. See *P. Oxy.* 12 (*FGrH* 255), 5, with N.G.L. Hammond, 'The Koina of Epirus and Macedonia', *ICS* 16 (1991), pp. 183–92.
45. Diodorus 16.89.1–3, Justin 9.5.1–7; cf. [Demosthenes] 17. See further Ryder, *Koine Eirene*, pp. 102–6 and 150–62, Ellis, *Philip II*, pp. 204–10, Griffith, *Macedonia* 2, pp. 623–46; cf. the commentary of Rhodes and Osborne, *Greek Historical Inscriptions*, no. 76, pp. 376–9.
46. Diodorus 16.89, Justin 9.5.4–7. On the concept of panhellenism, see, for example, M.B. Sakellariou, 'Panhellenism: From Concept to Policy', in M.B. Hatzopoulos and L.D. Loukopoulos (eds), *Philip of Macedon* (Athens: 1980), pp. 128–45.
47. Cf. Isocrates 4.16–17, 4.99, 4.173.
48. Lysias 33.5–6.
49. Onesicritus, *FGrH* 134 F 19 = Plutarch, *Alexander* 60.6.
50. Polybius 3.6.12–13.
51. Cf. Demosthenes 18.201, Polybius 9.33.7, [Plutarch], *Moralia* 240a. See also the discussions of Ellis, *Philip II*, pp. 204–9 and Griffith, *Macedonia* 2, pp. 623–46.
52. Diodorus 16.89.1–2, 16.91.2.
53. Justin 9.5.1–7.
54. Demosthenes 17, a speech delivered in either 333 (W. Will, 'Zur Datierung der Rede Ps.-Demosthenes XVII', *RhM* 125 [1982], pp. 202–13) or more likely 331 (G.L. Cawkwell, 'A Note on Ps.-Demosthenes 17.20', *Phoenix* 15 [1961], pp. 74–8).
55. See especially Ryder, *Koine Eirene*, pp. 102–6 and 150–62, on the character of the settlement and its significance in strengthening Philip's hold on Greece, and Griffith, *Macedonia* 2, pp. 610–12.
56. The translation is that of Rhodes and Osborne, *Greek Historical Inscriptions*, pp. 373–5.
57. See Ian Worthington, '*IG* ii² 236 and Philip's Common Peace of 337', in L.G.

Mitchell (ed.), *Greek History and Epigraphy: Essays in Honour of P. J. Rhodes* (Swansea: 2008).

58. Justin 9.5.6–7.
59. As is argued by Cawkwell, *Philip*, pp. 173–4.
60. Pausanias 5.17.4, 5.20.9–10.
61. At a later date the statues of Olympias and Eurydice were moved to the Temple of Hera at Olympia.
62. On the building, see further S.G. Miller, 'The Philippeion and Macedonian Hellenistic Architecture', *Athenische Mitteilungen* 88 (1973), pp. 189–218, R.F. Townsend, 'The Philippeion and Fourth-Century Athenian Architecture', in O. Palagia and S.V. Tracy (eds), *The Macedonians in Athens, 322–229 BC* (Oxford: 2003), pp. 93–101 and especially P. Schultz, 'Leochares' Argead Portraits in the Philippeion', in P. Schultz and R. von den Hoff (eds), *Early Hellenistic Portraiture: Image, Style, Context* (Cambridge: 2007), pp. 205–33.
63. On this, see especially Townsend, 'The Philippeion and Fourth-Century Athenian Architecture', pp. 93–101.
64. Schultz, 'Leochares' Argead Portraits in the Philippeion', pp. 209–10. Schultz along the way makes some nice parallels with the time it took for far larger monumental buildings to be constructed, such as the Parthenon (nine years) and the Temple of Asclepius at Epidaurus (less than five years). Moreover, as he says, the 111th Olympiad was scheduled for 336 at Olympia, and it would hardly have been good for Philip's public image if his Philippeion were not finished for that event.
65. Schultz, 'Leochares' Argead Portraits in the Philippeion', pp. 208–9 and 213–16.
66. *Ibid.*, pp. 220–1. Other examples of gilded statues included Praxiteles' portrait of Phryne (Pausanias 10.15.1), and Schultz also notes that Alexander I erected a gilded statue of himself at Delphi and Olympia, as did Alexander the Great at Delphi. Schultz argues (e.g., pp. 217–21) that the image of Philip was meant to be heroic or even had a 'divinising' purpose, but the latter is harder to accept (see Appendix 5).
67. E. Carney, *Women and Monarchy in Macedonia* (Norman, OK: 2000), p. 77.
68. See Schultz, 'Leochares' Argead Portraits in the Philippeion', pp. 221–5, on the setting and effect of the shape of the building.
69. Diodorus 16.52.3; cf. Ellis, *Philip II*, p. 92.
70. Curtius 6.4.25; cf. Arrian 3.22.1.
71. Aristobulus, *FGrH* 139 F 11 = Plutarch, *Alexander* 21.7.
72. Diodorus 16.60.4–5.
73. Argos seems an odd place to identify as a co-leader of this force, unless Isocrates was pandering to the Macedonians' Argive ancestry: see further Appendix 2.
74. On the *To Philip*, see Hammond, *Philip*, pp. 88–9, 96, Ellis, *Philip II*, pp. 128–30, Cawkwell, *Philip*, pp. 111–13; cf. S. Perlman, 'Isocrates' "Philippus" – A Reinterpretation', *Historia* 6 (1957), pp. 306–17. On Isocrates, see S. Usher, *Greek Oratory* (Oxford: 1999), pp. 296–323 and now T. Papillon, 'Isocrates', in Ian Worthington (ed.), *Blackwell Companion to Greek Rhetoric* (Oxford: 2006), pp. 58 and 74.
75. *Contra* Ellis, *Philip II*, pp. 91–2, and see further below.
76. J.R. Ellis, 'The Dynamics of Fourth-Century Macedonian Imperialism', *Ancient Macedonia* 2 (Institute for Balkan Studies, Thessaloniki: 1977), pp. 103–14, which is developed and becomes the central thesis of his *Philip II*; cf. Borza, *Shadow of Olympus*, pp. 228–30. Cawkwell, *Philip*, p. 111, also suggests that in 346 Philip wanted an alliance as well as peace with Athens as he had decided by then to invade Persia.
77. See J. Buckler, 'Philip II's Designs on Greece', in R.W. Wallace and E.M. Harris (eds), *Transitions to Empire: Essays in Honor of E. Badian* (Norman, OK: 1996), pp. 77–97.

78. R.M. Errington, 'Review-Discussion: Four Interpretations of Philip II', *AJAH* 6 (1981), pp. 69–88; cf. his *History of Macedonia*, pp. 88–9.

79. E.A. Fredricksmeyer, 'On the Final Aims of Philip II', in W.L. Adams and E.N. Borza (eds), *Philip II, Alexander the Great, and the Macedonian Heritage* (Lanham, MD: 1982), pp. 85–98.

80. Arrian 2.14.5.

81. Demosthenes 10.32 (fourth *Philippic*, delivered in 341).

82. Cf. Errington, 'Four Interpretations', pp. 77–84.

83. Plutarch, *Timoleon* 37. On Timoleon, see further R.J. Talbert, *Timoleon and the Revival of Greek Sicily, 344–317 BC* (London: 1974).

84. This is disputed by H. Montgomery, 'The Economic Revolution of Philip II – Myth or Reality?', *SO* 60 (1985), pp. 37–47, who uses the spurious nature of Alexander's speech at Opis as 'evidence' that Philip's economic reforms were nonexistent. His views are rebutted by N.G.L. Hammond, 'Philip's Innovations in Macedonian Economy', *SO* 70 (1995), pp. 22–9.

85. Diodorus 16.8.6–8. For Athens' income, see Theopompus, *FGrH* 115 F 166, Demosthenes 10.37–8.

86. Demosthenes 19.265–7, Diodorus 16.53.2.

87. Cf. Justin 8.3.8.

88. Diodorus 16.53.3.

89. Theopompus, *FGrH* 115 F 224, Justin 9.8.6–7.

90. Aristobulus, *FGrH* 139 F 4, Duris, *FGrH* 70 F 40, Onesicritus, *FGrH* 134 F 2 = Plutarch, *Alexander* 15.2, Arrian 7.9.6, Curtius 10.2.24, [Plutarch], *Moralia* 327d, 342d.

91. See Fredricksmeyer, 'Final Aims of Philip II', pp. 85–98; cf. his 'Alexander the Great and the Kingship of Asia', in A.B. Bosworth and E.J. Baynham (eds), *Alexander the Great in Fact and Fiction* (Oxford: 2000), pp. 136–66. The question is important in assessing Alexander's aims in his invasion: whether he had the grand designs of his father as argued by Fredricksmeyer, or merely took up the simpler plan of Asia Minor and later extended it; cf. P.A. Brunt, 'The Aims of Alexander', *G&R²* 12 (1965), pp. 205–15, Griffith, *Macedonia* 2, pp. 485–9 and 517–22; cf. E. Bloedow, 'Why Did Philip and Alexander Launch a War against the Persian Empire?', *L'Ant. Class.* 72 (2003), pp. 261–74 and see further, Chapter 16.

92. Diodorus 16.91.2, Pausanias 8.7.6.

93. Diodorus 17.39.1–2, 17.54.1–6, Arrian 2.25, Curtius 4.1.7–14, 4.11.1–5, Plutarch, *Alexander* 29.7–8, Justin 9.12.1–10. The sources are controversial here; for discussion, see A.B. Bosworth, *A Historical Commentary on Arrian's History of Alexander* 1 (Oxford: 1980), pp. 227–33 and 256–7. On the background, cf. Ian Worthington, *Alexander the Great, Man and God*, rev. and enl. edn (London: 2004), pp. 124–5.

94. Isocrates 5.120, *Letter* 2.11, Diodorus 16.91.4, 16.92.4; the source problems are noted by Fredricksmeyer, 'Final Aims of Philip II', p. 90 n. 14.

95. Diodorus 16.91.3–4. Cf. Diodorus 16.92.4, but how could he have known what Philip was thinking about the Persian king?

96. Diodorus 17.17.2.

Chapter 13: Assassination

1. Athenaeus 13.557d, Diodorus 16.93.9, Justin 9.5.8–9; see E. Carney, *Women and Monarchy in Macedonia* (Norman, OK: 2000), pp. 70–5. Arrian 3.6.5 says that he renamed her Eurydice after the marriage; cf. W. Heckel, 'Cleopatra or Eurydice?', *Phoenix* 32 (1978), pp. 155–8. However, the renaming is most likely Arrian's error: E. Badian, 'Eurydice', in W. L. Adams and E. N. Borza (eds), *Philip II, Alexander the Great, and the Macedonian Heritage* (Lanham, MD: 1982), pp. 99–110.

2. Athenaeus 13.557b–e; cf. 13.560c. See in detail on Satyrus' list A.D. Tronson, 'Satyrus the Peripatetic and the Marriages of Philip II', *JHS* 104 (1984), pp. 116–26; cf. Ellis, *Philip II*, pp. 212–14, Griffith, *Macedonia* 2, pp. 214–15 and 220–30. The following translation is that of Tronson, pp. 119–20.

3. See Ellis, *Philip II*, pp. 212–14, for arguments that Philip never divorced anyone and that all were wives as opposed to some being merely mistresses.

4. See further Carney, *Women and Monarchy in Macedonia*, pp. 55–7.

5. Ellis, *Philip II*, p. 111, translates the phrase as 'military purposes', which could preclude actual warfare, but this does not accurately reflect the Greek.

6. See further Tronson, 'Satyrus the Peripatetic', pp. 120–6.

7. Cf. Justin 10.1.1, that Artaxerxes II (405–359) had 115 sons from concubines, but 'only three fathered within a legitimate marriage'.

8. See Tronson, 'Satyrus the Peripatetic', pp. 120–6; cf. Carney, *Women and Monarchy in Macedonia*, pp. 53–5.

9. Carney, *Women and Monarchy in Macedonia*, pp. 73–4.

10. On Olympias, see Carney, *Women and Monarchy in Macedonia*, pp. 62–7 and 79–81 (during Philip's reign), and her *Olympias, Mother of Alexander the Great* (London: 2006).

11. Plutarch, *Alexander* 9.5.

12. Plutarch, *Alexander* 5.7.

13. Plutarch, *Alexander* 77.8.

14. Justin 9.8.3.

15. Plutarch, *Alexander* 77.7–8 [Plutarch], *Moralia* 1.3, Justin 9.8.2, 13.2.11, 14.5.2.

16. Isocrates, *Letter* 5.

17. Arrian, *Succ.* 1.22. See also W.S. Greenwalt, 'The Search for Arrhidaeus', *Anc. World* 10 (1985), pp. 69–77.

18. Carney, *Women and Monarchy in Macedonia*, pp. 69–70.

19. Arrian 1.5.4.

20. Cf. Plutarch, *Alexander* 9.5–6, Athenaeus 13.557d, 560c (they say that this marriage more than anything else caused a rift in Philip's household). See also W. Heckel, 'Philip and Olympias (337/6 BC)', in G.S. Shrimpton and D.J. McCargar (eds), *Classical Contributions: Studies in Honor of M.F. McGregor* (Locust Valley, NY: 1981), pp. 51–7.

21. Plutarch, *Alexander* 9.5.

22. Plutarch, *Alexander* 9.6–11, Athenaeus 13.557d from Satyrus; cf. Justin 9.7.3–4. See further Ellis, *Philip II*, pp. 214–16, on the whole incident and Attalus' remark.

23. Plutarch, *Alexander* 9.10, Justin 9.7.4; *contra* Athenaeus 557e, who omits the incident with Philip.

24. Plutarch, *Alexander* 9.4–5, Athenaeus 13.557d, Justin 9.7.5. Perhaps Alexander went to the court of Langarus, the Agrianian chieftain, since the two were friends; he would later support Alexander when he became king: Arrian 1.5.2–3.

25. Cf. Justin 9.7.7.

26. [Plutarch], *Moralia* 179c; see further Plutarch, *Alexander* 9.6–14, Justin 9.7.6.

27. Cf. Plutarch, *Alexander* 10.1–3.

28. Diodorus 16.91.4, Justin 9.7.7. On this Cleopatra, see Carney, *Women and Monarchy in Macedonia*, pp. 75–6.

29. Justin 9.5.9 and 9.7.2 talks of Philip 'repudiating' Olympias, and at 9.7.12 he says that Olympias 'forced Cleopatra, for whom Philip had divorced her, to hang herself', which is accepted by Hammond, *Philip*, p. 172. Justin is wrong here; among other things, he calls Cleopatra Attalus' sister.

30. See further Heckel, 'Philip and Olympias (337/6 BC)', pp. 51–7.

31. For example, Buckler, *Aegean Greece*, pp. 520–1.

32. Cf. Diodorus 16.91.4, 17.2.3–4.

33. Carney, *Women and Monarchy in Macedonia*, pp. 40–1.

34. Plutarch, *Alexander* 10.1–5.
35. Plutarch, *Demosthenes* 10.3.
36. Arrian 3.6.5, Plutarch, *Alexander* 10.1–4.
37. See M.B. Hatzopoulos, 'A Reconsideration of the Pixodaros Affair', in B. Barr-Sharrar and E.N. Borza (eds), *Macedonia and Greece in Late Classical and Early Hellenistic Times: Studies in the History of Art* 10 (Washington, DC: 1982), pp. 59–66; cf. Hammond, *Philip*, pp. 173–4.
38. Plutarch, *Alexander* 5.4.
39. On this and how it affected Alexander as king, the classic study of E. Badian still needs to be read first: 'Alexander the Great and the Loneliness of Power', in E. Badian, *Studies in Greek and Roman History* (Oxford: 1964), pp. 192–205.
40. Diodorus 16.91.2, 17.2.4, Justin 9.5.8.
41. See A.J. Hesisserer, *Alexander the Great and the Greeks: The Epigraphic Evidence* (Norman, OK: 1980), no. 2.
42. Arrian 1.17.11.
43. Polyaenus 5.44.4.
44. Diodorus 16.91, 17.7.8; cf. Arrian 1.17.10–11.
45. Sources: Aristotle, *Politics* 5.1311b1–3, Diodorus 16.93–4, 17.2.3–6, Plutarch, *Alexander* 10.4–7, [Plutarch], *Moralia* 327c, Justin 9.6.4–7.14; cf. Arrian, *FGrH* 156 F 9 and 22.
46. Diodorus 16.91.4–93.4, Justin 9.6.1–3.
47. Diodorus 16.91.5, 16.91.6.
48. Athenaeus 13.557e. Pausanias 8.7.7 and Justin 11.2.3 (cf. 9.7.3) have it that Cleopatra gave birth to a son, Caranus, and Justin later says (12.6.14) that the daughter was killed; Diodorus 17.2.3 merely says Cleopatra bore a child (he uses the neuter noun *paidion*). Since we know that Cleopatra did give birth to a daughter and that Olympias killed both mother and daughter upon Philip's death, there is not enough time for her to have been pregnant twice. On Europa, see Carney, *Women and Monarchy in Macedonia*, pp. 77–8.
49. Diodorus 16.92.5, 16.95.1.
50. Justin 9.6.3.
51. Diodorus 16.93.1–2.
52. Diodorus 16.93.3–95, Justin 9.6.4. N.G.L. Hammond, 'The Various Guards of Philip II and Alexander III', *Historia* 40 (1991), pp. 396–417, argues that the assassination took place in an entry passage, not in the actual orchestra.
53. Note the view of A.B. Bosworth, 'Philip II and Upper Macedonia', *CQ*² 21 (1971), pp. 95–6, that Pausasias may simply have tripped and been captured, and that the version we have was embellished for dramatic effect. Yet if Pausanias had been taken alive, we would expect to hear of it.
54. Justin (at 9.8.1) says he was forty-seven, but he means he was in his forty-seventh year, hence Philip was forty-six.
55. Aristotle, *Politics* 5.1311b, Diodorus 16.93–4, Plutarch, *Alexander* 10.6–7, Justin 9.6.5–7.9.
56. See, for example, E. Badian, 'The Death of Philip II', *Phoenix* 17 (1963), pp. 244–50 (Alexander involved), R. Develin, 'The Murder of Philip II', *Antichthon* 15 (1981), pp. 86–99 (Olympias involved); cf. Griffith, *Macedonia* 2, pp. 684–91, J.R. Fears, 'Pausanias, the Assassin of Philip', *Athenaeum* 53 (1975), pp. 111–35, N.G.L. Hammond, 'The End of Philip', in M.B. Hatzopoulos and L.D. Loukopoulos (eds), *Philip of Macedon* (London: 1980), pp. 166–75 (cf. Hammond, *Philip*, pp. 170–6) and E. Carney, 'The Politics of Polygamy: Olympias, Alexander and the Murder of Philip II', *Historia* 41 (1992), pp. 169–89 (Pausanias alone was responsible and neither Alexander nor Olympias had anything to do with it). Still the best and most thorough study is J.R. Ellis, 'The Assassination of Philip II', in H.J. Dell (ed.), *Ancient*

Macedonian Studies in Honour of C.F. Edson (Thessaloniki: 1981), pp. 99–137, which, while leaning towards a personal motive on Pausanias' part, wisely concludes that all explanations are still only theories.

57. Diodorus 16.93.8–9.
58. Justin 9.6.7.
59. Justin 9.7.1; see also 9.7.1–11 for their involvement in a conspiracy.
60. Plutarch, *Alexander* 10.6. The final clause is missing from the Penguin translation though the Greek text is secure.
61. Diodorus 16.94.4, Justin 9.7.9.
62. Cf. Carney, *Women and Monarchy in Macedonia*, pp. 79–81.
63. Diodorus 16.94.1.
64. Plutarch, *Demosthenes* 19.1. The last line of the quotation is omitted from the Penguin translation.
65. For more on this angle, see the arguments of E. Fredricksmeyer, 'Alexander and Philip: Emulation and Resentment', *CJ* 85 (1990), pp. 300–15, Ian Worthington, *Alexander the Great, Man and God*, rev. and enl. edn (London: 2004), pp. 37–43.
66. My view (which is not novel) is excluded by Carney, 'Politics of Polygamy', pp. 169–89, who also considers the other theories.
67. Plutarch, *Alexander* 27.8–10; cf. Diodorus 17.51.2–3, Curtius 4.7.27, Justin 11.11.2–12.

Chapter 14: After Philip

1. Aeschines 3.77; cf. Plutarch, *Demosthenes* 22.1 (Demosthenes had secret intelligence of Philip's death).
2. Aeschines 3.77, 3.160; cf. Plutarch, *Demosthenes* 22.3, *Phocion* 16.6, [Plutarch], *Moralia* 847b. The quotation is from Plutarch, *Demosthenes* 22.3.
3. Justin 11.1.1–6.
4. Arrian 1.25.1–2, Curtius 6.9.17, 6.10.24, [Plutarch], *Moralia* 327c; cf. Justin 12.6.14.
5. Polyaenus 4.2.3. Their involvement is suspect, and Alexander may have implicated them in order to draw attention away from himself: cf. E. Badian, 'The Death of Philip II', *Phoenix* 17 (1963), pp. 244–50.
6. Cf. Errington, *History of Macedonia*, p. 43 and see further A.B. Bosworth, 'Philip II and Upper Macedonia', *CQ²* 21 (1971), pp. 93–105, that they represented a very real threat.
7. Justin 11.1.7–10.
8. Diodorus 17.2.1–2.
9. On the purges, and Alexander's first couple of years as king, see in detail Ian Worthington, *Alexander the Great, Man and God*, rev. and enl. edn (London: 2004), pp. 44–65.
10. Diodorus 17.2.4–6, 17.5.1–2, Curtius 7.1.3, Justin 11.5.1.
11. Justin 9.7.12, Pausanias 8.7.7.
12. Diodorus 17.3.6–4.9, Arrian 1.1.2–3. On the historical background, see A.B. Bosworth, *Conquest and Empire: The Reign of Alexander the Great* (Cambridge: 1988), pp. 188–92 and Worthington, *Alexander*, pp. 50–3.
13. Diodorus 17.4.1; cf. Justin 11.3.2.
14. Diodorus 17.4.9, Arrian 1.1.2, [Plutarch], *Moralia* 240a–b, Justin 11.2.5. The major sticking point for the Spartans seems to have been the independence of Messenia, which was guaranteed under the Common Peace. However, they also refused to recognise anyone as master of Greece but themselves: cf. Justin 9.5.3.
15. See Ian Worthington, 'Alexander's Destruction of Thebes', in W. Heckel and L.A. Tritle (eds), *Crossroads of History: The Age of Alexander the Great* (Claremont, CA: 2003), pp. 65–86.

16. He marched 250 miles (400 km) through rugged terrain in thirteen days (Arrian 1.7.5).

17. Diodorus 17.8.3–14, Arrian 1.7.1–8.8, Plutarch, *Alexander* 11.10–12; cf. *Demosthenes* 23.2, Justin 11.3.8, and see Bosworth, *Conquest and Empire*, pp. 32–3 and 194–6, Worthington, *Alexander*, pp. 58–63 and his 'Alexander's Destruction of Thebes', pp. 65–86.

18. Aristobulus, *FGrH* 139 F 2b = [Plutarch], *Moralia* 259d–260d.

19. On the numbers, see D. Engels, *Alexander the Great and the Logistics of the Macedonian Army* (Berkeley and Los Angeles, CA: 1978), pp. 146–7 (Table 4).

20. Dinarchus 1.34, Diodorus 17.63.1–3, Curtius 6.1, and see Worthington, *Alexander*, pp. 77–8, 105–6 and 111.

21. Especially Athens, thanks to the administration of Lycurgus, who virtually tripled annual revenue from the sorry level to which it had sunk two or three decades earlier: Diodorus 16.88.1, [Plutarch], *Moralia* 841b–844a, and see E.M. Burke, 'Lycurgan Finances', *GRBS* 26 (1985), pp. 251–64 with F.W. Mitchel, 'Lykourgan Athens: 338–322', *Semple Lectures* 2 (Cincinnati, OH: 1970), Bosworth, *Conquest and Empire*, pp. 204–15 and M. Faraguna, *Atene nell'età di Alessandro: problemi politici, economici, finanziari* (Rome: 1992). On prosperity in the Peloponnese down to the Roman occupation in the second century BC, see G. Shipley, 'Between Macedonia and Rome: Political Landscapes and Social Change in Southern Greece in the Early Hellenistic Period', *BSA* 100 (2005), pp. 315–30.

22. [Plutarch], *Moralia* 847c, 848e; cf. Plutarch, *Phocion* 21.1.

23. Aeschines 3.164. On Demosthenes during this period, see my 'Demosthenes' (In)activity during the Reign of Alexander the Great', in Ian Worthington (ed.), *Demosthenes: Statesman and Orator* (London: 2000), pp. 90–113.

24. Aeschines 3.49–50, 3.101, 3.236–7, Demosthenes 18.57–8.

25. On the trial, see E.M. Burke, '*Contra Leocratem* and *De Corona*: Political Collaboration?', *Phoenix* 31 (1977), pp. 330–40, N. Sawada, 'Athenian Politics in the Age of Alexander the Great: A Reconsideration of the Trial of Ctesiphon', *Chiron* 26 (1996), pp. 57–84, J. Buckler, 'Demosthenes and Aeschines', in Ian Worthington (ed.), *Demosthenes: Statesman and Orator* (London: 2000), pp. 145–8.

26. On oratory as source material, see Appendix 1.

27. On the weaknesses in Aeschines' case, see, for example, E.M. Harris, 'Law and Oratory', in Ian Worthington (ed.), *Persuasion: Greek Rhetoric in Action* (London: 1994), especially pp. 142–8; see also his *Aeschines and Athenian Politics* (Oxford: 1995), pp. 142–8.

28. [Plutarch], *Moralia* 840d–e.

29. On the Harpalus affair and Demosthenes' downfall, see in detail Ian Worthington, *A Historical Commentary on Dinarchus: Rhetoric and Conspiracy in Later Fourth-Century Athens* (Ann Arbor, MI: 1992), pp. 41–77; cf. Worthington, *Alexander*, pp. 243–4 and 263–5.

30. On the war, see N.G.L. Hammond and F.W. Walbank, *A History of Macedonia* 3 (Oxford: 1988), pp. 107–17, for example. Contemporary Greeks called it 'The Greek War' until about 301 when Lamian War became the norm: N.G. Ashton, 'The Lamian War – stat magni nominis umbra', *JHS* 94 (1984), pp. 152–7.

31. Diodorus 18.18.4–5.

32. Plutarch, *Demosthenes* 29.4–7, [Plutarch], *Moralia* 847b, [Lucian], *Enc. Dem.* 28, 43–9.

33. See, for example, C.W. Wooten, *Cicero's Philippics and their Demosthenic Model* (Chapel Hill, NC: 1983).

34. Cicero, *ad Att.* 1.16.12, Horace, *Odes* 3.16, Juvenal, *Satires* 12.47 (of Olynthus in 348), Seneca, *Con.* 10.5.6.

35. F.M. Turner, *The Greek Heritage in Victorian Britain* (London: 1981), p. 187.

36. For example, A.W. Pickard-Cambridge, *Demosthenes and the Last Days of Greek Freedom* (London: 1914), G. Clemenceau, *Démosthènes* (Paris: 1926), P. Cloché, *Démosthène et la fin de la démocratie athénienne* (Paris: 1957). Clemenceau, *Démosthènes*, p. 10, blamed the Athenian people's demise on their failure to listen to Demosthenes from the outset.

37. See G.L. Cawkwell's views in his various articles on Demosthenes' policy, for example, 'Aeschines and the Peace of Philocrates', *REG* 73 (1960), pp. 416–38, 'Demosthenes' Policy after the Peace of Philocrates I and II', *CQ*² 13 (1963), pp. 120–38 and 200–13; cf. 'The Crowning of Demosthenes', *CQ*² 19 (1969), pp. 163–80, all synthesised in his biography *Philip of Macedon*, R. Sealey, *Demosthenes and His Time: A Study in Defeat* (Oxford: 1993), T.T.B. Ryder, 'Demosthenes and Philip II', in Ian Worthington (ed.), *Demosthenes: Statesman and Orator* (London: 2000), pp. 45–89 and Buckler, 'Demosthenes and Aeschines', pp. 114–58. However, Athens' readiness and ability to oppose Philip is positively argued by P.E. Harding, 'Athenian Foreign Policy in the Fourth Century', *Klio* 77 (1995), pp. 105–25.

Chapter 15: Philip in Retrospect: King, Man – and God?

1. Diodorus 16.95, Justin 9.8.
2. Errington, *History of Macedonia*, p. 101.
3. H. Montgomery, 'The Economic Revolution of Philip II – Myth or Reality?', *SO* 60 (1985), pp. 37–47, believes this connection did not exist and that Philip was not responsible for the economic reforms with which he is generally credited. Montgomery bases much of his argument on Alexander's speech at Opis, which he believes is rhetorical falsehood. However, his views have been rebutted by N.G.L. Hammond, 'Philip's Innovations in Macedonian Economy', *SO* 70 (1995), pp. 22–9. On Philip's economic revolution, see also Hammond, *Macedonia* 2, pp. 657–71 and his *Macedonian State*, pp. 177–87.
4. See F. Papazoglou, *Les villes de Macédoine à l'époque romaine* (Paris 1988); cf. M. Siganidou, 'Urban Centres in Macedonia', in J. Vokotopoulou (ed.), *Greek Civilization: Macedonia, Kingdom of Alexander the Great* (Athens: 1993), pp. 29–31.
5. See V. Poulios, 'Macedonian Coinage from the 6th Century to 148 BC', in J. Vokotopoulou (ed.), *Greek Civilization: Macedonia, Kingdom of Alexander the Great* (Athens: 1993), pp. 83–103; see too Hammond, *Macedonia* 2, pp. 662–6 and especially G. Le Rider, *Le monnayage d'argent et d'or de Philippe II frappé en Macédoine de 359 à 294* (Paris: 1977).
6. See A. Adams, 'Philip *Alias* Hitler', *G&R* 10 (1941), pp. 105–13.
7. On Philip's use of diplomacy throughout his reign, see T.T.B. Ryder, 'The Diplomatic Skills of Philip II', in Ian Worthington (ed.), *Ventures into Greek History: Essays in Honour of N.G.L. Hammond* (Oxford: 1994), pp. 228–57; see too J. Buckler, 'Philip II's Designs on Greece', in R.W. Wallace and E.M. Harris (eds), *Transitions to Empire: Essays in Honor of E. Badian* (Norman, OK: 1996), pp. 77–97 and G.L. Cawkwell, 'The End of Greek Liberty', Wallace and Harris, *Transitions to Empire*, pp. 98–121.
8. Cf. Diodorus 16.95.2–3, from Ephorus.
9. For Philip as general, see G.T. Griffith, 'Philip as a General and the Macedonian Army', in M.B. Hatzopoulos and L.D. Loukopoulos (eds), *Philip of Macedon* (Athens: 1980), pp. 48–57; cf. Cawkwell, 'End of Greek Liberty', pp. 108–12.
10. Justin 8.5.7–6.2.
11. Justin 8.3.8–9.
12. See further Ian Worthington, 'Alexander, Philip, and the Macedonian Background', in J. Roisman (ed.), *Brill's Companion to Alexander the Great* (Leiden: 2003), pp. 94–6.
13. The first was at the Hyphasis river in 326: see A.B. Bosworth, *Conquest and Empire:*

The Reign of Alexander the Great (Cambridge: 1988), pp. 132–3, Ian Worthington, *Alexander the Great: Man and God*, rev. & enl. edn (London: 2004), pp. 214–17. The second was at Opis in 324: see Bosworth, *Conquest and Empire*, pp. 159–61, Worthington, *Alexander*, pp. 248–52. See also E. Carney, 'Macedonians and Mutiny: Discipline and Indiscipline in the Army of Philip and Alexander', *CP* 91 (1996), pp. 19–44.

14. Theopompus, *FGrH* 115 F 224, Justin 9.8.6–7. On the sources for Philip, see Appendix 1.
15. Cf. Justin 8.3.8; but at 8.3.4 Justin says the king did not honour the contracts.
16. Griffith, *Macedonia* 2, p. 671.
17. Diodorus 16.92.5.
18. See in detail E.A. Fredricksmeyer, 'On the Final Aims of Philip II', in W.L. Adams and E.N. Borza (eds), *Philip II, Alexander the Great, and the Macedonian Heritage* (Lanham: 1982), pp. 85–98, especially pp. 94–8, his 'Divine Honors for Philip II', *TAPA* 109 (1979), pp. 39–61 and his 'On the Background of the Ruler Cult', in H.J. Dell (ed.), *Ancient Macedonian Studies in Honor of C.F. Edson* (Thessaloniki: 1981), pp. 145–56; cf. his 'Alexander the Great and the Kingship of Asia', in A.B. Bosworth and E.J. Baynham (eds), *Alexander the Great in Fact and Fiction* (Oxford: 2000), pp. 136–66; cf. (surprisingly) Borza, *Shadow of Olympus*, p. 250. Against this view, see E. Badian, 'The Deification of Alexander the Great', in H.J. Dell (ed.), *Ancient Macedonian Studies in Honor of C.F. Edson* (Thessaloniki: 1981), especially pp. 67–71, Griffith, *Macedonia* 2, pp. 682–4 and 695.
19. Cf. P.A. Brunt, 'The Aims of Alexander', *G&R²* 12 (1965), pp. 205–15, Griffith, *Macedonia* 2, pp. 484–9 and 517–22.
20. See the criticisms of Hammond, *Philip*, pp. 70–8.
21. Theopompus, *FGrH* 115 F 237 = Athenaeus 77d–e, Demosthenes 18.295–96.
22. Justin 8.1.1–2.
23. *Letter* 7 (e.g., 324c–326b).
24. See especially Isocrates 5.119–23; cf. *Epistle* 3.
25. Cawkwell, 'End of Greek Liberty', p. 115.
26. Demosthenes 18.19; cf. 18.61.
27. G.L. Cawkwell, 'Philip and Athens', in M.B. Hatzopoulos and L.D. Loukopoulos (eds), *Philip of Macedon* (Athens: 1980), pp. 100–10 and T.T.B. Ryder 'The Diplomatic Skills of Philip II', in Ian Worthington (ed.), *Ventures into Greek History: Essays in Honour of N.G.L. Hammond* (Oxford: 1994), pp. 228–57 (Philip and Athens: pp. 251–7).
28. Demosthenes 11.22 ('wounded in every limb') and 18.67; on Demosthenes' description of Philip's wounds and how they were embellished over the years for literary effect, see A.S. Riginos, 'The Wounding of Philip II of Macedon: Fact and Fabrication', *JHS* 114 (1994), pp. 103–19.
29. The analogy is that of Hammond, *Macedonian State*, p. 198.
30. Diodorus 17.117.5.

Chapter 16: Philip and Alexander: Like Father, Like Son?

1. See A.B. Bosworth, *From Arrian to Alexander* (Oxford: 1988), pp. 101–13; cf. H. Montgomery, 'The Economic Revolution of Philip II – Myth or Reality?', *SO* 60 (1985), pp. 39–40, 44; *contra* N.G.L. Hammond, 'Philip's Innovations in Macedonian Economy', *SO* 70 (1995), pp. 22–9.
2. Bosworth, *From Arrian to Alexander*, p. 108, calls this part of the speech absurd, rightly pointing out that the archaeological evidence shows the Macedonians had a highly developed and cultured society, and he thinks it is a product of Arrian's literary talents (pp. 109–10). However, he (like Montgomery, 'Economic Revolution of Philip II') believes the passage refers to all the people, not just those of Upper Macedonia (who

did not live in cities like their Lower Macedonian counterparts: archaeological evidence has not revealed the same level of artistic sophistication there).

3. Arrian 7.9.6–10.7.
4. The following draws on my *Alexander the Great, Man and God*, rev. and enl. edn (London: 2004), pp. 299–303 ('Philip's Ghost'); cf. pp. 37–43.
5. Diodorus 17.17.2. However, note the reservations of E. Bloedow, 'Why Did Philip and Alexander Launch a War against the Persian Empire?', *L'Ant. Class.* 72 (2003), pp. 261–74.
6. Arrian 2.3, Plutarch, *Alexander* 18.2–4 (both from Aristobulus).
7. Arrian 3.3–4, Plutarch, *Alexander* 26.10–27. See further, for example, A.B. Bosworth, 'Alexander and Ammon', in K. Kinzl (ed.), *Greece and the Ancient Mediterranean in History and Prehistory* (Berlin: 1977), pp. 51–75, Worthington, *Alexander*, pp. 113–25 and especially pp. 273–83 ('Man and God').
8. Aristobulus, *FGrH* 139 F 13 = Arrian 3.3.2.
9. For this and other stories, see Plutarch, *Alexander* 2.3–6, 3.6–7.
10. For example, Curtius 6.2.1–10, Plutarch, *Alexander* 45.1–4 (Alexander wearing Persian clothes and adopting Persian practices), Plutarch, *Alexander* 54.2–55.4, Curtius 8.5.5–6.1, Justin 12.7.1–3 (*proskynesis*), Curtius 6.6.6 (use of the Persian royal seal), Arrian 7.8.2 (reasons for the outbreak of the Opis mutiny).
11. Arrian 7.8.3; Curtius 10.2.13 talks of the men 'having no respect for the king'.
12. Demosthenes: Hyperides 5.31; Damis: [Plutarch], *Moralia* 219e.
13. Plutarch, *Alexander* 64.9.
14. Aristobulus, *FGrH* 139 F 55 = Arrian 7.20.1.
15. On this, see D. Gilley, 'Alexander and the Carmanian March of 324 BC', *AHB* 20 (2007), pp. 9–14.
16. Arrian 4.8, Curtius 8.1.27–37, Plutarch, *Alexander* 50–1.
17. Ephemerides, *FGrH* 117 F 2a = Aelian, *Varra Historia* 3.23, where his drinking is one of the things that is 'not good' about him.
18. Ephippus, *FGrH* 126 F 5 = Athenaeus 12.537e.
19. Diodorus 17.16.2.
20. Ptolemy, *FGrH* 138 F 30 = Arrian 7.26.3, Diodorus 17.117.4.
21. Diodorus 17.117.3, 18.2.4, Curtius 10.5.4, Justin 12.15.12.
22. On this period (its historical, social, intellectual and cultural aspects), see the essays in A. Erskine (ed.), *Blackwell Companion to the Hellenistic World* (Oxford: 2003), citing further bibliography.
23. When one evaluates him as a kingly 'package' as opposed to merely as a general, a very different picture emerges: see Worthington, *Alexander*, pp. 284–98.

Appendix 1: The Sources of Information

1. For a good survey of the ancient evidence, see E.N. Borza, *Before Alexander: Constructing Early Macedonia* (Claremont, CA: 1999), pp. 5–26 and 53–5.
2. N.G.L. Hammond and F.W. Walbank, *A History of Macedonia* 3 (Oxford: 1988), p. 27; see too W. Heckel, 'Marsyas of Pella: Historian of Macedon', *Hermes* 108 (1980), pp. 444–62.
3. The fragments of these earlier writers are collected in F. Jacoby, *Die Fragmente der griechischen Historiker* ('The Fragments of the Greek Historians'), commonly abbreviated as *FGrH*. This is a multi-volume collection of the Greek texts of the fragmentary earlier histories and Jacoby's commentaries on many of them. A new edition of this work entitled *Brill's New Jacoby* is in progress (all in English), to be published online by E.J. Brill in biannual instalments from July 2007 to December 2013.
4. See the new commentary of J. Engels on Theagenes, *Brill's New Jacoby* 774 (Leiden: 2007).

5. See further G.S. Shrimpton, *Theopompus the Historian* (Montreal: 1991) and his 'Theopompus' Treatment of Philip in the *Philippica*', *Phoenix* 31 (1977), pp. 123–44, W.R. Connor, 'History without Heroes: Theopompus' Treatment of Philip of Macedon', *GRBS* 8 (1967), pp. 33–154 and most recently M.A. Flower, *Theopompus of Chios* (Oxford: 1994), especially Chapters 5–6 on Theopompus and Philip.

6. Theopompus, *FGrH* 115 F 27.

7. Demosthenes 3.295 (he names twenty-seven individuals who betrayed their cities); cf. Diodorus 16.54.2, who uses the same terminology.

8. Justin 9.8.6.

9. Diodorus 16.93.3–4, Justin 8.6.5–8, and see in general Justin 9.8 (translated in Chapter 15 of this book).

10. Satyrus in Athenaeus 13.557d–e.

11. Plutarch, *Alexander* 9.5.

12. On this, see Flower, *Theopompus of Chios*, pp. 98–104.

13. Buckler, *Aegean Greece*, p. 386.

14. See Flower, *Theopompus of Chios*, pp. 136–47.

15. Philip's marriages: Athenaeus 13.557b–e; cf. A.D. Tronson, 'Satyrus the Peripatetic and the Marriages of Philip II', *JHS* 104 (1984), pp. 116–26.

16. On Diodorus, see K. Sacks, *Diodorus Siculus and the First Century* (Princeton, NJ: 1990); see too his 'Diodorus and his Sources: Conformity and Creativity', in S. Hornblower (ed.), *Greek Historiography* (Oxford: 1994), pp. 213–32. There is a brief treatment of this book by E.I. McQueen, *Diodorus Siculus. The Reign of Philip II. The Greek and Macedonian Narrative from Book XVI* (Bristol: 1995).

17. *FGrH* 73; cf. Diodorus 16.14.3–5, 16.76.5–6.

18. On sources, see further N.G.L. Hammond, 'The Sources of Diodorus XVI', *CQ* 31 (1937), pp. 79–91 and 32 (1938), pp. 37–51.

19. Diodorus 16.95.2–3.

20. See further J.M. Alonso-Núñez, 'An Augustan World History: The *Historiae Philippicae* of Pompeius Trogus', *G&R*[2] 34 (1987), pp. 56–72, N.G.L. Hammond, 'The Sources of Justin on Macedonia to the Death of Philip', *CQ*[2] 41 (1991), pp. 496–508, W. Heckel and R. Develin, *Justin, Epitome of the Philippic History of Pompeius Trogus* (Atlanta, GA: 1994) and now J.C. Yardley, *Justin and Trogus: A Study of the Language of Justin's Epitome of Trogus* (Toronto: 2003).

21. See R. Syme, 'The Date of Justin and the Discovery of Trogus' *Historia*', *Historia* 37 (1988), pp. 358–71, which considers all dates and argues for the later one.

22. Justin 8.3.1–5.

23. On Plutarch, see D.A. Russell, *Plutarch* (London: 1973), T. Duff, *Plutarch's Lives* (Oxford: 1999) and C. Pelling, *Plutarch and History* (London: 2002).

24. [Demosthenes] 7 and 12, respectively.

25. See, for example, T.T.B. Ryder, 'Demosthenes and Philip II', in Ian Worthington (ed.), *Demosthenes: Statesman and Orator* (London: 2000), pp. 45–89, whose analysis of Demosthenes' anti-Macedonian policy portrays a cynical yet politically astute Demosthenes, who switches policy for his own ends and uses scare-tactic rhetoric to alarm the people and so give himself an edge over opponents in the political arena.

26. Most recently, J. Buckler, 'Demosthenes and Aeschines', in Worthington (ed.), *Demosthenes: Statesman and Orator*, pp. 114–58, discusses the limitations of their speeches and analyses their differing policies to Macedonia. On the false embassy speech (19), see also D.M. MacDowell, *Demosthenes: On the False Embassy* (Oxford: 2000).

27. See further Ian Worthington, 'Greek Oratory, Revision of Speeches and the Problem of Historical Reliability', *Cl. & Med.* 42 (1991), pp. 55–74 and his 'History and Oratorical Exploitation', in Ian Worthington (ed.), *Persuasion: Greek Rhetoric in Action* (London: 1994), pp. 109–29, with bibliography cited, and M. Nouhaud,

L'utilisation de l'histoire par les orateurs attiques (Paris: 1982); cf. M. H. Hansen, 'Two Notes on Demosthenes' Symbouleutic Speeches', *Cl. & Med.* 35 (1984), pp. 57–70.

28.   See further S. Perlman, 'The Historical Example, its Use and Importance as Political Propaganda in the Attic Orators', *SH* 7 (1961), pp. 150–66 and L. Pearson, 'Historical Allusions in the Attic Orators', *CP* 36 (1941), pp. 209–29.

29.   On this, see P.E. Harding, 'Rhetoric and Politics in Fourth-Century Athens', *Phoenix* 41 (1987), pp. 25–39.

30.   On the speeches as sources, see the cogent remarks of Buckler, 'Demosthenes and Aeschines', pp. 148–54.

31.   This is taken as a given by T.T.B. Ryder, 'The Diplomatic Skills of Philip II', in Ian Worthington (ed.), *Ventures into Greek History: Essays in Honour of N.G.L. Hammond* (Oxford: 1994), pp. 228–57; see too C. Tuplin, 'Demosthenes' *Olynthiacs* and the Character of the Demegoric Corpus', *Historia* 47 (1998), pp. 276–320.

32.   Philip's coinage is mentioned several times in this book. The best and most wide-ranging work on Philip's coinage is G. Le Rider, *Le monnayage d'argent et d'or de Philippe II frappé en Macédoine de 359 à 294* (Paris: 1977). See also V. Poulios, 'Macedonian Coinage from the 6th Century to 148 BC', in J. Vokotopoulou (ed.), *Greek Civilization: Macedonia, Kingdom of Alexander the Great* (Athens: 1993), pp. 83–103.

33.   They are too numerous to mention here, but a very good, succinct survey, with reference to the archaeologists involved (albeit outdated now), is given by M. Andronikos, 'Archaeological Discoveries in Macedonia', in J. Vokotopoulou (ed.), *Greek Civilization: Macedonia, Kingdom of Alexander the Great* (Athens: 1993), pp. 5–11. In the same volume the finds and excavations at many principal sites are discussed on pp. 32–67, and for excellent photographs of finds in the classical period, see pp. 197–241.

34.   See D. Pandermalis, *Dion: The Archaeological Site and Museum* (Athens: 1997).

35.   See M. Andronikos, *Vergina: The Royal Tombs* (Athens: 1984; repr. 2004) and S. Drougou and C. Saatsoglou-Paliadeli, *Vergina: Wandering through the Archaeological Site* (Athens: 2004).

Appendix 2: The Question of Macedonian Ethnicity

1.   The ancient evidence is exhaustively collected and discussed by M.B. Sakellariou, 'The Inhabitants', in M.B. Sakellariou (ed.), *Macedonia, 4000 Years of Greek History and Civilization* (Athens: 1983), pp. 48–63 and E.N. Borza, 'Greeks and Macedonians in the Age of Alexander: The Source Traditions', in R.W. Wallace and E.M. Harris (eds), *Transitions to Empire: Essays in Honor of E. Badian* (Norman, OK: 1996), pp. 122–39; cf. J. Vokotopoulou, 'Macedonia in the Literary Sources', in J. Vokotopoulou (ed.), *Greek Civilization: Macedonia, Kingdom of Alexander the Great* (Athens: 1993), pp. 71–3. For a succinct overview of the problem, see E.N. Borza, *Before Alexander: Constructing Early Macedonia* (Claremont, CA: 1999), pp. 27–43 and his *Shadow of Olympus*, pp. 77–97.

2.   On this latter vexed issue, see, for example, L.M. Danforth, *The Macedonian Conflict* (Princeton, NJ: 1995); cf. his 'Alexander the Great and the Macedonian Conflict', in J. Roisman (ed.), *Brill's Companion to Alexander the Great* (Leiden: 2003), pp. 347–64, H. Poulton, *Who Are the Macedonians?* (Bloomington, IN: 2000).

3.   Herodotus 1.56, 5.22.1, 8.43, 8.137–9.

4.   See further N.G.L. Hammond, *A History of Macedonia* 1 (Oxford: 1972), pp. 432–34 and Borza, *Shadow of Olympus*, pp. 80–4 and 110–13.

5.   Herodotus 5.22; cf. P. Roos, 'Alexander I in Olympia', *Eranos* 83 (1985), pp. 162–8. See the cautionary remarks of Borza, *Shadow of Olympus*, pp. 111–12; *contra* Hammond, *Macedonia* 2, pp. 4–5. See further R. Scaife, 'Alexander I in the Histories

of Herodotus', *Hermes* 117 (1989), pp. 129–37, questioning Herodotus' portrayal of Alexander I, and hence his Greek descent; cf. E. Badian, 'Herodotus on Alexander I of Macedon; A Study in Some Subtle Silences', in S. Hornblower (ed.), *Greek Historiography* (Oxford: 1994), pp. 107–30.

6. Hammond, *Macedonia* 2, p. 98.
7. Thucydides 2.99.2–6; cf. 5.80.2 on the Argive connection.
8. Isocrates 5.32; cf. 6.17–18. The translation is that of T.L. Papillon, *Isocrates* 2 (Austin, TX: 2004), *ad loc.*
9. Strabo 7.8.
10. L. Moretti, *Olympionikai: i vincitori negli antichi agoni Olimpici* (Rome: 1957), pp. 110–11.
11. *Ibid.*, p. 124.
12. See further on the word, E.M. Anson, 'The Meaning of the Term *Makedones*', *Anc. World* 10 (1984), pp. 67–8.
13. See further F. Papazoglou, *Les villes de Macédoine à l'époque romaine* (Paris: 1988), Hammond, *Macedonia* 2, pp. 39–54; cf. Hammond, *Macedonian State*, pp. 12–15.
14. Polybius 28.8.9.
15. Aeschines 3.72.
16. A longer extract from this speech is given at the start of Chapter 1.
17. Cf. Hammond, *History of Macedonia* 1, pp. 420–3.
18. See D. Gilley, 'Alexander the Great and the Carmanian March of 324 BC', *AHB* (2007), pp. 9–14.
19. See especially Sakellariou, 'The Inhabitants', pp. 54–9.
20. See the discussion of B. Millis in his commentary on F1 of the anonymous author no. 311 in *Brill's New Jacoby* (Leiden: 2008).
21. Plutarch, *Alexander* 51.6. On these episodes, see A.B. Bosworth, *Conquest and Empire: The Reign of Alexander the Great* (Cambridge: 1988), pp. 101–3 (Philotas) and 114–15 (Cleitus) and Ian Worthington, *Alexander the Great, Man and God*, rev. and enl. edn (London: 2004), pp. 164–9 (Philotas) and 184–6 (Cleitus).

Appendix 3: Macedonia before Philip II

1. Cf. N.G.L. Hammond, 'The Kingdoms in Illyria circa 400–167 BC', *BSA* 61 (1966), pp. 239–53; cf. his *History of Macedonia* 1 (Oxford: 1972), pp. 420–3.
2. On the history, see further Hammond, *History of Macedonia* 1, pp. 430–41 and his *Macedonian State*, pp. 4–12 and 36–41; see too Hammond, *Macedonia* 2, pp. 54–69.
3. See Hammond, *Macedonian State*, pp. 81–9.
4. On the league, see A.B. West, *The History of the Chalcidic League* (Madison, WI: 1918). There is a crying need for a new history of the league that would take into account the more recent archaeological discoveries.
5. See Borza, *Shadow of Olympus*, pp. 98–131 (Alexander I) and pp. 132–60 (Perdiccas II), Hammond, *Macedonia* 2, pp. 98–104 (Alexander I) and pp. 115–36 (Perdiccas II) and his *Macedonian State*, pp. 43–7 (Alexander I) and 71–3 (Perdiccas II), and Errington, *History of Macedonia*, pp. 10–24.
6. See J.W. Cole, 'Perdiccas and Athens', *Phoenix* 28 (1974), pp. 55–72.
7. On whom, see Hammond, *Macedonia* 2, pp. 137–41, Borza, *Shadow of Olympus*, pp. 161–77, Errington, *History of Macedonia*, pp. 24–8.
8. On the importance of Archelaus' coinage, and its impact on his successors and on Macedonia itself, see especially W.S. Greenwalt, 'The Production of Coinage from Archelaus to Perdiccas III and the Evolution of Argead Macedonia', in Ian Worthington (ed.), *Ventures into Greek History: Essays in Honour of N.G.L. Hammond* (Oxford: 1994), pp. 105–34.
9. Thucydides 2.100.2.

10. *Contra* M.B. Hatzopoulos, 'Strepsa: A Reconsideration, or New Evidence on the Road System of Lower Macedonia', in *Two Studies in Ancient Macedonian Topography*, *Meletemata* 3 (Athens: 1987), pp. 41–4, who argues for a date during the reign of Amyntas III. On the status of Pella in the time of Archelaus, cf. Borza, *Shadow of Olympus*, pp. 166–8.

11. Aristotle, *Rhetoric* 2.23.8.

12. Diodorus 17.16.3; cf. Arrian 1.11.1 (wrongly saying it took place at Aegae).

13. In other words, a counter-Olympics, to use Badian's phrase: see E. Badian, 'Greeks and Macedonians', in B. Barr-Sharrar and E.N. Borza (eds), *Macedonia and Greece in Late Classical and Early Hellenistic Times: Studies in the History of Art* 10 (Washington, DC: 1982), p. 35; the argument and phrase are taken up by E.N. Borza, 'The Philhellenism of Archelaus', *Ancient Macedonia* 5 (Institute for Balkan studies, Thessaloniki: 1993), pp. 241–2 (cf. *Shadow of Olympus*, pp. 174–5), who argues that Archelaus founded the festival because he was not recognised as Greek and hence not allowed to take part in the Olympic Games.

14. Xenophon, *Hellenica* 5.2.13, [Plutarch], *Moralia* 177a–b, Athenaeus 8.345d.

15. Plato, *Gorgias* 471a–d.

16. Diodorus 14.37.6; see Hammond, *Macedonia* 2, pp. 167–72, Borza, *Shadow of Olympus*, pp. 177–9, Errington, *History of Macedonia*, pp. 28–9.

17. Diodorus 14.89.2; on Amyntas, see Hammond, *Macedonia* 2, pp. 172–80, Borza, *Shadow of Olympus*, pp. 180–9, Errington, *History of Macedonia*, pp. 29–34. See further W.S. Greenwalt, 'Amyntas III and the Political; Stability of Argead Macedonia', *Anc. World* 18 (1988), pp. 35–44.

18. Xenophon, *Hellenica* 5.2.11–13 and Diodorus 14.92.3–4 speak only of Olynthus' backing, but Thebes may also have played a role in this venture, for a fragment from an account of Theban opposition to Macedonia says: 'With regard then to their acts of hostility directed against your kingdom and the dynasty of your companions, though you are probably aware of them, I have thought it worthwhile to write you a brief account of them, lest you should think that they have escaped me. The Thebans in the first place attempted with the aid of the Olynthians to expel Amyntas, the father of Philip, from the country and to deprive him of his kingdom, although he had done them no previous injury': *FGrH* 153 F 1; the translation is that of the editors, Grenfell and Hunt, as given in C.A. Robinson, *The History of Alexander the Great* 1 (Providence, RI: 1953), p. 270.

19. On the northern involvement, see generally J. Heskel, *The North Aegean Wars, 371–60 BC* (Stuttgart: 1997).

20. Diodorus 15.67.4, [Plutarch], *Moralia* 178c, Justin 7.5.2–3. On the following historical background, see Hammond, *Macedonia* 2, pp. 180–8, Borza, *Shadow of Olympus*, pp. 189–97, Errington, *History of Macedonia*, pp. 35–7.

21. Diodorus 15.61, 15.67.4, 16.2.2–3, Plutarch, *Pelopidas* 26.4–5, Justin 6.9.7, 7.5.1–3. On Philip in Thebes, see Chapter 3.

22. Marsyas, *FGrH* 135/6 F 3 = Athenaeus 14.629d.

23. On regents and challenges to the throne in the period down to and including Philip II, see M.B. Hatzopoulos, 'Succession and Regency in Classical Macedonia', in *Ancient Macedonia* 4 (Institute for Balkan Studies, Thessaloniki: 1986), pp. 279–92.

24. Whether this was the same Pausanias who made another attempt on the Macedonian throne when Perdiccas died, this time backed by one of the Thracian kings, is unknown. *IG* iv² 94/95.13 records a Pausanias in a list of 360/59 at Epidaurus beside the town of Calindia in Mygdonia, but this proves nothing. Pausanias was a very common name, and the Pausanias of the inscription may have been an entirely different man.

25. Diodorus 16.2.1.

Appendix 4: Pella

1. Cf. Hammond, *Philip*, pp. 56–7.
2. On Pella, see in detail the Greek Ministry of Culture Publications of M. Siganidou and M. Lilimbaki-Akamati, *Pella* (Athens: 2003), P. Petsas, *Pella, Alexander the Great's Capital* (Thessaloniki: 1978), M. Lilimbaki-Akamati and I. Akamatis, *Pella and its Environs* (Athens: 2004); cf. M. Lilimbaki-Akamati, 'Pella', in J. Vokotopoulou (ed.), *Greek Civilization: Macedonia, Kingdom of Alexander the Great* (Athens: 1993), pp. 41–4. All of these works are lavishly illustrated.
3. See Lilimbaki-Akamati and Akamatis, *Pella and its Environs*, pp. 142–6.

Appendix 5: Philip's Apparent Divinity

1. Diodorus 16.92.5.
2. Diodorus 16.95.1.
3. For a good analysis of the ancient evidence and summary of modern scholars' views, see E. Baynham, 'The Question of Macedonian Divine Honours for Philip II', *Mediterranean Archaeology* 7 (1994), pp. 35–43.
4. *Letter* 3.5.
5. Diodorus 16.35.5, Justin 8.2.3.
6. From a much later source (Aelius Aristides): see C. Habicht, *Gottmenschentum und griechische Städte* (1970), pp. 11–17, E.A. Fredricksmeyer, 'Divine Honors for Philip II', *TAPA* 109 (1979), pp. 50–1.
7. *SEG* 38.658.
8. We are told that in 334 (when Alexander invaded Asia) those who had despoiled the Temple of Artemis and cast down Philip's statue were punished: Arrian 1.17.11.
9. Clement, *Protrepticus* 4.54.5.
10. For example, Isocrates 9.57 talks of the *eikones* of Conon (of Athens) and Evagoras (King of Cyprus), but of the *agalmata* of Zeus Soter in the Athenian Agora.
11. Cf. Diodorus 16.54, where he echoes Demosthenes in his belief that Philip took fortified towns by bribery rather than by assault.
12. Duris, *FGrH* 76 F 71.
13. See further M. Flower, 'Agesilaus of Sparta and the Origins of the Ruler-Cult', *CQ*[2] 38 (1988), pp. 123–34.
14. Cf. E.A. Fredricksmeyer, 'On the Final Aims of Philip II', in W.L. Adams and E.N. Borza (eds), *Philip II, Alexander the Great, and the Macedonian Heritage* (Lanham, MD: 1982), pp. 94–5.
15. Justin 8.2.7.
16. Baynham, 'Question of Macedonian Divine Honours for Philip II', pp. 39–40.
17. Cf. Griffith, *Macedonia* 2, p. 683.
18. Fredricksmeyer, 'Divine Honors for Philip II', pp. 52–6, *contra* Griffith, *Macedonia* 2, pp. 692–5.
19. Pausanias 5.20.10.
20. Griffith, *Macedonia* 2, p. 694.
21. Cf. K. Lapatin, *Chryselephantine Statuary in the Mediterranean World* (Oxford: 2001), pp. 117–18.
22. P. Schultz, 'Leochares' Argead Portraits in the Philippeion', in P. Schultz and R. von den Hoff (eds), *Early Hellenistic Portraiture: Image, Style, Context* (Cambridge: 2007), pp. 205–33.
23. On the importance of the setting, see further, Schultz, *ibid.*, pp. 221–4.
24. For arguments in support, see *ibid.*, pp. 209–10.
25. Griffith, *Macedonia* 2, pp. 720–1, citing bibliography.
26. See E. Badian, 'The Deification of Alexander the Great', in H.J. Dell (ed.), *Ancient*

Macedonian Studies in Honor of C.F. Edson (Thessaloniki: 1981), 40–1, Fredricksmeyer, 'Divine Honors for Philip II', p. 51.

27. Demosthenes 19.261.

28. See the commentary of A. D'Hautcourt on Aethlios of Samos, *Brill's New Jacoby* 536 (Leiden: 2007), *ad* F3.

29. Badian, 'Deification of Alexander', pp. 67–71; cf. Fredricksmeyer, 'Divine Honors for Philip II', p. 59 n. 56.

30. J.M. Williams, 'Demades' Last Years, 323/2–319/8 B.C.: A "Revisionist" Interpretation', *Anc. World* 19 (1989), pp. 23–4.

31. Hyperides 6.21; cf. [Demades] 1.48, for statues of Alexander and also shrines and altars to him, accepted by N.G.L. Hammond and F.W. Walbank, *A History of Macedonia* 3 (Oxford: 1988), p. 82 with n. 3; cf. G.L. Cawkwell, 'The Deification of Alexander the Great: A Note', in Ian Worthington (ed.), *Ventures into Greek History: Essays in Honour of N.G.L. Hammond* (Oxford: 1994), pp. 293–306.

32. Ellis, *Philip II*, p. 307 n. 58, Griffith, *Macedonia* 2, p. 683. On the Hellenistic ruler-cult, see especially A. Chaniotis, 'The Divinity of Hellenistic Rulers', in A. Erskine (ed.), *Blackwell Companion to the Hellenistic World* (Oxford: 2003), pp. 431–45.

Appendix 6: The Vergina Royal Tombs

1. For the identification, see N.G.L. Hammond, *A History of Macedonia* 1 (Oxford: 1972), pp. 156–7 and his 'The Location of Aegae', *JHS* 117 (1997), pp. 177–9.

2. M. Andronikos, *Vergina: The Royal Tombs and the Ancient City* (Athens: 1984; repr. 2004); cf. his 'The Royal Tombs at Aigai (Vergina)', in M.B. Hatzopoulos and L.D. Loukopoulos (eds), *Philip of Macedon* (London, 1980), pp. 188–231; cf. S. Drougou and C. Saatsoglou-Paliadeli, *Vergina: Wandering through the Archaeological Site* (Athens: 2004).

3. M. Andronikos, *Vergina: The Royal Tombs* and his 'The Finds from the Royal Tombs at Vergina', *PBA* 65 (1979), pp. 355–67 and 'Some Reflections on the Macedonian Tombs', *BSA* 82 (1987), pp. 1–16.

4. For example, N.G.L. Hammond, 'Philip's Tomb in Historical Context', *GRBS* 19 (1978), pp. 331–50, his 'The Evidence for the Identity of the Royal Tombs at Vergina', in W.L. Adams and E.N. Borza (eds), *Philip II, Alexander the Great, and the Macedonian Heritage* (Lanham, MD: 1982), pp. 111–27, and 'The Royal Tombs at Vergina', *BSA* 86 (1991), pp. 69–82 and P. Green, 'The Royal Tomb at Vergina: A Historical Analysis', in W.L. Adams and E.N. Borza (eds), *Philip II, Alexander the Great, and the Macedonian Heritage* (Lanham, MD: 1982), pp. 129–51.

5. P.W. Lehmann, 'The So-Called Tomb of Philip II: A Different Interpretation', *AJA* 84 (1980), pp. 527–31, her 'Once Again the Royal Tomb at Vergina', *AAA* 14 (1981), pp. 134–44 and 'The So-Called Tomb of Philip II: An Addendum', *AJA* 86 (1982), pp. 437–42, E.N. Borza, 'The Royal Macedonian Tombs and the Paraphernalia of Alexander the Great', *Phoenix* 41 (1987), pp. 105–21; cf. Borza, *Shadow of Olympus*, pp. 256–66.

6. Diodorus 19.11.3–9, 19.52.5, Justin 14.5.10.

7. See S.I. Rotroff, 'Royal Saltcellars from the Athenian Agora', *AJA* 86 (1982) and 'Spool Saltcellars in the Athenian Agora', *Hesperia* 53 (1984), pp. 343–54.

8. See in detail A. Bartsiokas, 'The Eye Injury of King Philip II and the Skeletal Evidence from the Royal Tomb II at Vergina', *Science* 288 Issue 5465 (April 2000), pp. 511–14.

9. O. Palagia, 'Hephaestion's Pyre and the Royal Hunt of Alexander', in A.B. Bosworth and E.J. Baynham (eds), *Alexander the Great in Fact and Fiction* (Oxford: 2000), pp. 167–206.

10. Pliny, *NH* 35.110.

11. For example, W.L. Adams, 'The Royal Macedonian Tomb at Vergina: An Historical

Interpretation', *Anc. World* 3 (1980), pp. 67–72 and his 'Cassander, Alexander IV, and the Tombs at Vergina', *Anc. World* 22 (1991), pp. 27–33, E.D. Carney, 'The Female Burial in the Antechamber of Tomb II at Vergina', *Anc. World* 22 (1991), pp. 17–26.

12. See in detail Borza, 'Royal Macedonian Tombs and the Paraphernalia of Alexander the Great'; cf. his *Shadow of Olympus*, pp. 263–5.

13. Pliny, *NH* 35.109, says that Nicomachus painted a scene like this. On the identification of the remains, see E. Carney, 'Tomb I at Vergina and the Meaning of the Great Tumulus as a Historical Monument', *Archaeological News* 17 (1992), pp. 1–11.

14. J.H. Musgrave, 'Dust and Damn'd Oblivion: A Study of Cremation in Ancient Greece', *BSA* 85 (1990), p. 280, and see pp. 279–80 for his forensic analysis of the remains in Tomb I.

15. Diodorus 17.2.3.

16. For example, M.B. Hatzopoulos, 'Some Reflections on the Macedonian Tombs', *BSA* 82 (1987), pp. 1–16 and R.A. Tomlinson, 'The Architectural Content of the Macedonian Vaulted Tombs', *BSA* 82 (1987), pp. 305–12.

17. Plutarch, *Alexander* 10.4.

18. See in detail Musgrave, 'Dust and Damn'd Oblivion', pp. 278–9.

19. A point made to me by Professor Prag in email correspondence, but see Musgrave's study cited in the previous note.

20. In this I disagree with the common opinion (cf. Borza, *Shadow of Olympus*, p. 260), which is that Alexander was so angry at what his mother had done to Cleopatra and the baby girl that he had them buried.

21. Cf. Hammond, 'Philip's Tomb in Historical Context', p. 336.

22. On what follows, see Musgrave, 'Dust and Damn'd Oblivion', p. 279, citing other bibliography.

23. E.N. Borza, *Before Alexander: Constructing Early Macedonia* (Claremont, CA: 1999), p. 69 n. 42.

24. See Andronikos, *Vergina: The Royal Tombs*, pp. 102–18, with superb photos.

25. See further, *ibid.*, pp. 221–4.

26. Cf. Green, 'Royal Tomb at Vergina', pp. 135–6.

27. See A.S. Riginos, 'The Wounding of Philip II of Macedon: Fact and Fabrication', *JHS* 114 (1994), pp. 116–18.

28. See N.I. Xirotiris and F. Langenscheidt, 'The Cremations from the Royal Macedonian Tombs of Vergina', *Arch. Eph.* (1981), pp. 142–60.

29. See J.H. Musgrave, R.A.H Neave and A.J.N.W. Prag, 'The Skull from Tomb II at Vergina: King Philip II of Macedon', *JHS* 104 (1984), pp. 60–78, A.J.N.W. Prag, 'Reconstructing the Skull of Philip of Macedon', in E.C. Danien (ed.), *The World of Philip and Alexander* (Philadelphia, PA: 1990), pp. 17–37 and his 'Reconstructing King Philip II: The "Nice" Version', *AJA* 94 (1990), pp. 237–47.

30. For example, see Bartsiokas, 'Eye Injury of King Philip II', pp. 511–14.

31. See A.J.N.W. Prag, J.H. Musgrave and R.A. Neave, 'Twenty-first Century Philippic', in G.J. Oliver and Z. Archibald (eds), *The Power of the Individual in Ancient Greece. Essays in Honour of J.K. Davies* (Stuttgart: 2008), citing all relevant previous bibliography. I am very grateful to them for allowing me to see a copy of their essay in advance of its publication and to refer to it.

32. Alexander 'had no more than seventy talents in the treasury, maintenance for only thirty days, he owed two hundred talents, and had to borrow 800': Aristobulus, *FGrH* 139 F 4, Duris, *FGrH* 70 F 40, Onesicritus, *FGrH* 134 F 2 = Plutarch, *Alexander* 15.2, Arrian 7.9.6, Curtius 10.2.24, [Plutarch], *Moralia* 327d and 342d.

33. Diodorus 19.105.2 says that he was nearing adulthood (cf. 19.52.4).

BIBLIOGRAPHIC ESSAY

The following essay deals only with modern books, not articles. Information on the latter can be found by consulting the notes in the various books. On the ancient source material, see in more detail Appendix 1.

There are numerous books on the geography, history, culture and archaeological finds of ancient Macedonia. Two excellent introductions, which are mines of information on many towns and cities in Macedonia as well as on many aspects of Macedonian life, and are lavishly illustrated, are M.B. Sakellariou (ed.), *Macedonia, 4000 Years of Greek History and Civilization* (Athens: 1983) and (part of an international exhibition) J. Vokotopoulou (ed.), *Greek Civilization: Macedonia, Kingdom of Alexander the Great* (Athens: 1993). That of Sakellariou covers the Bronze Age to contemporary Macedonia, while that of Vokotopoulou covers the Bronze Age to the Hellenistic period. Also of note are the collections of essays in R. Ginouvès (ed.), *Macedonia: From Philip II to the Roman Conquest* (Princeton, NJ: 1994) and B. Barr-Sharrar and E.N. Borza (eds), *Macedonia and Greece in Late Classical and Early Hellenistic Times: Studies in the History of Art* 10 (Washington, DC: 1982), though the latter mostly focuses on Macedonian art and architecture in the later Classical and Hellenistic periods.

The best guides to the ancient sites and their finds are those published by the Greek Ministry of Culture. Some of these are cited in the notes for this book.

More detailed studies of ancient Macedonia are N.G.L. Hammond's magisterial three-volume *A History of Macedonia* (Oxford: 1972–88), the second volume written in collaboration with G.T. Griffith and the third with F.W. Walbank. This work is highly specialised, requires some prior knowledge of the history, and not all the Greek in it is translated. The topography and earlier history of Macedonia are dealt with in the first volume, which in many parts is obsolete because of archaeological discoveries made in the intervening decades. The second volume deals with Macedonian history from 550 to 336 BC (and includes a section on Philip's reign by Griffith), and the third with the history from Alexander the Great to 167 BC (Roman annexation of Greece). Somewhat more accessible is N.G.L. Hammond, *The Macedonian State: Origins, Institutions, and History* (Oxford: 1989), which gathers together views from the three-volume history within one set of covers. However, the subject matter is not always arranged chronologically and many aspects are treated thematically, so readers need to be on the ball at all times. Philip's reign is dealt with on pp. 100–204, although many references to Alexander's reign are folded into it.

Also detailed but less wide-ranging is R.M. Errington, *A History of Macedonia*, trans. C. Errington (Berkeley and Los Angeles, CA: 1990), which deals with the period from the fifth century to the reign of Philip. Its focus is on political and military history, and archaeological advances and evidence are largely neglected. Philip's reign is dealt with thematically (not chrono-logically) by geographical area on pp. 38–102. E.N. Borza, *In the Shadow of Olympus: The Emergence of Macedon* (Princeton, NJ: 1992), usefully considers literary and archaeological evidence for the history of Macedonia down to the end of Philip's reign in 336. Borza's careful treatment of Philip's reign, which is chronological and by area, is on pp. 198–230. There are good review essays of these works on Macedonian history by E. Carney, 'Review Essays on Macedonian History', *AHB* 5 (1991), pp. 179–89 and R.M. Errington, 'Review-Discussion: Four Interpretations of Philip II', *AJAH* 6 (1981), pp. 69–88. Another book worth singling out is E. Carney, *Women and Monarchy in Macedonia* (Norman, OK: 2000), which discusses the neglected role of women in royal policy and at court, and in doing so sheds much light on these factors as well as on social customs in Macedonia in general.

The number of books on Philip is small compared to the truckload on Alexander (which in introductory chapters treat Philip's reign but in necessarily summary fashion). Further, the books on Philip are written generally from the political and military viewpoints, and almost all are outdated and/or out of print. The earliest serious book was that of D.G. Hogarth, *Philip and Alexander of Macedon: Two Essays in Biography* (London: 1897; repr. 1971) – Philip is on pp. 4–157. Though outdated now, this was valuable because it was based on the author's own travels in Greece and it separated Macedonian history from Greek history (cf. E.N. Borza, 'David George Hogarth: Eighty Years After', *Anc. World* 1 [1978], pp. 97–101). Indeed, it also shone the spotlight firmly on Philip, referring to him and Alexander as 'the two Makers of Macedon' (in the preface).

Much attention still remained focused on the exploits of Alexander the Great, however, and it was some time before the next books about Philip appeared. Of note are A. Momigliano, *Filippo il Macedone* (Florence: 1934), F.R. Wüst, *Philipp II von Makedonien und Griechenland in den Jahren 346 bis*

339 (Munich: 1938), which covers the second half of the king's reign, and P. Cloché, *Un fondateur d'empire. Philippe II, roi de Macédoine* (Paris: 1955). Cloché followed his biography with a narrative treatment of Macedonia (including Philip's reign) in his *Histoire de la Macédoine jusqu'à l'avènement d'Alexandre le Grand* (Paris: 1960). Then it was the English-speaking world's turn, with J.R. Ellis, *Philip II and Macedonian Imperialism* (London: 1976) and G.L. Cawkwell, *Philip of Macedon* (London: 1978), on which I comment below. Next appeared D. Kienast, *Philip II von Makedonien und das Reich der Achaimeniden* (Munich: 1973), D. Tsimboukides, *Philip II the Macedonian* (Athens: 1985), which is more general and in Greek, and G. Wirth, *Philipp II* (Stuttgart: 1985), a very good analysis (written in German). A.S. Bradford, *Philip II of Macedon: A Life from the Ancient Sources* (Westport, CT: 1992) is an account of the king's life as told by selected ancient sources in translation. As such, there is no discussion of events and the like, but having the sources between a single set of covers is very useful. Finally, we have N.G.L. Hammond, *Philip of Macedon* (London: 1994), and, what amounts to a biography within a book because of its length, G.T. Griffith's section in N.G.L. Hammond and G.T. Griffith, *A History of Macedonia* 2 (Oxford: 1979), on pp. 203–698 (pp. 647–74 are by Hammond). I comment on these two books below. Of all these (to the best of my knowledge) only Hammond's book is still in print, and it is now well over a decade old.

Two other books on Philip must be mentioned. The first is M.B. Hatzopoulos and L.D. Loukopoulos (eds), *Philip of Macedon* (Athens: 1980). This is a gorgeously and generously illustrated collection of more narrative-type papers by leading scholars on various aspects of Philip's personality and achievements. The second is S. Perlman (ed.), *Philip and Athens* (Cambridge: 1973), which reprints several important journal articles and sections from books on Philip's career and policy.

Like the ancient sources, modern scholars differ in their opinions of Philip (and of Demosthenes), and here I restrict myself to the four major English works cited above. The best scholarly book with much detailed discussion and copious notes is that of Ellis, *Philip II and Macedonian Imperialism*, written from the perspective of Philip, not that of the Greeks, for a change. To him, Philip was first and foremost a diplomat, wanting peace and alliance with the Greeks. For Ellis the Peace of Philocrates in 346 was Philip's exit policy from Greece, given (argues Ellis) he was looking at Asia by then, not merely seeking a breathing space in some overall plan to reduce Greece. Only when diplomacy failed, thanks mostly to Demosthenes, did he resort to military force and subjugate Greece.

Cawkwell's book, *Philip of Macedon*, is a synthesis of many of his earlier and vastly influential articles on fourth-century Greek history. He bases his account primarily on the ancient sources, and sees Philip as a great man who transformed the ancient world: he confronted the city-states of Greece with the nation-state of Macedonia and was therefore a serious menace to the liberty of Greece. Like Ellis, Cawkwell is critical of Demosthenes, whose policies were almost entirely misconceived and caused Philip to be opposed less effectively than he might have been. While Demosthenes did try to be a defender of liberty, for Cawkwell 'he did it badly' (p. 10).

Hammond, in *Philip of Macedon*, is rightly eulogistic of Philip's accomplishments, which vividly showed up the weakness of the Greeks' political system, and is noncommittal about Demosthenes. His book is light on notes and documentation, and prior knowledge of Greek history is needed on the reader's part to be able to follow his discussion.

Griffith's treatment in *A History of Macedonia* 2 focuses on Philip's political and military activities. His account is a masterpiece of information and discussion anchored in critical analysis of the sources. His relaxed writing style makes his discussion easier to read than other parts of the book, but again there is some expectation that readers will have prior knowledge of the background and sources.

Also of relevance to Philip's reign are R. Sealey, *Demosthenes and his Time: A Study in Defeat* (Oxford: 1993), which focuses on Demosthenes' policy regarding Macedonia, and Ian Worthington (ed.), *Demosthenes: Statesman and Orator* (London: 2000), a collection of original essays by leading scholars dealing with various aspects of Demosthenes' life and career as a politician and orator. For brief biographies of many of the individuals mentioned in the present book, together with further bibliography, see W. Heckel, *Who's Who in the Age of Alexander the Great* (Oxford: 2006).

For additional information on earlier episodes in Greek history that are referred to in my book (for example, the Persian Wars, the Peloponnesian War, the Spartan and Theban hegemonies), any good history of Greece can be consulted; especially recommendable is S. Hornblower, *The Greek World, 479–323 BC* (London: 1983), and J. Buckler, *Aegean Greece in the Fourth Century BC* (Leiden: 2003). Both are detailed (that of Buckler especially so) as well as being written in an engaging style so that the reader does not get confused or mired in excessive citation. Buckler's narrative also has the advantage of drawing on the author's eyewitness topographical information based on his numerous visits to Greece.

Biographies abound of Philip's famous son Alexander the Great (with background on Macedonia and Philip). Of special note are A.B. Bosworth, *Conquest and Empire: The Reign of Alexander the Great* (Cambridge: 1988), P. Cartledge, *Alexander the Great: The Hunt for a New Past* (London: 2003), P. Green, *Alexander of Macedon* (Harmondsworth: 1974), N.G.L. Hammond,

Alexander the Great: King, Commander and Statesman[2] (Bristol: 1989) and his *The Genius of Alexander the Great* (London: 1997), and Ian Worthington, *Alexander the Great, Man and God*, rev. and enl. edn (London: 2004). On military matters, see especially D.W. Engels, *Alexander the Great and the Logistics of the Macedonian Army* (Berkeley and Los Angeles, CA: 1978) and Major-General J.F.C. Fuller, *The Generalship of Alexander the Great* (New Brunswick, NH: 1960). For details on these and other books on Alexander, see the bibliographic essay in Worthington, *Alexander the Great*, pp. 320–32.

SELECT BIBLIOGRAPHY

Adams, A., 'Philip *Alias* Hitler', *G&R* 10 (1941), pp. 105–13

Adams, W.L., 'The Royal Macedonian Tomb at Vergina: An Historical Interpretation', *Anc. World* 3 (1980), pp. 67–72

—, 'Macedonian Kingship and the Right of Petition', in *Ancient Macedonia* 4 (Institute for Balkan Studies, Thessaloniki: 1986), pp. 43–52

—, 'Cassander, Alexander IV, and the Tombs at Vergina', *Anc. World* 22 (1991), pp. 27–33

— and E.N. Borza (eds), *Philip II, Alexander the Great, and the Macedonian Heritage* (Lanham, MD: 1982)

Adcock, F.E. and D.J. Mosley, *Diplomacy in Ancient Greece* (London: 1974)

Alonso-Nunez, J.M., 'An Augustan World History: The *Historiae Philippicae* of Pompeius Trogus', *G&R*[2] 34 (1987), pp. 56–72

Andrewes, A., *The Greek Tyrants* (London: 1974)

Andronikos, M., 'The Finds from the Royal Tombs at Vergina', *PBA* 65 (1979), pp. 355–67

—, 'The Royal Tombs at Aigai (Vergina)', in M.B. Hatzopoulos and L.D. Loukopoulos (eds), *Philip of Macedon* (London: 1980), pp. 188–231

—, 'Art during the Archaic and Classical Periods', in M.B. Sakellariou (ed.), *Macedonia, 4000 Years of Greek History and Civilization* (Athens: 1983), pp. 92–110

—, *Vergina: The Royal Tombs and the Ancient City* (Athens: 1984; repr. 2004)

—, 'Some Reflections on the Macedonian Tombs', *BSA* 82 (1987), pp. 1–16

—, 'Archaeological Discoveries in Macedonia', in J. Vokotopoulou (ed.), *Greek Civilization: Macedonia, Kingdom of Alexander the Great* (Athens: 1993), pp. 5–11

Anson, E.M., 'The Meaning of the Term *Makedones*', *Anc. World* 10 (1984), pp. 67–8

Ashton, N.G., 'The Lamian War – stat magni nominis umbra', *JHS* 94 (1984), pp. 152–7

Badian, E., 'The Death of Philip II', *Phoenix* 17 (1963), pp. 244–50

—, 'Alexander the Great and the Loneliness of Power', in E. Badian, *Studies in Greek and Roman History* (Oxford: 1964), pp. 192–205

—, 'The Deification of Alexander the Great', in H.J. Dell (ed.), *Ancient Macedonian Studies in Honor of C.F. Edson* (Thessaloniki: 1981), pp. 27–71

—, 'Greeks and Macedonians', in B. Barr-Sharrar and E.N. Borza (eds), *Macedonia and Greece in Late Classical and Early Hellenistic Times: Studies in the History of Art* 10 (Washington, DC: 1982), pp. 33–51

—, 'Eurydice', in W.L. Adams and E.N. Borza (eds), *Philip II, Alexander the Great, and the Macedonian Heritage* (Lanham, MD: 1982), pp. 99–110

—, 'Philip II and Thrace', *Pulpudeva* 4 (1983), pp. 51–71

—, 'Herodotus on Alexander I of Macedon: A Study in Some Subtle Silences', in S. Hornblower (ed.), *Greek Historiography* (Oxford: 1994), pp. 107–30

—, 'The Ghost of Empire: Reflections on Athenian Foreign Policy in the Fourth Century', in W. Eder (ed.), *Die athenische Demokratie im 4. Jahrhundert v. Chr.* (Stuttgart: 1995), pp. 79–106

—, 'Philip II and the Last of the Thessalians', *Ancient Macedonia* 6 (Institute for Balkan Studies, Thessaloniki: 1999), pp. 109–22

—, 'The Road to Prominence', in Ian Worthington (ed.), *Demosthenes: Statesman and Orator* (London: 2000), pp. 9–44

Barr-Sharrar, B. and E.N. Borza (eds), *Macedonia and Greece in Late Classical and Early Hellenistic Times: Studies in the History of Art* 10 (Washington, DC: 1982)

Bartsiokas, A., 'The Eye Injury of King Philip II and the Skeletal Evidence from the Royal Tomb II at Vergina', *Science* 288 Issue 5465 (April 2000), pp. 511–14

Baynham, E., 'The Question of Macedonian Divine Honours for Philip II', *Mediterranean Archaeology* 7 (1994), pp. 35–43

Bloedow, E., 'Why Did Philip and Alexander Launch a War against the Persian Empire?', *L'Ant. Class.* 72 (2003), pp. 261–74

Borza, E.N., 'David George Hogarth: Eighty Years After', *Anc. World* 1 (1978), pp. 97–101

—, 'Some Observations on Malaria and the Ecology of Central Macedonia in Antiquity', *AJAH* 4 (1979), pp. 102–24

—, 'The Natural Resources of Early Macedonia', in W.L. Adams and E.N. Borza (eds), *Philip II, Alexander the Great, and the Macedonian Heritage* (Lanham, MD: 1982), pp. 1–20

—, 'The Symposium at Alexander's Court', *Ancient Macedonia* 3 (Institute for Balkan Studies, Thessaloniki: 1983), pp. 45–55

—, 'Timber and Politics in the Ancient World: Macedon and the Greeks', *Proceedings of the American Philosophical Society* 131 (1987), pp. 32–52

—, 'The Royal Macedonian Tombs and the Paraphernalia of Alexander the Great', *Phoenix* 41 (1987), pp. 105–21

—, *In the Shadow of Olympus: The Emergence of Macedon* (Princeton: 1990)

—, 'The Philhellenism of Archelaus', *Ancient Macedonia* 5 (Institute for Balkan Studies, Thessaloniki: 1993), pp. 241–2

—, 'Greeks and Macedonians in the Age of Alexander: The Source Traditions', in R.W. Wallace and E.M. Harris (eds), *Transitions to Empire. Essays in Honor of E. Badian* (Norman, OK: 1996), pp. 122–39

—, *Before Alexander: Constructing Early Macedonia* (Claremont, CA: 1999)

Bosworth, A.B., 'Philip II and Upper Macedonia', *CQ*^{2} 21 (1971), pp. 93–105

—, 'Alexander and Ammon', in K. Kinzl (ed.), *Greece and the Ancient Mediterranean in History and Prehistory* (Berlin: 1977), pp. 51–75

—, *A Historical Commentary on Arrian's History of Alexander* 1 (Oxford: 1980)

—, *Conquest and Empire: The Reign of Alexander the Great* (Cambridge: 1988)

—, *From Arrian to Alexander* (Oxford: 1988)

Bradford, A.S., *Philip II of Macedon: A Life from the Ancient Sources* (Westport, CT: 1992)

Bradford Welles, C., *Diodorus Siculus 16.66–95*, Loeb Classical Library 8 (Cambridge, MA: 1963; repr. 1970)

Brunt, P.A., 'The Aims of Alexander', *G&R*^{2} 12 (1965), pp. 205–15

—, 'Euboea in the Time of Philip II', *CQ*^{2} 19 (1969), pp. 245–65

—, *Arrian, History of Alexander*, Loeb Classical Library, 2 vols (Cambridge, MA: 1976–83)

Buckler, J., *The Theban Hegemony* (Cambridge, MA: 1980)

—, *Philip II and the Sacred War* (Leiden: 1989)

—, 'Philip II's Designs on Greece', in W.R. Wallace and E.M. Harris (eds), *Transitions to Empire: Essays in Honor of E. Badian* (Norman, OK: 1996), pp. 77–97

—, 'Demosthenes and Aeschines', in Ian Worthington (ed.), *Demosthenes: Statesman and Orator* (London: 2000), pp. 114–58

—, *Aegean Greece in the Fourth Century* BC (Leiden: 2003)

Burke, E.M., '*Contra Leocratem* and *De Corona*: Political Collaboration?', *Phoenix* 31 (1977), pp. 330–40

—, 'Lycurgan Finances', *GRBS* 26 (1985), pp. 251–64

Burn, A.R., *Persia and the Greeks*[2] (London: 1984)

Campbell, D.B., *Ancient Siege Warfare: Persians, Greeks, Carthaginians and Romans, 576–146 BC* (London: 2005)

Carey, C., *Aeschines* (Austin, TX: 2000)

Cargill, J., *The Second Athenian League* (Berkeley: 1981)

Carney, E., 'The Female Burial in the Antechamber of Tomb II at Vergina', *Anc. World* 22 (1991), pp. 17–26

—, 'Review Essays on Macedonian History', *AHB* 5 (1991), pp. 179–89

—, 'Tomb I at Vergina and the Meaning of the Great Tumulus as a Historical Monument', *Archaeological News* 17 (1992), pp. 1–11

—, 'The Politics of Polygamy: Olympias, Alexander and the Murder of Philip II', *Historia* 41 (1992), pp. 169–89

—, 'Macedonians and Mutiny: Discipline and Indiscipline in the Army of Philip and Alexander', *CP* 91 (1996), pp. 19–44

—, *Women and Monarchy in Macedonia* (Norman, OK: 2000)

—, *Olympias, Mother of Alexander the Great* (London: 2006)

Carter, J.M., 'Athens, Euboea and Olynthus', *Historia* 20 (1971), pp. 418–29

Cartledge, P., *Agesilaos and the Crisis of Sparta* (Baltimore, MD: 1987)

—, *Alexander the Great: The Hunt for a New Past* (London: 2003)

Cawkwell, G.L., 'Aeschines and the Peace of Philocrates', *REG* 73 (1960), pp. 416–38

—, 'A Note on Ps.-Demosthenes 17.20', *Phoenix* 15 (1961), pp. 74–8

—, 'The Defence of Olynthus', *CQ*[2] 12 (1962), pp. 122–40

—, 'Eubulus', *JHS* 83 (1963), pp. 47–67

—, 'Demosthenes' Policy after the Peace of Philocrates I and II', *CQ*[2] 13 (1963), pp. 120–38 and 200–13

—, 'The Crowning of Demosthenes', *CQ*[2] 19 (1969), pp. 163–80

—, 'Epaminondas and Thebes', *CQ*[2] 22 (1978), pp. 254–78

—, *Philip of Macedon* (London: 1978)

—, 'Philip and Athens', in M.B. Hatzopoulos and L.D. Loukopoulos (eds), *Philip of Macedon* (Athens: 1980), pp. 100–10

—, 'Athenian Naval Power in the Fourth Century', *CQ*[2] 34 (1984), pp. 334–45

—, 'The Deification of Alexander the Great: A Note', in Ian Worthington (ed.), *Ventures into Greek History: Essays in Honour of N.G.L. Hammond* (Oxford: 1994), pp. 293–306

—, 'The End of Greek Liberty', in R.W. Wallace and E.M. Harris (eds), *Transitions to Empire: Essays in Honor of E. Badian* (Norman, OK: 1996), pp. 98–121

Chaniotis, A., 'The Divinity of Hellenistic Rulers', in A. Erskine (ed.), *Blackwell Companion to the Hellenistic World* (Oxford: 2003), pp. 431–45

Clemenceau, G., *Démosthènes* (Paris: 1926)

Cloché, P., *Un fondateur d'empire: Philippe II, roi de Macédoine* (Paris: 1955)

—, *Démosthène et la fin de la démocratie athénienne* (Paris: 1957)

—, *Histoire de la Macédoine jusqu'à l'avènement d'Alexandre le Grand* (Paris: 1960)

Cole, J.W., 'Perdiccas and Athens', *Phoenix* 28 (1974), pp. 55–72

Connor, W.R., 'History without Heroes: Theopompus' Treatment of Philip of Macedon', *GRBS* 8 (1967), pp. 33–154

Daitz, S.G., 'The Relationship of the *De Chersoneso* and the *Philippika quarta* of Demosthenes', *CP* 52 (1957), pp. 145–62

Danforth, L.M., *The Macedonian Conflict* (Princeton, NJ: 1995)

—, 'Alexander the Great and the Macedonian Conflict', in J. Roisman (ed.), *Brill's Companion to Alexander the Great* (Leiden: 2003), pp. 347–64

Davidson, J., *Courtesans and Fishcakes* (London: 1997)

Davies, J.K., 'The Tradition about the First Sacred War', in S. Hornblower (ed.), *Greek Historiography* (Oxford: 1994), pp. 193–212

Dell, H.J., 'The Western Frontier of the Macedonian Monarchy', *Ancient Macedonia* 1 (Institute for Balkan Studies, Thessaloniki: 1970), pp. 115–26

D'Hautcourt, A., 'Aethlios, no. 546', *Brill's New Jacoby* (Leiden: 2007)

de Ste. Croix, G.E.M., 'The Alleged Secret Pact between Athens and Philip II Concerning Amphipolis and Pydna', *CQ*² 13 (1963), pp. 110–19

Develin, R., 'The Murder of Philip II', *Antichthon* 15 (1981), pp. 86–99

— and W. Heckel, *Justin, Epitome of the Philippic History of Pompeius Trogus* (Atlanta, GA: 1994)

Drougou, S., and C. Saatsoglou-Paliadeli, *Vergina: Wandering through the Archaeological Site* (Athens: 2004)

Duff, T., *Plutarch's Lives* (Oxford: 1999)

Ehrhardt, C., 'Two Notes on Philip of Macedon's First Interventions in Thessaly', *CQ*² 17 (1967), pp. 296–301

Ellis, J.R., 'The Order of the *Olynthiacs*', *Historia* 16 (1967), pp. 108–11

—, 'Population-Transplants by Philip II', *Makedonika* 9 (1969), pp. 9–17

—, 'The Security of the Macedonian Throne under Philip II', *Ancient Macedonia* 1 (Institute for Balkan Studies, Thessaloniki: 1970), pp. 68–75

—, 'The Stepbrothers of Philip II', *Historia* 22 (1973), pp. 350–4

—, *Philip II and Macedonian Imperialism* (London: 1976)

—, 'The Dynamics of Fourth-Century Macedonian Imperialism', *Ancient Macedonia* 2 (Institute for Balkan Studies, Thessaloniki: 1977), pp. 103–14

—, 'The Unification of Macedonia', in M.B. Hatzopoulos and L.D. Loukopoulos (eds), *Philip of Macedon* (Athens: 1980), pp. 36–47

—, 'The Assassination of Philip II', in H.J. Dell (ed.), *Ancient Macedonian Studies in Honour of C.F. Edson* (Thessaloniki: 1981), pp. 99–137

—, 'Philip and the Peace of Philokrates', in W.L. Adams and E.N. Borza (eds), *Philip II, Alexander the Great, and the Macedonian Heritage* (Lanham, MD: 1982), pp. 43–59

Engels, D., *Alexander the Great and the Logistics of the Macedonian Army* (Berkeley and Los Angeles: 1978)

Engels, J., 'Theagenes no. 774', *Brill's New Jacoby* (Leiden 2008)

Errington, R.M., 'Macedonian Royal Style and its Historical Significance', *JHS* 94 (1974), pp. 20–37

—, 'Arybbas the Molossian', *GRBS* 16 (1975), pp. 41–50

—, 'Review-Discussion: Four Interpretations of Philip II', *AJAH* 6 (1981), pp. 69–88

—, *A History of Macedonia*, trans. C. Errington (Berkeley: 1990)

Erskine, A., 'The *Pezêtairoi* of Philip II and Alexander III', *Historia* 38 (1989), pp. 385–94

— (ed.), *Blackwell Companion to the Hellenistic World* (Oxford: 2003)

Faklaris, P.B., 'Aegae: Determining the Site of the First Capital of the Macedonians', *AJA* 98 (1994), pp. 609–16

Faraguna, M., *Atene nell'età di Alessandro: problemi politici, economici, finanziari* (Rome: 1992)

Fears, J.R., 'Pausanias, the Assassin of Philip', *Athenaeum* 53 (1975), pp. 111–35

Fisher, N., *Aeschines, Against Timarchos* (Oxford: 2001)

Flower, M.A., 'Agesilaus of Sparta and the Origins of the Ruler-Cult', *CQ*² 38 (1988), pp. 123–34

—, *Theopompus of Chios* (Oxford: 1994)

Fontenrose, J.E., *The Delphic Oracle, its Responses and Operations, with a Catalogue of Responses* (Berkeley and Los Angeles: 1978)

Fredricksmeyer, E.A., 'Divine Honors for Philip II', *TAPA* 109 (1979), pp. 39–61

—, 'On the Background of the Ruler Cult', in H.J. Dell (ed.), *Ancient Macedonian Studies in Honor of C.F. Edson* (Thessaloniki: 1981), pp. 145–56

—, 'On the Final Aims of Philip II', in W.L. Adams and E.N. Borza (eds), *Philip II, Alexander the Great, and the Macedonian Heritage* (Lanham, MD: 1982), pp. 85–98

—, 'Alexander and Philip: Emulation and Resentment', *CJ* 85 (1990), pp. 300–15

—, 'The Kausia: Macedonian or Indian?', in Ian Worthington (ed.), *Ventures into Greek History: Essays in Honour of N.G.L. Hammond* (Oxford: 1994), pp. 135–58

—, 'Alexander the Great and the Kingship of Asia', in A.B. Bosworth and E.J. Baynham (eds), *Alexander the Great in Fact and Fiction* (Oxford: 2000), pp. 136–66

Fuller, J.F.C., *The Generalship of Alexander the Great* (New Brunswick: 1960)

Garlan, Y., *Recherches de poliorcétique grecque* (Paris: 1974)

Gilley, D., 'Alexander and the Carmanian March of 324 BC', *AHB* 20 (2007), pp. 9–14

Ginouvès, R. (ed.), *Macedonia, From Philip II to the Roman Conquest* (Princeton, NJ: 1994)

Green, P., *Alexander of Macedon* (Harmondsworth: 1974)

—, 'The Royal Tomb at Vergina: A Historical Analysis', in W.L. Adams and E.N. Borza (eds), *Philip II, Alexander the Great, and the Macedonian Heritage* (Lanham, MD: 1982), pp. 129–51

—, *The Greco-Persian Wars* (Berkeley: 1996)

Greenwalt, W.S., 'The Search for Arrhidaeus', *Anc. World* 10 (1985), pp. 69–77

—, 'Amyntas III and the Political Stability of Argead Macedonia', *Anc. World* 18 (1988), pp. 35–44

—, 'Polygamy and Succession in Argead Macedonia', *Arethusa* 22 (1989), pp. 19–45

—, 'The Production of Coinage from Archelaus to Perdiccas III and the Evolution of Argead Macedonia', in Ian Worthington (ed.), *Ventures into Greek History: Essays in Honour of N.G.L. Hammond* (Oxford: 1994), pp. 105–34

Griffith, G.T., 'The Macedonian Background', *G&R*² 12 (1965), pp. 125–39

—, 'Philip of Macedon's Early Intervention in Thessaly (358–352 B.C.)', *CQ*² 20 (1970), pp. 67–80

—, 'Athens in the Fourth Century', in P.D.A. Garnsey and C.R. Whittaker (eds), *Imperialism in the Ancient World* (Cambridge: 1978), pp. 127–44

—, 'Philip as a General and the Macedonian Army', in M.B. Hatzopoulos and L.D. Loukopoulos (eds), *Philip of Macedon* (Athens: 1980), pp. 58–77

Habicht, C., *Gottmenschentum und griechische Städte* (Munich: 1970)

Hall, J.M., 'Contested Ethnicities: Perceptions of Macedonia within Evolving Definitions of Greek Identity', in I. Malkin (ed.), *Ancient Perceptions of Greek Ethnicity* (Cambridge, MA: 2001), pp. 159–86

Hamilton, C.D., 'Philip II and Archidamus', in W.L. Adams and E.N. Borza (eds), *Philip II, Alexander the Great, and the Macedonian Heritage* (Lanham, MD: 1982), pp. 61–77

—, *Agesilaus and the Failure of Spartan Hegemony* (Ithaca, NY: 1991)

Hammond, N.G.L., 'The Sources of Diodorus XVI', *CQ* 31 (1937), pp. 79–91 and 32 (1938), pp 37–51

—, 'The Kingdoms in Illyria circa 400–167 BC', *BSA* 61 (1966), pp. 239–53

—, *Epirus* (Oxford: 1967)

—, *A History of Macedonia* 1 (Oxford: 1972)

—, 'Philip's Tomb in Historical Context', *GRBS* 19 (1978), pp. 331–50

—, 'Training in the Use of the Sarissa and its Effect in Battle 359–333 BC', *Antichthon* 14 (1980), pp. 53–63

—, 'The End of Philip', in M.B. Hatzopoulos and L.D. Loukopoulos (eds), *Philip of Macedon* (London: 1980), pp. 166–75

—, 'The Western Frontier in the Reign of Philip II', in H.J. Dell (ed.), *Ancient Macedonian Studies in Honour of C.F. Edson* (Institute for Balkan Studies, Thessaloniki: 1981), pp. 199–217

—, 'The Evidence for the Identity of the Royal Tombs at Vergina', in W.L. Adams and E.N. Borza (eds), *Philip II, Alexander the Great, and the Macedonian Heritage* (Lanham, MD: 1982), pp. 111–27

—, *A History of Greece*³ (Oxford: 1986)

—, *The Macedonian State: Origins, Institutions, and History* (Oxford: 1989)

—, 'The Battle between Philip and Bardylis', *Antichthon* 23 (1989), pp. 1–9

—, *Alexander the Great: King, Commander and Statesman*[2] (Bristol: 1989)

—, 'The Koina of Epirus and Macedonia', *ICS* 16 (1991), pp. 183–92

—, 'The Royal Tombs at Vergina', *BSA* 86 (1991), pp. 69–82

—, 'The Sources of Justin on Macedonia to the Death of Philip', *CQ*[2] 41 (1991), pp. 496–508

—, 'The Various Guards of Philip II and Alexander III', *Historia* 40 (1991), pp. 396–417

—, *Philip of Macedon* (London: 1994)

—, 'Philip's Innovations in Macedonian Economy', *SO* 70 (1995), pp. 22–9

—, 'The Location of Aegae', *JHS* 117 (1997), pp. 177–9

—, *The Genius of Alexander the Great* (London: 1997)

— and G.T. Griffith, *A History of Macedonia* 2 (Oxford: 1979)

— and F.W. Walbank, *A History of Macedonia* 3 (Oxford: 1988)

Hansen, M.H., 'The Theoric Fund and the *Graphe Paranomon* against Apollodorus', *GRBS* 17 (1976), pp. 235–46

—, 'Two Notes on Demosthenes' Symbouleutic Speeches', *Cl. & Med.* 35 (1984), pp. 57–70

—, *The Athenian Assembly in the Age of Demosthenes* (Oxford: 1987)

—, *The Athenian Democracy in the Age of Demosthenes* (Oxford: 1991)

Harding, P.E., 'Rhetoric and Politics in Fourth-Century Athens', *Phoenix* 41 (1987), pp. 25–39

—, 'Athenian Foreign Policy in the Fourth Century', *Klio* 77 (1995), pp. 105–25

Harris, E.M., 'Law and Oratory', in Ian Worthington (ed.), *Persuasion: Greek Rhetoric in Action* (London: 1994), pp. 130–50

—, *Aeschines and Athenian Politics* (Oxford: 1995)

Harvey, F.D., '*Dona Ferentes*: Some Aspects of Bribery in Greek Politics', in P.A. Cartledge and F.D. Harvey (eds), *Crux: Essays in Greek History Presented to G.E.M. de Ste. Croix on his 75th Birthday* (London: 1985), pp. 76–117

Hatzopoulos, M.B., 'The Oleveni Inscription and the Dates of Philip II's Reign', in W.L. Adams and E.N. Borza (eds), *Philip II, Alexander the Great, and the Macedonian Heritage* (Lanham, MD: 1982), pp. 21–42

—, 'A Reconsideration of the Pixodaros Affair', in B. Barr-Sharrar and E.N. Borza (eds), *Macedonia and Greece in Late Classical and Early Hellenistic Times: Studies in the History of Art* 10 (Washington, DC: 1982), pp. 59–66

—, 'Succession and Regency in Classical Macedonia', in *Ancient Macedonia* 4 (Institute for Balkan Studies, Thessaloniki: 1986), pp. 279–92

—, 'Strepsa: A Reconsideration, or New Evidence on the Road System of Lower Macedonia', in *Two Studies in Ancient Macedonian Topography* (Athens: 1987), pp. 41–4

—, 'Some Reflections on the Macedonian Tombs', *BSA* 82 (1987), pp. 1–16

—, 'La lettre royale d'Oleveni', *Chiron* 25 (1995), pp. 163–85

—, *Macedonian Institutions under the Kings* 1 and 2, *Meletemata* 22 (Athens: 1996)

— and L.D. Loukopoulos (eds), *Philip of Macedon* (Athens: 1980)

Heckel, W., 'Cleopatra or Eurydice?', *Phoenix* 32 (1978), pp. 155–8

—, 'Marsyas of Pella: Historian of Macedon', *Hermes* 108 (1980), pp. 444–62

—, 'Philip and Olympias (337/6 BC)', in G.S. Shrimpton and D.J. McCargar (eds), *Classical Contributions: Studies in Honor of M.F. McGregor* (Locust Valley, NY: 1981), pp. 51–7

—, 'Polyxena the Mother of Alexander the Great', *Chiron* 11 (1981), pp. 79–96

—, *Who's Who in the Age of Alexander the Great* (Oxford: 2006)

— and R. Develin, *Justin, Epitome of the Philippic History of Pompeius Trogus* (Atlanta, GA: 1994)

Hesisserer, A.J., *Alexander the Great and the Greeks: The Epigraphic Evidence* (Norman, OK: 1980)

Heskel, J., 'Philip II and Argaios: A Pretender's Story', in R.W. Wallace and E.M. Harris (eds), *Transitions to Empire: Essays in Honor of E. Badian* (Norman, OK: 1996), pp. 37–56

—, *The North Aegean Wars, 371–60 BC* (Stuttgart: 1997)

Hogarth, D.G., *Philip and Alexander of Macedon: Two Essays in Biography* (London: 1897; repr. 1971)

Hornblower, S., *The Greek World, 479–323 BC* (London: 1983)

Jacoby, F., *Die Fragmente der grieschischen Historiker* (Berlin/Leiden: 1926–)

Kagan, D., *The Peloponnesian War* (London: 2003)

Keyser, P.T., 'The Use of Artillery by Philip II and Alexander the Great', *Anc. World* 15 (1994), pp. 27–49

Kienast, D., *Philip II von Makedonien und das Reich der Achaimeniden* (Munich: 1973)

Kraay, C.M., *Archaic and Classical Greek Coins* (Berkeley and Los Angeles: 1976)

Lapatin, K., *Chryselephantine Statuary in the Mediterranean World* (Oxford: 2001)

Le Rider, G., *Le monnayage d'argent et d'or de Philippe II frappé en Macédoine de 359 à 294* (Paris: 1977)

—, 'The Coinage of Philip and the Pangaion Mines', in M.B. Hatzopoulos and L.D. Loukopoulos (eds), *Philip of Macedon* (Athens: 1980), pp. 48–57

Lehmann, P.W., 'The So-Called Tomb of Philip II: A Different Interpretation', *AJA* 84 (1980), pp. 527–31

—, 'Once Again the Royal Tomb at Vergina', *AAA* 14 (1981), pp. 134–44

—, 'The So-Called Tomb of Phillip II: An Addendum', *AJA* 86 (1982), pp. 437–42

Lilimbaki-Akamati, M., 'Pella', in J. Vokotopoulou (ed.), *Greek Civilization: Macedonia, Kingdom of Alexander the Great* (Athens: 1993), pp. 41–4

— and I. Akamatis, *Pella and its Environs* (Athens: 2004)

MacDowell, D.M., *The Law in Classical Athens* (London: 1978)

—, *Demosthenes: On the False Embassy* (Oxford: 2000)

McQueen, E.I., *Diodorus Siculus. The Reign of Philip II. The Greek and Macedonian Narrative from Book XVI* (Bristol: 1995)

Markle, M.M., 'Support of Athenian Intellectuals for Philip: A Study of Isocrates' *Philippus* and Speusippus' *Letter to Philip*', *JHS* 96 (1976), pp. 80–99

Marsden, E.W., *Greek and Roman Artillery* (Oxford: 1969)

—, 'Macedonian Military Machinery and its Designers under Philip and Alexander', *Ancient Macedonia* 2 (Institute for Balkan Studies, Thessaloniki: 1977), pp. 211–23

Meiggs, R., *Trees and Timber in the Ancient Mediterranean Word* (Oxford: 1962)

Miller, S.G., 'The Philippeion and Macedonian Hellenistic Architecture', *Athenische Mitteilungen* 88 (1973), pp. 189–218

—, 'Macedonian Tombs: Their Architecture and Architectural Decoration', in B. Barr-Sharrar and E.N. Borza (eds), *Macedonia and Greece in Late Classical and Early Hellenistic Times: Studies in the History of Art* 10 (Washington, DC: 1982), pp. 153–71

Millis, B., 'Anonymous no. 311', *Brill's New Jacoby* (Leiden: 2008)

Mitchel, F.W., 'Lykourgan Athens: 338–322', *Semple Lectures* 2 (Cincinnati: 1970)

Momigliano, A., *Filippo il Macedone* (Florence: 1934)

Montgomery, H., 'The Economic Revolution of Philip II – Myth or Reality?', *SO* 60 (1985), pp. 37–47

Moretti, L., *Olympionikai: i vincitori negli antichi agoni Olimpici* (Rome: 1957)

Musgrave, J.H., 'Dust and Damn'd Oblivion: A Study of Cremation in Ancient Greece', *BSA* 85 (1990), pp. 271–99

—, R.A.H. Neave and A.J.N.W. Prag, 'The Skull from Tomb II at Vergina: King Philip II of Macedon', *JHS* 104 (1984), pp. 60–78

Natoli, A.F., *The Letter of Speusippus to Philip II* (Stuttgart: 2004)

Nouhaud, M., *L'utilisation de l'histoire par les orateurs attiques* (Paris: 1982)

Palagia, O., 'Hephaestion's Pyre and the Royal Hunt of Alexander', in A.B. Bosworth and E.J. Baynham (eds), *Alexander the Great in Fact and Fiction* (Oxford: 2000), pp. 167–206

Pandermalis, D., 'Monuments and Art in the Roman Period', in M.B. Sakellariou (ed.), *Macedonia, 4000 Years of Greek History and Civilization* (Athens: 1983), pp. 208–21

—, *Dion: The Archaeological Site and Museum* (Athens: 1997)

Papazoglou, F., *Les villes de Macédoine à l'époque romaine* (Paris 1988)

Papillon, T.L., *Isocrates* II (Austin, TX: 2004)

—, 'Isocrates', in Ian Worthington (ed.), *Blackwell Companion to Greek Rhetoric* (Oxford 2006), pp. 58–74

Parke, H.W., *A History of the Delphic Oracle* (Oxford: 1939)

— and J. Boardman, 'The Struggle for the Tripod and the First Sacred War', *JHS* 77 (1957), pp. 276–82

Pearson, L., 'Historical Allusions in the Attic Orators', *CP* 36 (1941), pp. 209–29

Pelling, C., *Plutarch and History* (London: 2002)

Perlman, S., 'Isocrates, "Philippus" – A Reinterpretation', *Historia* 6 (1957), pp. 306–17

—, 'The Historical Example, its Use and Importance as Political Propaganda in the Attic Orators', *SH* 7 (1961), pp. 150–66

— (ed.), *Philip and Athens* (Cambridge: 1973)

—, 'Greek Diplomatic Tradition and the Corinthian League of Philip of Macedon', *Historia* 34 (1985), pp. 153–74

—, 'Fourth Century Treaties and the League of Corinth of Philip of Macedon', in *Ancient Macedonia* 4 (Institute for Balkan Studies, Thessaloniki: 1986), pp. 437–42

Petsas, P., *Pella, Alexander the Great's Capital* (Thessaloniki: 1978)

Pickard-Cambridge, A.W., *Demosthenes and the Last Days of Greek Freedom* (London: 1914)

Poulios, V., 'Macedonian Coinage from the 6th Century to 148 BC', in J. Vokotopoulou (ed.), *Greek Civilization: Macedonia, Kingdom of Alexander the Great* (Athens: 1993), pp. 83–103

Poulton, H., *Who Are the Macedonians?* (Bloomington, IN: 2000)

Prag, A.J.N.W., 'Reconstructing the Skull of Philip of Macedon', in E.C. Danien (ed.), *The World of Philip and Alexander* (Philadelphia, PA: 1990), pp. 17–37

—, 'Reconstructing King Philip II: The "Nice" Version', *AJA* 94 (1990), pp. 237–47

—, J.H. Musgrave and R.A. Neave, 'Twenty-First-Century Philippic', in G.J. Oliver and Z. Archibald (eds), *The Power of the Individual in Ancient Greece: Essays in Honour of J.K. Davies* (Stuttgart: 2008)

Prestianni Gialombardo, A.M., '*Philippika* I: Sul "Culto" di Filippo II di Macedonia', *Siculorum Gymnasium* 28 (1975), pp. 1–57

Rahe, P.A., 'The Annihilation of the Sacred Band at Chaeronea', *AJA* 85 (1981), pp. 84–7

Rhodes, P.J., *The Athenian Boule* (Oxford: 1972)

— and R. Osborne (eds), *Greek Historical Inscriptions, 404–323 BC* (Oxford: 2003)

Richter, G.M.A., *The Portraits of the Greeks* (Ithaca, NY: 1984)

Riginos, A.S., 'The Wounding of Philip II of Macedon: Fact and Fabrication', *JHS* 114 (1994), pp. 103–19

Robertson, M., 'Early Greek Mosaics', in B. Barr-Sharrar and E.N. Borza (eds), *Macedonia and Greece in Late Classical and Early Hellenistic Times: Studies in the History of Art* 10 (Washington, DC: 1982), pp. 241–9

Robinson, C.A., *The History of Alexander the Great*, 2 vols (Providence, RI: 1953)

Roebuck, C., 'The Settlement of Philip II with the Greek States in 338 B.C.', *CP* 43 (1948), pp. 73–92

Roos, P., 'Alexander I in Olympia', *Eranos* 83 (1985), pp. 162–8

Rotroff, S.I., 'Spool Saltcellars in the Athenian Agora', *Hesperia* 53 (1984), pp. 343–54

Rowe, G.O., 'Demosthenes' First Philippic: The Satiric Mode', *TAPA* 99 (1968), pp. 361–74

Russell, D.A., *Plutarch* (London: 1973)

Ryder, T.T.B., *Koine Eirene* (Oxford: 1965)

—, 'Demosthenes and Philip's Peace of 338/7 B.C.', *CQ*² 26 (1976), pp. 85–7

—, 'The Diplomatic Skills of Philip II', in Ian Worthington (ed.), *Ventures into Greek History: Essays in Honour of N.G.L. Hammond* (Oxford: 1994), pp. 228–57

—, 'Demosthenes and Philip II', in Ian Worthington (ed.), *Demosthenes: Statesman and Orator* (London: 2000), pp. 45–89

Sacks, K., *Diodorus Siculus and the First Century* (Princeton, NJ: 1990)

—, 'Diodorus and his Sources: Conformity and Creativity', in S. Hornblower (ed.), *Greek Historiography* (Oxford: 1994), pp. 213–32

Sakellariou, M.B., 'Panhellenism: From Concept to Policy', in M.B. Hatzopoulos and L.D. Loukopoulos (eds), *Philip of Macedon* (Athens: 1980), pp. 128–45

— (ed.), *Macedonia, 4000 Years of Greek History and Civilization* (Athens: 1983)

—, 'The Inhabitants', in M.B. Sakellariou (ed.), *Macedonia, 4000 Years of Greek History and Civilization* (Athens: 1983), pp. 48–63

Saunders, A.N.W., *Greek Political Oratory*, Penguin Classics (Harmondsworth: 1970; repr. 1984)

Sawada, N., 'A Reconsideration of the Peace of Philocrates', *Kodai* 4 (1993), pp. 21–50

—, 'Athenian Politics in the Age of Alexander the Great: A Reconsideration of the Trial of Ctesiphon', *Chiron* 26 (1996), pp. 57–84

Scaife, R., 'Alexander I in the Histories of Herodotus', *Hermes* 117 (1989), pp. 129–37

Schultz, P., 'Leochares' Argead Portraits in the Philippeion', in P. Schultz and R. von den Hoff (eds), *Early Hellenistic Portraiture: Image, Style, Context* (Cambridge: 2007), pp. 205–33

Scott-Kilvert, I., *Plutarch, The Age of Alexander*, Penguin Classics (Harmondsworth: 1973)

Sealey, R., *Demosthenes and His Time: A Study in Defeat* (Oxford: 1993)

Sekunda, N.V., 'The Sarissa', *Acta Universitatis Lodziensis, Folia Archaeologica* 23 (2001), pp. 13–41

Sherman, C.L., *Diodorus Siculus 16.1–65*, Loeb Classical Library 7 (Cambridge, MA: 1952; repr. 1971)

Shipley, G., 'Between Macedonia and Rome: Political Landscapes and Social Changes in Southern Greece in the Early Hellenistic Period', *BSA* 100 (2005), pp. 315–30

Shrimpton, G.S., 'Theopompus' Treatment of Philip in the *Philippica*', *Phoenix* 31 (1977), pp. 123–44

—, *Theopompus the Historian* (Montreal: 1991)

Siganidou, M., 'Urban Centres in Macedonia', in J. Vokotopoulou (ed.), *Greek Civilization: Macedonia, Kingdom of Alexander the Great* (Athens: 1993), pp. 29–31

— and M. Lilimbaki-Akamati, *Pella* (Athens: 2003)

Sivignon, M., 'The Geographical Setting of Macedonia', in M.B. Sakellariou (ed.), *Macedonia, 4000 Years of Greek History and Civilization* (Athens: 1983), pp. 12–26

Snodgrass, A.M., *Arms and Armour of the Greeks* (London: 1967)

Sordi, M., *La Lega Thessala fino ad Alessandro* (Rome: 1958)

Sprawski, S., *Jason of Pherai* (Krakow: 1999)

—, 'Philip II and the Freedom of the Thessalians', *Electrum* 9 (2003), pp. 61–4

—, 'Were Lycophron and Jason Tyrants of Pherae? Xenophon on the History of Thessaly', in C. Tuplin (ed.), *Xenophon and his World* (Stuttgart: 2004), pp. 437–52

—, 'All the King's Men: Thessalians and Philip II's Designs on Greece', in D. Musial (ed.), *Society and Religions: Studies in Greek and Roman History* (Torun: 2005), pp. 31–49

Syme, R., 'The Date of Justin and the Discovery of Trogus' *Historia*', *Historia* 37 (1988), pp. 358–71

Talbert, R.J., *Timoleon and the Revival of Greek Sicily, 344–317 BC* (London: 1974)

Thomas, C.G., *Alexander and his World* (Oxford: 2006)

Tod, M.N., *Greek Historical Inscriptions* 2 (Oxford: 1948)

Tomlinson, R.A., 'Ancient Macedonian Symposia', *Ancient Macedonia* 1 (Institute for Balkan Studies, Thessaloniki: 1970), pp. 308–15

—, 'The Architectural Content of the Macedonian Vaulted Tombs', *BSA* 82 (1987), pp. 305–12

Touratsoglou, J., 'Art in the Hellenistic Period', in M.B. Sakellariou (ed.), *Macedonia, 4000 Years of Greek History and Civilization* (Athens: 1983), pp. 170–91

Townsend, R.F., 'The Philippeion and Fourth-Century Athenian Architecture', in O. Palagia and S.V. Tracy (eds), *The Macedonians in Athens, 322–229 BC* (Oxford 2003), pp. 93–101

Tritle, L., *The Peloponnesian War* (Westport, CT: 2004)

Tronson, A.D., 'Satyrus the Peripatetic and the Marriages of Philip II', *JHS* 104 (1984), pp. 116–26

—, 'The Relevance of *IG* II² 329 to the Hellenic League of Alexander the Great', *Anc. World* 12 (1985), pp. 15–19

Trundle, M., *Greek Mercenaries from the Late Archaic Period to Alexander* (London: 2004)

Tsimboukides, D., *Philip II the Macedonian* (Athens: 1985)

Tuplin, C., 'Demosthenes' *Olynthiacs* and the Character of the Demegoric Corpus', *Historia* 47 (1998), pp. 276–320

Turner, F.M., *The Greek Heritage in Victorian Britain* (London: 1981)

Usher, S., *Greek Oratory* (Oxford: 1999)

—, 'Symbouleutic Oratory', in Ian Worthington (ed.), *Blackwell Companion to Greek Rhetoric* (Oxford: 2006), pp. 220–35

Vokotopoulou, J. (ed.), *Greek Civilization: Macedonia, Kingdom of Alexander the Great* (Athens: 1993)

—, 'Macedonia in the Literary Sources', in J. Vokotopoulou (ed.), *Greek Civilization: Macedonia, Kingdom of Alexander the Great* (Athens: 1993), pp. 71–81

Wallace, R.W., *The Areopagos Council, to 307 B.C.* (Baltimore, MD: 1989)

West, A.B., *The History of the Chalcidic League* (Madison, WI: 1918)

Westlake, H.D., *Thessaly in the Fourth Century BC* (London: 1935; repr. Chicago: 1993)

Whitehead, D. and P.H. Blyth, *Athenaeus Mechanicus, On Machines* (Stuttgart: 2004)

Will, W., 'Zur Datierung der Rede Ps.-Demosthenes XVII', *RhM* 125 (1982), pp. 202–13

Williams, J.M., 'Demades' Last Years, 323/2–319/8 B.C.: A "Revisionist" Interpretation', *Anc. World* 19 (1989), pp. 19–30

Wirth, G., *Philipp II* (Stuttgart: 1985)

Wooten, C.W., *Cicero's Philippics and their Demosthenic Model* (Chapel Hill, NC: 1983)

Worthington, Ian, 'The Authenticity of Demosthenes' Fourth *Philippic*', *Mnemosyne* 44 (1991), pp. 425–8

—, 'Greek Oratory, Revision of Speeches and the Problem of Historical Reliability', *Cl. & Med.* 42 (1991), pp. 55–74

—, *A Historical Commentary on Dinarchus: Rhetoric and Conspiracy in Later Fourth-Century Athens* (Ann Arbor, MI: 1992)

—, 'History and Oratorical Exploitation', in Ian Worthington (ed.), *Persuasion: Greek Rhetoric in Action* (London: 1994), pp. 109–29

— (ed.), *Demosthenes: Statesman and Orator* (London: 2000)

—, 'Demosthenes' (In)activity During the Reign of Alexander the Great', in Ian Worthington (ed.), *Demosthenes: Statesman and Orator* (London: 2000), pp. 90–113

—, 'Alexander, Philip, and the Macedonian Background', in J. Roisman (ed.), *Brill's Companion to Alexander the Great* (Leiden: 2003), pp. 69–98

—, 'Alexander's Destruction of Thebes', in W. Heckel and L.A. Tritle (eds), *Crossroads of History: The Age of Alexander the Great* (Claremont, CA: 2003), pp. 65–86

—, *Alexander the Great, Man and God*, rev. and enl. edn (London: 2004)

—, review of the film *Alexander*, written and directed by Oliver Stone (2004), *American Historical Review* 110 (2005), pp. 533–4

—, 'Rhetoric and Politics in Classical Greece: Rise of the *Rhêtores*', in Ian Worthington (ed.), *Blackwell Companion to Greek Rhetoric* (Oxford: 2006), pp. 255–71

—, *Demosthenes: Speeches 60 and 61, Prologues, Letters* (Austin, TX: 2006)

—, '*IG* ii² 236 and Philip's Common Peace of 337', in L.G. Mitchell (ed.), *Greek History and Epigraphy: Essays in Honour of P. J. Rhodes* (Swansea: 2008)

Wüst, F.R., *Philipp II von Makedonien und Griechenland in den Jahren 346 bis 339* (Munich: 1938)

Xirotiris, N.I., and F. Langenscheidt, 'The Cremations from the Royal Macedonian Tombs of Vergina', *Arch. Eph.* (1981), pp. 142–60

Yardley, J.C., *Justin and Trogus: A Study of the Language of Justin's Epitome of Trogus* (Toronto: 2003)

Yunis, H., *Demosthenes Speeches 18 and 19* (Austin, TX: 2005)

INDEX